WYCLIF

POLITICAL IDEAS AND PRACTICE

Papers by Michael Wilks

Selected and introduced by Anne Hudson

Oxbow Books

WYCLIF
POLITICAL IDEAS AND PRACTICE

Papers by Michael Wilks

Michael Wilks

WYCLIF

POLITICAL IDEAS AND PRACTICE

Papers by Michael Wilks

Selected and introduced by Anne Hudson

Oxbow Books
2000

Published by
Oxbow Books, Park End Place, Oxford OX1 1HN

ISBN 1 84217 009 0

A CIP record for this book is available from the British Library

Printed in Great Britain
at the Short Run Press, Exeter

CONTENTS

CONTENTS

ACKNOWLEDGEMENTS

All the papers by Michael Wilks in this volume have been published before with the exception of the last; the first appeared in French but is here reproduced from the original typescript in English. The last paper was Michael Wilks's inaugural lecture as Professor of Medieval History, given at Birkbeck College on 5 November 1980. The published papers have been reprinted without alteration or updating. To the inaugural lecture Dr Diana Wood has added a brief bibliography of primary sources and recent critical literature. Had Michael Wilks prepared this lecture for publication he would doubtless have provided much more information than this, especially in quotation from Wyclif's polemic against the Crusade; but footnotes added by an editor would alter the original informality of this paper.

Full details for the original place of publication for the papers included are given in the list below. We are greatly indebted to the original publishers for permission to reprint, and especially to the Ecclesiastical History Society in the main series and in the Subsidia series of whose *Studies in Church History* nine of the papers first appeared. Warm thanks are also given to the authorities of the Prague National (formerly University) Library for permission to use the photograph of one of their manuscripts on the cover. Especial thanks are due to Stella Wilks, Michael's widow, for her help in putting this volume together, and particularly for the photograph of Michael and for the typescript of the first chapter.

SOURCES

The articles here first appeared in the following places, and are reprinted by kind permission of the original publishers.

1 *Dictionnaire de spiritualité,* fascicules CVI–CVII (vol. xvi) (Beauchesne, Paris, 1994), cols. 1501–1512 (in French).

2 *Studies in Church History* 2 (1965), 220–36.

3 *Studies in Church History* 5 (1969), 69–98.

4 *Studies in Church History* 9 (1972), 109–30.

5 *Studies in Church History* 11 (1975), 147–61.

6 *The Church in a Changing Society: CIHEC Conference in Uppsala, 1977* (Uppsala, 1978), 63–70.

7 *Studies in Church History, Subsidia* 5 (1987), 135–63.

8 *Studies in Church History* 24 (1987), xv–xlv.

9 *Studies in Church History, Subsidia* 10 (1994), 39–63.

10 *Studies in Church History* 33 (1997), 177–93.

11 *Studies in Church History, Subsidia* 12 (1999), 57–86.

Note: the picture on the cover appears at the start of a copy of Wyclif's *De veritate sacre scripture,* and is presumably intended as a representation of the author. The manuscript is in a Bohemian hand of *c.* 1410. It is now Prague National (formerly University) Library MS VIII.C.3 (1472), where the miniature is on f.2r. Reproduction is by kind permission of the Library authorities in Prague.

The pages in this volume are numbered in the top left and right corners. The numbers at the bottoms of the pages refer to the original pagination of the articles in *Studies in Church History.*

ABBREVIATIONS

The following list covers abbreviations used in some or all of the ensuing chapters. Because of the varying styles of periodicals and publishers, there may be minor differences in punctuation and typography from that shown below. Not included are those works whose short titles are indicated on first occurrence in a paper's footnotes.

BIHR   *Bulletin of the Institute of Historical Research* (London, 1923–)
BJRL   *Bulletin of the John Rylands Library* (Manchester, 1903–)
CathHR   *Catholic Historical Review* (Washington, DC, 1915–)
CPR   *Calendar of Patent Rolls in the Public Record Office* (London, 1882–)
CHB   *Cambridge History of the Bible,* ii, ed. G. W. H. Lampe (Cambridge, 1969)
EETS   *Early English Text Society* (London, 1864–)
EHR   *English Historical Review* (London, 1886–)
Fasciculi Zizaniorum, ed W. W. Shirley (*RS* 1858)
HJ   *Historical Journal* (Cambridge, 1958–)
HThR   *Harvard Theological Review* (New York/Cambridge, MA, 1908–)
JEH   *Journal of Ecclesiastical History* (Cambridge, 1950–)
JMedH   *Journal of Medieval History* (Amsterdam, 1975–)
JTS   *Journal of Theological Studies* (Oxford, 1899–)
OMT   *Oxford Medieval Texts* (Oxford, 1971–)
PL   *Patrologia Latina,* ed. J. P. Migne (Paris, 1841–)
PP   *Past and Present* (London, 1952–)
Rot.Parl.   *Rotuli Parliamentorum* (7 vols., London, 1832)
RS   *Rolls Series* (London, 1858–1911)
SCH   *Studies in Church History* (London/Oxford, 1964–)
ScHR   *Scottish Historical Review* (Edinburgh/Glasgow, 1904–)
SCH.S   *Studies in Church History: Subsidia* (Oxford, 1978–)
TRHS   *Transactions of the Royal Historical Society* (London, 1871–)
TU   *Texte und Untersuchungen zur Geschichte der altchristlichen Literatur* (Leipzig/Berlin, 1822–)

Vox Clamantis, ed. G. C. Macaulay, *The Complete Works of John Gower* 4 (Oxford, 1902)

Walsingham, *Chronicon Angliae,* ed. E. M. Thompson (*RS*, 1874)

Walsingham, *Historia Anglicana,* ed. H. T. Ridley (2 vols., *RS*, 1863–4)

WB	*Wycliffite Bible*
Wilkins	*Concilia Magnae Britanniae et Hiberniae A.D. 446–1717,* ed. D. Wilkins (4 vols., London 1737)
WS	*Wyclif Society* (London, 1884–1922)
YAJ	*Yorkshire Archaeological Journal* (London/Leeds, 1870–)

The following abbreviated titles of works by Wyclif are sometimes used (all are edited in the *WS* series):

De civ.dom.	*De civili domino*
De eccles.	*De ecclesia*
De euch.	*De eucharistia*
De off.reg.	*De officio regis*
De pot.pap.	*De potestate pape*
De ver.sac.scr.	*De veritate sancte scripture*
Serm.	*Sermones*

Note: where an Arabic figure stands before the (volume and) page number in reference to one of Wyclif's works, the chapter is indicated.

INTRODUCTION

Michael Wilks's first published paper on Wyclif appeared in 1965, the last after his death in 1999. The earliest, 'Predestination, Property, and Power: Wyclif's Theory of Dominion and Grace', announced in its title a new departure in Wyclif studies. In 1965 views of Wyclif amongst scholars and students of fourteenth-century England were largely controlled by the age-old tradition of Wyclif as the 'morning-star of the Reformation', a tradition which originated amongst the sixteenth-century reformers themselves and which continued to be repeated and refuted through the ensuing periods. Immediately in 1965 the dominant authority on Wyclif was Bruce McFarlane's *John Wycliffe and the Beginnings of English Nonconformity*, a work originally published in 1952 but reprinted several times later. McFarlane certainly did not subscribe to the reformers' enthusiasm for Wyclif, or to the assumption that his followers in the Lollard movement had had a serious impact on English religious life in the hundred years after Wyclif's death, but his biography was still shaped by the immediate political concerns of that tradition. Its accessible format and appearance in a widely disseminated series ensured that McFarlane's picture was widely adopted as the modern authority on Wyclif, whilst McFarlane's skills as a lecturer and tutor influenced the work of a number of Oxford graduates who engaged in research under his direction.[1] McFarlane's biography, because of its place of publication, was produced without annotation; but it is clear that its sources were predominantly the chronicles of the late fourteenth century, the documents of the secular administration and the printed episcopal registers.

Wilks came to Wyclif from a completely different direction. The area in which he had done his doctoral research had been within the history of ideas: the development of the theory of sovereignty in favour of the papal monarchy, with particular

---

[1] Notably J. A. F. Thomson and Margaret Aston, though only the latter had published before 1965.

reference to the writings of Augustinus Triumphus of Ancona. The outcome of that research appeared in 1964 as *The Problem of Sovereignty in the Later Middle Ages: the Papal Monarchy with Augustinus Triumphus and the Publicists.* He had been supervised by Walter Ullmann, himself a historian of very different interests and temperament from McFarlane, and he was a product of the Cambridge history school.[2] Ullmann remained to the end a supreme authority.[3] It is thus no surprise that the Wyclif who emerges from Wilks's papers is a very different person, that Wyclif's own writings form the major focus of interest, and that Wyclif appears as one in a tradition of political thought stretching from Aristotle to Locke and Hobbes.

To take each of these three points in turn, though in reverse order since that best reflects the sequence of Wilks's own concern. At a casual glance it may seem initially surprising that one trained on the writings of papal propagandists, mostly Italian or at least working in Italy, should turn to an English author notorious for his opposition to papal claims. The clue to the train of interest that led Wilks to the later writer is perhaps best seen in his second publication 'The Early Oxford Wyclif: Papalist or Nominalist?' (1969). His familiarity with the arguments and with the vocabulary of papalists enabled Michael Wilks to trace an inheritance, albeit turned on its head, in Wyclif: Wyclif, he reminded his readers, had repeatedly alluded to his 'conversion' from early errors, and these, he argued, had not been those of a nominalist turning to realism, but of a papalist converted to a theory closer to being described as regalian – hierocratic still, but with a new focus. In the first paper, and in others published later (notably nos 7 and 8), the ramifications of this understanding are worked out and demonstrated. The important source texts for Wyclif were Aristotle and Augustine (both amply acknowledged within his own writings), Aquinas (less frequently mentioned, but regularly with more reverence as 'sanctus Thomas' than Wyclif's

---

[2] So was J. A. Robson, author of *Wyclif and the Oxford Schools* (1961), whose supervisor had been Professor David Knowles. Robson's careful analysis of the position of Wyclif's *Summa de ente* in relation to Oxford philosophy in the third quarter of the fourteenth century remains the only full study of that important work.

[3] See, for instance, the 1999 paper, p. 60, n. 9.

later reputation might lead one to expect), and (though largely submerged and possibly indirectly) Ockham and Marsilius. To understand Wyclif's significance, Wilks constantly indicated, the modern historian must know his sources and his position in this long sequence.

But preeminently Wilks was a reader of Wyclif's own all too prolific writings: repetitive they may be, couched in a Latin that is less than transparent, difficult to date because of processes of revision, but they are the key to understanding. The footnotes of all but the last paper (no. 11) are dominated by quotations and references across Wyclif's texts; this published attestation is only a tiny selection of the mass of notes from those texts, notes which were clearly amplified by constant rereading, that constitute one of the largest sections of the material that Wilks left at his death. The twelve parts of the *Summa theologie*, to which Wilks usually added the preceding *De dominio divino* and the ensuing *De eucharistia*,[4] attracted most attention, but the mass of the *Sermones* and some shorter works were within his mastery.[5]

Interest in Wyclif's political ideas in regard to the office of king and pope led inevitably to the question of why, when Wyclif had apparently had so much to offer Edward III, the young Richard II and their royalist supporters, he had personally ended his days in disgrace at Lutterworth, and his followers had so quickly come to be regarded as incipient traitors as well as heretics. Wilks's paper on '*Reformatio regni*: Wyclif and Hus as Leaders of Religious Protest Movements' is perhaps his most eloquent production, written with a fluency of argument and a conviction beyond the earlier Wyclif papers, and perhaps also the later works. The key to Wyclif's thought is now clearer: it is that of double substances, whether that is applied to the deity, to the eucharist or to political authority. Wyclif wanted a *reformatio regni* to be led from the top downwards; he was defeated as much by bad luck (the papal schism and especially the Peasants' Revolt)

---

[4] This explains Wilks's description of the *Summa* as made up of fourteen books (see p. 9).

[5] Though Wilks recognized, of course, the early *Sermones quadraginta* grouping, he never seems entirely to have discarded Loserth's description of volume 4 of his edition as '*Sermones mixti*' (in which he followed the arrangement of the base text, Trinity College Cambridge B.16.2): that name has no authorial justification.

as by his own mistakes or intemperance. For a brief time Hus, whom Wilks saw as closely following Wyclif's ideas,[6] gained the kind of support from Wenceslas that Wyclif had looked in vain to the English king to find. Later papers, notably nos 6 and 11, explore the immediate political reasons for this English outcome, tracing the hopes of success Wyclif might have had from John of Gaunt, later amongst the royalist party of the late 1370s to early 1380s. In his last paper, no.11, Wilks identifies as crucial in the outcome the role of Thomas Arundel, brother of one of the Appellants, archbishop successively of York and Canterbury – and Arundel he likewise accused of being the key figure in the deposition of Richard II, king-maker and simultaneously unmaker of reform.

Despite the continuance of certain ideas throughout more than 35 years of work on Wyclif, it is possible to trace changes in Michael Wilks's approach and to see that his mind continued to address new issues. Certainly the footnotes to these papers attest to the breadth of his reading on topics contemporary with Wyclif, whether on Chaucer, Langland or Margery Kempe, or on the possible influence of Bohemian art on the court culture of Richard II. As time went on there seems to be an increase in the attention paid to the detailed political context within which Wyclif's ideas were formed and published: the minutiae of chroniclers are increasingly combed for clues about the manoeuvres of the dominant figures in the Wyclif story, and the complexity of ever-changing alliances is traced through public documents. Wilks remained, however, almost entirely within the domain of printed materials: he rarely cites unprinted evidence, whether from the Public Record Office, from episcopal documentation or from unpublished texts, even those by Wyclif himself. This doubtless explains the reliance on the tangled analysis of Wycliffite Bible manuscripts,[7] a reliance that perhaps weakens his argument in 'Misleading manuscripts: Wyclif and the non-Wycliffite Bible' (no.5).

---

[6] Wilks possibly did not realise the extent of the Czech debate on this issue, though he alludes to some of its early stages.

[7] As published, at the date of the paper's publication in 1975, by Fristedt, Lindberg and Hargreaves.

For several years before his untimely death Michael Wilks had been working on a book-length new biography of Wyclif, one which would be 'a political life'; he had spoken of this as nearly complete. Unfortunately the only biography of the figure who had preoccupied Michael for so long that was completed was the brief outline that appeared in 1994 in the *Dictionnaire de spiritualité*. Valuable though that is, it is a minnow beside the whale that the full-length study would have been. Furthermore, the concerns of the encyclopedia in which it was to appear have inevitably shaped its proportions: there is a brief account of the life, followed by longer sections on Wyclif's thought, and a short section on the group of preachers who disseminated that thought. But the thought which is here most closely analysed concerns Wyclif's basic philosophical and theological ideas (though even here there is nothing on his views of oral confession and absolution), and there is little on Wilks's primary concern (and expertise), namely the relation of church and state. Whether anything can be salvaged from Michael's papers to produce the biography he did not live to complete is as yet uncertain – initial impressions, despite that wealth of notes, is that the argument for the biography existed in Michael's head but not on paper.

This collection is necessarily only one aspect of Michael Wilks's contribution to the understanding of Wyclif, even if it is the one easiest to record. The conference *From Ockham to Wyclif*, held in Oxford in April 1985, and the volume which published its proceedings, owed much to his organization, genius for conviviality and patience with participants: it was he who suggested the yoking, improbable at first mention but triumphantly successful in outcome, of the two Oxford masters whose anniversaries (Ockham's probable birth in 1285, Wyclif's death on 31 December 1384) were celebrated. Not only at that conference, but more frequently at the two annual meetings of the Ecclesiastical History Society (whose Treasurer he was for many years, and President in 1985-6), his friendly interest in the concerns of colleagues and young research students, together with his own contributions, kept Wyclif studies at the forefront of interest. And he responded quickly and sympathetically, notwithstanding many other commitments and later ill-health, to queries and to offprints, however improbable their source or content.

The thirty-five years of Michael Wilks's publication on Wyclif saw considerable developments not only in scholarly understanding of Wyclif himself but also in perceptions of what is needed to provide a proper comprehension of the long distant past. Straightforward political history, taken from the unquestioned documents of the time, is no longer sufficient: those documents embody a perspective, often a polemical and propagandist perspective, which must be probed; evidence of a more varied kind than the documents of state must be analysed; ideas and artefacts must be factored in to the picture. The most recently published papers (nos 9-11) show how acutely aware Michael Wilks was of these developments, even though his own starting point had been in the forefront of the new interests. In some ways Wyclif studies have still not caught up with his expertise: there remain few if any with his command of Wyclif's writings, none who understand so much of the theoretical background to Wyclif's ecclesiological ideas. Others recently may have worked more extensively on Wyclif's directly logical and philosophical contribution, or on the mutations of Wyclif's thought in the vernacular writings of his followers. But for many of the most central issues of Wyclif's thought, readers at the beginning of the new century will return with gratitude to the perceptions and rigorous analysis given in Michael Wilks's papers.

Anne Hudson

1
JOHN WYCLIF, REFORMER, *c.*1327–1384

1. *Biography.*

John Wyclif was probably born about 1327 into the minor gentry family who held the village of Wycliffe in Teesdale, North Yorkshire. He was ordained deacon at St. Mary's, and priest at the Minster in York under Archbishop William de la Zouche during 1351, but after 1352 was apparently assimilated into the household of the new archbishop, the noted reformer John Thoresby. It is possible that he was already at Oxford, perhaps intended for a career in law, but by 1356 he seems to have graduated in arts and had become a fellow of Merton College. He was appointed, presumably under Thoresby's patronage, Master of Balliol College by 1360. He was obliged to resign when given his first living in May 1361, but had returned to Oxford by 1363, from which time he occupied rooms in Queen's Hall. Early in 1366 Simon Islip, archbishop of Canterbury, appointed him to the wardenship of Canterbury College; but opposition from the Benedictines, including the new archbishop Simon Langham, led to Wyclif's dismissal in 1367, although the subsequent legal dispute was not settled until 1371. In that year, having pursued the theology course during the late 1360s, Wyclif incepted as doctor of theology. [1]

Thoresby had secured for him the rectory of Fillingham, Lincs. (11 May 1361), and in 1362 he was given the canonry and prebend of Aust at Westbury-on-Trym, Glos. On 12 November 1368 he exchanged Fillingham for Ludgershall, Bucks., and on 7 April 1374 replaced this with Lutterworth, Leics. Promise of a prebend at Lincoln by Gregory XI (January 1371, repeated December 1373) did not materialize when Caistor became available in 1375, and Wyclif is reputed to have been disappointed at his failure to obtain the see of Worcester when it was vacant between November 1373 and September 1375. By the

This is the original English text of the article published in French in *Dictionnaire de Spiritualité*, fascicules CVI-CVII (vol. xvi, 1994), cols. 1501–1512.

mid-1370s, however, Wyclif was not only acknowledged at Oxford as the outstanding teacher of his time, but was also the leader of a reform movement of 'poor priests', inspired by Franciscan ideals of apostolic poverty, for whom the obtaining of high office was not a prime consideration.

Wyclif was already well established in royal service. John of Gaunt, the effective ruler of England, was the feudal superior of the Wycliffe area, and Wyclif himself enjoyed the patronage of two of Gaunt's Exchequer officials, William Askeby, archdeacon of Nottingham, and Richard, Lord Scrope of Bolton and Masham, who was Treasurer from 1371. Wyclif seems to have had an appointment as a Household clerk *(clericus regis)* in the later 1360s, to have attended Parliament as an official in the early 1370s, and during the summer of 1374 took part in the negotiations at Bruges over the related issues of papal taxation and provisions and appeals to the apostolic see. By this period opposition to Wyclif's increasing anti-papalism was mounting, again with the Benedictines foremost, and a series of disputes greeted the publication of his views on ecclesiastical lordship, followed by an appeal to the papal court channelled through the Benedictine cardinal Adam Easton. During the crisis of the Good Parliament in 1376 Wyclif supported Gaunt in his struggle with the English bishops led by William of Wykeham (Winchester) and William Courtenay (London), and as a consequence Wyclif was summoned to appear before an episcopal court at St. Paul's on 19 February 1377, although the personal intervention of Gaunt and the Earl Marshall, Henry Percy, rendered the hearing abortive. The reception of a papal condemnation on nineteen propositions drawn from Wyclif's work on lordship, issued by Gregory XI on 22 May, led to a period of house arrest in Oxford and another trial at Lambeth Palace in March 1378, although this too was frustrated by royal intervention. Wyclif gained some revenge by attacking Nicholas Litlington, abbot of Westminster, who had excommunicated Gaunt's officers for sanctuary violation, at the Gloucester Parliament in October. But his hopes that the accession of the young Richard II would prove a turning point for the success of the reform programme proved illusory.

The outbreak of the Great Schism, in which Wyclif initially wrote in defence of the English government's support for Urban VI, effectively put a stop to the process against him. But in 1380

Wyclif was unwise enough to embark on a campaign against the
religious orders, in part for their failure to adopt his reform
programme, and a year later changed circumstances provided
ample scope for new moves against him. The outbreak of the
Peasants' Revolt, for which (despite the Revolt's attack on Gaunt)
Wyclif expressed some sympathy, and which led to Courtenay's
appointment as archbishop of Canterbury, and the publication of
a full restatement of his eucharistic doctrine fuelled complaints
that he was guilty of both sedition and heresy. After a
condemnation by a commission at Oxford appointed by the
chancellor William Barton, Courtenay summoned a council to
meet at the London Blackfriars on 17–21 May 1382 which
declared that of 24 alleged Wycliffite propositions – although
Wyclif was not mentioned by name – ten were heretical and the
rest erroneous. Wyclif himself had already withdrawn to
Lutterworth, and so escaped the archiepiscopal visitation of
Oxford during the summer and autumn of 1382. But he continued
in retirement to be as productive as ever, now condemning both
popes of the Schism as Antichrist, advocating peace with France,
supporting Gaunt's opposition to the bishop of Norwich's
crusade in Flanders in 1383 and defending him during the
summer of 1384 in the mysterious affair of the mad Carmelite.
Already ill, he seems to have suffered a stroke on 28 December
1384, died on 31 December, and was buried at Lutterworth.
Following a more extensive condemnation of his teaching by the
Council of Constance in May 1415, his remains were burnt in the
spring of 1428 and the ashes thrown into the nearby river Swift.
His followers, already being vilified as 'Lollards', formed a
movement which survived in England into the Reformation of the
sixteenth century, but it was in Bohemia during the Hussite
Revolt that his teaching had most immediate effect.

2. *Works.*

The bulk of the three hundred Latin works attributed to Wyclif,
and now admirably catalogued by Williel Thomson, were edited
and published in 36 volumes by the Wyclif Society between 1882
and 1922, but the authenticity of any of the alleged English works
remains an open question. Dating the works has, however,

proved to be an extremely hazardous operation, since the three *summae* and a number of other major writings are clearly compilations of earlier lectures and tracts, with the additional problem that there seems to have been later revision either by Wyclif himself or by his followers. None of his very early work appears to have survived, and may well have been deliberately destroyed by Wyclif to mask his rejection of extreme philosophical Realism and orthodox Augustinianism. This 'conversion' (to quote Beryl Smalley) had clearly taken place well before 1370, by which time Wyclif was already lamenting his 'youthful errors'.

The three parts of the *Summa logica*, containing lectures on Aristotelian logic, provide much of the earliest surviving material and probably date to the period 1360–3, although there is evidence of later revision, and both the *De actibus animae* and the *De insolubilibus* would seem to be subsequent additions. The *Summa intellectualium* or *Summa de ente* is still incomplete, but consisted of some fifteen sections grouped into two parts, and dates to the later 1360s. A fragmentary series of debates with John Kenningham in 1371 marks the transition to the first of the 'theological' works, the *De benedicta incarnatione*, which includes remnants of Wyclif's lectures on the *Sentences*, whilst the magisterial *Postilla super totam Bibliam*, the first commentary on the whole of the Bible since Nicholas of Lyra, was in progress but may not have been completed until the mid-1370s.

Between 1373 and 1381 Wyclif produced the massive fourteen volumes of the *Summa theologiae*, beginning with six books on the various types of law and lordship, four dealing with the Bible, the Church and its government, and finally four volumes defending his eucharistic theory and savaging his opponents, now including the friars. Amongst some thirty other tracts written in his later years mention may be made of the *De officio pastorali* (1379), commentaries on Matthew xxiii–xxiv, the *Trialogus* of 1382 and *Dialogus* of 1383, and the *Opus evangelicum* completed late in 1384. Of the four volumes of collected sermons, parts I, II and III are in fact a treatise couched in the form of specimen sermons (1381–2), and only part IV contains the reordered texts of two sermon collections, the *Quadraginta sermones* dating to the second half of the 1370s and the *Sermones viginti* of 1382–3.

Of the dozen or so English works attributed to Wyclif, one might conjecture that the tracts on the Ten Commandments, on confession, the commentaries on Matthew, on lordship and the church would be most likely to be his, but all this is doubtful. Similarly it is clear that by 1382 Wyclif was aware that the gospels had been translated into English, but again there is no proof that he took any active part in the work of translation itself.

3. *Doctrine.*

Wyclif's encyclopaedic system may be characterized as a more finely balanced and elastic form of Thomism adapted to the requirements of a national monarchy ruling an independent church-state. He came to believe that extreme Realism in philosophy was being used to underpin a perverted Augustinianism in theology which gave total universal power to the papacy at the expense of national communities, and therefore all branches of learning were in urgent need of reform. As he emphasised in the fragmentary record of his disputes with the Carmelite John Kenningham in 1371, the same principles must apply in philosophy, theology and politics, and all his surviving work bears this out. Although he repeatedly confessed to youthful philosophic errors, by which he appears to mean primarily that he accepted the current hierocratic theory of papal supremacy (subsequently rejected as a childish notion accepted only by 'boys'), there are no writings from this early period. Wyclif had entered an Oxford which still reverberated from the disputes associated with Richard Fitzralph on such matters as predestination and free will, the states of natural innocence, lordship and grace, and the relationship between the friars and parish clergy, and all this would be amply reflected in his own later work. But what is probably now most of the earliest material is contained in the as yet unpublished commentary on Aristotle's *Physics,* which underlines how much Wyclif owed to the 'school' of mathematical science at Merton – his opponent William Woodford subsequently ridiculed him for applying mathematical concepts to the eucharist – and helps to explain the considerable following he attracted from amongst his colleagues at Merton, a college with its own strong Augustinian and royalist tradition.

Combined with Euclidean geometric principles and the optical theories of Witello the Pole, Wyclif used the commentaries on the *Physics* by both Grosseteste and Aquinas, together with the various Arabic commentators, to argue that every matter must be viewed from opposite directions before these views are harmonized, so reinforcing Aristotle's teaching on the need for a mean between the divinity of Platonic realism and the materialism of the Sophists. Just as the sun produces both day and night, or a pillar can be either tall or deep, it is essentially a question of where it is seen from. Nature contains two orders, upwards and downwards *(ordines ascendi et descendi)*: divine grace coming down from above is to be balanced by man's own use of right reason towards God – although it had to be recognized that the present corruption of human reason had produced profound disharmony. But in a rightly-ordered system there has to be a 'two-way contingency' with everything seen from opposite poles so that both directions can be taken together. On this basis Wyclif was able throughout the whole of his thought to apply the Aristotelian principle of equivocation, deriving from the logicians' technique of dealing with 'insolubles' or contradictions. This enabled Wyclif to accept both sides of any equation, confusing his opponents and subsequent ages by his habit of emphasising one side at the expense of the other as circumstances dictated, without making it clear that it was an equation and he therefore half-agreed with them. Such doublesidedness meant that all other contemporary scholars could be condemned for single-minded extremism: the 'modern sign-doctors', whose sophistries he repeatedly denounced, might be at opposite ends of the spectrum to each other, but, as with a horseshoe, the ends curved towards the other side – they were both equidistant from the central truth. 'I take the middle way', he declared, the *via media* which requires that opposites are blended together. All theories are right – or rather, all are wrong, for not recognising that every other one is partially right too.

Wyclif's answer to the vexed question of universals illustrates the difficulty one often experiences in retaining the flavour of what he appears to be saying whilst conveying the meaning of what was intended. It is very easy to assume that his apparent rejection of Ockhamist nominalism or conceptualism made Wyclif into an extreme Realist in the Platonic sense. But this is not case.

God, he said, is lord of both universals and individuals. Both have substance in the sense that one cannot be a lord without something or someone to lord it over: individuals become as necessary to God as his own reality (and on this ground Wyclif followed Anselm in claiming that philosophy could prove the existence of God). Accordingly both universals and accidents are true beings which cannot normally and properly exist in isolation from each other, although they can be thought of as separate things, and may occasionally need to be treated as such. Universals have downward reality as the divine ideas by which God creates whatever exists outside himself; they also have upward reality as concepts, like genera and species, constructed in the human mind, but in this sense essentially as human creations; and thirdly, both the preceding senses can and should be taken together, equivocally, by seeing them as signs of what really exists, images which would not be there if, as in a mirror, there was either nothing to reflect or no one to look at them. The true existence of universals relates both to themselves as such – they have *quidditas* as substantial forms – and to their individual accidents. Universal and individual, substance and accidents, form and matter, all express the same duality. They really are *per se* and *per accidens:* they have potentially separate existences but actually, usually, should be seen together. It was a principle of double substance which Wyclif applied directly to the doctrine of the eucharist, rejecting the old-fashioned Humbertine-Gregorian definitions in the process. What, he queried, is this small, white substance? In rational human terms the communion bread, as bread, has the substance of bread and looks like bread; it remains *(remanet)* bread after consecration both in appearance and quiddity. But the act of consecration also converts it into a second body, the *corpus Christi,* since the Bible records that Christ took bread and said 'This is my body', and therefore it must now be seen by the eye of faith as Christ himself. The great book of Christianity teaches us to use two eyes, actual and mystical. Double substance theory means that the eucharist is not actually Christ – the faithful at mass are not cannibals – but an image of Christ, an instrumental vehicle or sign of grace: but in this restricted sacramental or figurative sense transubstantiation has effectively taken place. Equivocation solves all problems, although having sketched the outlines of the theory in his early works,

Wyclif did not elaborate his eucharistic teaching until his discussion of the nature of the Church made this unavoidable, and he was able to attack the Fourth Lateran Council's version of transubstantiation as part of his campaign to discredit the memory of Innocent III, in his view the worst of all popes, because he had initiated a whole new era in the exaltation of papal sovereignty.

If, Wyclif argued, the official papal theory of transubstantiation, by which the sacramental bread and wine ceased to be bread and wine, was to be maintained, it would require a miracle to take place every time the mass was celebrated. Miracles would become a normal part of human life in the Church, which would not only be unreasonably divisive in separating the miracle-working priesthood from the laity, but would also mean that God would have to exercise his absolute power, by which acts against the natural order of earthly things were brought about, as a matter of course at human pleasure and command. But this would deny the whole basis of the Creation: God could not be allowed to annihilate what he had created. Such use of his omnipotence would offend against the whole principle of equity, of moderation and self-restraint, which was essential to goodness, and God was nothing if not good. God cannot escape from his own nature: he is never free to do what is wrong. God cannot contradict himself (perhaps an odd statement for someone whose whole system was based on the principle that contradiction was the mark of truth). But by this he meant that God must limit his own omnipotence, his absolute divine potency to do whatever he pleased, by making it normally impossible for himself to act otherwise than as he does through his ordained power by which the natural order was established and upheld. The Creation was necessary because, again, God could not be the Lord unless he had a world to be lord of. The natural order is as necessary to God as he is to it as its creator: there is a dual necessity. Realists would make everything basically divine, denying the rationale of the natural world; Ockhamists would deny the Bible by allowing only material things to exist, so that matter itself becomes the eternal principle; both are to be condemned and accommodated. Aristotle was clearly wrong to assert the eternity of matter as regards the beginning of the world, but once created it raised the question of whether God would ever really want to do without the world. God had apparently ordained that the world would end, but it remained theoretically possible that he might decide otherwise on the Day of Judgement. But what God decided about eternity was not a question for man to be concerned with here and now. The two levels of divine power, absolute and ordained, meant two versions of time. There was divine time *(duratio)* in which past and future were eternally present, and there was human time *(tempus)* measured in this world by successive ages. Once more the appeal was to Aristotelian physics: a line could be seen either as a single thing or as a succession of dots next to each other. There was both a single eternity and a history composed of a series of instants following each other. It all depended which was under consideration. But there was no problem about predestination and human free will. In the eternal present of divine time all was foreknown. But this does not create difficulties on earth because man cannot know what God has decided, and it is always possible that God will change his mind. Divine foreknowledge is theoretical, not actual in practice. Necessity, as Wyclif put it following Grosseteste, is ambiguous: we must distinguish between what God can know by virtue of his omnipotence, i.e. 'absolute necessity', and what he has bound himself not to know on earth, what hypothetically he could know if he wanted to but does not. Wyclif was not the complete terminist he was assumed to be by the Council of Constance. As Augustine had said, the sinner was a man beside himself like a virtuous image seen in a mirror by one's actual evil self, but only the one person was visible. By the same token in reverse, signs of damnation – and Wyclif had no difficulty in compiling enormous lists, which grew ever longer as he grew older, of damnable abuses amongst the clergy of his day, which suggested that they were amongst the *praesciti* – were valid enough in terms of time and human reason, but God can always determine otherwise in eternity. Mortal sin did not guarantee hellfire any more than taking the eucharist ensured salvation and made one a member of the elect *(praedestinati)* who alone formed the true Church in heaven. The love of God which gave the damned grace in this world is to be contrasted with the lack of earthly grace enjoyed by the righteous, but there was no certain correlation between salvation and human behaviour.

In what he regarded as a return to traditional English theology as it had been defined by authors as diverse as Anselm and the Anglo-Norman Anonymous, Wyclif emphasised the importance of the Incarnation as 'squaring the circle of human existence'. Christ, the *Deus-homo,* a golden mean uniting the divine with the human, was the supreme example of necessary duality: two natures which could be taken in isolation but were made one in himself. Since the national kingdom, being both a *regnum* and an *ecclesia,* was itself a *corpus Christi* this same duality should operate in English society. King and pope, respectively heads of the lay and sacerdotal orders, were both vicars of Christ: but the king was vicar of Christ as God whilst the pope was only vicar of Christ as a man. The ideal relationship between them was accordingly one of wealth versus poverty, since all belonged to God. The king ruled in power and majesty, whilst the pope, like all clergy, should be distinguished by humility and suffering, as had been the case in the first age of the apostolic Church. Wyclif's notorious thesis (which he adapted from papal theory) that lordship *(dominium)* was dependent on grace meant for practical purposes the king's grace as vicar of God. The *ecclesia Anglicana* had originated as a royal proprietary church in which the king was patron in chief and the source of all grants made by himself and other lords. But as the world declined into a second age, defined by the Donation of Constantine injecting the venom of imperialism and possessiveness, ownership of property and power, into the clergy, so the relative standing of kings and popes had had to be adjusted. Kings, like God, were obliged to restrict their own absolutism and accept that they were no longer the only *caput ecclesiae:* there was a duality, two swords, in the way that John of Salisbury had described it as a cooperation of separate temporal and spiritual jurisdictions. To overstep the bounds of self-limitation became a mark of tyranny, an act of self-deposition. Yet the interminable papal demands for more, the way in which the crusades made the clergy more like Mohammedans than Christians in their lust for conquest, led to a further degeneration *c.*1200 into the present third age, the age of Antichrist in which the popes claimed total sovereignty and clerical *cupiditas* swallowed up whole kingdoms. An unreformed clergy, especially the 'possessioners' of the monastic orders, devoted their lives to litigation, flinging excommunication and charges of heresy against all who would withstand them.

The predominant theme of Wyclif's later writings therefore became a constantly reiterated plea for a great purification *(reformatio)*, a return to the apostolic Church, to be achieved by a royal dispossession of the *possessionati* and the compulsory adoption by the clergy of a life of evangelical poverty. It was a case of necessity, when the ruler might act *casualiter*, reverting to his original absolute power for the common good of the realm. The pope, as the bishop of Rome, should confine himself to the affairs of a local Italian church. If not, he could be dealt with under the same terms of a case of necessity as defined by the canon lawyers of the twelfth century, by which a general council should be summoned to determine that he was a heretic who had deposed himself from his own office.

A central feature of Wyclif's repudiation of sacerdotal separatism and arrogant superiority was his constant rejection of humanly devised ecclesiastical 'rites and ceremonies' which in his view had no apostolic foundation. In the same way that merely taking in the eucharistic *corpus Christi* did not make the alleged Christian into a Christ-like being, so the true Christ-dweller *(Christicola)* was required to perform an imitation of Christ *in vita et moribus*, a covenant with God to change or convert his whole way of life so that his will was brought into conformity with the divine will. Christianity could not just be a matter of externals. Ultimately it was an inner religion, a way of love *(caritas)* associated with the secret teachings of St. John, which had its own mystical theology and could change the believer into an *imago Christi*, a mirror reflecting God himself. Truth could be sought through both the active and the contemplative lives, but the third way, the inner life of charity, was best, a mixed way equally applicable to both clergy and laity. The clergy might justifiably claim to know more, but too much knowledge was liable to generate the besetting sin of pride, so that 'unknowing' might be a safer guide to salvation. What was needed beyond the clerical and lay *ordines* was another order, the *ordo Christi*, of poor, simple, apostolic man – idiots of God but members of the *scola Christi* – who were pure in heart and devoted their lives to the good works of humility: prayer and penitence, teaching and pastoral care for others. The supreme guide and example was

naturally Christ himself, and accordingly study of the Bible was
of paramount importance. The Bible, especially the Gospels, was
the book of evangelical living, the only source for Christ himself,
and Christ was the *liber vitae*, a living exponent of the true way
to live. But the Bible in this context meant not only one shorn of
textual impurities and human accretions, but more importantly
a work in the hands of those who could appreciate 'the logic of
scripture': true theology required right-minded philosophers who
understood the principles which governed universals and
equivocation. Whereas the papalist would turn the Bible into
arcana imperii, a mass of divine mysteries, and the nominalist
would see it simply as mere words to be taken at face value only,
Wyclif argued that the Biblical texts should be seen both as marks
on a page of manuscript and as signs of inner mystical meanings.
Following Aquinas, he insisted that the true sense was the literal
sense, the sense that God intended, whichever that might be. But
although the Bible contained all truth, and was therefore the sole
source of truth, scripture could be mediated through other
vehicles like prayers, creeds and decrees so long as it was
understood that it was the content of truth that mattered *(sola
scriptura)* rather than the context. Wyclif did not envisage a
conflict between scripture and authentic tradition: both were part
of the *corpus Bibliae scripturae*. The true teachings of the Church,
its councils and saints, were fully acceptable, and on the whole
he adopted Gratian's *Decretum* as a statement of the 'good old
law' approved by both divine and natural law. It was the insane
novelties of the *Decretales*, full of papal decrees which were to be
branded as lies seeking to falsify scripture itself. But God would
not have created the natural order without giving men the
capability of knowing what was right, and accordingly religion
had to be reasonable. Reading the Bible was a co-operation
between God and man, divine authority from above and human
reason from below. If something was true, it was of course
entirely reasonable for Christians to accept it; on the other hand,
even pagans as reasonable men had an innate ability, albeit
limited, to ascertain divine truth. Christianity should be neither
a continual swallowing of incredible mysteries nor a collection of
fallacious human opinions: it should be a harmonious blend of
reason and faith, whose tenets were always open to scrutiny –
and he repeatedly challenged any opponents to demonstrate that

he was in error so that he could administer self-correction. A simple reasonable and righteous faith was preferable to an elaborate theology, and whilst Wyclif freely admitted that the intricacies of truth (not least his habit of using new words or old words with new meanings) might need to be tempered to the needs of the illiterate, he also felt that the laity, if properly taught, were much more reliable than learned exegetes. It was therefore of vital importance that the Bible, especially the New Testament, should be easily available. But whilst this was obviously helped by translation of the scriptures into English, it was preaching which became the supreme duty of the pastor. Vernacular translation of the Bible and other religious works was desirable primarily as an aid to preaching rather than as a subject for independent study and direct reading. What was needed above all was a body of preachers who would spread the truth. How can one preach unless there are those who can be sent? The formation of an order of preachers steadily became Wyclif's prime concern. His colleagues at Oxford were encouraged to engage in preaching missions, but Wyclif seems to have relied much more on the training of clergy who would spread his principles in the households of the aristocracy and the courts of princes. In course of time the *ordo Christi* was designed to become under royal patronage an order to end all others – and from this angle the exceedingly acrimonious antimendicantism of his later years was not simply a matter of pique at lack of support – although this objective lies uneasily with his view that the order of Wycliffite preachers should also be an elite with a much more apocalyptic function. Drawing on Joachimite and Spiritual Franciscan inspiration, Wyclif prophesied that his adherents would become a saving remnant of suffering servants who would revive the ideal of martyrdom on the model of St. Paul and the early Church. Their persecution by the forces of Antichrist would be a corporate crucifixion for the benefit of the English *populus Dei*, a redemptive process out of which a perfect society would be resurrected at the end of time. To demonstrate that the Last Days had indeed been reached, Wyclif was forced to accept the fiction that Urban VI (of all popes!) would prove to be the long promised *papa angelicus*. Although this notion provided useful propaganda for the English government's choice of popes in the Great Schism of 1378, it did not long survive the failure of the forlorn appeals made to the Roman church, and it is difficult to imagine that these were seriously intended to be anything but delaying tactics in Wyclif's struggle with the opposition party amongst the English bishops.

4. *Manuscripts and Editions.*

There is a full list in Williel R. Thomson, *The Latin Writings of John Wyclyf* (Toronto, 1983). The bulk of the published works are to be found in the collected edition of *Wyclif's Latin Works* (Wyclif Society, 36 volumes, London, 1882–1922, reprinted Frankfurt am Main, 1968), but to these should be added the earlier editions by G. Lechler of the *De officio pastorali* (Leipzig, 1863) and the *Trialogus* (Oxford, 1869); the *Fasciculi zizaniorum magistri Johannis Wyclif* (ed. W. W. Shirley, Rolls Series, London, 1858) contains a number of tracts and is an indispensible, but hostile, source of biographical information. More recent material includes the editions by S. Harrison Thomson of parts of the *Summa de ente* (Oxford, 1930), the *De trinitate* by Allen duPont Breck (Boulder, Colorado, 1962), and subsequent to Thomson's catalogue the *De universalibus* (ed. I. J. Mueller, trans. A. Kenny, 2 vols., Oxford, 1985), and the *Summa insolubilium* (ed. P. V. Spade and G. A. Wilson, Binghamton, 1986). The three main collections of alleged English works are T. Arnold, *Select English Works of John Wyclif* (3 vols., Oxford, 1869–71), *The English Works of Wyclif hitherto unprinted* (ed. F. D. Matthew, Early English Text Society Original Series 74, London 1880, revd. edn. 1902, reprinted Millwood, 1973), and *Wyclif: Select English Writings* (ed. H. E. Winn, Oxford, 1929), but, as stated above, these are of doubtful authenticity and relate to the history of Lollardy rather than Wyclif himself. The same applies to the *English Wycliffite Sermons* (ed. A. Hudson and P. Gradon, 5 vols., Oxford, 1983–96) and the Wycliffite Bible (ed. J. Forshall and F. Madden, 4 vols., Oxford, 1850, reprinted New York, 1982), on which a further bibliography is provided in the second volume of the *Cambridge History of the Bible* (ed. G. W. H. Lampe, Cambridge, 1969).

Studies.

The classic work by H. B. Workman, *John Wyclif* (2 vols., Oxford, 1926) is still the basic account, but should be supplemented by more recent literature, including K. B. McFarlane, *John Wycliffe and the Beginnings of English Nonconformity* (London, 1952), republished as *Wycliffe and English Non-Conformity* (Harmondsworth, 1972); J. H. Dahmus, *The prosecution of John Wyclyf* (New Haven, 1952, reprinted Hamden, Conn., 1970); J. A. Robson, *Wyclif and the Oxford Schools* (Cambridge, 1971); G. A. Benrath, *Wyclifs Bibelkommentar* (Berlin, 1966); F. de Boor, *Wyclifs Simoniebegriff: die theologischen und kirchenpolitischen Grundlagen der Kirchenkritik John Wyclifs* (Halle, 1970); J. Hughes, *Pastors and Visionaries: Religion and Secular Life in Late Medieval Yorkshire* (Woodbridge, 1988). Further reading may be found in recent collections of essays: A. Kenny (ed.), *Wyclif in his Times* (Oxford, 1986); A. Hudson and M. Wilks (eds.), *From Ockham to Wyclif (Studies in Church History, Subsidia 5*, Oxford, 1987); M. Aston, *Lollards and Reformers: Images and Literacy in Late Medieval Religion* (London, 1984). For the most up to date accounts of the relationship between Wyclif and the Wycliffite movement reference should be made to A. Hudson, *The Premature Reformation: Wycliffite Texts and Lollard History* (Oxford, 1988), and J. I. Catto and T. A. R. Evans (eds.), *The History of the University of Oxford ii: Late Medieval Oxford* (Oxford, 1992).

2

Predestination, Property, and Power: Wyclif's Theory of Dominion and Grace

MICHAEL WILKS

Lecturer in History, Birkbeck College, University of London

For nearly six hundred years the significance of Wyclif's theory of dominion and grace has been in dispute, although it is generally agreed that his chief claim to fame as a political figure rests upon it. It has recently been described as his main contention,[1] and there can be no doubt that it was a thesis of which he was inordinately proud. It became a major feature in both the papal condemnation of 1377 and that of the Blackfriars Council five years later; it looms even more largely in the forty-five Wycliffite propositions condemned at Prague in 1403, at Rome in 1413, and subsequently by the Council of Constance in 1415.[2] Hus's defence of the theory was an important factor in bringing him to the stake. But if Wyclif's contemporaries had little hesitation in recognising a destructive potential, modern scholars have been far more cautious in assessing its political value. Neither R. L. Poole nor Workman could reach a firm judgement. Poole described it as a unique conception which justified its author's title to be considered as the father of modern Christianity, but at the same time he referred to a philo-

[1] M. McKisack, *The Fourteenth Century*, 1959, 512; cf. C. H. McIlwain, *The Growth of Political Thought in the West*, 1932, 315, 'the pivot on which his whole philosophic system turns.'

[2] For Gregory XI's bulls of 22 May 1377, which condemn eighteen articles, see Walsingham, *Historia Anglicana*, ed. H. T. Riley, 1863, I, 345-6. The twenty-four conclusions deemed either heretical or erroneous in 1382 are listed in *Fasciculi Zizaniorum*, ed. W. W. Shirley, 1858, 277–82. These were augmented at Paris by a further twenty-one articles, and used by the German masters at Prague, to form the forty-five eventually condemned at Constance in the eighth session of the council on 4 May 1415: H. von der Hardt, *Magnumo ecumenicum Constantiense concilium*, Frankfurt-Leipzig 1697-1700, IV, 153-4; also in F. Palacký, *Documenta Mag. Johannis Hus*, Prague 1869, 329-31; cf. Hefele-Leclercq, *Histoire des conciles*, Paris 1907-38, VII, pt 1, 223-6. Another 260 articles were condemned in the following session.

sophy of fruitless ingenuity which was never intended to have any immediate, practical effect.[1] Similarly Workman emphasised its Utopian nature, but nevertheless declared that Wyclif had swept away much of the Catholic system as then practised.[2] Most textbooks of political thought[3] have preferred to follow Trevelyan's savage comment that it was a metaphysical juggle, contradictory, still-born, and not repeated by Wyclif in later life.[4] On the other hand it has been widely accepted that Wyclif's aim was to bestow divine rights of power and possession upon all good Christians, thereby discarding the existing hierarchies of government which stood between God and his people.[5] More recent discussions of the subject have therefore tended to present a rather different picture. The late Professor Betts spoke of it as a revolutionary idea, indicative of profound social change, 'which was able to unmake popes, to trample episcopacy underfoot, to mutilate monasticism,' and whose effects could be seen not only in the Reformation, but in the Dutch revolt under Philip II as much as in the Czech rejection of Sigismund.[6] So too Professor Dahmus believes that Wyclif wanted the principle of dominion to be implemented by an immediate dispossession of the clergy, and that this would have had a catastrophic effect.[7] And a few months ago another American scholar, Howard Kaminsky, depicted dominion

[1] R. L. Poole, *Illustrations of the History of Medieval Thought and Learning*, 2nd ed. London 1920, repr. New York 1960, 267, 261. It is also characterised as impracticable and 'devoid of all worldly wisdom' by J. Stacey, 'The Character of John Wyclif,' *London Quarterly and Holborn Review*, CLXXXIV (1959), 133-6 at 135.

[2] H. B. Workman, *John Wyclif*, 1926, I, 259; II, 13-15. Earlier, Workman had referred to 'the weakest point of Wyclif's system. This was the doctrine of dominion founded on grace, the assertion that office, whether civil or spiritual, lapsed with mortal sin': see his edition of *The Letters of John Hus*, 1904, 70. Cf. K. B. McFarlane, *John Wycliffe and the Beginnings of English Nonconformity*, 1952, 92: its practical bearing is far from clear but gives his thought 'a destructive, almost an anarchistic, tendency.'

[3] E.g. R. W. and A. J. Carlyle, *History of Mediaeval Political Theory in the West*, VI (1950,), 62, 'his conception of dominion had little real significance, at least in political theory'; E. Lewis, *Medieval Political Ideas*, 1954, 106. B. L. Manning, 'Wyclif,' *Cambridge Medieval History*, VII, 498, remarked on the 'irritating refusal to adjust theories to practice.'

[4] G. M. Trevelyan, *England in the Age of Wycliffe*, 4th ed. 1909, 199-200.

[5] E.g. M. Deanesly, *The Lollard Bible*, 1920, 226-8, who maintains that this logically led to the need for a vernacular Bible.

[6] R. R. Betts, 'Richard FitzRalph, Archbishop of Armagh, and the Doctrine of Dominion,' *Essays in British and Irish History in honour of J. E. Todd*, ed. H. A. Cronne, T. W. Moody, D. B. Quinn, 1949, 46-60 at 46-8.

[7] J. H. Dahmus, *The Prosecution of John Wyclif*, New Haven 1952, 24, 53; cf. M. Hurley, '*Scriptura Sola*: Wyclif and his Critics,' *Traditio*, XVI (1960), 275-352 at 286-7, 'That this was theological dynamite, capable of blowing up the whole fabric of society, lay and ecclesiastical, needs no elaboration.'

and grace as a vital element in a new political theory which 'opened
up the secular order to all the forces of reform that were built into
Western Christianity.' It helped to create what he terms 'an ideology
of revolution.' [1]

Stated in its simplest form, Wyclif's theory asserts that *dominium*
—the right to hold power and possessions: to govern, to confer the
sacraments, to own land and other property—is dependent upon
grace. It must be a divine right of possession. Consequently *dominium*
in its true sense pertains only to those who are in a state of grace, the
elect or *praedestinati*, the righteous whose salvation is assured. This
lordship therefore relates to the Church only in the limited sense of
the predestined, the *universitas fidelium praedestinatorum*:[2] all things
belong in common to the just—they are the rulers of the world.[3] But
those who have sinned mortally without repentance, the *praesciti* or
foreknown, are mere usurpers of what they hold, for they are pre-
ordained to damnation and cannot righteously possess anything.[4]
They are St Paul's 'slaves of sin,' and slaves have neither property
rights nor power to rule. They may therefore expect to be dispossessed by the just. These statements are then followed by a series
of diatribes on the wickedness of a clergy bloated with temporal
possessions, and especially the iniquity of a Caesarean papacy motivated by pride and lust for power. They are to be deprived of their
unjust possessions by the laity and restored to the pristine purity of
the apostolic age. This is the main trend of the argument, but the
theory would seem to be capable of almost indefinite extension. For
example, Wyclif appears to be reviving the old notion that a sinful

[1] H. Kaminsky, 'Wyclifism as Ideology of Revolution,' *Church History*, XXXII (1963),
57–74.
[2] *De Ecclesia*, ed. J. Loserth, 1886, 2, 37; 3, 58–9. For his distinction between the two
Ecclesiae or bodies of damned and elect: 3, 60–1; 4, 70; 5, 102–3, 112. John of Salisbury,
Policraticus, VIII, 17, ed. C. C. J. Webb, 1909, II, 348–9, had written of a *respublica
impiorum* which was to be contrasted with the *respublica* of the just: V, 2 (I, 282–98);
also V, 17; VI, proem.; VI, 19.
[3] E.g. *De civili dominio*, I, ed. R. L. Poole, 1885, 11, 76, 'quilibet innocens vel iustus
dominatur toti mundo sensibili et beati regnant tamquam veri reges super omnia bona
Dei.'
[4] *De civili dominio*, I, 1, 1–2, 'Intendo itaque pro dicendis ostendere duas veritates
quibus utar tamquam principiis ad dicenda: prima, quod nemo ut est in peccato mortali
habet iustitiam simpliciter ad donum Dei; secunda, quod quilibet existens in gratia
gratificante finaliter nedum habet ius sed in re habet omnia bona Dei . . . Omne ius
humanum praesupponit causaliter ius divinum . . . ergo omne dominium iustum ad
homines praesupponit iustum dominium quoad Deum. Sed quilibet existens in peccato
mortali caret, ut sic, iusto dominio quoad Deum, ergo et simpliciter iusto dominio.' This
is elaborated in chs. 1–14 *passim*.

priest could not confer valid sacraments;[1] or to be maintaining that
those who ruled without divine approval were both usurpers and
tyrants, and lost their right to govern.[2] Understandably, on the face
of it, Wyclif's theory seems to be justifying something not far short
of anarchy.

This theory has been criticised on three grounds. First, that it
had nothing new to say. Basically Wyclif was simply restating the
traditional mediaeval principle that divine righteousness (*iustitia*)
must stand behind all human rulings and institutions;[3] that the
peculiar formulation of this point in Wyclif's version had been
borrowed from FitzRalph (which Wyclif would not have denied);
and that FitzRalph in his turn had been developing a series of
statements made in the first quarter of the fourteenth century by the
Augustinian theologians in defence of papal supremacy.[4] It has even
been suggested that the condemnation of Wyclif's—and Hus's—
theory of lordship by the Council of Constance was an implicit
rejection of the original papal doctrine.[5] Secondly, the complaint is
made that Wyclif never really made it clear how one was to distinguish between the elect and the damned, so that it was virtually
impossible to tell who had a right to rule and possess, and who did
not. In this way the theory was robbed of a great deal of its practical
significance. And thirdly, that Wyclif had developed his thesis in
order to support the expropriation of the clergy by the laity, just as
FitzRalph had used it on behalf of the seculars against the friars, but
that neither author had shown how a connection was to be made
between the righteous and the expropriators.[6] On what grounds were
Wyclif's dispossessing laity to be equated and identified with the
praedestinati, the just who possess all and therefore revoke the title
of possession from those who stand in mortal sin?

These criticisms, however, seriously underestimate Wyclif's
intellectual shrewdness and perspicacity, as well as his grasp of

[1] God does not necessarily confirm the acts of a priest by a grant of power to those
actions: 'illi quorum potestas a Deo suspenditur per peccatum vel ex inhabilitate
numquam acceperant potestatem,' *De potestate papae*, ed. J. Loserth, 1907, 9, 203-5; cf.
2, 34-5.

[2] E.g. *De civili dominio*, I, 1, 7-8.

[3] W. A. Dunning, *History of Political Theories, Ancient and Medieval*, 1905, 264; cf.
Carlyle, op. cit. VI, 61-2; McIlwain, op. cit. 315-16.

[4] See further A. Gwynn, *The English Austin Friars in the Time of Wyclif*, 1940, 59-73,
234-6; also D. Knowles, *The Religious Orders in England*, 1948-59, II, 61-8.

[5] Lewis, op. cit. 105-6.

[6] Gwynn, op. cit. 68; McFarlane, op. cit. 60-1.

practical political issues. Since the second criticism—if criticism it is—was acknowledged by Wyclif himself, we may perhaps consider it first: namely, that Wyclif was too confused or too idealistic to deal with the practical problem of distinguishing between the elect and the damned. On the contrary Wyclif never really intended that they should be so distinguished. He repeatedly emphasised that a human separation of *praedestinati* and *praesciti* was impossible. The *Ecclesia militans* exists as a composite body of damned and elect, a *corpus bipartitum*, until the Day of Judgement.[1] Until the divine decision is finally declared, any man's status in terms of grace remains a matter of complete uncertainty,[2] and therefore the question is best ignored. Otherwise, he points out, for fear of honouring a prelate whom we suspect of being damned, we should be tempted to disobey him, and the Church would be thrown into confusion.[3] To all intents and purposes matters may be left as they are under the present system of earthly justice (*secundum praesentem iustitiam*), with the damned classified as real members of the Christian community,[4] retaining what they unjustly hold by divine permission.[5] Even the tyrant is to be left undisturbed in the improper enjoyment of his power and possessions 'lest scandal should be caused by tumultuous contention.'[6] It may not be a divine right of tyranny, since technically a tyrant is devoid of rights, but in practice it amounts to very much the same thing. At all events it is far from being a theory of revolution.

[1] *De civili dominio*, I, 2, 11-12; *De Ecclesia*, 4, 71-2, 'Ecclesia mixta'; also 4, 89; 5 104; 9, 201-2; 17, 408-9; cf. Ecclus. xlvii, 23. As Wyclif states, this was adopted from Augustine's commentary on the rules of Tychonius: see the *De doctrina christiana*, III, 31, 44 (PL, xxxiv, 82); and for discussion and further literature, S. J. Grabowski, *The Church: An Introduction to the Theology of St Augustine*, St Louis 1957, 551-64, also 620-1, 627-9.

[2] *De Ecclesia*, 3, 64, 'de tali finali inhaerentia est nobis dubium.' God alone knows who is to be saved, 'caeteris autem est illud incognitum qui sunt columbae et qui corvi' (an allusion to Gen. viii, 6f.); 9, 202, 'Et rationes omnium istorum sunt nobis absconditae . . . Nam secretum divinae ordinationis dies nostrae mortis et dies finalis divisionis ideo sunt a mortalibus occultati.'

[3] *De Ecclesia*, 6, 141, 'quia tunc esset tanta vel maior ambiguitas de praelatis utrum sint membra Ecclesiae . . . quia suspicionem probabilem habemus de mortali . . . et periret obedientia praelatis, cum non sic debemus honorare membra diaboli . . . et sic contra testimonia sanctorum nimis perturbaretur Ecclesia.' In any case the committing of mortal sin was no certain guide, since the predestined could commit such a sin and yet be saved.   [4] *De civili dominio*, I, 39, 288.

[5] *De civili dominio*, I, 2, 12, 'quod peccator, licet videatur in facie Ecclesiae errantis habere dona Domini, non tamen vere est dotarius, sed ex permissione divina iniuste occupat haec ad tempus'; cf. I, 3, 22, 'quod Deus non approbat sed permittit.'

[6] 'non contentione tumultuosa scandalisando': see *De civili dominio*, I, 6, 42-6.

It was, however, beyond Wyclif's nature to let the matter rest there: he could never resist the temptation to play a game of cat and mouse with his readers. Of course, he remarks, we may know the truth of the matter if God should tell us: it is possible for the identity of the damned and the elect to be known by revelation.[1] On the other hand it would surely be contrary to the nature of God for him to tell us. As a power for good, he cannot deny goodness to others. And this means that he cannot deprive men of the virtues of faith and hope. But if he was to reveal the fact of a man's impending salvation, he would deny him the merit of believing; just as a revelation of his future damnation would destroy his ability to hope. It would also ruin any determination he might have to be good, and since God cannot be a force for evil purposes, he must allow men to continue in faith and hope of salvation to come, but in their present state of uncertainty.[2]

No doubt it was true, Wyclif admitted, that there were certain aspects of a prelate's behaviour which might be considered as infallible signs of his later damnation, or which would at least justify a probable guess as to his standing with God: his attitude towards secular rights, his love of justice and desire to profit the Christian society, his willingness to hear the word of God.[3] But even if this was the case, there was another consideration to be borne in mind.

[1] *De Ecclesia*, 1, 5, 18; 4, 84-5.

[2] *De statu innocentiae*, ed. J. Loserth and F. D. Matthew, 1922, 8, 514, 'cum Deus non potest, ut tenetur communiter, revelare homini suam dampnationem, quia tunc daret occasionem, ymmo Deus necessitaret hominem, ad desperandum, et abiectis virtutibus in servitio diaboli conversandum ... Hic videtur mihi quod omnis homo, sive praescitus sive praedestinatus, debet sperare suam beatitudinem, cum Deus non potest dampnare hominem nisi suum demeritum sit in causa.' See also *De Ecclesia*, 1, 25; 4, 90-1. It is interesting to notice that Hus used this argument to defend Wyclif: it was not known for certain whether Wyclif was a heretic, and in default of revelation it was proper to hope that a man was saved, and therefore it was to be presumed that he was not heretical. See his reply to the charges made in the archiepiscopal court at Prague in August, 1408: Palacký, *Documenta*, 153-5; also his *Replica contra Ioannem Stokes* in *Historia et monumenta J. Hus et Hieron. Pragensis*, Nuremberg 1715, 1, 108; and *Super IV Sententiarum libros*, IV, xx, 3, ed. V. Flajšhans, *Sebrané spisy*, Prague 1903-8, 11, 621.

[3] *De Ecclesia*, 9, 185, 'Talis itaque finalis praeponderantia saecularis privilegii est signum infallibile membri diaboli'; *De civili dominio*, III, ed. J. Loserth, 1903-4, 25, 595-6, 'Et ita sicut nemo scit, nisi cui revelatum est distincte, utrum sit praedestinatus vel praescitus, ... sed spem debet habere et signum firmans spem talem; signum est si post soporem temptationis redeat penitentia fructuosa, vigil reminiscentia de hora mortis et die iudicii, et tertio si habet zelum iustitiae et processus prosperi domus Dei; ... Et ne quis praesumat ex scintilla istorum signorum peccare audacius, posuit Deus probabilitatem in hiis signis et non absolutam veritatem connexionis'; *De officio regis*, ed. A. W. Pollard and C. Sayle, 1887, 11, 255, 'Unde data sunt quaedam signa et manifesta salutis iudicia per quae indubitabile sit eum esse de numero salvandorum, in quo haec

Grace was essentially a personal matter: its absence deprived a person of right to power and office. But the office continued to exist because it had a necessary function to fulfil in the organisation of society.[1] However much the prelate himself was damned, the divine power still flowed through his office. A man might deprive himself of his office in the eyes of God, but on the terrestrial level God continued to work through that office—with the officer, so to speak, a sleeping partner in the business—in order that his subjects should not be deprived of the divine benefits. From the prelate's point of view, his personal merits determined his possession of office: but from his subjects' point of view, the office made the man. And this applied to the jurisdictional power of the ruler as much as to the sacramental power of the priest.[2] As far as men were concerned, the damned priest could still confer sacramental grace or pronounce a valid sentence of excommunication.[3] The tyrant was to be obeyed by right of office, although by right of personal *dominium* founded on grace he was no longer a king.[4] A pope was still to be recognised even if it was apparent that he was numbered amongst the fore-

signa permanserunt. Maxime autem signum confidentiae electorum est illud verbum Domini, *Ioh.*, viii, [47], Qui ex Deo est, verba Dei audit.'

[1] *De potestate papae*, 6, 131, 'cum manet eius dignitas cum peccato.'

[2] *De civili dominio*. I, 3, 23-4, 'Ad tertium dicitur quod argumentum est verum sicut conclusio, scilicet quod donum caracteris, donum prophetandi, et potestas utendi clavibus cum peccato mortali stat . . . Sed est notandum quod licet exercens potestatem ordinis vel iurisdictionis peccet mortaliter, tamen Deus, in cuius nomine ministrat, supplet quod capacibus proficiat ac si iustus uteretur debite potestate, excepto quod in abutente meritum personale subtrahitur . . . quod si in culpa facit bonum opus de genere, contingit, ut supradictum est, quod sibi proderit et alii mereantur.' Hus was to make exactly the same distinctions: see his reply to article 4 of the Wycliffite propositions in the *Defensio articulorum* of July 1412, and at Constance; also the *Postil* of 1413, as cited by M. Spinka, *John Hus and the Czech Reform*, Chicago 1941, 55, 58-9.

[3] E.g. *De Ecclesia*, 19, 448, 'Videtur autem mihi quod praescitus etiam in mortali peccato actuali ministrat fidelibus, licet sibi dampnabiliter, tamen subiectis utiliter sacramenta.' His powers had an indelible character until the Day of Judgement, whereas the *praedestinatus* had this indelible character without qualification (p. 444). Cf. *De civili dominio*, I, 40, 301, 'persona praescita auctoritate Ecclesiae excommunicat.' This may be compared with orthodox hierocratic theory: e.g. Augustinus Triumphus, *Summa de potestate ecclesiastica*, Rome 1584, XXIX, 3 and 3 ad 1, 177, 'Papa in dando indulgentiam habet se in ratione instrumenti quo relaxatio poena sit, non in ratione subiecti cui gratia sacramentalis tribuatur . . . Sed sicut papa existens in mortali [peccato] potest gratiam sacramentalem conferre administrando officium . . . Papa existens in mortali [peccato] non habet gratiam indulgentiae ad propriam salutem, sed habet eam ad ministerium salutis aliorum.'

[4] *De officio regis*, 1, 17, 'tales non remanerent reges nisi aequivoce, licet habeant potestatem regalem abusam; et sic *realiter* habent potestatem et dignitatem consequentem secundum quam regunt, licet demeritorie. Et sic tyrranni, etiam praesciti, qui solum nominetenus sunt reges vel domini, habent potestatem informem ad regendum et

known.[1] And when Hus returned similar answers to the so-called forty-five Wycliffite propositions at his trial in 1415, we may consider that he knew his Wyclif a great deal better than the holy fathers of Constance.[2]

Now in fact neither Wyclif nor Hus denied that a ruler's subjects had the right to declare him deposed. But this was on the quite different grounds that he had broken the law.[3] For this was a denial of his official capacity, a failure to carry out his divinely ordained function. It was the law which made him king or pope, as the case might be, and he could be removed for breach of it. But this is a quite separate issue: it had nothing to do with his personal status, his standing under *dominium* and grace, and need not therefore detain us

dominandum, *sed illa potestas non est dominium*. Statum ergo potestatis regalis habent et multas rationes bonorum gratuitorum secundum quas remanent vicarie honorandi.' Similarly Hus replied in answer to article 15 of the Wycliffite propositions that 'no man is a civil lord, a bishop or prelate, whilst he is in mortal sin,' that this was true *quoad meritum* but not *quoad officium*: the sinner officially retained his function and possessions in the sight of men, although not entitled to them by merit before God.

[1] Having made the point that a pope is not automatically *caput Ecclesiae* when he may in fact be damned, Wyclif adds that he may still keep his power and possessions because his wickedness is suspended as regards punishment in this life: 'Et si quaeratur quid meretur praescitus existens in gratia secundum praesentem iustitiam, dicitur quod apud rectiloquos et non aequivocantes numquam meretur beatitudinem . . . sed meretur perpetuam mitigationem poenae aeternae cum aliis bonis temporalibus . . . malitia per temporalem gratiam est suspensa. Et sic praesciti, sive saeculares sive clerici, quantumcunque iuste videantur praefici bonis Dei, hoc est, dumtaxat secundum quid dum sunt in gratia temporali . . .' In reply to article 8 of the Wycliffite propositions (that a pope foreknown to be a member of the Devil had no power over the faithful), Hus denied that he ever held it, and affirmed that 'even the worst pope has the power by virtue of his office, through which God acts': cf. Spinka, op. cit. 60-3.

[2] The weakness of the current view that Hus was basically independent of Wyclif, and thus more orthodox, seems to rest upon a facile acceptance of Wyclif's radicalism: cf. now P. de Vooght, *L'Hérésie de Jean Hus* and *Hussiana*, Louvain 1960. This standpoint is adopted by Spinka, although he recognises that the Wycliffite articles did not necessarily represent Wyclif's true position (56). This point had been made by the Czech masters, including Hus, in 1403.

[3] *De Ecclesia*, 19, 465, 'Obediendum est tamen tali praetenso praeposito, salva semper obedientia legi Christi.' Even if the cardinals found that they had elected an *apostaticus*, and not an *apostolicus*, he was to be accepted unless he contravened the law of God: 'Non enim licet humanitus reprobare ut ex fide supponitur, nisi ut Deus *ex sua lege* docuerit reprobandum,' *De potestate papae*, 9, 214. Similarly Hus accepted that no one should obey a lord or prelate who issued commands contrary to the faith: Workman, *Letters*, no. 8, 46-7. In this way both Wyclif and Hus were able to remain within the limits of the old argument that a pope could only be deposed for heresy: e.g. Augustinus Triumphus, *Summa*, XXIX, 3, 177, 'sed papa pro culpa mortali non amittit potestatem iurisdictionis nisi talis culpa haeresim haberet annexam . . .'; V, 8, 55, 'Nam potestas praelationis est donum gratiae gratis datae, non donum gratiae gratis facientis. Sed tale donum gratiae gratis datae non tollitur in papa per aliquod peccatum, nisi solum per unum, puta pro crimine haeresis . . . per tale enim peccatum solum papa desinit esse papa.'

here. Wyclif may have justified the right of resistance—indeed he did so clearly enough on other occasions—but also on other grounds, the rights of men under natural law to good government. A ruler could be deposed, but dominion and grace were not involved in the process.

After Wyclif had put so much stress upon his theory of lordship and grace, a feeling of exasperation at reaching this point is doubtless pardonable. But one thing is clear. Wyclif never intended that men should draw a distinction between those who were in grace and those who were not: man was not to play the part of God. He cannot be criticised for not making the distinction clear, because he never thought that it should be made, or that it would have any practical significance if it was. No doubt Wyclif was not averse to giving a contrary impression: he always delighted in proving the opposite of what he apparently set out to demonstrate. If, as seems likely, his *Summa theologiae* is largely made up of lectures given at Oxford, this would explain not only the lack of order and endless repetition in the work, but might also account for his technique. His audience might well leave the lecture hall with the point, the constantly repeated point that lack of grace destroyed lordship, firmly fixed in their minds—having fallen asleep or failed to catch the subsequent disclaimer that this had any practical effect—but a disclaimer which Wyclif could hope would protect him from a charge of heresy. Like Ockham, Wyclif took particular pleasure in indulging in lengthy speculation about divine possibilities (thereby creating great alarm and confusion) but knowing full well that this speculation was to have no immediate results for human life.[1] The location of grace could not be known: but even if it was, it made no practical difference. From the human point of view, then, why bother with divine grace? Indeed from this angle Wyclif's theory of *dominium* and grace exemplifies the trend of Oxford thought in the fourteenth century to

---

[1] Thus Wyclif's elaborate insistence that only God, and not the human electors, can create a true pope (*De potestate papae*, chs.8–9) is concluded with the decision that men must accept the elected candidate for lack of proof that he was not chosen by God. Only if the pope subsequently proved himself fallible could the *communitas fidelium* proceed to his deposition on the plea that it was now realised that God had not elected him after all. In both cases the human decision holds good, in spite of Wyclif's constant harping upon the essentially divine nature of the choice. FitzRalph had argued that human ordinances were to be accepted precisely because they were of dubious validity: one could never be sure that God had not approved of them, *De pauperie Salvatoris*, ed. R. L. Poole [Bks. 1–4] as an appendix to Wyclif, *De dominio divino*, 1890, IV, 1, 436.

drive a wedge between God and human affairs.[1] Whether a ruler was to retain his position was to be determined by law, not by grace; by a present human decision, not a future divine judgement of salvation; by man, not by God.[2] It was an acknowledgement that human life *secundum praesentem iustitiam* bore little relationship to the realities of the divine world; that there were two levels of truth, human and divine, co-existent but contradictory;[3] that, in effect, human life could be considered with small reference to God. The attributes of divine justice could be considered at immense length for the very reason that they were to have little practical, earthly significance. The result was to leave man—at least within the limits of this mortal life—as the virtual master of his own world.

His discussion of *dominium* and grace in terms of divine right as opposed to earthly realities would, Wyclif recognised, be ridiculed as being of no political consequence. 'I know,' he writes, 'that I shall be laughed to scorn by the politicians and mundane-minded men.' [4] But because the theory had no practical significance for Wyclif in this one respect, it would be most unwise to assume that it had none at all: so far we have merely been looking for the wrong sort of significance. And here Wyclif's debt to papal-hierocratic theory is all-important. Wyclif derived the framework of his theory from FitzRalph, and we are so accustomed to thinking of FitzRalph as a sort of prototype of Wyclif that we sometimes tend to forget that he was a publicist in the Roman curia at Avignon, elaborating a concept which had been developed earlier in the century by such men as Aegidius Romanus and Augustinus Triumphus. And their version of

---

[1] Cf. the studies of G. Leff, *Bradwardine and the Pelagians*, 1957, and *Gregory of Rimini*, 1961.

[2] Men should never be afraid to act now by law for their own convenience through fear that the subsequent divine judgement might be otherwise: 'Melius ergo est pro ordine universi quod peccantes puniantur secundum leges hominum iam statutas, et dampnentur plurimi finaliter delinquentes, quam quod maneat Ecclesia militans ab offensis adextra exercitantibus inquieta,' *De dominio divino*, III, 2, 215-6. In 1412 Hus told Stephen of Dolein that he was entitled to condemn Wyclif's words now, but that he had no right to condemn Wyclif's soul, a decision which must await the future judgement of God: Workman, *Letters*, no. 14, 76-7.

[3] The same effect was achieved by the idea that a final choice of salvation was vouchsafed to man immediately before death: D. Knowles, *The Historian and Character*, 1963, 143-4. This principle may be found in Wyclif, *De dominio divino*, IV, 4, 235, but note his refusal to give an opinion in the celebrated case of Trajan, *De mandatis divinis*, 23, ed. J. Loserth and F. D. Matthew, 1922, 321, on the grounds that Trajan was already predestined to salvation.

[4] 'Scio enim quod ista sententia deridebitur a politicis et mundanis': see the *De dominio divino*, III, 6, 255-7.

the doctrine of dominion and grace had made it clear that its prime aim[1] was to deny to men in general any form of innate or 'natural' rights of property. They had insisted that all possessions—power and property—were divine gifts bestowed upon men as acts of grace through the medium of the papacy: this applied to kingship as well as to landed estates and movable goods.[2] The pope, as the earthly

---

[1] It could also be used to deny the validity of non-Christian governments: e.g. Aegidius Romanus, *De ecclesiastica potestate*, III, 11, ed. R. Scholz, Weimar 1929, 201, 'Immo apud infideles non solum non sunt regna neque imperia, cum apud eos regna et imperia sint latrocinia, immo etiam apud eos non sunt aliqua iusta dominia, ut non sit aliquis infidelis iustus dominus sive iustus possessor domus suae vel agri sui vel vineae suae vel cuiuscumque rei suae; quia . . . qui non vult subesse Domino suo, dignum est quod nihil subsit sub dominio suo.' Similarly Augustinus Triumphus said that rulers who were not appointed by the *sacerdotium* had no just title to lordship, but only 'dominium usurpatum et tyrannicum,' *Summa*, XXXVI, 1, 212; and for Thomas of Strassburg on this, see Gwynn, op. cit. 73. In this connection it is important not to take out of its context the well-known passage in FitzRalph, *Summa in quaestionibus Armenorum*, X, 4, Paris 1511, f. 75va:

> Unde, quantum mihi videtur, nullus existens in peccato mortali habet aliarum creaturarum verum dominium apud Deum, sed tyrannus aut fur sive raptor merito est vocandus, quamvis nomen regis aut principis aut domini propter possessionem seu propter successionem haereditariam aut propter approbationem populi sibi subiecti aut propter aliam legem humanam retineat.

FitzRalph was discussing the case of a kingdom seized by conquest, and argued that there could be no natural right of government there—as expressed in the free consent of the people to the new ruler—since natural rights had been lost by sin in the Garden of Eden (ff. 75^{rb-va}), which is the position developed at length in the *De pauperie Salvatoris*. Men could confer nothing on an elected prince because they had nothing to give. What power a prince rightly possessed must come from God, either in the form of direct divine authority, or by ecclesiastical recognition, or by the prince showing the fidelity and repentance of a true Christian where he was accepted by the free will of the *populus*. Either way he must be a *christianus* and *fidelis*, obedient to God.

> R. Cum autem populi ad hoc concurrit gratuita non extorta voluntas, quoniam tunc approbatur a Deo talis potestas si aliud malum in praesidente et subiectis non obstet, aut cum auctoritate spirituali Dei aut suae Ecclesiae confirmetur, huius dominium vere regalis potestas seu dignitas dici potest, et qui aliquo horum modorum regnum ingreditur, intrat per ostium quod est Christus, et est a furto et latrocinio alienus . . .
>
> J. Dic expressius quod sentis cum dicis, 'si aliquod malum in praesidente et subiectis non obstet.'
>
> R. Infidelitatem intelligo, quoniam infidelis nullum iustum dominium temporalium obtinet apud Deum, et ideo eius dominium non approbatur sed reprobatur a Deo . . . et ideo Deus eos frequenter a dominio proicit (X, 3-4, f. 75rb).

The mortal sin in the first passage cited here refers specifically to the sin of unbelief: 'quia potest unusquisque princeps talis esse, scil. peccator et infidelis, etiam si gratuitus consensus populi approbet possessionem illius quod detinet; ideo superius adieci "si aliud malum etc." ' This enabled FitzRalph to argue that, if all true rulers were to be *fideles*, then they must also be subject to the pope.

[2] Augustinus Triumphus, *Summa*, XL, 3, 231, 'derivantur enim dona spiritualia ab eo [scil. papa] tamquam a fonte in imperatorem et in omnes filios Ecclesiae.'

source of divine grace,[1] could alone be regarded as having an effective right of ownership: all *dominium* belongs to him in place of Christ.[2] Accordingly, all that men have they hold from him.[3] This followed from the corporate nature of the Christian community. As a corporation the *Ecclesia universalis* possessed a real personality of its own: in theological terms, all Christians formed one man in heaven, Christ, a mystical person or body comprising all the faithful members. Since sovereignty resided in this corporate personality, so Christ was, strictly speaking, the ultimate owner of all things in creation. Christ, it was said, held the two treasuries of grace: of jurisdictional power, of offices, and the ownership of corporeal things on the one hand; of orders, sacramental power, and spiritual benefits on the other. But gifts from these twin *thesauri* were distributed to the faithful on earth through the agency of the vicar of Christ, who acted as the terrestrial expression of the sovereign personality of the society. The recipients of these donations of grace could not therefore claim any absolute rights of ownership: earthly men were merely stewards of God and the pope, and could be dispossessed of what they held at will. True ownership remained with that abstraction, the celestial community of the faithful, the *corpus Christi mysticum*.[4]

Wyclif had a knowledge and understanding of papal-hierocratic theory that might have been envied by many papalists themselves, and he never hesitated to make use of a papal idea when he could turn it to his own advantage.[5] When this is borne in mind, it is not difficult to appreciate what Wyclif meant by his repeated statements that all things are owned by the just in common. It is a fundamental mistake to consider the *praedestinati* in terms of earthly men: on the contrary the just are the saints, those heavenly beings who alone are

---

[1] Note the use of Jn. i, 16 and Eph. iv, 7 in favour of the pope by Augustinus Triumphus, *Summa*, XIX, 2, 118; LXXI, 2, 372; LXXVII, 3 ad 1 and 3, 398.

[2] Augustinus Triumphus, *Summa*, CI, 7, 499, 'planum est papam vice Christi dominium et usum rerum habere non solum clericorum immo omnium laicorum. Est enim ipse Christus dominus Ecclesiae et omnium illorum quibus Ecclesia plena est.'

[3] In the stylised phraseology of papal theory a man owes 'omne quod habet' to the pope as *persona Ecclesiae*: e.g. Augustinus Triumphus, *Summa*, I, 1, 5; Aegidius Romanus, *De ecclesiastica potestate*, II, 4, 51. The phrase derives from Josh. vii, 24 where it relates to the idea of collective punishment.

[4] See further my *Problem of Sovereignty*, 1963, especially 174-83; also *Studia Patristica*, Berlin 1962, VI, 533-42.

[5] Cf. W. A. Pantin, *The English Church in the Fourteenth Century*, 1955, 130. For another example of this practice with Wyclif see my 'The *Apostolicus* and the Bishop of Rome,' *JTS*, XIII-XIV, 1962-3.

in the fullness of grace, and as such form a celestial 'whole' or person, the *corpus mysticum* of Christ himself.[1] The just have no direct relevance here to human individuals in this life. The theory has to be taken in a divine sense,[2] and we can now appreciate why Wyclif warned that only a theologian would be able to understand his teaching on lordship.[3] This point had, incidentally, been perfectly clear to Hus, who emphasised its Augustinian basis.[4] All things belong to Christ, who is the aggregate person (*persona aggregata*) of the elect,[5] to the Church in the sense of that abstract reality, the *Ecclesia praedestinatorum* or Church Triumphant.[6] Wyclif is saying

[1] *De civili dominio*, I, 14, 103, 'corpus Christi mysticum habet omnia bona mundi'; I, 43, 360, 'Illud autem unum est corpus Christi misticum ex omnibus praedestinatis aggregatum'; *De dominio divino*, III, 3, 223, 'omnis creatura beata per manus Mediatoris Dei et hominum habebit omnia, Deum supra se ut dominum, concives ut socios, et omnia alia possidebit tamquam subservitores cedentes eis ad gloriam; et sic omnes et singuli erunt reges, haeredes Dei et cohaeredes Christi, habentes omnia in communi'; *De Ecclesia*, I, 20–1, 'Nam sancti doctores dicunt concorditer quod omnes electi a principio mundi usque ad diem iudicii sunt una persona, quae est mater Ecclesia,' quoting in support the statement of Gregory I 'quod Christum et Ecclesiam unam personam credimus, hoc etiam unius personae actibus significari videamus'; also 9, 187; 14, 303. The elect are the 'membra Christi mistici' (17, 391), united 'per *incorporationem* in corpus Christi misticum' (6, 138), who form the *Ecclesia* considered 'secundum se totum in patria' (6, 117). Similarly in the *De mandatis divinis*, 7, 60, the 'tota generatio iustorum sit unus Dei Patri Filius' who together form 'regni coelorum dominus.'

[2] Wyclif was careful to state at the beginning that this had to be understood *simpliciter* or *finaliter*: *De civili dominio*, I, 1, 1; I, 2, 8–9; cf. *De Ecclesia*, 14, 313, '*Quando enim triumphantes vitam aeternam possidebunt*, Deus eos constituet super omnia bona sua.'

[3] *De dominio divino*, I, *prologue*, 1, 'ideo ut caecitas hominum sit melius ad sensum scripturae professoribus huius scientiae declarata, consonum videtur a dominio inchoandum. Innitar autem in ordine procedendi rationibus et sensui scripturae, cui ex religione et speciali obedientia sum professus. Scio enim ipsam in modo loquendi ...' FitzRalph, too, had made the point that he was using special theological terminology, *De pauperie Salvatoris*, II, 1, 335; II, 4, 339–40. But this may also be found in Ockham.

[4] Hus, *De Ecclesia*, 18, ed. S. H. Thomson, Boulder, Colorado and Cambridge, England 1956, 170–1, citing Augustine, *Enarratio in Psal.*, CXXI, 9 (PL, xxxvii, 1626), 'Qui sunt isti nisi iusti? Qui sunt coeli nisi iusti? Qui coelum ipsi coeli? Quia quae Ecclesia ipsi Ecclesia; sic sunt multa ut una sit, sic ergo et iusti; ita sunt iusti coelum, ut coeli sint. In ipsis autem sedet Deus.' Wyclif himself pointed out, *De civili dominio*, I, 14, 103, that the outline of the theory, with appropriate Biblical quotations, is in Augustine, *Ep.* CLXXX, 9, 35–7 (PL, xxxiii, 808–9), and that the passage concludes with the *christiani imperatores* despoiling the goods of the Donatist churches; also Augustine, *Ep.* CLIII, 26 (PL, xxxiii, 665), cited Wyclif, *De civili dominio*, I, 1, 5–6. Wyclif also follows Augustine in equating the just with the poor, since their ownership is a heavenly possessing only: 'membra [Ecclesiae] sunt pauperes saturati, quia deserti sunt in hoc saeculo,' Augustine, *Enarratio in Psal.*, CXXXI, 23 (PL, xxxvii, 1726) = Wyclif, *De Ecclesia*, 1, 6; cf. FitzRalph, *De pauperie Salvatoris*, III, 27, 419–20. See also *Studia Patristica*, VI, 537.

[5] *De civili dominio*, I, 43, 365; also 359, 'aggregatio bonorum'; and see *De Ecclesia*, 6, 123: Christ is the 'caput aggregatum Ecclesiae,' comprising all the predestined.

[6] *De civili dominio*, II, 10, 104. The use of the expression *Ecclesia praedestinatorum*

no more than that the power and wealth of a Christian society are held by its corporate personality,[1] which may be identified with God.[2] Earthly possessions form the *patrimonium Christi*,[3] the treasury of Christ, who is the heavenly embodiment or sovereign essence of the community.[4]

Wyclif's so-called communism, as in the traditional papal version, does not then relate to the community in terms of individual people, but to an abstract personification of society really existing on the heavenly level. It asserts what we may regard as a State-ownership of property. Common possession by the good means ownership by the abstract reality of the community—the 'ecclesia' or 'regnum' (the terms are synonymous)[5]—which is represented for practical purposes by the ruler. For this reason Wyclif defines the lay prince as the vicar of God[6]: he is the physical expression of the divine State-personality, the *communitas regni* given human form.[7] As the visible representative of the State he acts for the *Ecclesia praedestinatorum* by distributing to his subjects such powers and possessions, offices and rights, as are deemed necessary for the common good.[8]

is of course quite innocuous if understood in this heavenly sense, and had been used by the Augustinian theologians earlier in the fourteenth century.

[1] The unjust act against Christ because they steal from his body: 'Nam eo ipso quod quis iniuste, invito vel ignorante Domino, capit bona aliena, furtum committit vel latrocinia: cum ergo omnis iniustus iniuste capit bona corporis sui . . . quae omnia sunt cuiuscunque iusti . . .,' *De civili dominio*, I, 5, 34.

[2] *De civili dominio*, I, 12, 80-1: the *praedestinati* are the 'dives in Deum'; cf. I, 19, 134, 'omnia sint bona Domini.' See also *De mandatis divinis*, 21, 275, where the kingdom of heaven is described as the souls of the saints, as a *thesaurus*, and, since he possesses all, as the ruler, God or Christ, himself.

[3] *De Ecclesia*, 14, 311, 'nam iusti sunt omnia iure poli [i.e. iure divino] . . . omnia bona Ecclesiae, sive in laicos sive in clero, sunt de patrimonio crucifixi; ipse enim est haeres habens in capite omnia bona mundi'; cf. 15, 342, 347; *De mandatis divinis*, 30, 459-60; and for *thesaurus*: *De civili dominio*, I, 13, 96.

[4] 'Dominus simpliciter,' *De Ecclesia*, 13, 280: therefore only Christ can make perpetual grants of property.

[5] Cf. Kaminsky, art. cit. 62.

[6] *De civili dominio*, I, 19, 134; III, 25, 596; *De Ecclesia*, 12, 254; *De potestate papae*, 12, 378; *De officio regis*, 1, 4-5; 3, 54-5; 6, 121; cf. 1, 17, 'imago Trinitatis.'

[7] *De officio regis*, 3, 56, 'Et per idem sic est de quolibet eius [scil. Dei] vicario, qui non solum ex persona propria sed ex vi communitatis totius regni sui mandat ut sic legaliter procedatur'; cf. 5, 91, 'Totum regnum cum rege est una persona, ut hic supponitur, cuius caput vel cor est rex influens criminis conservationem sensum et motum'; 6, 131, 'et quod rex praedestinatus et sui unam personam constituunt quae agit opera sua tam clericalia quam laicalia auctoritate regia'; *De civili dominio*, I, 26, 187, 'ergo communitatis vel personae est peccatum tale corrigere.'

[8] *De civili dominio*, I, 19, 132, 'quia officium civiliter dominantis est custodia possessorum a capitali terreno domino [scil. Deo] vel communitate secundum formam adinventionis humanae recipere, res possessas ad utilitatem reipublicae custodire, et

Recalling the Roman law basis of this conception, Wyclif speaks of the fisc, the celestial storehouse of the realm,[1] of which the prince acts as treasurer, a bailiff of God[2] dispensing private property rights (in Wyclif's terminology, *civile dominium*)[3] to the members of the community, whether lay or clerical. These have no absolute right to what they hold, and therefore no immunity from royal jurisdiction.[4] Wyclif had no real objection to clerical possession of *temporalia*, provided that they were held with a full recognition of their private right status.[5] What he deplored was the notion that private property rights were immutable—that there was a perpetual *civile dominium* inherent in ecclesiastical tenure—which would effectively deny the superior public right—the divine lordship—of the king's grace.[6] And from this premise Wyclif had little difficulty in defining the regalian rights of the king over his clergy:[7] his position as the source

secundum regulas civilis iustitiae, ut communitati expedit, distribuere'; II, 3, 24, 'et cum iusti sunt omnia bona mundi, patet quod tunc domini temporales meritorie distribuerent bona ex sua parte occupantium.' These are the 'goods of the poor' which the king administers on behalf of Christ: II, 4, 30-1; *De officio regis*, 7, 180-1, 184.

[1] The clergy are to remain 'contenti de stipendiis a communi aerario saecularie ministratis,' *De civili dominio*, II, 3, 21; cf. 'corporale regni sui suffragium,' *De officio regis*, 5, 104; 6, 119, which may be compared with the 'spirituale suffragium' (7, 181) administered by the king to the extent that he is responsible for appointing good priests, although he himself does not have sacramental power as such (8, 196-7; cf. *De civili dominio*, II, 5, 46). For a similar theory applied to the French king in the contemporary *Somnium viridarii* see Wilks, *Problem of Sovereignty*, 430.

[2] *De dominio divino*, III, 6, 255, 'Unde expediret dominos temporales recognoscere quod non sunt nisi ministri vel ballivi Domini, ut sic omnia quaecunque fecerint, in nomine Domini Dei sui faciant.' In the same way Dante had maintained (*Monarchia*, II, 12; III, 10; III, 13) that the *patrimonium* of the poor of Christ was administered by the emperor, who duly made grants from it to the clergy. Thus the clergy did not have true *dominium*, but only a delegated duty of guardianship.

[3] E.g. *De civili dominio*, III, 21, 430, 'Unde ius civile est ius particulare . . . ad stabiliendum proprietatem possessionibus humanitus constitutum.'

[4] *De civili dominio*, II, 8, 81, 'Inconsonum est christianum temporalia possidere et legibus regum non subici.'

[5] *De potestate papae*, 5, 89, 'Notandum tamen quod temporalia non occasione ab eis data sed male accepta venenant ecclesiam. Si enim totus clerus diceret effectualiter quod omnia temporalia quae habemus ut clerici forent purae elemosynae saecularium et bona communia pauperum . . . possemus proprietate usus et ministerii occupare licite omnia temporalia quae habemus.'

[6] Hence his attacks on the notion of free use of one's possessions without corresponding obligations: e.g. *De civili dominio*, I, 19, 136-7, 143.

[7] *De potestate papae*, 12, 347, 'Quoad secundum patet quod oportet esse unum caput ad beneficia ecclesiastica partiendum, nam lex Christi est ad illud sufficiens, et *persona populi*, cui praeficeretur talis praepositus, foret optimus iudex ad discernendum talem praepositum episcopo praesentandum. Sic enim fuit in primitiva Ecclesia, nec cessat ratio quare non sic foret hodie. Nam illa persona tenerrime provideret de mediis ad salutem animae necessariis cuiusmodi est pastor discretus; si enim providet de mediis

of ecclesiastical property; his rights of patronage—to reserve benefices, to appoint bishops, to tax the clergy, and to extract oaths of
allegiance from them; his duty to make laws for the regulation of the
priesthood; his capacity to punish delinquent clerics; his power to
revoke his original grants by withholding ecclesiastical revenues or
by outright confiscation of church property in time of need—all the
very familiar features of an ecclesiastical polity over which the prince
stands supreme as king and priest.[1]

The practical significance of Wyclif's doctrine of dominion and
grace was therefore the reverse of revolutionary. Behind a smoke-
screen of predestinarian speculation it enabled him to reconstruct
the old lay ideal of a theocratic monarchy and a proprietary church.
He was able to confer upon the lay prince a sacred character[2]
befitting one who was the visible expression of the mystical entity of
the 'State,' the community of the righteous.[3] And whilst the king was
elevated into a supreme proprietor, the clergy were reduced to being
no more than the stewards of royal estates.[4] It was indeed true that
this system is seen on closer examination to suffer from the same
congenital weakness as most other lay theories: it was silent on the

corporis nutritivis, fides necessitat quod infinitum plus provideat de mediis animae
nutritivis'; cf. *De civili dominio*, II, 12, 142-3. That the *populus* referred to here should
be understood in the sense of the abstract community is indicated by corresponding
passages: e.g. *De officio regis*, 11, 258, 'Cum autem corpus misticum Christi dici poterit
ipse Christus . . . multitudo populi dici poterit Christus, quia eius Ecclesia'; *De civili
dominio*, II, 11, 120, 'Ecclesia enim, in cuius nomine [imperator] fit correptio[nem
papae], est quacunque persona infinite superior'; cf. II, 8, 69-70, 75.

[1] E.g. *De officio regis*, 7, 152: ecclesiastical legislation 'pertinet ad regem, qui debet
esse sacerdos et pontifex regni sui . . . quia lex Dei, et per consequens lex ecclesiae, est
lex regis,' although he makes it clear that 'principes saeculi sunt pontifices' in the sense
of having episcopal jurisdiction, not *potestas ordinis* (6, 147, 149); cf. *De potestate papae*,
12, 373-4, 'saecularis dominus ac superior clericus.'

[2] E.g. *De potestate papae*, 12, 377-8, 'Et ex istis primo patet quod rex Angliae primo
et principaliter daret operam ad regulandum clerum suum et specialiter episcopos ut
vivant similius legi Christi; totum enim regnum est unum corpus quod tueri atque
mederi spectat ad regis officium . . . Secundo patet quod sive Romanus pontifex sive
quicumque alius ex praesumptione infundabili impedierit hoc sacrum regis officium,
habet rationem haeretici et pessimi Antichristi. Patet ex hoc quod talis est capitalis in
haeresi talis regis, . . . ideo hoc temptans contra reges, qui sunt Dei vicarii, temptat
sacrilege contra sanctam Ecclesiam et per consequens contra Deum.'

[3] Offences against the royal law, and so against the king's majesty, are offences against
both the *respublica* and God. Accordingly crime and sin may be equated, and rebellion
classified as heresy: see *De civili dominio*, I, 4, 30-1; II, 5, 42-3; II, 17, 248.

[4] E.g. *De civili dominio*, I, 19, 134, 'Nec est possibile quemquam dominari civiliter
nisi fuerit custos, balivus vel villicus super bonis domini dominorum'; I, 36, 159,
'Similiter omnis homo est pure praestarius, accomodarius et balivus Dei sui': as applied
to bishops, III, 12, 211. Cf. *De mandatis divinis*, 30, 459-60.

crucial point of how the king became a *vicarius Dei*, the treasurer of heaven on earth. In the long run this problem would prove fatal to Wyclif's design, since it forced him back—like so many contemporary writers—to an acceptance of the principle that the voice of the people was the voice of God in the creation of a prince,[1] and this in its turn opened up possibilities of contractual government, reciprocal rights, and legal limitation which were fundamentally incompatible with rule by divine grace. It forced him to create a second theory of dominion, of *dominium* and nature, based on Aristotelian and Thomistic principles of natural law which were alien to the whole notion of *dominium* and grace. But that is another story. For present purposes it only needs to be repeated that Wyclif's theory of dominion and grace *was* diametrically opposed to any system of popular rights.

[1] E.g. *De civili dominio*, I, 30, 212, 'Et patet ex sententia Aristotelis, tertium *Politicorum*, capitulo xxviii [III, 17] recitata, quod virtus superexcellens in rege est praecipua causa regnandi civiliter. Ipsa enim per se sufficit ad regnandum evangelice, et est sufficiens cum approbatione populi ad regnandum civiliter.' Cf. *De potestate papae*, 8, 177, on the need for the 'approbatio subditorum' even if only a consenting function 'praeter electionem instituentium.' He concludes, 'Sic enim populus eligit dominum quando effectualiter acceptat quod ille sit dominus suus, et spondet fideliter se esse sibi ut domino serviturum. Unde quando successione haereditaria vadit dominium, adhuc est alia electio subditorum.' But he still refers frequently to the divine appointment of the ruler by God: e.g. *De civili dominio*, I, 18, 130; *De officio regis*, 4, 78.

3

The Early Oxford Wyclif:
Papalist or Nominalist?

M. J. WILKS

*Reader in the History of Political Thought, Birkbeck College,
University of London*

From time to time it has been pointed out that Wyclif had a quite exceptional grasp of papal-hierocratic theory. [1] Although its bitter opponent, his extensive knowledge of the refinements of the theory, his almost intuitive appreciation of its most fundamental principles, indicate a depth of penetration into hierocratic ideology which many supporters of papal supremacy must themselves have envied. His effectiveness as an anti-papal writer during the polemics of the 1370s and 1380s lay less in the novelty and originality of his own system of thought, and in the consistency with which he repeated himself, but rather in his superior ability to detect the weakest points in his adversaries' chain of argument. He not only knew exactly where to thrust between the links, but, more important, how to aim for the pivots of the system, so that the whole hierocratic theory might be turned on its head. This was something which could only be done by one who knew and understood the papal system through and through. But how did Wyclif acquire this understanding, this capacity for putting himself within the minds of his opponents? There is only one slight indication that he may have read a typical late medieval treatise on papal sovereignty: he refers to a certain Nicholas Putanensis, ostensibly, it seems, writing a commentary on St Paul's *Epistle to the*

[1] See my 'The *Apostolicus* and the Bishop of Rome,' *JTS*, n. s., XIII-XIV, (1962-3), and 'Predestination, Property and Power: Wyclif's Theory of Dominion and Grace,' *SCH*, II (1965); also W. A. Pantin, *The English Church in the Fourteenth Century*, 1955, 130.

Romans—but this has so far resisted all attempts at identification.[1] He was of course familiar with the classic authorities—Augustine, Bernard, [2] Hugh of St Victor, John of Salisbury—but he apparently understood them as supporting his own point of view. There is FitzRalph: but FitzRalph was by no means an unambiguous papal champion, and Wyclif does not seem to have absorbed FitzRalph's writings until well into the 1370s. No doubt mid-fourteenth-century Oxford could provide him with a conspectus of canonistic teaching, [3] and indeed Wyclif's knowledge of canonistics is so good that Workman was once led to venture the suggestion that Wyclif had begun to train as a lawyer himself. [4] Unfortunately there is no real evidence for this, and it would wreak havoc with the generally accepted chronology of his life. Nevertheless, Workman may have pointed in the right direction. There is a good deal of evidence from Wyclif himself to suggest that the reason why he had such an ample grasp of the hierocratic theory, the political Platonism of the Middle Ages, was that he had once been a papalist himself.

It is well known that there are a number of passages in his works in which Wyclif confesses that as a youth (*iunior, parvulus*) he had languished in error and ignorance. Little weight, however, has been attached to these statements. A number of modern scholars during the past fifty years have briefly mentioned two or three of them in passing, but the general attitude

[1] *De Ecclesia*, 14, 319-26. All references, unless specified, are to the Wyclif Society editions of Wyclif's works. According to Wyclif, Nicholas denied the current lay theory of dual monarchy, stressing the perfection of sacerdotal government on earth and the subjection of all kings to the absolute will of the pope. This was justified on the grounds that the pope received imperial power direct from Christ, as shown by his ability to create and depose the Roman emperor, and act as emperor himself during an imperial vacancy. He represents the too numerous group of maniacal lawyers, who, despite their lack of theological training, have induced many bishops to follow them in their blasphemous madness (321).

[2] Cf. P. de Vooght, 'Du *De consideratione* de Saint Bernard au *De Potestate papae* de Wiclif,' *Irénikon*, XXVI (1953), 114f.

[3] L. Boyle, 'The *Summa Summarum* and Some Other English Works of Canon Law,' *Proceedings of the Second International Congress of Medieval Canon Law*, Vatican City, 1965, 415-56.

[4] H. B. Workman, *John Wyclif*, 1926, I, 102-3.

has been that too much should not be made of them. If Wyclif admitted to having made mistakes in his youth, this does not represent a well-established position, but rather a period of doubt and uncertainty before he could determine his later views. [1] If we are to talk (as Wyclif did) of a conversion, then the term must be put into inverted commas. [2] Yet it may be questioned whether these confessions can be shrugged off quite so cavalierly. Wyclif makes such statements on no less than twenty-two occasions and, granted that he was the sort of writer who put so much value on what he said that he often said the same thing twenty times over, he was nonetheless making these statements in sixteen different works, which span the whole of his literary career as we know it. Provided that the usual dating of his early works is reliable, he began this series of confessions early in the 1360s, and it does not terminate until 1384, the year of his death. It may surely be argued that something stated on average every year for twenty years is a point which the author, at least, thought to be of quite special importance.

In these passages Wyclif admits that he was once a sophist who agreed with the modernists, the *doctores moderni*, and was thereby led into heresy and falsehood. It has been generally accepted without much question that he is here admitting to have trifled with nominalism, to have adopted the Ockhamism with which an arts student at Oxford was immediately bound to have come into contact. [3] Only when he passed on to the study of theology did Wyclif come to realise that too great a concern with the

[1] Workman, *op. cit.*, I, 139, 333; S. H. Thomson, 'The Philosophical Basis of Wyclif's Theology,' *Journal of Religion*, XI (1931), 86-116 at 88-9; J. A. Robson, *Wyclif and the Oxford Schools*, 1961, 145.

[2] B. Smalley, 'The Bible and Eternity: John Wyclif's Dilemma,' *Journal of the Warburg and Courtauld Institutes*, XXVII (1964), 73-89 at 79-80. Dr Smalley suggests two stages in this initial development: first a period of scepticism about Biblical truth, followed by a second phase in which this truth was accepted for the wrong reasons and with the wrong arguments. Then came 'conversion' to realism.

[3] As originally put forward by M. H. Dziewicki, 'An Essay on Wyclif's Philosophical System,' *Johannis Wyclif Miscellanea Philosophica*, 1902, I, v-xxvii at vi.

logic of the schools had led him into unorthodoxy. [1] And he now hastened to correct himself—perhaps over-correct himself— by espousing an Augustinian, Neoplatonic realism of the most extreme kind. This is so much the current account of the affair that it does not need to be elaborated here. [2]

It would however be advisable to begin the process of reinvestigation by making an analysis of what Wyclif actually says, and what his repeated statements have to tell us about the nature of his 'juvenile deliria'. [3] He confesses to errors in philosophy—about the nature of universals, [4] the relationship of matter and form, the theory of time; [5] in theology—concerning

[1] Robson, *op. cit.*, 224; and cf. review by Smalley, *Medium Aevum*, XXX (1961), 200-3; also now J. Crompton, *JEH*, XVIII (1967), 265, 'in some ways he was haunted by guilt at having once embraced the opinions of those modern doctors whose positions he later so violently attacked, who were expounding the new logic of Ockham and his successors.'

[2] For example see further G. V. Lechler, *John Wiclif and his English Precursors*, 1878, II, 6-12; J. T. McNeill, 'Some Emphases in Wyclif's Teaching', *Journal of Religion*, VII (1927), 447-66; S. H. Thomson, 'The Philosophical Basis', 95f., and *Europe in Renaissance and Reformation*, 1963, 173-6; R. R. Betts, 'The University of Prague: The First Sixty Years', *Prague Essays*, ed. R. W. Seton-Watson, 1949, 53-68 at 69-70; M. Hurley, '*Scriptura sola*: Wyclif and His Critics,' *Traditio*, XVI (1960), 275-352 at 280-2; Robson, *op. cit.*, 141f., 220; Smalley, 'The Bible and Eternity,' and 'Wyclif's *Postilla* on the Old Testament and his *Principium*', *Oxford Studies Presented to D. Callus*, 1964, 253-96 at 278-9; J. Crompton, 'Wyclif', *Lexikon für Theologie und Kirche*, X (1965), 1279-80; M. Spinka, *John Hus at the Council of Constance*, New York, 1965, 27, and *John Hus' Concept of the Church*, Princeton, 1966, 22, 32.

[3] *De compositione hominis*, 4, 67, 'Sed post percepi dicta huiusmodi esse deliramenta iuvenilia'. *Deliramenta* is a favourite expression with Augustine for false doctrines contrary to scriptural truth: e.g. as applied to the teaching of the Jews, *Contra adversarios legis et prophetarum*, II, 2, 6 (*PL*, XLII, 642).

[4] *De universalibus*, 10, 'Et sic quando fui iunior involvebam ignoranter universalia sicut forte faciunt multi hodie qui pertinaciter universalia detestantur': as cited by Thomson, 'Philosophical Basis', 89; Robson, *op. cit.*, 145.

[5] See the passage cited by Robson, *op. cit.*, 180, from the *De scientia Dei* in which Wyclif says that he used to reject Augustinian teaching and restrict the meaning of 'present time' to a particular moment: '... quod quondam concessi quando restrinxi verba de praesenti ad unum instans, sed stat quod illud est contra sensum Augustini ... '. There is a similar passage in which he appears to say that he once denied the notion of divine eternity,

the eucharist, the scope of divine omnipotence, predestination, [1] and the proper mode of interpreting scripture; and he adds that he had a false conception of the right relationship between philosophy and theology, reason and faith, themselves. [2] We notice at once that the list is not concerned solely with matters of logic and philosophical speculation: at least half the items of declared fantasy are specifically theological, and the remainder have close connections with theological considerations. Wyclif seems to be admitting that he was once, not just a callow, ignorant student of arts, but a bad theologian as well. And if, for present purposes, we take a somewhat closer look at these theological positions, considerable doubt must be cast upon the nominalism attributed to him in his youth by modern scholar-

Responsiones ad R. Strode, 176, 'Quando autem incarceravi verba temporis, respuendo modum loquendi scripturae, longe aliter sum locutus. Sed modo videtur michi quod ista locutio sit plena brigis et, additis omnibus pictatiis, nimis falsa et fidelibus loquentibus onerosa'. Dziewicki, *art. cit.*, xiv, has pointed out that Wyclif's later position must be located between a realist acceptance of eternity and a nominalist denial of it. On this basis Wyclif's admission that he rejected the principle of eternity in his youth would automatically classify him as a nominalist at that time. However it should be noted that in the *Responsio* passage Wyclif is discussing the question in connection with the meaning of the *Ecclesia*, and emphasises that he no longer understands this to mean the 'present Church' of pope and clergy, but as the eternal Church, the *Ecclesia praedestinatorum*. From this point of view an admission that he once restricted time to the present is simply another way of acknowledging that he used to accept papal authority, but now looks beyond that authority to the true Church of the elect. This either puts the young Wyclif in the absurd position of having been both a papalist and a nominalist, or we must recognise that the whole question of nominalism is a red herring in this context.

[1] Note also *Trialogus*, IV, 13, 289-90, where he states that he once thought that men on earth could regulate the amount of punishment that they would suffer in hell, but now believes this is already determined: 'Ideo dixi quando fui iunior quod quantitas poenae damni attenditur penes quantitatem commodi quod damnatus haberet si ipsemet non poneret obicem in peccando. Sed modo apparet mihi istud inbrigabile propter multa: primo quia positivum et privativum non sic poterunt coaequari; secundo quia, cum omnia quae evenient de necessitate evenient, absolute necessarium est quod damnatus ponat obicem in peccando ...'. The discussion is inconclusive — '*Sed relinquendo materiam istam iuvenibus ...*' — but would seem to be related to his later attacks on the efficacy of authorised methods of acquiring additional grace like indulgences and pilgrimages.

[2] *Sermones*, II, 52-3, ii, 384.

ship. Indeed it may be of more significance to notice that contemporaries only began to accuse him of Ockhamist leanings in the last decade of his life.[1]

One of the topics which many study from their boyhood, he tells us, is the subject of divine necessity. I used to hold the view, he continues, that things were necessary only if God willed that they should be so, and for no other reason.

Propter difficultatem istius materiae multi qui a iuventute studuerunt istam materiam contrarie sunt locuti, ut hii propter istud specialiter negantes quod aliqua necessario sunt futura nisi ad istum sensum, *quem quondam tenui*, quod sunt futura necessitate ex suppositione: hoc est, Deus vult quod erunt; et necessario, si Deus vult quod erunt, ipsa erunt; et cum ista necessitate stat summa contingentia. [2]

Everything depended upon the absolute will of God, and there was no place left for human rationality and the exercise of man's free will. But now, he adds in a later passage, I have changed my view and see that divine necessity and human freedom of action must go hand in hand. [3] In short, Wyclif is saying that he once accepted the absolute omnipotence of God, a view which he clearly does not hold in any of his extant works, which are full of long lists of things which God cannot do lest he infringe man's right to choose his own manner of life. Now it is easy to understand from this why it has been assumed

---

[1] See the charges levelled against Wyclif by a doctor of theology who had once been one of his supporters at Oxford, as reported in *De veritate sacrae scripturae*, 12, i, 346-54, with Wyclif's replies in defence of Ockham. This opponent may have been William of Rymington, prior of Salley Abbey, Yorks., who accused Wyclif of being *doctor errorum modernorum*.

[2] *De statu innocentiae*, 9, 518.

[3] *Responsiones ad R. Strode*, 177, 'Et aliae conclusiones quae olim videbantur michi mirabiles, iam videntur michi catholice defendendae: quando enim eram parvulus in notitia fidei, loquebar ut parvulus et sapiebam ut parvulus, putans tamquam necessarium quod omnes actus humani forent in sua libertate contradictionis, sic quod liberrime possem facere oppositum aeternae Dei ordinantiae repugnando, sicut infans ductu nutricis ambulare incipiens putat ex se libere sine necessitatione nutricis quorsumcunque voluerit ambulare; quando autem ex Deo factus sum vir, evacuavi ex sua gratia cogitatus, qui erant parvuli, concedens quod homo in gradu suo habet liberum arbitrium, et tamen necessitatem omnium suorum operum futurorum'.

that the early Wyclif was an Ockhamist. The Ockhamist stressed the unlimited nature of the divine omnipotence, even if he also carefully refrained from allowing this omnipotence any activity in the human world in order to make room for the creation of an autonomous sphere of human right. God's absolute power might only be a hypothetical one, but the Ockhamist made tremendous play with it. Nevertheless, as Dr Leff has pointed out, most recently in his study of FitzRalph, [1] the conservative Augustinian theologian, such as Bradwardine, would equally readily assert that all power belonged to God, although he would add that this could only mean that there was therefore none left for men. In fact an acceptance of divine omnipotence had long been an indispensable basis for the papal claim to total sovereignty as the vicariate of God. [2] There was, then, a superficial similarity between Ockhamist and Augustinian in that they both claimed to accept the omnipotence of God— although whereas the Ockhamist permitted it virtually no play upon earth for practical purposes, the Augustinian insisted that it governed all human affairs, and recognised no effective distinction between heaven and earth.

That Wyclif adopted the omnipotence of God in this latter, Augustinian version would seem to be made clear by his supporting remarks that this was a question closely related to the problem of matter and form, body and soul, earthly and divine things. [3] Once, he tells us, I imagined that matter and form, although two distinct entities, could nevertheless be turned into one thing in the same way that two liquids seem to be blended together in a bottle: 'et ex illis coextensis resultare unum ad aliqualem motum quo duo liquida ymaginantur ad invicem commisceri'. [4] It was as if we could

---

[1] G. Leff, *Richard FitzRalph, Commentator of the Sentences*, 1963, 5-6, 9.

[2] Cf. my *Problem of Sovereignty in the Later Middle Ages*, 1963, esp. 151f., 293f. Notice the close relationship between Wyclif's limitation of divine omnipotence and the demand for limited government in *De logica*, III, 7, *passim*, and his use of Aristotle's *Physics* in support of this relationship.

[3] *De statu innocentiae*, 7, 511-12; and note the reference here to Bradwardine.

[4] *De logica*, III, 9, iii, 120.

say that colour and clay combined into a single substance called coloured clay. [1] The fact that this supposed reduction of two substances into one leaves one set of accidents to exist in isolation did not worry me — although now 'procul a me ista positio!' [2] But this meant that at the time I could not recognise the separate existence of body and soul: I made the soul the essence of the body, which effectively obliterated human nature and made all things spiritual and divine. [3] In short the material substance was annihilated. Yet Wyclif's admission that he was formerly an annihilationist again points to a realist, Augustinian position, particularly when the principle is applied (as Wyclif had always realised that it must be) to the character of the eucharist. He acknowledged that he had begun by holding the orthodox theory of transubstantiation,

> Unde licet quondam laboraverim ad describendum transsubstantiationem concorditer ad sensum prioris Ecclesiae, tamen modo videtur michi quod contrari[at]ur, posteriora Ecclesia oberrante, [4]

in which the material substance (the bread and wine) vanished as a substance, and was replaced by the spiritual substance of Christ's body and blood. Here again the divine obliterates the material. But I did not at that time recognize, he writes, that there could be multiple essences, that two substances could coexist together: 'quando autem variavi ab ista sententia non cog-

[1] III, 9, iii, 68. He adds that Aristotelian physics (as derived through Avicenna) now make it clear to him that coloured clay is still colour and clay, which may amalgamate, but never really lose their separate identities, iii, 79-83.

[2] III, 9, iii, 120, 'Et illis superaddi accidentia tamquam res abstractas quae possunt per se existere.'

[3] *De compositione hominis*, 2, 36, 'Quondam autem dixi . . . et ad istum sensum concessi animam esse corpus vel substantiam sensibilem, et sic essentialiter omne quod est homo. Sed quia *tunc* videtur quod anima sit materia prima, natura divina natura humana, et sic de multis fidei dissonis, . . . ideo mihi videtur *modo* quod rationabiliter sit tacenda'. He remarks that he could never understand how dead bodies still moved and appeared to have a 'life' of their own 'quando ymaginabar animam esse essentiam separabilem, materiae coliniatam', 4, 67.

[4] *De eucharistia*, 2, 52, in which he refers back to his earlier rejection of annihilation in the *Summa intellectualium*. As shrewdly indicated by J. H. Fisher, *John Gower*, New York, 1964, 162, 357, Wyclif saw annihilation, the creation of nothingness, as a symbol of sin: thus a realist theory of the

novi, ut modo, quomodo res habet multiplex esse' [1] —which was the basis of his fully developed theory of the eucharist. True, one might perhaps argue again that there is a sort of similarity here with nominalism, which is also a one-substance theory (as Wyclif himself recognised [2]), but nominalism would assert the continued existence of the material substance of bread and wine alone in isolation. Yet no one has ever suggested that Wyclif was orginally a nominalist in the matter of the eucharist, and there is no reason why they should. It seems inexplicable, however, that so many eminent scholars should be prepared to accept that Wyclif was initially a nominalist whilst recognising his original realism in regard to the eucharist. Since Wyclif repeatedly underlined his point that the principles of philosophy must be applied, through the medium of one's conception of matter and form, to the theory of the eucharist, [3] this modern interpretation amounts to a charge of illogical thinking against Wyclif. Wyclif admitted to many youthful errors, but self-contradiction was not one of them.

So far the young Wyclif has appeared as one who stressed the supremacy of divine power and spiritual substances at the expense of corporeal, human, material things. There is no real difficulty in recognising this to be the attitude of a realist and a papalist, an Augustinian. But when acknowledging his early errors in biblical interpretation, it was his carnal

---

eucharist which insisted upon the annihilation of substances was symptomatic of the evil which infected the whole papal system. This is the counterpart to the familiar canonistic theory that the pope can create *ex nihilo* as an attribute of his divine righteousness.

[1] *De Ecclesia*, 5, 107.

[2] See the combined attack on both realists and nominalists in *De apostasia*, 15, 204-5, for creating *accidens sine subiecto* by their theories of the *corpus Christi*: 'Et ista est maior blasfemia, quia illud accidens vel nichil est vel vacuum, et concedere hoc de corpore et Deo foret summa blasfemia'.

[3] Thus in the *De eucharistia* itself Wyclif stipulates three possible views on the nature of the eucharist: e.g. 2, 29, 'In qua materia sunt tres viae'; also 7, 222. These are orthodox papal real presence, Ockhamist commemorative, and Wyclif's dual substance theories, which are to be equated with realist, nominalist and intermediate philosophical positions. His own position is defined as one combining matter and form, or reason ('Aristoteles vel ratio') and faith: 3, 67, 78.

acceptance of words at their face value, his readiness to adopt a human interpretation of scripture without regard for the spiritual or mystical intent, of which he accuses himself.

> ... non enim debeo carnaliter dicta intelligere ... sicut intellexi quando fui ignarus gramaticae et aequivocationis, quas sancti doctores exprimunt de scripturis, sed debeo intelligere personas vel notiones divinas sicut sancti doctores dilucidant. Et sic per tunicam, pallium, oculum vel maxillam debent intelligi vires et habitus interioris hominis, habendo sensum scripturae in dictis consilis et non partes aut vestimenta exterioris hominis quae corporaliter intuentur. [1]

He admitted that he had been guilty of erecting man alongside God as an exponent of truth. [2] Obviously, one will say, a nominalist position. But before drawing hasty conclusions, it is worthwhile to consider the context in which these remarks were made. Wyclif is here, in the *De veritate sacrae scripturae*, condemning the attribution of divine authority to papal decrees, the assumption which, he says, makes the pope into an *alter Deus*,

---

[1] *De civili dominio*, III, 1, 404; also *De veritate sacrae scripturae*, 6, i, 114, 'Unde quando loquebar ut parvulus fui anxie intricatus ad intelligendum ac defendendum istas scripturas de virtute sermonis ... et demum Dominus ex gratia sua apperuit michi sensum ad intelligendum aequivocationem praedictam scripturae, et sic intellexi scripturam sacram nunc loqui ad literam singulariter de scriptura primo modo dicta, nunc pluraliter de scriptura secundo et tertio modo dicta, ... Et per istas distinctiones intellexi scripturam infringibiliter veram ad literam'. Cf. 5, i, 100, 'Quando autem fui minor, abieci locutiones misticas ...'. For the development of the principle that the literal sense involved both the actual words and their spiritual or allegorical meaning see further B. Smalley, *The Study of the Bible in the Middle Ages*, 2nd. ed., 1952.

[2] *De veritate sacrae scripturae*, 6, i, 124-5, 'Quandoque autem contendebam distinguendo hos quatuor sensus ex opposito per rangas inutiles, vocando sensum non solum veritatem quam auctor asserit de scriptura, sed agregatum ex illo et modo intelligendi nostro: post vero visum est michi modum loquendi esse infundabilem et superflue onerosum'. The objection to admitting human interpretations is that these may vary ('secundum modos intelligendi hominum variatur'), and therefore only the divine meaning should be considered: 'Et tunc videtur quod solum ille sit sensus scripturae quem Deus et beati legunt in libro vitae'. Cf. the attack on the *sophista* who would make 'hominum ascendere in coelum et esse Deum, cum quotlibet ridiculis' in the *De ente in communi*, ed S. H. Thomson, 1930, 2, 33.

another God. [1] Elsewhere, when making a similar confession of
juvenile foolishness, he comments that he used to believe that
a man could interfere with God's will as to who should be
saved and who damned: again he appears to have in mind the
papal claim to bind and loose in heaven and earth, to open and
close the gates of paradise. [2] But this at once suggests that in
speaking of man being erected alongside God, Wyclif had in
mind a particular man, namely the pope, rather than humanity
in general. [3] He did not mean that he had been splitting the
cosmos into equal portions between man and God in an Ockhamist fashion, but that he had allowed himself to believe that a
man—the pope—could become divine, and that a carnal being
could interpret the divine word by his own power. It might be
true that the Ockhamist, with his conception of an earthbound
humanity, was also guilty of deification, of making man into
his own god: in this sense the Ockhamist did seek to make men

[1] *De veritate sacrae scripturae*, 6, i, 116, 'bullae vel epistolae papales dicuntur
sacrae'; 15, i, 394, 'Ideo dicere quod omnes bullae papales sunt paris aucto-
ritatis aut certitudinis veritatis cum sacra scriptura foret blasfeme sibi
imponere quod [papa] sit Christus'; 20, ii, 134-5, this would allow the
pope to dispense with the Bible and become 'Deus in terris'. For *alter
Deus*, e.g. *De civili dominio*, I, 38, 283.

[2] Note the way in which the attack upon pope and clergy for claiming the
power 'iudicandi absolutionem simpliciter quoad Deum et Ecclesiam tri-
umphantem' in *Sermones*, I, i, 341, leads to the assertion that God alone can
determine grace and punishment after death, and an admission that he
once denied this ('Quando autem fui iunior negavi quod quidquam sit
debitum nisi debeatur simpliciter quoad Deum . . . ', i, 357) as taking no
account of humanly determined merits and demerits: 'Quondam autem
dixi quod relationes huius rationis habent meritum et demeritum pro
tempore suo succedens . . . Sed tota ista difficultas est logicalis et inanis'.
Cf. his attack on 'istam blasfemiam quod Deus non potest dare rem sacra-
menti nisi ipsi [scil. moderni] adiuverint ministrando signa', *De blasfemia*,
9, 139.

[3] See also his complaint about the heresy of the 'modern Pelagians': 'qui
ponunt esse possibile quod homo operetur cum hoc quod Deus non
cooperetur cum eo', *De volutione Dei*, 7, 195. This might apply to Augustinian or nominalist, but it may be remarked that elsewhere it is the hierocrats
who are accused (of all things) of being individualist: e.g. the *praelati* who
are 'singularibus dediti', *Purgans errores circa universalia in communi*, l, 31;
and the attribution of the view that a man should seek his individual good
to the sophists in the middle of a discussion of papal power, *De civili
dominio*, II, 14, 184.

divine. But so, according to Wyclif, does the papal realist, [1] and since it is the papalist who is inflating the importance of a created being, who is trying to humanise God in the person of the pope, then it is the papalists who can more appropriately be described as the materialist, carnal-minded thinkers. They are the *grossi politici et mundani*, because their boosting of divine values is simply intended to elevate their own earthly position. [2] If they stress the efficacy of the divine power it is in order to deify themselves as its possessors. If they place limitations upon it, this is to secure a share in its manipulation. By treating divine things in a human, material manner, they destroy the distinction between God and man. When Wyclif confessed to humanism, he was telling his readers, in an oblique and deliberately misleading manner, that he had once been a supporter of the papal-hierocratic system.

It is as well to emphasize that this obscurity was deliberate. Wyclif had a definite purpose in making it difficult for his readers to distinguish between Ockhamist nominalism and papal realism. [3] The reason is that in later life he wanted to use exactly the same arguments against both positions, and therefore found it desirable to accuse both sides of

[1] Conversely both papalists and nominalists can be condemned for trying to deny that Christ was a king upon earth by divine right, one side by making this a matter of civil rulership, the other by denying it altogether. Both are 'moderni ignari scripturae. ... nescientes distinguere inter dominationem vel regnationem evangelicam et civilem': *De civili dominio*, III, 5, 69.

[2] For the identification of the *moderni* with the *politici* see for example *De civili dominio*, I, 4, 32-3: they are the 'ecclesiastici nostri temporis'; who advocate the total supremacy of the ruler (I, 14, 100), substitute a secular conception of the *Ecclesia* for its true spiritual nature (I, 24, 173), and who include the canonists amongst their writers about law and politics (II, 12, 128-9).

[3] Accordingly the Ockhamists were also to be attacked as *moderni* 'sign doctors', and accused of misinterpreting Aristotle, along with the realists. For a good example of both classes of *moderni* being dealt with together over the question of universals see *Purgans errores circa universalia in communi*, l, 29-31, 'de universalibus quidam nimis *pueriliter* et quidam subtiliter obiciunt'. For the nominalists as *moderni* in this respect, *De Trinitate*, ed. A. duP. Breck, Boulder, Col., 1962, 9, 100; *De benedicta incarnatione*, 6, 86; 9, 144. But we cannot accept Robson's view, *op. cit.*, 187, that this is 'a term which invariably refers, in Wyclif's works, to Ockhamists'.

exactly the same errors. Both parties were to be rejected as extremists, who failed to make any allowance for their opponents being partially right. He came to realise, as he 'grew up', that opposites were not opposed: they were simply extensions on one side or another of a central truth. [1] The trouble with both realists and nominalists was that they would insist on dealing with divine things in isolation. The Ockhamist maintained that divine truths were knowable by faith alone: he dared not use reason in theology, since reason appeared to give him a series of totally different answers. Similarly the papalist maintained that faith alone ('nuda fides') was the only certain guide to truth: reason was thereby devalued and ultimately could be neglected altogether. Neither side would allow, as Wyclif stressed must be the case, that reason and faith should go together as integral elements in divine truth.

... et tenent nimis multi sed fatue quod lumen fidei et lumen naturale sunt contraria ... Sed veritas est quod lumen naturale, ordinatum a Deo ut inducat in fidem, non est contrarium lumini fidei, sed in fidem catholicam inductivum ... cum ratio naturalis rectificata inducit et praeparat ad cunctos articulos fidei cognoscendos.[2]

Wyclif himself therefore stood in opposition to both extremes, according them a greater similarity with each other than of either to his own position. Extremes, he argued, may be at opposite poles, but, as in a magnet, the curve of the metal means that they are not really very far apart. The distribution of the opposing schools resembles a horseshoe, in which the middle section appears as the opposite of the two extremities, which are

[1] This is reflected in his refusal to allow that theological propositions could be dealt with by simple 'yes' and 'no' answers: for an example of this 'sic et non' technique, see *De volutione Dei*, 16, 262, on the question of whether sin is pleasing to God. Thus he later attacked his opponents for demanding that one should 'simpliciter concedere vel negare', *De blasfemia*, 5, 73. Hus employed the same device against the charges put to him at Constance.

[2] *Sermones*, I, 25, i, 170; *De dominio divino*, I, 11, 89, 'Videtur michi quod moderni magis exorbitant qui ponunt lumen fidei, tamquam contrarium, confundere quae videmus in lumine naturali. Econtra equidem est dicendum quod lumen supernaturale est forma perfectiva luminis naturalis ...'. Heresy is therefore to be defined as a defect of both faith and reason: *De civili dominio*, II, 7, 59.

themselves much closer together than they are to the centre. To obtain his own central position it was necessary for Wyclif to pick and choose from both sides, as well as to attack them, and to allow that one side had as much or as little right about it as the other extreme. It is very noticeable that in about a third of the passages under discussion here he attributes his early misguidedness to his inability to equivocate—'quando fui ignarus gramaticae et aequivocationis quas sancti doctores exprimunt de scripturis' [1] —to achieve a middle way [2] by balancing one extreme against the other, 'cum in aequivocis non sit contradictio', alternately denying and accepting the truth of any extreme proposition taken in isolation. [3] This gives us an indication of what it was that brought about his conversion. Wyclif's own accounts of this process are, on the surface, hopelessly conflicting: at various times he credits his coming of age to having read Augustine, [4] or Aristotle either in the radical version presented by

---

[1] *De civili dominio*, III, 19, 404; also III, 21, 443, 'Unde quando fui iunior, ignorans aequivocationem scripturae'; *De veritate sacrae scripturae*, 6, i, 114; *De bendicta incarnatione*, 6, 103; *Sermones*, I, 54, i, 357. Equivocation will solve the problem of universals and harmonise the views of the holy doctors on the relationship of signs to things: *De ente in communi*, 3, 39.

[2] *Supplementum Trialogi*, ed. G. Lechler, 1869, 2, 414, 'In neutram tamen istarum partium incido, sed evitans Scyllam et Caribdim, transeo per medium, dictum meum non diffiniens. Nec scio excusare praelatos modernos ab haeresi, . . .'; *De ente praedicamentali*, 14, 127, 'Sed theologus medians inter has duas vias, notata distinctione praedicta de agentia, dicit *et* Deum agere omnem rem positivam actam *et* communicare creaturis potentiam ad agendum'.

[3] Cf. *De benedicta incarnatione*, 1, 13, 'Concordo secundo cum approbatis doctoribus ut Augustino, Ieronimo et caeteris . . . Concordo tertio cum novellis . . . Et ad istum sensum concedo affirmativas, modifico negativas'. This is to be achieved by equivocation: *prologus*, 1-2; 1, 3; 7, 115. See also *De materia et forma*, 7, 223, 'Ideo, exemplativo sensu, dicit post quod hoc est ut *sic* et est ut *non*, ad modum loquendi Aristotelis in tali materia. Et sic sophistice volentes extorquere rationem simpliciter potest eligi alterutra pars, negando reliquam ad sensum contradictorium: vel tertio, negando utrumque ad sensus aequivoco, et cum in aequivocis non sit contradictio, non conceditur falsum. Et illa responsio plus decet theologum qui non affectat apparentiam sophisticam, . . .': this technique is similarly attributed to Aristotle in *De ente praedicamentali*, 2, 15f.; *Trialogus*, ed. G. Lechler, 1869, I, 9, 66.

[4] See the important passage in *De materia et forma*, 4, 190-1, in which he says that when he started as a student of philosophy he could not interpret

Averroes, [1] or in the more moderate form used by Aquinas. [2] Since each of these represents one of the three main philosophical positions available in the fourteenth century, it seems extraordinarily difficult to imagine what his position can have been before he was familiar with any of these authors. However, on closer examination, we can begin to eliminate. When he tells us that he read Augustine and so achieved maturity, he meant that he now understood for the first time what Augustine really meant: [3] that he had been misunderstanding Augustine up to this point. And armed with the realization of what Augustine really, i.e. ought to have, meant to say, he came to see the value of Aristotle and Averroes, that is, of what they too should really mean. In other words, Wyclif was saying, he came to appreciate that Augustinianism and Averro-Aristotelianism were not truly opposed, and that both were needed for a complete synthesis of the truth. Once having reached this point, we need have little

Aristotle on prime matter correctly and babbled, until Augustine showed him how to make Aristotle conform to theology—which suggests that he began by attacking Aristotle: 'Ista verba etsi saepe audivi et balbutiendo protuli quando incoepi philosophari, legendo libros Aristotelis, longe tamen fui a sensu verborum, sicut forte alii mihi similes, quousque fui paululum illustratus in notitia materiae primae secundum sensum scripturae a sanctis doctoribus mihi expositum, et specialiter a beato Augustino exponente illud *Gen.*, I [1], In principio creavit Deus coelum et terram ... Et iste est sensus beati Augustini et concorditer aliorum philosophorum ponentium quod Deus est prius naturaliter quam aliquod genus, et sic est principium cuiuslibet generis'. Cf. *Responsiones ad R. Strode*, 197.

[1] Having cited Aristotle and Averroes on the unity of body and soul, *De compositione hominis*, 4, 55-7, he remarks, 'Et ignorantia huius methaphisicae de anima fui ego et forte alii mei similes plurimum excaecatus, sompnians quod anima et specialiter humana sit res quae peterit a corpore separari'. Note his discussion of the Platonic view of the relationship of matter and form in *De logica*, III, 9, iii, 121, with the comment, 'Sed sermo Aristotelis est michi placentior'. Aristotle and Averroes are cited some forty times in this work in contrast to only one reference to Augustine.

[2] *De civili dominio*, III, 21, 443; and note that he states that he changed his theory of time after reading the commentaries on Aristotle's *Physics* and *Metaphysics*: 'Unde propter tales evidentias fui primo motus ad ampliandum tempus, quia non vidi quomodo philosophus vel theologus posset negare huiusmodi successiva'. The former may be identified as Aquinas, *Expositio in VII libros Physicorum*, IV, 15-23, 558-637.

[3] See his account of how he came to understand the meaning of a statement by Augustine, *Responsiones ad R. Strode*, 197.

hesitation in deciding that the crucial event in Wyclif's majority
was his reading of Aquinas, who showed me, he writes in one
instance, [1] the way to a truer understanding of the Bible and the
Fathers. On this basis we can confidently assert that Wyclif was
once an Augustinian realist, rejecting the radical Aristotelian
principles of the nominalists, until Aquinas showed him that
both extremes could be modified and harmonized. [2] Indeed we
might argue that all Wyclif's written work as we have it is an
attempt to reinterpret Augustine, to bring about a grand review
of traditional Augustinian and papal principles in order that
they might be brought to terms with the Aristotelian revolution.
There was ample reason to describe Wyclif as 'John, son of
Augustine', [3] but at the same time one may suspect that that most
eminent of Church Fathers would have vigorously contested

[1] Thus in *De civili dominio*, III, 21, 443, he apparently confesses to having
once taught that the pope was *rex et sacerdos* (which is the main topic of the
section), but changed his view once Aquinas had shown him how to equivocate about this: 'Unde quando fui iunior . . . reputavi pro magna victoria deducere quod dominus est pars clerici et tamen idem dominus non
est pars clerici. Postea autem quando detecta est loyca Christi, apostoli,
Augustini et aliorum sanctorum, humiliter et subtiliter asserentium quod
in aequivocis non est contradictio, stabat Iohannes [*John*, I, 29, occasionally applied by Wyclif to himself] confusus et ignarus idiota, quid ulterius
replicaret quando, detecta aequivocatione scripturae, deduxerat quod re-
pugnaretur inconveniens, sed verecunde deficiens prae ignorantia fecit
finem. Nec licet sic respondere destruendo scolam arguendi in concedendo
contradicenda praeter signa, sed solum quando sufficienti auctoritate
scripturae aequivocatio tollens repugnantiam est fundata; et istum sensum explanat sanctus Thomas, secunda secundae, quaestione clxxxv,
articulo v in fine . . .'. The passage cited (Aquinas, *Summa theologiae*, II, II,
clxxxv, 6 ad 3) does not in fact illustrate this principle, only Wyclif's infinite
capacity for sheering off at a tangent to attack clerical property rights.

[2] It seems clear enough that the principle of the duality of substances
('una est substantia immaterialis et alia substantia materialis'), which is the
method used to harmonise extremes, was derived by Wyclif from Aquinas:
'Et super illam considerationem credo sanctum Thomam et alios loquentes
de esse et essentia pro magna parte fundari', *De materia et forma*, 4, 187 and
184 respectively. The Aristotelian concept of the mean is of course a basic
feature of Thomistic thinking and was widely used by Aquinas: e.g.,
Comm. in Nich. Eth., II, 7, 324 (ed. Spiazzi), 92, 'Virtus ipsa est quaedam
medietas inter duas malitias et inter duos habitus vitioses'.

[3] 'Sui discipuli vocabant eum famoso et elato nomine Ioannem Augustini',
according to Thomas Netter, *Doctrinale antiquitatum fidei Ecclesiae catholicae*,
I, 34 (ed. Venice, 1571), I, 105.

his paternity in this case. The prime influence on the shaping of Wyclif's system of thought was Aristotle, even though an Aristotle masquerading as Augustine. If we ourselves are to accept this as 'Augustinianism', we must appreciate that it was Augustine revised to a point beyond recognition. And Wyclif was shrewd enough, and, in his devious way, honest enough, to know it and admit it.

Nevertheless it was from Augustine that Wyclif derived his whole conception of boyhood as used in these passages. When he called himself a child or youth, we need not doubt that he was referring to himself as a much younger man —perhaps a very young one—but these expressions must be understood as having a figurative rather than a literal meaning (or, as Wyclif would have put it, they were used literally in the sense of having a more important spiritual connotation behind them). Just as Augustine had stressed the ignorance and intellectual vulnerability of childhood, [1] and by analogy had condemned non-Christians for the puerility of their learning, [2] so Wyclif defined childishness as a species of infidelity, a condition of inept understanding of the faith to be contrasted with the mature appreciation of divine righteousness displayed by the true theologians following in the footsteps of the saints and elders of the Church: 'Patet ergo quod antiqui theologi laborarunt ad cognoscendum sensum scripturae et dimittendum alios sensus infidelium seu puerorum'. [3] When I was a child, he para-

---

[1] E.g. *De libero arbitrio*, III, 23, 68 (*PL*, XXXII, 1304); *Epp.*, CLXVI, 6, 16 (*PL*, XXXIII, 727); *De Trinitate*, XIV, 5, 7 (*PL*, XLII*, 1040-1). Note the emphasis here that irrational ignorance is a sin against the will of God.

[2] *De doctrina christiana*, II, 28, 42 (*PL*, XXXIV, 53), ' . . . historia plurimum nos adiuvat ad sanctos libros intelligendos, etiamsi praeter Ecclesiam puerili eruditione discatur'.

[3] *De veritate sacrae scripturae*, 3, i, 44; also 6, i, 118, 'Ex quo patet quod inepti sunt ad discendum hanc scripturam pueri et superbi', adding that the term *pueri* is used in the sense that Augustine uses it (although again the actual reference given to his source is incorrect). Cf. the contrast of *sensus puerilis* with *sensus catholicus* in *De civili dominio*, III, 19, 403. In *Sermones*, III, 33, iii, 269, he urges bishops to be like the elders of *Rev.*, IV, 4, who are 'maturi in moribus quia in scientia divina populo seniores'.

phrased *Corinthians*, I thought as a child, and did not understand. [1] He spoke of his blind groping after truth in his infancy, [2] for childhood is an age puffed up with pride, [3] and it is pride which blinds the young and makes them secular-minded. [4] All this, it can be seen, was particularly applicable to papalists. [5] They were the children of pride, blinded by lust for secular wealth and power, inspired by the *cupiditas* which stood opposed to *iustitia*. [6] The hierocratic system was suitable only for juveniles,

[1] *De benedicta incarnatione*, 6, 103, 'Et quando sapiebam ut parvulus putabam istum sanctum [Ambrose] multum ignarum logicae'; *Responsiones ad R. Strode*, 177. The reference is to I *Cor.*, XIII, 11, also cited *De veritate sacrae scripturae*, 3, i, 44.

[2] *De materia et forma*, 6, 211, 'Quando autem minus sapui scripturam et solum fluctuavi in tortura animi, nunc negando informitatem materiae, nunc dicendo quod non est informis nisi quoad illud instans naturae, sed non ex hoc sequitur quod est informis . . . Et sic de quibuslibet de caeculis a veritate, quae caecati circumpalpitantes veritatem langwide suspicantur'.

[3] See his repeated admissions to having been motivated by pride: e.g. *De veritate sacrae scripturae*, 5, i, 100, 'Quando autem fui minor abieci locutiones misticas partim propter meam superbiam . . . '; cf. 2, i, 23, 'Unde de ista vana gloria confiteor saepe tam arguendo quam respondendo prolapsus sum a doctrina scripturae, cupiens simul apparentiam famae in populo . . .'; *De civili dominio*, III, 21, 443, 'Unde quando fui iunior . . . ac sitiens redargutionem auditorii apparentem . . .'; *Responsiones ad R. Strode*, 197, 'confitetur tamen se multipliciter peccasse praesumptione et arrogantia'. Also *Purgans errores circa universalia in communi*, 1, 31.

[4] *Trialogus*, IV, 15, 298, 'quando populus magis fuit affectus temporalibus tamquam iuvenis et non sapiens coelestia'; *Supplementum Trialogi*, I, 410, 'Cum ergo patres legis veteris erant in puerili aetate saeculi manuducendi bonis temporalibus . . .'; *De logica*, III, 10, iii, 181, 'quia mentes iuvenum infectae et corporalium fantasmum mutabilitate plenae non concipiunt . . .'.

[5] Thus in attacking the material wealth of the clergy he says 'ut loquar pueris qui mundum sapiunt', *Sermones*, II, 6, ii, 38; cf. I, 58, i, 348, 'tales bullae sunt tumores aquae vel pueriles nolae et non evangelium'. In the English version of the *De officio pastorali*, ed. F. D. Matthew, 1880 (*EETS*, 74), 31, 455, he says that children would be just as good priests as the existing ones.

[6] For a good example of the antithesis of *cupiditas* to the apostolic mean see *De officio pastorali*, ed. G. V. Lechler, Leipzig, 1863, I, 2, 8-9: the former is regarded as the hallmark of tyranny, I, 4 and 7, 11 and 14. The evils of *cupiditas* were stressed by most medieval theologians, notably Augustine and Aquinas, but the specific opposition of this concept to apostolic truth derives from the sixth-century Greek commentary on *I John*, IV, 4-8, attributed to Oecumenius, but now regarded as a spurious work: see further T. P. Dunning, *Piers Plowman*: *An Interpretation of the A Text*, 1937, esp. 42-3. Wyclif's usage shows a close connection with contemporary

since it took its adherents no further than the legal ceremonies of the Jewish synagogue, the Church in its infancy. [1] On other occasions he condemned his opponents as mad boys who objected to Aristotle and refused to use philosophy to understand the Bible properly:

> ... in toto intellectu scripturae oportet supponere rectam logicam et naturalem philosophiam, et tunc discoli adversantes veritati scripturae sunt tamquam deliri pueri deridendi. [2]

Thus, for Wyclif, it was the papalist, as much as the Ockhamist, [3] who was the sophist and falsifier, [4] the modernist propounding

poetic convention which ascribed bad counsel, the cause of tyranny, to the bad advice of young men: cf. A. B. Ferguson, *The Articulate Citizen and the English Renaissance*, Durham, N. Carolina, 1965, 70f. The use of the child to represent a tyrant, based on *Eccles.*, X, 16, is a commonplace of fourteenth-century political thought.

[1] *Sermones*, III, 8, iii, 57,' ... Deus educavit Ecclesiam, nam in principio quando Ecclesia erat parvula aetate et scientia, et sic petulans et indiscreta, servivit sub partibus mundi ... Unde tota lex vetus dicitur quasi alphabetum, quod pro lege veteri discebatur a populo Hebraeorum'. But under Christ's law of grace the *Ecclesia* achieved its fullness, only to be thrown back by the 'infundabiles ceremoniae Antichristi', so that *nostra Ecclesia* today 'in discibilibus et operabilibus saluti suae inutilibus plus quam iuvenis Ecclesia insolentius et multiplicius evagatur ... et sic tamquam anus decrepita in modis puerilibus iuvenescitur'.

[2] *Expositio Matthaei XXIV*, 7, 373; and see also *De actibus animae*, II, 3, 112-13, where he opposes Aristotle to the *modernus*, who is 'stultius ... quam bestiam, puerum vel dementem'.

[3] In this sense he can still speak of having been opposed to the *sophistae* in his youth: e.g. *De civili dominio*, III, 21, 443, 'Unde quando fui iunior ... et timens elationem sophisticam'; *De veritate sacrae scripturae*, 5, i, 100, 'Quando autem fui minor abieci locutiones misticas partim propter meam superbiam et partim ad destruendum inanem gloriam sophistarum'; cf. 2, i, 23, 'cupiens simul apparentiam famae in populo et denudationem arrogantiae sophistarum'. As with *moderni*, the term is used interchangeably, and each usage must be considered in relation to the circumstances in which it appears.

[4] See his paraphrase of *Prov.*, XII, 22, 'Abominatio est Domino labia mendacia', as 'qui sophistice loquitur est Deo odibilis', *De iuramento Arnaldi*, ed. G. V. Lechler, *John Wiclif and his English Precursors*, 1878, II, 345; and his attacks on the sophists for evading the truth in *De logica*, III, 1 and 8, ii, 21 and 226. The character 'False-thinker' or Pseustis in the *Trialogus* expounds extreme Aristotelian and extreme papal views against both Alithia, 'solidus philosophus', and Phronesis, 'subtilis theologus et maturus', who are allied in opposition to him. Wyclif appears to have been modelling himself upon Augustine in his condemnation of the 'academics',

profane novelties: [1] and when Wyclif confessed to having once been a *modernus*, we should beware of understanding this to mean that he had been a nominalistic student of arts. Like Grosseteste, who had never of course heard of Ockham, the *modernus* was an opponent who impugned the use of Aristotle. [2] All this was simply an admission that he had once supported the hierocratic system at a time when, according to his own phraseology, he was blinded by infantile piety. [3] And when he was eventually denounced to the papal curia in 1376, he put the blame for this

e.g. the falsely reasoning sophists of *De doctrina christiana*, II, 31 (*PL*, XXXIV, 58). In contemporary literature attacks on sophism are a recognised feature of anti-clerical propaganda: in *Piers Plowman* the priest is the sophist who understands the letter but not the spirit of Truth's pardon, N. Coghill, 'The Pardon of *Piers Plowman*', *Proceedings of the British Academy*, XXX (1944), 319; J. Burrow, 'The Action of Langland's Second Vision,' *Essays in Criticism*, XV (1965), 261-2. Without entering into the problem of Wyclif's acquaintance with the *Defensor pacis* of Marsilius of Padua, it may be noted that Marsilius had accused the papalists of sophism in claiming that the pope had a plenitude of power, an utterly pernicious opinion: *Defensor pacis*, ed. R. Scholz, Hanover, 1932-3, I, i, 3-4, 5-6; I, i, 8, 9; II, xxiii, 2, 441; II, xxiv, 17, 466. They gave words false meanings so that things which were properly secular appeared to be spiritual: II, xxix, 7, 582; cf. II, i, 1, 137-9.

[1] In the *De veritate sacrae scripturae* 'nostri doctores moderni', whom Wyclif accuses of heresy by falsifying the Bible, are those who attach a plenitude of power to the pope and 'laborant ad curiam Romanam': 16, ii, 1f ; 17, ii, 43 and 57; 20, ii, 133; 28, iii, 107; 32, iii, 284. They are represented by the canonists whose *novellae* and *extravagantes* allow the pope to dispense against God, 27, iii, 69-70. These are the Caesarean clergy of the *moderna ecclesia*: *De potestate papae*, 1, 1; *Opus evangelicum*, I, 8, i, 27; I, 27, i, 93; *Supplementum Trialogi*, 2, 414-6; *De septem donis Spiritus Sancti*, 4, 215.

[2] 'Haec adduximus contra quosdam modernos qui nituntur contra ipsum Aristotelem et suos expositores . . .' (*Hexaemeron*): see B. Smalley, 'The Biblical Scholar', *Robert Grosseteste, Scholar and Bishop*, ed. D. A. Callus, 1955, 79. See *De actibus animae*, I, 3, 45, for Aristotle classified with the apostles and *antiqui doctores* in opposition to the *moderni theologi*: therefore Aristotelian metaphysics and theology are to be used together 'pro intellectu scripturae et pro tollendis argutiis sophistarum', *De dominio divino*, II, I, 178; II, 4, 191-2. The habit of labelling one's opponents as *moderni* may also derive from Averroes.

[3] *Opus evangelicum*, IV, 3, ii, 297, 'multa videntur absurda pueris pietate infantili caecatis, quae apparent satis catholica in fundamentis fidei stabilitis'. When he changed his attitude towards universities after his expulsion from Oxford in 1382 he compared himself to St. Paul 'quondam pharisaeus', *Dialogus*, 26, 54.

betrayal upon the *pueri*, Black Dog's boys, the English papalists. [1]

We may, then, expect little help from the texts in estimating Wyclif's actual age at the time of his conversion. Since he remarks that it was a slow process, [2] any particular date would necessarily be imprecise. In any case the very doubtful chronology of Wyclif's early life would make any answer purely speculative. We are dying, Wyclif liked to say, again in imitation of

---

[1] In the early summer, probably June, of 1382 Wyclif complained that a certain *canis niger*, named Tolstan or Colstan, and his yelping whelps ('balbutientes catuli'), who had originally reported him to the Roman curia over the question of lordship, were again attacking him for his views on the religious orders and the eucharist: *Sermones*, III, 24 and 30-2, iii, 188-90, 246-56, 261-2. Black Dog is described as a teacher of idiot boys at Oxford: he is toothless when he bites because lacking in wisdom, and his puppies are blind (iii, 190, 247, 252, 262). Wyclif accuses them of being ignorant of equivocation, and urges them to learn the elementary logic of harmonising contradictory statements from Aristotle and Augustine, lest they foul their own kennels (iii, 190, 218-19). According to Walsingham, *Historia Anglicana*, I, 357, and *Chronicon Angliae*, 184, Wyclif had said at Lambeth early in 1378 that 'per pueros reportata est sententia fidei quam dixi in scholis et alibi, ac magis, per pueros etiam usque ad Romanam curiam transportata'. Numerous candidates for the identity of Black Dog have been put forward. Cardinals Easton and Langham, Bishop Brinton of Rochester, Abbot Littlington of Westminster, William Woodford, O. F. M., Robert Waldby, O. E. S. A., and William Binham (prior of Wallingford, Berks., from at least 1379) can be excluded, since Wyclif specifies that he was 'de ordine Benedicti' (iii, 246; cf. 252, 255-6, 261) and was still actually teaching at Oxford in 1382 (iii, 188-90). As pointed out by M. Hurley, 'Scriptura sola: Wyclif and his Critics', *Traditio*, XVI (1960), 275-352 at 316, this must also discount Workman's suggestion, I, 296, that he was Uthred of Boldon, who had already left Oxford for Finchdale before 1382; and he therefore prefers Workman's other suggestion, II, 123-4, that he was John Welles of Ramsey, prior of Gloucester College, and known to be in Oxford at the required times (cf. Emden, III, 2008). Welles certainly seems to have regarded himself as the target of the accusation, to judge by his reply in *Fasciculi zizaniorum*, 239. On the basis of Biblical texts like *Prov.*, XXVI, 11-12, and *Matt.*, VII, 7, and XV, 26, the dog had become a common symbol in patristic and medieval exegesis for the sinner, heretic, or enemy of truth—the beast-like man to be ejected from the community because unclean.

[2] *Responsiones ad R. Strode*, 197, 'Unde homo quem novistis in scolis circa istam materiam, secundum mensuram quam Deus sibi dederat, laboravit et paulative veritates secundum quod credit esse Deo beneplacitum et expediens Ecclesiae declaravit'.

St Augustine, from the moment that we begin to live. [1] We know that he completed the process on 3 December, 1384, but we have no very certain idea of when he began to die, and he has been variously estimated as taking between 45 and 60 years to do it. Current opinion, making no allowance for interruptions in his career, tends to assume that he completed his seven years of arts courses and two years as regent master by 1361, and began his theology course two years later. On the normal pattern he might then have been about 26. [2] Since the unregenerate Wyclif seems to have held some theological views, his 'conversion' would appear to have begun after this date: we might therefore propose a period in the mid-1360s, although it should be borne in mind that he had been an ordained priest since at least 1361, [3] and may very well be attributing his erroneous theological opinions to this time.

[1] E.g. *De dominio divino*, I, *prologue*, 1; *De mandatis divinis*, 22, 304; cf. Augustine, *De civitate Dei*, IV, 5; V, 17.

[2] Robson, *op. cit.*, 13-14; cf. J. A. Weisheipl, 'Curriculum of the Faculty of Arts at Oxford in the Early Fourteenth Century', *Mediaeval Studies*, XXVI (1964), 143-85. Also V. Murdoch, *The Wyclyf Tradition* (Toronto Ph. D. Thesis, 1960), 118. These would suggest a date of birth between 1335 and 1338. Robson's evidence would seem to dispose of Workman's suggestion, I, 94, that there was a more prolonged gap between Wyclif's arts and theology courses, but does not cover Workman's other point, I, 82-3, that the plague in Oxford during 1349-53 may have created a delay of up to five years in his career. Accordingly Workman's own preference, I, 21-2, 52, for a date of birth c. 1330 is still feasible, and has most recently been followed by J. H. Dahmus, *William Courtenay, Archbishop of Canterbury, 1381-1396*, 1966, 293 n. 25. Nineteenth-century opinion (e.g. Lewis, Shirley, Lechler) had assumed that he was born as early as 1324. There are obvious advantages in thinking that Wyclif was older rather than younger, not only to explain his otherwise rather early death and to allow a greater space of time into which to fit his enormous literary output, but also to suggest the comparative maturity of his pro-papal period. There is however one slight indication that current estimates are correct. In the *De benedicta incarnatione*, 6, 94, he refers to Christ's sufferings 'in media aetate', i.e. aged 33, which is interesting in view of the fact that on these estimates Wyclif himself would be approximately the same age at the time of writing (1371/2), although Wyclif's habit of comparing himself to the crucified Christ develops rather later in his career.

[3] Workman, *op. cit.*, I, 151: Wyclif must have been ordained by the time of his institution to Fillingham on 14 May, 1361, presumably by the archbishop of York, John Thoresby, since it was normal for priests to be ordain-

Unfortunately, whether we specify either the early or the middle years of the 1360s, it becomes impossible to avoid the very vexed problem of the books on logic. On present dating the first half of the 1360s was the period when Wyclif produced his first known work, the *Summa logicae*, [1] consisting perhaps of eight books, of which six or seven may be identifiable. [2] In this work he describes himself, appropriately, as being a *logicus*, one who has not yet become a theologian. [3] Now Wyclif tells us that his age of ignorant infancy occurred when he was a *logicus*, [4] occupied with dubious pursuits like the study of optics [5] and

---

ed by the bishop of the diocese in which they were born. There is no evidence that he obtained special permission to be ordained elsewhere, and official documents describe him as a priest of York.

[1] For the evidence that the works on logic originally formed a *Summa* see Robson, *op. cit.*, 128, 225-7. For dating see S. H. Thomson, 'The Order of Writing of Wyclif's Philosophical Works', *Českou Minulosti: Essays presented to V. Novotny*, Prague, 1929, 146-66 at 163-6; and revised chronology and order in 'Unnoticed MSS and Works of Wyclif', *JTS*, XXXVIII (1937), 24-36, 139-48 at 142.

[2] This suggestion hinges upon the *De actibus animae*, which is clearly part of some larger work (note the opening line: *'restat* tractare . . .'), and which contains references to other books numbered one to eight. Since books 6-8 are said to be awaiting composition, the *De actibus* must be book 5 in the series. According to Thomson, 'Unnoticed MSS', 142, there were four works written by Wyclif before the *De actibus*, namely, the *De logica* and the three tracts of its continuation. The *De actibus* also states (II, 2, 88; cf. I, 1, 28) that the final book will deal with the problem of insolubles, which is presumably the as yet unpublished *De insolubilibus*: on which see Thomson, *art. cit.*, 139-44. There is a possibility that one of the two other books is the *De physica* (also unpublished, but cf. Thomson, *art. cit.*, 144-8), described as a commentary on Aristotle's *Physics*, which are themselves used in the *De logica* (e.g. III, 7, ii, 162 and 174; III, 9, ii, 82-3). Since, according to Robson, *op. cit.*, 226, the *Summa* had a section on quantity and quality, this would seem to be appropriate.

[3] *De logica*, III, 9, iii, 20, 'humilis logicus': he repeatedly uses the phrase 'relinquo theologis', as if to say that he is not one of their number, e.g. III, 6, 7, 9 and 10, ii, 127, 174-5, and iii, 74, 204.

[4] *De statu innocentiae*, 7, 511, 'Quando fui logicus . . .'; *Responsiones ad argumenta cuiusdam aemuli veritatis*, 15, 305, 'Hic dixerunt sophistae quando fui iunior . . . et sic non repugnat Porphirio vel veritati logici . . .'; and note the description of a former opinion as 'logicalis et inanis', *Sermones*, I, 52, i, 347.

[5] *Sermones*, II, 53, ii, 384, 'Quando fui iunior et in delectatione vaga magis sollicitus, collegi diffuse proprietates lucis ex codicibus perspectivae

56   *Studies in Church History 5 (1969), 69–98*

other time-wasting philosophy. He had not yet progressed on to a proper study of theological subjects, [1] although he had already begun to expound the Bible, [2] perhaps as a priest. This clearly fits the period of the *Summa logicae*, which does in fact deal with optics to some extent, [3] and when Wyclif tantalisingly hints that he actually published his erroneous opinions, [4] we might expect the books on logic to fill the bill. Yet these works, as we have them, are quite evidently the work of the converted Wyclif, condemning the sophists, [5] employing the notion of double substances, [6] his rejection of annihilation already certain and applied to the eucharist, [7] and, moreover, a declaration that he is now pursuing the techniques of equivocation. I am, he writes, no longer one of the *pueri*. Indeed he now considered himself to be *senex*, an old man: [8] and whilst this may be no more than just another figurative statement that he had at last

et alias veritates mathematicas, . . .', with a series of references to the *Perspectivae* of Witello of Cracow.

[1] *De benedicta incarnatione*, 10, 165-6, 'Et in ista methaphisica vellem me studuisse quando sollicitabam me si quantitas, motus et caetera accidentia distinguantur. Subtilior enim est distinctio humanitatis a Verbo quam accidentis huiusmodi a subiecto'.

[2] *Sermones*, I, 54, i, 357, 'Quando autem fui iunior negavi quod quidquam sit debitum nisi debeatur simpliciter quoad Deum . . . et sic *exposui scripturam* et negavi de virtute sermonis verba doctorum in ista materia'.

[3] *De logica*, III, 5, 7 and 9, ii, 105, 176-81, and iii, 51, 61; *De actibus animae*, I, 3, 46; cf. I, 1, 12-18.

[4] See his statement that he 'publicavit' views which he now regrets, *Responsiones ad R. Strode*, 197. He usually remarks that he said ('dixi') these things, but *dicere* is commonly used in other instances to refer back to previous writings, and so does not necessarily imply that the statements were purely verbal ones.

[5] *De logica*, III, 1, 3 and 9, ii, 16, 21, 58-9, and iii, 45-6.

[6] *De logica*, III, 8, ii, 226; III, 9, *passim*.

[7] *De logica*, II, 4, i, 196; III, 9, iii, 32, 93, III, 10, iii, 134-8, 204.

[8] *De logica*, III, 10, iii, 145, 'Ideo expedit scire utramque scolam, sed puerilis scola imbrigabiliter onerosa. Scola autem etiam theologorum est levis, dissensiones sophisticas statim executiens correspondenter ad conditiones hominum quibus conveniunt istae scolae. Nunc autem sum nimis senex ad poenaliter incarcerandum me in scola prior[e]. Ideo, propter facilitatem indulgendum senibus, sequor secundam [scolam], intelligendo scripturam et aequivocando quando colloquentes locuntur ut parvuli'. As the editor points out, the text of this passage is very corrupt, and I have changed the order of words in the last sentence. He also calls himself 'senior', iii, 199.

attained to wisdom, it is possible that he was again thinking of Augustine, who had apparently regarded old age as beginning in one's forties. [1] Yet if Wyclif produced his *Summa logicae* in his forties,[2] and the usual dating is correct, the work would have to be located in the early 1380s. Since the date 1383 is in fact cited at one point,[3] and Wyclif speaks of having prepared the work for the benefit of his followers, [4] it seems probable that Workman was right to suggest (although no other scholar seems to have agreed with him) that the logical *Summa* was heavily revised at the end of Wyclif's life [5]—unwilling as anyone must be to add yet another burden to those fantastically productive

[1] There is an ambiguous remark in II, 12, i, 169, '[Deus] potest tamen facere quod ego non sum nec fui futurus quadragenarius in hoc instanti,' which might suggest either that he was on the point of being forty, or that he was in his forties. Augustine had said that a man entering upon old age might still have half his life before him. Old age in this sense can hardly begin later than fifty, and a decade earlier may well be intended. I am grateful to Dr R. A. Markus for this information.

[2] There is also the obscure debate about being forty years old in *De actibus animae*, II, 3, 106: discussing the point that what is false now may be true later and vice versa, so that true and false need not necessarily be in conflict, he cites as an example 'ut iam falsum est quod ego vixi 40 annis, et illud falsum non erit verum, quia illud falsum iam non est'. Whatever the significance of these remarks, they are curious coming from one who, on the present dating of these works, would have been in his twenties.

[3] *De logica*, III, 10, iii, 183, from the birth of Christ 'nunc sunt mille trecenti et 83 anni'. Both the editor, Dziewicki, *Introduction*, I, vii, and Thomson, 'Order of Writing', 163, dismiss this as a scribal error.

[4] *De logica*, I, *proemium*, i, 1, 'Motus sum per quosdam legis Dei amicos certum tractatum ad declarandum logicam sacrae scripturae compilare'; II, 10, i, 152, 'me et meos sequaces'. There are numerous references to *iuvenes* who will be reading the work: II, *proemium*, 2, 14 and 18, i, 75, 171, 195, 234; and according to Thomson, 'Unnoticed MSS', this is also a feature of the *De insolubilibus*. Such remarks become common in Wyclif's works from 1382: e.g. *Trialogus*, IV, 13, 290.

[5] Workman, *op. cit.*, I, 333. Note the scribe's statement in *De logica*, III, 10, iii, 227, that the work had been 'fideliter correctus'. This would meet Dziewicki's argument, 'An Essay', xiv, that the *De logica* was written after the *Summa de ente*. Since the latter, as Robson rightly suggests, *op. cit.*, 130-5, incorporates Wyclif's commentary on the *Sentences*, this would seem to be an unlikely procedure-although not impossible: Ockham seems to have produced a logical *Summa* for the benefit of his pupils after his commentary on the *Sentences*: see C. K. Brampton, 'The Probable Order of Ockham's Non-Polemical Works', *Traditio*, XIX (1963), 469-83 at 481-2.

final years. There is, incidentally, good evidence that he was revising his early sermons for a collected edition at this date. [1] But if this revision of the books on logic really took place, why should Wyclif in 1383, condemned for heresy and daily becoming more venomously anti-papal, have thought it necessary to hide traces of early Ockhamist leanings? By that time there would hardly seem to be much point. If on the other hand it was realism, Augustinianism, papalism, which needed to be covered up and revised out of recognition, this is readily understandable. His disciples could not be allowed to come into possession of works by their master which would lend support to the very system which he was now so forcibly denouncing.

Leaving speculation aside, we may more profitably conclude by considering the wider significance of Wyclif's early Oxford career. Our understanding of the errors from which Wyclif was apparently converted in the years around 1365 must affect our whole interpretation of his thought. For, if we are right in thinking that the young Wyclif was an Augustinian realist and hierocrat, content to accept the principle of papal supremacy, then the one thing which the elder Wyclif—the Wyclif we know and whose writings we can read—cannot be, is an extreme realist of the Augustinian school. This was precisely the 'infidelity' which he had now renounced. Yet virtually every writer about Wyclif during the present century has taken it for granted that Wyclif's philosophy as it survives in the *Summa de ente* and elsewhere is that of an extreme realist. It would be tedious to

---

[1] *Sermones, Praefatio*, i, v, 'Et ideo, ut sententia Dei sit planior et servus suus inutilis excusabilior, videtur quod *in illo otio quo a scholasticis otiamur* et in particulari aedificationi Ecclesiae *in fine dierum nostrorum* sollicitamur, sint sermones rudes ad populum *colligendi*'. Workman, *op. cit.*, II, 208, was surely right to say that this statement must have been made after Wyclif had left Oxford, although W. Mallard, 'Dating the *Sermones Quadraginta* of John Wyclif', *Medievalia et Humanistica*, XVII (1966), 86-105, has now argued that the editing was done at Oxford before the summer of 1381. Since *Sermones*, IV, includes sermons written at least as late as mid-1383, this collection and revision of his sermons should be dated to 1384. There is also the point that the English translator of the sermons, who was certainly at work during 1383, did not use *Sermones*, IV, but only worked from I-III, composed in 1381-2, and therefore all that was available to him in 1383.

list authorities on this point, although it would be fair to add that a few scholars of exceptional acumen in this field—we may perhaps mention Knowles and Kalivoda [1]—have already expressed reservations and suggested that a more heterodox and eclectic position should be discerned in some respects. Now it seems that we shall need to reconsider the entire subject of Wyclif's philosophy—and one shudders to think of the repercussions this may have on the study of Hus and 'Prague realism'. But it may be confidently predicted that Wyclif, far from being an extreme Augustinian realist, will emerge as another example of that curious hybrid species, the Christian Aristotelian, utilising the Thomistic principle of the mean to achieve a *via media*, employing the Aristotelian technique of equivocation to harmonise traditional Christian teachings with the secular humanism of the classical past. As Wyclif indicates himself, he began writing the great *Summa theologiae* with the Bible open at one hand and Averroes' commentary on Aristotle at the other: [2] what he himself wrote was bound to be placed, both physically and metaphorically, in between the two extremes, a judicious combination of both sides. Theology would perfect what the pagan philosophy had taught by reason: [3] conversely, as he

[1] D. Knowles, 'The Censured Opinions of Uthred of Boldon', *Proceedings of the British Academy*, XXXVII (1951), 305-42=*The Historian and Character and Other Essays*, 1963, 129-70 at 152; R. Kalivoda, 'Joannes Wyclifs Metaphysik des extremen Realismus und ihre Bedeutung im Endstadium der mittelalterlichen Philosophie', *Miscellanea Medievalia*, II, *Die Metaphysik im Mittelalter*, ed. P. Wilpert, Berlin, 1963, 716-23. At one point Workman, *op. cit.*, I, 104-5, had suggested some Thomistic influence, but generally regarded him as a realist, and was therefore misled by Wyclif into characterising both papalism and Ockhamism as nominalism, I, 113-14, 136, 140-2.

[2] See the use of Paul, *Romans*, and Averroes' commentary on the *Ethics* of Aristotle at the beginning of the *De dominio divino*.

[3] E.g. *De mandatis divinis*, 3, 21, 'Et hinc ordinavit Deus rationabiliter quod voluntas sua non foret abscondita ut voluntates hominum, sed plurimum patula cuiuscunque ... Sed quia generalis notitia philosophorum non sufficit, ideo condidit duo testamenta in quibus expressit multas suas abditas voluntates. Et hinc quodam instinctu naturali omnes ritus hominum passim sibi vendicant notitiam scripturae ... quia nemo potest iuste iudicare, operari vel vivere vel quamcunque scientiam aliam *perfecte* cognoscere sine illa'; cf. 7, 60-1, 'Totus quidem mundus sensibilis est liber quidam

pointed out, it would be necessary to read Aristotle for an explanation of what the Bible really meant. [1] If grace perfects nature, then it is only just to allow nature to perfect grace. [2] That, for Wyclif, was the divine reciprocity; and since the same principle of reciprocity [3] ran through all his political writings, we may reasonably expect to find the same ambiguous attitude dominating his consideration of the papacy and other governmental institutions. At least we shall no longer have to grapple with the problem, made much of recently by Gewirth and Leff, [4] that Wyclif is a glaring exception to the rule that the papal system was the political counterpart of Augustinian realism, and that antipapalism must reflect a degree of Averro-Aristotelian nominalism. Wyclif was an Augustinian ultra-realist—before 1365;

quem naturales in quibusdam suis partibus cognoscentes, quasi elementa alphabeti considerant', but one must also go 'ultra hunc librum sensibilem legere intelligibiliter librum vitae, cognoscendo omnem creaturam secundum suum esse intelligibile in aeternis rationibus libri vitae'. See also *De civili dominio*, III, 10, 148-51; *De veritate sacrae scripturae*, 4, i, 72-3, 'In talibus itaque figuris locutionis scripturae latet omne genus philosophiae naturalis, quae ex intellectu scripturae suscepit *ultimum complementum*. Nam philosophia naturalis usque adeo deficit ab ultimo complemento, quousque gravidata fuerit moralitate vel alio sensu mistico scripturae. Et sic tam logica quam omnis alia philosophia recipit in scriptura sacra *perfectionem ultimam* in Deum propinquius dirigentem'.

[1] E.g. *De civili dominio*, II, 1, 5-6, 'ut innuit tam textus *Genesis* quam exponentes textum Aristotelis'; and see the use of Aristotle's *Ethics* to explain the meaning of *Galatians*: II, 2, 8-9; III, 1, 2. It is significant that the *De veritate*, a work on scripture, should begin with an evaluation of Aristotelian philosophy. The recent assessment of E. Delaruelle, 'Réforme et hérésie Wyclif', *L'Église au temps du Grand Schisme et de la crise conciliaire*, Paris, 1964, 943-88 at 955, that Wyclif's outlook was so essentially Christian and theological that Aristotle was of little significance to him seems unfortunate.

[2] *De statu innocentiae*, 3, 493, 'Nec obest probabili ratione convincere multa quae fuissent in statu innocentiae, licent in scriptura non fuerint expressata'; cf. 1, 475, 'pro cuius indagine utendum est testimonio scripturae, dictis sanctorum, et probabili ratione'; hence the Bible, Augustine, and Aristotle are to be used together, e.g. 2, 485; 5, 500.

[3] Cf. Aristotle, *Nicomachean Ethics*, V, 5, 1132b-3a; *Politics*, II, 2, 1261a.

[4] A. Gewirth, 'Philosophy and Political Thought in the Fourteenth Century', *The Forward Movement of the Fourteenth Century*, ed. F. L. Utley, Columbus, Ohio, 1961, 125-64 at 133-53, esp. 140-1, 151; G. Leff, 'The Apostolic Ideal in Later Medieval Ecclesiology', *JTS*, *n.s.*, XVIII (1967), 58-82.

and he was a virulently antipapal writer—after 1375. But we should never again make the mistake of confusing these two distinct episodes in his intellectual career.

Nor can that career itself ever look quite the same again. The long debate about when Wyclif began to expound his eucharistic heresy assumes a degree of artificiality. It now seems clear that Wyclif realised from the beginning that his denial of divine omnipotence and conversion to a dual substance theory must have a profound effect upon his interpretation of the eucharist and the question of the remanence of bread and wine after transsubstantiation. It had been clear for nearly a century that the adoption of Thomistic and Aristotelian principles must logically lead to difficulties in the interpretation of the eucharist. [1] But, as in the case of his opposition to the friars, where he openly admitted that political prudence (an Aristotelian concept which he highly prized) caused him for many years to omit the mendicant orders from his condemnation of the *possessionati*, so Wyclif was ready to dissemble about the relationship of his philosophy to the sacraments as long as possible. [2] This may do much to explain the peculiarity of a theologian who could spend the better part of a decade writing a voluminous *summa* of theology and yet hardly mention

[1] Cf. F. J. Roensch, *Early Thomistic School*, Dubuque, Iowa, 1964, 178-81, 205; cf. 99-103, 276-87.

[2] E.g. *De materia et forma*, 4, 189, 'Illud tamen secundum naturam potest converti in quodcunque, manens idem secundum materiam, ut post dicetur. De conversione autem panis in corpus Christi, quam Ecclesia vocat transsubstantiationem, est longus sermo et mihi adhuc inscrutabilis'; also *Purgans errores circa universalia in communi*, 5, 43; *De potentia productiva Dei ad extra*, 12, 289. The suggestion that Wyclif's eucharistic heresy is a direct outcome of his philosophical opinions during the 1360s had been made by F. D. Matthew, *English Works of Wyclif*, 1880, xxii-xxiv, but the change is usually dated to the 1370s, and his views are sometimes said to have passed through several stages, e.g. Dziewicki, 'An Essay', xxii-xxiv; Thomson, 'Order of Writing', 163, on the basis of Woodford's testimony: see *Fasciculi zizaniorum*, xv n.4. It would be more accurate to consider the three stages suggested as orthodox, dissembling, and overtly heretical phases. As numerous references in the *De apostasia* indicate, there was a close connection in Wyclif's mind between the friars and transubstantiation in that he saw both deriving from the blasphemous pope Innocent III: cf. *De eucharistia*, 9, 278.

that central feature of all Christian theology, the true body of Christ. Nor need we waste a great deal of time speculating whether it was lack of preferment or entry into the royal service which served to spark off Wyclif's antipapalism. The ground for this had already been prepared when he came to terms with Aristotle. Fundamentally his opposition to the papacy was an intellectual affair, and had been predetermined by a philosophical conversion. Small wonder that he later wrote with the enthusiasm of a convert, the savage fury of a renegade. It may well be this conversion from papalism which explains his lack of promotion, not the other way round. [1] He had after all committed the unforgivable offence of presuming that he was right against the whole establishment of ecclesiastical authority and university doctors. He stressed that when he was a young man he had been a great sinner, and yet other people had agreed with him —'Quando autem fui iunior . . . locutus sum cum aliis' [2]—which was really his way of saying what great sinners so many people were for disagreeing with him now. It is sometimes difficult to avoid a pang of fellow-feeling.

[1] As early as 1366 or thereabouts he complained in the *Purgans errores circa universalia in communi*, 1, 31, about the papalists only giving promotion to bishoprics and other offices to those who were 'de affinitate sua', although the first reference to lack of his own preferment comes about three or four years later in the *De volutione Dei*, 1, 125-6. Having consoled himself for not being a bishop ('Fatui igitur est cum deliberatione absolute tristari de hoc quod homo non est episcopus, vel bonis naturalibus aut fortuitis plus dotatus'), he remarks that the long delay is causing both his patience and his *obedience* to wear thin: 'Et indubie talis diutina mora, ymaginando talia, retraxit de mea patientia et humili subditione divinae ordinantiae, omittendo alia quibus debui interne deservire, . . .'. The reference to not getting his domestic deserts may relate to the Canterbury Hall affair, which Wyclif later said that he lost because the post usually went to the *pueri*: *De officio regis*, 4, 75. Caistor, too, went to a *iuvenis*, *De civili dominio*, III, 17, 334. It sounds as if Wyclif was blacklisted by the hierocratic party from an early date for no longer being 'one of the boys'.
[2] *Sermones*, I, 54, i, 357; cf. *De actibus animae*, II, 1, 73, where he says that he will now use Aristotle ('secundum logicam Aristotelis . . . et illud sequar ego in futurum') aginst the 'sophistae et maior pars hominum'.

4
REFORMATIO REGNI:
WYCLIF AND HUS AS LEADERS OF
RELIGIOUS PROTEST MOVEMENTS

by MICHAEL WILKS

IN May 1382 William Courtenay, archbishop of Canterbury since the murder of his predecessor Sudbury during the Peasants' Revolt the previous year, declared it to be a matter of frequent complaint and common report that evil persons were going about his province preaching without authority, and spreading doctrines which threatened to destroy not only ecclesiastical authority but civil government as well. They were the adherents, he was informed, of a certain teacher of novelties at Oxford, named John Wyclif, whose sect broadcast the seeds of pestiferous error so widely in the pastures of Canterbury that only the most savage hoeing would root them out.[1] The chroniclers hastened to confirm this account. According to their accounts, by 1382 Wyclif had been able, through his writings and the preaching of his followers, to seduce the laity, including great lords and members of the nobility, over a great part of the realm. Even members of the clergy and scholars were not free from infection. Thus Knighton commented that – at least in the area around Leicester – every other person one met was a Lollard.[2] Thirty years later it is the same story in Bohemia. As the carthusian prior Stephen of Dolany complained, despite the condemnation of Wyclif's teachings at the university of Prague in 1403, the Wycliffites swarmed everywhere: 'in the state apartments of princes, in the schools of the students, in the lonely chambers of the monks, and even in the cells of the Carthusians'.[3]

---

[1] *Fasciculi Zizaniorum*, ed W. W. Shirley, *RS* 5 (London 1858) p 275; [D.] Wilkins, *Concilia* (London 1737) III pp 158 and 172.

[2] [Henry] Knighton, *Chronicon*, ed J. R. Lumby, *RS* 92, 2 vols (London 1889–95) II p·191; compare pp 176, 183, 185; *Eulogium Historiarum*, first continuation, ed F. S. Haydon, *RS* 9, 3 vols (London 1858–63) III pp 351, 354–5; compare [Thomas of] Walsingham, *Historia Anglicana*, ed H. T. Riley, *RS* 28, 2 vols (London 1863–4) I p 325; II pp 50, 53; *Chronicon Angliae*, ed E. M. Thompson, *RS* 64 (London 1874) p 396. Although outdated in some respects, the best survey of this material is still H. L. Cannon, 'The Poor Priests: A Study in the Rise of English Lollardy', *Annual Report of the American Historical Association for 1899* (Washington 1900) I pp 451–82.

[3] Cited H. B. Workman and R. M. Pope, *The Letters of John Hus* (London 1904) p 11.

Yet I do not need to remind this audience that Courtenay's action in
and after 1382 destroyed Wyclifism as a movement for the next
generation. Whilst making allowance for the events culminating in
the Oldcastle Rising of 1414, it is still true to say that Lollardy was in
effect driven underground in England for the rest of the medieval
period. In Bohemia, under the inspiration of Wyclif's teachings, the
Hussite reform movement succeeded in creating a national church-
state which was to triumph over all the forces of christian universalism
– pope, emperor and general council – so that it may fairly be said that
the Reformation began in Bohemia a century before the rest of Europe.[1]
Why? What was the essential difference which made Wyclifism an
abject failure in England and an astonishing success story in Bohemia?

It is now nearly half a century since Workman published the
magisterial two volumes which remain the authoritative account of
Wyclif's life.[2] An enormous amount of more recent scholarship,
particularly in the past two decades, has produced a bewildering variety
of different interpretations (and permutation of other people's interpretations) on individual points. But it now seems to be generally
accepted that the reasons for Wyclif's failure must be sought in a
radical phase of his career, beginning about 1379 and continuing with
increasing intensity until his death at the end of 1384.[3] It is agreed that
the years immediately following 1379 were a time when Wyclif
committed two acts of indescribable folly and suffered one piece of
appalling bad luck. He resolved his earlier doubts about the remanence
of bread and wine in the eucharist, and was so elated by his newfound
certainty that he flung discretion to the winds and published the *De
eucharistia*. The work followed the usual pattern of being made up of a
series of very repetitive lectures already given in the schools at Oxford,
and this had been enough to cause many former friends and supporters, who had warmly applauded his demands for reform of the
clergy, to refuse to follow him into outright heresy on the matter of
the sacraments. Since many of these former supporters were friars,

---

[1] F. Zilka, 'The Czech Reformation and its Relation to the World Reformation',
Slavonic and East European Review, VIII (London 1929–30) pp 284–91; compare F.
Kafka, 'The Hussite Movement and the Czech Reformation', *Journal of World History*
(= *Cahiers d'histoire mondiale*), V (Paris 1960) pp 830–56.

[2] [H. B.] Workman,[*John Wyclif: A Study of the English Medieval Church*,] 2 vols (Oxford
1926).

[3] For example J. H. Dahmus, *The Prosecution of John Wyclif* (New Haven 1952) p 81;
[K. B.] McFarlane, [*John Wycliffe and the Beginnings of English Nonconformity*] (London
1952) pp 96–7; compare M. Hurley, '*Scriptura Sola*: Wyclif and his Critics', *Traditio*,
XVI (New York 1960) pp 275–352.

Wyclif was led to retaliate against this apostasy by launching into one of the most vigorous denunciations of the mendicant orders made by a secular master during the fourteenth century.

Wyclif's position was now extremely precarious. Condemned by the Barton committee at Oxford for heresy, suspended from teaching duties, and excommunicated, Wyclif published a defiant manifesto against his enemies in May 1381, and appealed to the government for protection. But the outbreak of the Peasants' Revolt at the end of the month made it impossible for the government to intervene on behalf of anybody accused of stirring up sedition, and it was not long before Wyclif and his remaining followers were being openly accused of having fomented the Revolt itself by their teachings. Forced out of Oxford, Wyclif retired to his parish of Lutterworth in time to escape the further condemnation of his teachings at the Blackfriars council of 1382 and Courtenay's subsequent purge of the university. His remaining years in retirement were a sad epilogue in which, ill and perhaps partly paralysed, he occupied himself with writing even more vitriolic attacks against his opponents, and with the production of enormous numbers of pamphlets, tracts and sermons for use by a steadily dwindling number of lollard preachers.

The implication of all this is that it was Wyclif's heresy, particularly in the matter of the eucharist, which is the key to his failure. Much has been made of the point that it was precisely on the question of denying transubstantiation that Hus refused to follow Wyclif, as if to suggest that Hus deserved to succeed, where Wyclif failed, for having been more orthodox than his master. Although Hus, most unfairly, paid the supreme penalty which Wyclif for not very obvious reasons somehow escaped, the Hussite movement is made to appear as a movement of religious dissent to be contrasted with the deliberate heresy of Lollardy. But this line of argument, it seems to me, is unfruitful. Heresy was a by-product of the Wycliffite system, a symptom rather than a cause; ultimately it was irrelevant in determining the success or failure of the movement either in England or Bohemia – and it does not therefore really matter from this point of view whether Hus *was* more orthodox than Wyclif. Wyclifism was above all a political movement, whose significance both in England and in Bohemia would be determined by political factors, by the policies pursued by political leaders, and by the interaction of political circumstances.

In the first place, the English bishops did not need an open declara-

tion by Wyclif that his theories would involve a drastic reinterpreta-
tion of eucharistic doctrine, nor his enmity with the friars, nor his
alleged complicity in the Peasants' Revolt, in order to secure his
condemnation. Although the two hearings held at St Paul's by
Wyclif's ecclesiastical superiors – one in February 1377, and the other
in January 1378 – had proved abortive, partly due to government
intervention and partly to the violence of the London mob, nevertheless
the fact remained that the reception of Gregory XI's bulls of May
1377 meant that Wyclif's teaching on lordship, dominion and grace,
and on the validity of papal and episcopal jurisdiction, had been
pronounced a matter of error by the supreme authority in the Church.[1]
Henceforth it was papal policy that the influence of his theories was
to be stamped out, and Wyclif himself was ordered to be put in prison
in chains or cited to the papal court itself. The legal process was in
fact extremely slow, and technically was never completed. But this
does not alter the point that from 1377 onwards the bishops had
unassailable legal justification for acting against Wyclif and his
followers whenever they deemed it expedient to do so. That the
bishops did not deem it expedient to act in haste, but allowed Wyclif
enough rope to hang himself several times over by the further elaboration of his principles over a period of four and a half years, should not
be allowed to conceal the fact that it was the political character of
Wycliffite theology which was so obnoxious, and was indeed the root
cause of all the trouble.

There is one other preliminary consideration. It would give a false
impression to suggest, as some recent commentators have done, that
Wyclif suddenly lurched into heresy on the sacraments on the rebound
from these early attempts to secure his condemnation. That he now
took a positive delight in emphasising the more radical aspects of his
system of thought, and that his language became increasingly vigorous
and vindictive, is not in doubt. But it was essentially a matter of emphasis, of tilting the balance, of elaborating and applying the principles
which he had already laid down in his philosophical works some ten
or twenty years before. Wyclif said nothing after 1378 that reasonably
astute opponents like William Woodford, William Binham, Uthred
of Boldon or John Cunningham, and particularly Adam Easton, were
not perfectly capable of deducing for themselves during the early 1370s.

The guiding principle of Wyclif's philosophy was the theme of
double substances and the need to combine them in christian teaching,

[1] Walsingham, *Historia Anglicana*, 1 pp 353ff.

whilst recognising that each substance retained a fundamental independence, integrity and identity, and that there could be a conversion from one to another without denying the reality – without annihilating – the former. God and man; the whole and the part; universal and accident; the divine and the natural; sacred scripture and human tradition; faith and reason; Augustine and Aristotle; papal power and civil government; headship and community; *societas Christiana* and pagan *polis*; *corpus Christi* and eucharistic bread – the proper relationship of all these things was susceptible in Wyclif's eyes to the techniques which he had evolved in dealing with the philosophical problem of insolubles. In a sense they were all aspects of the same central issue of how the apparently opposed and contradictory characteristics of divine and natural substances could be brought together in harmony and the contradictions 'solved' by equivocation. To take a simple example. In *c* 1370 Wyclif wrote a short work on the nature of man, *De compositione hominis*, the purpose of which was on the surface to make the quite unremarkable point that man was a combination of matter and form, natural and divine elements, in other words body and soul. Either part could exist in isolation (*per se intrinseco*),[1] just as man before baptism was pre-eminently body, and after death was pre-eminently soul, but for most of his life was a combination of two distinct parts neither of which ever totally surrendered its individual identity. Each part, he wrote, has its own life and its own substance: 'quia partes...habent vitam propriam et propriam quiditatem'.[2] There is a double nature, one divine and the other natural, both of which for practical purposes act together as one.[3]

The immediate application of the principle was in christology, since Christ, Wyclif argued, was the supreme expression of dual substances as God and man. By the incarnation God had demonstrated that man should play an equal part with God in earthly affairs – and he assiduously attached the phrase *Deus et homo* to every mention of Christ's

---

[1] *De compositione hominis*, 4, ed R. Beer, W[yclif] S[ociety] (London 1884) p 73.

[2] *De compositione hominis*, 4 p 58.

[3] *De compositione hominis*, I p 11; compare 2, p 35, 'homo est duae substantiae vel naturae'. Wyclif does of course emphasise that these are essentially theoretical distinctions, and that in practice the two natures should be taken together – each in isolation would be incomplete – so that it is possible to describe both together as a complete third nature: 'ut quilibet homo est natura spiritualis cui accidit esse animam; est iterum natura vel essentia corporea cui accidit esse corpus humanum; et haec duo incommunicabiliter sunt distincta; et est tertio natura ex corpore et anima integrata quae distingwatur ab utraque...Nec est negandum quin omnis persona hominis sit tres naturae, duae incompletae et tertia integra'. His immediate application of this is to the two ends of human life, p 13.

name to remind his readers of the principle. But he was already aware
that this could be directly transposed into political terms, 'nam homo
est pars populi'.[1] Like the Greek thinkers, he saw society as the
individual writ large, and realised that the same scheme of double
quiddities must apply to the Church, at once a heavenly *corpus mysticum*
and a conglomeration of natural human communities, a universal
society (a society having the nature of a universal) and a collection of
national semi-sovereign states. And when he came to write his eucharistic theory he was at pains to point out that he was saying nothing new,
but was simply adopting the same principle of double substances.
'Sacramentum altaris', he wrote in 1382, 'est verus corpus Christi et
verus panis *sicut Christus est verus Deus et verus homo.'*[2] There was here
a conversion, a switch of attention, from the corporeal *substantia panis*
to the spiritual *substantia Christi* – but like the Church itself, the eucharist was and remained on earth a combination of the two quiddities,
divine and natural, after the manner of man himself: 'Hoc dicit
pro pane et vino, et sic *duplicis substantiae* totum fibaret hominem,
scilicet hominem exteriorem et hominem interiorem, corpus et anima.'[3]

One may remark in parenthesis that if Hus was as good a *Wiclefista* as
he claimed to be, then the question of whether he actually followed
Wyclif into eucharistic heresy, as the Council of Constance accused
him of doing, becomes a relatively minor issue. Once Hus had adopted
Wyclif's philosophical principles, once he had accepted his definition

---

[1] *De compositione hominis*, 5 p 92. The work was specifically written to serve as an introduction to his discussion of lordship and obedience: 1 pp 1–2, 'Tria movent ad tractare
materiam de compositione hominis...Tertio quia antecedit ad tractatum humani
dominii, cum relatio non potest cognosci nisi per notitiam sui principii subiectivi.
Nec sciri potest quomodo homo naturaliter dominetur atque servat sibiipsi...nisi
praecognoscatur quomodo homo est duarum naturarum utraque, secundum quas
relatio servitutis et dominii in eodem supposito congregantur'.

[2] S. H. Thomson, 'John Wyclif's "Lost" *De fide sacramentorum'*, *JTS*, XXXIII (1932)
pp 359–65 at p 363; compare p 364, 'sic constat in sacramento altaris. Ibi est forma vel
substantia Christi humanitatis spiritualiter, et forma vel substantia panis corporaliter'.
For the correlation between eucharist, *Ecclesia* and the nature of Christ, see, for example, *De Ecclesia*, 1, ed J. Loserth, WS (London 1886) p 8; *De eucharistia*, 9, ed J.
Loserth, WS (London 1892) p 325.

[3] *De fide sacramentorum*, p 365; *De eucharistia*, 4 p 100, 'Et sic conversio illa non destruit
naturam panis, nec mutat naturam corporis inducendo in materiam aliam quidditatem,
sed facit praesentiam corporis Christi et tollit principalitatem panis'; cf. 3 p 82, 'potest
ergo dici quod panis et vinum convertuntur principaliter in corpus Christi et sanguinem
...nec panis aut vinum deterioratur sed melioratur...manet namque utraque natura'.
Both substances co-exist, but they are looked at in different ways, and by consecration
attention is switched from one to the other, in the same way that the stars are still
present but are ignored and not seen when the sun comes out: 5 pp 130, 137; 7
p 231.

of the *Ecclesia* – which he undoubtedly did[1] – then only by the grossest inconsistency could Hus have refused to accept a double-substance theory of the eucharist, the idea that after consecration you could eat your bread and still have it. The truth of the matter is that Hus saw the point and simply stopped short without committing himself. But in this he was merely following in his predecessor's footsteps. Wyclif himself had already worked out his eucharistic theory ten years before he wrote the *De eucharistia*, and simply refused to write it up because he was well aware that it would have disastrous effects on his friendship with many of the friars.[2] Later, when he had parted company with the mendicants, he bitterly reproached himself for this act of intellectual cowardice – and was all the more vicious towards the friars in consequence for failing to reciprocate. But during the 1370s Wyclif dissembled on the eucharist, pretending to agree with Woodford that he was always changing his mind and really did not know what he did think.

All this meant that when Wyclif began to write his great *Summa theologiae* in 1373, which was carefully planned and eventually reached to fourteen volumes, he decided to leave the theology out for as long as possible, and concentrate on its legal and political implications. Following Aquinas's four-fold classification of law, he produced *De dominio divino* on the eternal law by which God regulated himself; *De mandatis divinis*, the divine law for men; and correspondingly the *De statu innocentiae* outlining man's basic rights under natural law: and then proceeded to show how the divine and the natural came together in human law, in three volumes of the *De dominio civili*. The way in

[1] Compare M. Spinka, *John Hus' Concept of the Church* (Princeton 1966) pp 253–6, and G. Leff, *Heresy in the Later Middle Ages* (Manchester 1967) pp 638–9; 'Wyclif and Hus: A Doctrinal Comparison', *BJRL*, L (1967–8) pp 387–410 at 403ff, both of whom broadly accept the view of de Vooght that Loserth had been wrong to regard Hus as a slavish imitator of Wyclif and that Hus refused to follow him into error: for example P. de Vooght, 'Jean Hus et ses juges', *Das Konzil von Konstanz: Beiträge zu seiner Geschichte und Theologie*, ed A. Franzen and W. Müller (Freiburg, Basle, Vienna 1964) pp 152–73; and see also S. H. Thomson in the introduction to his edition of *Hus, Tractatus de Ecclesia* (Boulder, Col., and Cambridge 1956) pp viii–x, xxxiii. The continuing debate is well summarised by H. Kaminsky, *A History of the Hussite Revolution* (Berkeley and Los Angeles 1967) pp 35–7, who rightly follows R. Kalivoda, *Husitská ideologie* (Prague 1961) pp 151–91, in accepting the basic identity of doctrine between Wyclif and Hus. See now also F. Smahel, '*Doctor evangelicus super omnes evangelistas*: Wyclif's Fortune in Hussite Bohemia', *BIHR*, XLIII (1970) pp 16–34 at pp 26–8.

[2] G. A. Benrath, *Wyclifs Bibelkommentar* (Berlin 1966) pp 266–71, indicates that Wyclif had already accepted the principle of remanence in his *Postilla super totam Bibliam* and was dubious then about the accepted theory of transubstantiation. In the *De eucharistia*, 2 p 52, Wyclif says himself that his theory is a logical extension of his philosophical work on the question of annihilation.

which man and God acted together to interpret divine law was further treated in a separate volume, the *De veritate sacrae scripturae*, completed in 1378 but conceived six years earlier.[1] But if Wyclif's treatment of scripture was ostensibly Augustinian (the *De veritate* is supposedly modelled on Augustine's *De doctrina christiana*) his treatment of papal and royal government was distinctly Aristotelian. The *De officio regis* was written for the new king Richard II, and the *De potestate papae* to complement it, written for the new pope Urban VI. Wyclif not only professed to tell them how to govern, but in the *De Ecclesia* combined Augustine and Aristotle, again within a Thomistic framework, to emphasise the dual nature of the christian society over which popes and kings should act together in harmony. This completed the overtly political sections of the work, and by 1379 Wyclif had no option but to pass from the *corpus mysticum* to the *corpus verum* and expound much the same principles in terms of the eucharist. Finally the *Summa* was rounded off with a trilogy, three short and hurriedly written books on the subject of heresy, books which tend, understandably, to be much more autobiographical than the others.

Although, therefore, there was the closest of links between Wyclif's politics and his theology, this order of writing meant that Wyclif – convinced of the need for a great renewal of christian life and an extensive re-structuring of the christian society – was obliged to produce a design for an essentially political reformation with no more than a suggestion that doctrinal reform would follow once the new political order had been achieved. Unlike the movement led by Hus, in which the question of the eucharist was present from the beginning, and became for many of Hus's colleagues a symbol of the political movement itself, Wyclif's demand for a general *reformatio Ecclesiae* was a predominantly political one in the first instance, and may bear comparison with the *reformatio orbis* demanded by the Staufen emperors in previous centuries, and the course which the Reformation took in England during the sixteenth century.

Wyclif appears to have derived the actual term *reformatio* from Grosseteste,[2] who had used it in the sense of a correction of sinners

---

[1] Even the *De logica*, ed M. H. Dziewicki, WS (London 1893–9), appears to have envisaged the application of his philosophical principles to Biblical studies: 1 proem. (1 p 1), 'Motus sum per quosdam legis Dei amicos certum tractatum ad declarandum logicam sacrae scripturae compilare'; compare W. Mallard, 'John Wyclif and the Tradition of Biblical Authority', *Church History*, xxx (Chicago 1961) pp 50–60 at p 56.

[2] *Epistola* 127, ed H. R. Luard, *RS* 25 (London 1861) p 360, but cited by Wyclif in its version as a separate work *De cura pastorali*.

(meaning, of course, the correction of sinners by their bishops and clergy). But he linked this up with his own conception of a universal deformation – a *deformitas Ecclesiae*[1] – a world which had, he said, suddenly seemed to go mad under the impact of increasing papal and episcopal tyranny. 'I say "suddenly seemed" to be deformed,' he commented, 'since it has only just been realised, now that I have pointed it out.'[2] But in fact it was a process which had been going on for a long time, and had passed the point of tolerability in 1200 under the papacy of Innocent III. The beginning of the thirteenth century was in his eyes a climacteric moment in human affairs, initiating a period of permanent crisis. Wyclif saw the history of the Church, in Joachimist fashion, as having passed through three ages, each one worse than the one before, and each with its appropriate allocation of ecclesiastical jurisdiction between lay rulers and papacy. In the first age of true apostolicity, the age of innocence which the *Ecclesia primitiva* had enjoyed down to the fourth century, all governmental power and jurisdiction had been in the hands of lay priest-kings, and the clergy had contented itself with its duties of preaching true doctrine and administering the sacraments. But with the Donation of Constantine – the *donatio*, or rather *dotatio*, *Constantini* by which Constantine had embraced Christianity and married the papacy, granting it an endowment or marriage settlement of secular power – there had begun a second age of partnership between pope and lay ruler, a *dualitas*, in which ecclesiastical jurisdiction was shared between them, as depicted in the good old law of Gratian's *Decretum*. It was always therefore a matter of some importance for Wyclif to distinguish the true popes who came before 1200 from the tyrannical popes who came afterwards. On one occasion he goes to considerable lengths to demonstrate by quoting chronicles that Nicholas II was an earlier pope than Innocent III, and was therefore all the better for this priority.[3] But with Innocent there began the third, last and worst age, the age of Antichrist (the age, he added later, of the mendicant orders whom Innocent had instituted as pseudo-apostles) in which the popes had endeavoured to take all power into their own hands, to claim a plenitude of power, and make themselves into the real king in every kingdom. This was a characteristic, he commented, which had become markedly worse since the popes moved to Avignon. There was now an age of confusion, in which both jurisdictions, temporal and spiritual, had been fused

[1] For example *De Ecclesia*, 11 p 292.
[2] *De Ecclesia*, 12 p 265.   [3] *De eucharistia*, 5 pp 140–1.

together in the claims of the papal monarchs, aided and abetted by a satellite clergy in every realm.

Wyclif therefore conceived his reformation as a revolution in the traditional sense, which one still finds used in English thought by Locke and Burke, as a revolving or turning back to a past ideal situation.[1] The new order would essentially be a re-forming or recreation of the apostolic Church, a new age in which the tyrant-priests would be deprived of their wealth and political power by the lay rulers, and redeemed as new men into a primitive purity. Moreover, it was this insistence on the need for a great rebirth, for a *renovatio*, for the need for the clergy to be born again as new men and to undergo – so to speak – a process of baptism and emerge as *novi homines*, which explains Wyclif's obsessive demands for the confiscation of clerical wealth. It was not that Wyclif objected to property ownership, to wealth as such: otherwise it would hardly have been logical to require the pauperisation of the clergy in order to hand over their burden of sin to the laity. But for him the possession of wealth and political power by the clergy was a symbol of their status as alienated beings. It denoted that they were men who had become divorced from their rational, right-thinking christian selves, and were no longer their true selves but *possessionati*, men possessed by a diabolical other identity, which was reflected in their lust for power and property. Similarly his constant attacks on the clergy for seeking material comforts to the exclusion of spiritual virtues was an expression on a different level of the ancient notion that the clergy had become animal men as distinct from truly human, rational men: they were not themselves at all, and it was small wonder that they had become mad, the stuff of which tyrants and heretics were made, and that their only salvation lay in conversion to their true, ideal identities. The real purpose of dispossession was symbolic, a sign that the clergy were reborn as right-willing beings, had become themselves as they ought to be.

It was this deep sense of clerical self-alienation which goes far to explain why Wyclif looked to the king as the means of generating the reformation.[2] In the fashion of a Waldensian or Spiritual writer, he

---

[1] V. F. Snow, 'The Concept of Revolution in Seventeenth-Century England', *HJ*, v (1962) pp 167–74.

[2] See further my 'Predestination, Property and Power', *SCH*, II (1965) pp 220–36. For the importance of the idea of the *voluntas inordinata* in Wyclif's theory see now F. de Boor, *Wyclifs Simoniebegriff: Die theologischen und kirchenpolitischen Grundlagen der Kirchenkritik John Wyclifs* (Halle 1970), espec pp 64ff.

stipulated against the existence of an actually existing present Church of wrong-willing beings, an *Ecclesia malignantium*, the true reality of an *Ecclesia* of the just, the community of right-willing selves which was present with, or rather, in God – the *res publica* of the righteous. Only when the clergy shed their selfishness, their self-interest, and sought to identify themselves with their public selves in the *respublica Dei*, could there be a rebirth of apostolicity. And it was this abstraction, the *communitas iustorum* – the true State – which it was the function of the king to represent on earth. In order to achieve his true self, his public identity – in order to identify himself with the *respublica* of the just – every individual had to become a king's man, owing allegiance only to the king, in the first instance Christ, the heavenly king, and in practice his vicar, the lay ruler. And it was this conception of society as a heavenly *congregatio*, an abstract entity – in modern terms, a sovereignty – given a visible embodiment in the king, which enabled Wyclif, with devastating logic, to demand the dissolution of the religious orders in England by the monarchy. Sovereignty, as Bodin later pointed out, cannot recognise the existence as independent entities of any other corporate bodies; and Wyclif in his own way was making exactly the same point. It is sometimes suggested that Wyclif was trying to create his own order of friars, a preaching order modelled on the Franciscans, but the real purpose of his urge for the creation of an *ordo Christi* was to make all men equal as subjects under the king. It was to be an order to end all orders, an end to the divisive effects of independent ecclesiastical corporations, and to bring all together in unity under the crown. The new order in society, born out of the reformation, would mean a new order of political beings, of all men as citizens, giving obedience to the lay prince as both priest and king.

This is not to suggest, as some scholars have tended to do, that Wyclif did not seek to create his own sect, his own band of poor priests, of wandering preachers who would seek to instil into the community at large the principles of right living, and who would endeavour in their own lives to emulate the righteousness of their ideal identities. Wyclif saw himself as the prophet of the new age:[1] he sometimes liked to picture himself as the only sane person in a world

---

[1] *De vaticinatione seu prophetia*, 1, ed J. Loserth, *Opera Minora*, WS (London 1913) p 165, 'spectat ad officium doctoris evangelici prophetare'; and note his comparison of himself with St Paul and his sufferings, *De eucharistia*, 9 pp 294–5. He had already pointed out in the *Postilla* that a prophet would need to secure the help of lay lords to protect him from the persecution of evil priests, Benrath, p 89 n 212.

full of madmen,[1] and to harp upon his loneliness as the burden which a prophet had to bear. But he also conceived it his duty (again there are analogies with Joachism and Franciscan Spiritualism) to prepare the way through a group of itinerant priests whose preaching would usher in the new era, and whose suffering under persecution would only serve to emphasise their Christ-like character. That they were always a small number does not seem to be in doubt (although their opponents tended to see them lurking behind every bush), but Wyclif went out of his way to emphasise that they were a few speakers of truth, a minority pitted against the possessioners,[2] a saving remnant of the faithful. Some of them would appear to have been friars, but we know virtually nothing about them, and little is to be gleaned from Wyclif's oblique references except the fact of their existence, and that they considered themselves as forming a *fraternitas* or order. What can now be said with confidence, however, is that this select band of true priests, *viri apostolici*, was not a creation of Wyclif's later years when he had no other means of spreading his views, but was an integral part of his scheme for a *reformatio* in the years before 1378 – the earliest references do in fact date back to as early as 1372/3.[3] He seems to have viewed them as a species of Platonic philosopher guardians whose function was to guide kings and other lords in the way of truth, an academy of consultants to government, whose knowledge of righteousness, he once said, would give them more real power in government than a bad pope.[4] They were, in other words, the true rulers of the

[1] For example *De apostasia*, 13, ed M. H. Dziewicki, WS (London 1889) p 173, 'nunc Ecclesia nostra occidua in qua sunt multi maniaci'.

[2] For example *De Ecclesia*, 15 p 357, 'ideo propter multitudinem, propter famam et propter terrorem istorum satellitum exterriti sunt pauci simplices dicere veritatem'. Although only a year or so later (1379–80) he was claiming that 'certe sumus quod plures nobiscum sunt quam cum illis', *Responsiones ad Strode* (*Opera Minora*) p 198.

[3] See the numerous instructions on preaching given to the simple followers of Christ living an apostolic *vita* in the *Postilla*: Benrath, espec pp 179–90, 341–6; compare B. Smalley, 'Wyclif's *Postilla* on the Old Testament and his *Principium*', *Oxford Studies presented to D. Callus* (Oxford 1964) pp 253–96 at pp 280–1. As pointed out by W. Mallard, 'Dating the *Sermones Quadraginta* of John Wyclif', *Medievalia et Humanistica*, XVII (Boulder, Colorado 1966) pp 86–105 at p 99, there is a passage in a sermon (iv 59 p 462) firmly datable to 19 October 1376 which suggests that there was a recognisable group in existence: 'Et licet scribae nostri dicant praedicantes religionem istam esse blasphemos atque haereticos, destructionem Ecclesiae machinantes, tamen visis miraculis veritatem nostri ordinis confitentur'. It may perhaps be suggested that the series of sermons on the Ten Commandments (iv 35–45) of the spring of 1377, some addressed 'vestrae fraternitati', and which seem to have been given to mixed audiences in different places, may have been intended for a group or groups of adherents.

[4] *De blasphemia*, 2 p 37, 'Sacerdos enim mundo incognitus, qui similius sequitur Christum in moribus, habet potestatem regendi et aedificandi Ecclesiam excellentius, quia non

community, even if the community ignored their existence – again a very Platonic sentiment. But that he handpicked men of high quality and capacity may perhaps be indicated by the rapid promotion of the Oxford Lollards once they had recanted and come to terms with the ecclesiastical authorities.

Wyclif never made any secret of the fact that he hotly resented his own lack of ecclesiastical preferment, and one can appreciate the hostility of the ecclesiastical establishment towards a renegade priest whose early career seems to have been as an exponent of the hierocratic theme.[1] Nevertheless it is a little surprising that one who enjoyed the protection of Gaunt should not have secured more advancement during the mid-1370s, unless he himself came not to desire it, and preferred to see himself in the role of adviser behind the throne, the *specialis clericus* of the king. Yet it is difficult to tell whether Gaunt ever regarded Wyclif as anything but a propagandist and pamphleteer, who was useful to him in the incessant guerilla warfare which the English government carried on against the hierocratic tendencies of the bishops in a continuous struggle to secure control of the English clergy and to turn the *ecclesia Anglicana* into a proprietary church. It was traditional royal policy to regard the bishops as organs of government, and the Hundred Years War was emphasising the usefulness of the clergy in acting as expounders of government policy and whipping up support for campaigns against France.[2] If Gaunt was in favour of reform, it was essentially because he sought to strengthen this traditional royal control of the clergy. For this purpose Wyclif was useful. But he and his movement were not essential – as was to be demonstrated by the fact that between 1380 and the early fifteenth century the English government did come to exercise a very firm control over its bishops without Wycliffite assistance.[3]

But what Wyclif meant by reform was, as we have seen, something far more fundamental. He wanted a virtual refoundation of the *ecclesia Anglicana*, a clergy stripped of political character and reduced to naked

consistit regimen Ecclesiae in spoliatione…sed in meritoria operatione…Sic quod melius foret Ecclesiae non esse papam vel praelatos huiusmodi, sed, abiecta tota traditione caesarea, sacerdotes pauperes docere nude et familiariter legem Christi'; cf. 1 p 9, 'Unde potens est Deus illuminare et exercitare mentes paucorum fidelium qui constanter detegant et moneant, si digni sumus, ad destructionem huius versutiae Antichristi'.

[1] Compare Wilks, *SCH*, v (1969) pp 69–98.
[2] H. J. Hewitt, *The Organisation of War under Edward III* (Manchester 1966) pp 160–5.
[3] E. F. Jacob, *Henry Chichele and the Ecclesiastical Politics of his Age* (Creighton Lecture: London 1951) pp 2–3.

essentials, and he argued that no really effective reform could take place unless this was done first, a going back to the beginning and starting again. From this point of view, however, Gaunt proved to be far more dangerous to Wyclifism than Courtenay. He was a man of government, a statesman, in the sense in which these terms were later to be applied to Sir Robert Peel as a man who put the stability and political advantage of the realm above matters of principle, and beyond considerations of personal advantage. The crucial period was from 1377 to 1379, years in which Gaunt did to a very large degree have command of the government and become the *rex incoronatus* that his enemies at St Albans always accused him of being. The death of Edward III put a minor on the English throne: Richard II was ten years old in 1377. The outbreak of the Great Schism in 1378 effectively meant the immediate removal of papal control in England, and, incidentally, halted the process against Wyclif himself. Gaunt had a virtually free hand: for Wyclif it was the supreme opportunity, the very conditions most favourable for the implementation of the *reformatio* programme.

But neither Gaunt nor the English government generally saw it in these terms at all. To them the schism meant a splendid opportunity to embarrass the French by choosing to support Urban VI against his Avignonese rival. And having once chosen him, the government became obsessed by the unlimited opportunities for treason now open to the clergy in favour of Clement VII – there was constant alarm that the clergy in coastal areas might be acting as French spies[1] – and reacted by insisting all the more firmly on the necessity for obedience to Urban VI. Wyclif, of course, did his best in the circumstances. He talked half-heartedly about *noster Urbanus*, and even pretended to believe for a time that Urban (a quite incredible suggestion when one remembers what Urban VI was really like) might be the longed-for *papa angelicus* who would inaugurate the new age.[2] But it was a poor

[1] Compare Hewitt, *Organisation of War*, pp 165–8.
[2] For example *De simonia*, 5, ed S. Herzberg-Fränkel and M. H. Dziewicki, WS (London 1898) p 67, 'O quam gloriosum foret exemplar Ecclesiae si Urbanus noster VI renuntiaret omnibus mundi divitiis sicut Petrus, ita quod in Urbano I et VI compleatur circulus quo clerus religione Christi relicta in saecularibus evagatur'. But note 7 p 93, 'Tria autem remedia ex Dei gratia coniecturo. Primum quod Deus irradiet mentem papae exempli gratia Urbani VI quod...conquasset omnes huiusmodi symonias: sed illud foret inopinatum et immensum miraculum'; and by *De blasphemia*, 1 pp 7–8, he has decided that nothing is to be done but wait for Urban to die and hope for a better replacement: see the passage beginning 'O si regnum nostrum post mortem Urbani sexti non foret seductum per satrapas, sic quod liberet se a tali capite et generatione hac pessima'.

strait to be in for one arguing that the English church could manage without popes at all.

Similarly the minority of Richard II only served to convince Gaunt that the *stabilitas regni* was the prime consideration.[1] He would defend Wyclif against the bishops, since he was well aware that the prosecution of Wyclif was an oblique attack on his own position: but Wyclif was still to him just one more episode in the interminable series of political contests which he waged against the hierocrats, and in which the waging tended to be more rewarding than the winning. Overall Gaunt was prepared to come to an accommodation with the bishops in the interests of maintaining stable government during the minority (even indulging in a series of diplomatic absences when necessary), and he ultimately preferred to work with a relatively moderate primate like Sudbury (who became royal chancellor in 1380) in order to maintain the functioning of government, rather than plunge the realm into the sort of turmoil that a Wycliffite reformation would have engendered. As Wyclif complained, in a very revealing passage written in late 1378 or early 1379,[2] he was encountering all the arguments against sudden change which it seems in the nature of bureaucracies to produce automatically: that the *reformatio* would produce too much upheaval; that it might not even then succeed; or that if it could be achieved, now was still not the right time to attempt it. It might be the right thing to do, but the present difficult circumstances made it inadvisable to act within the foreseeable future. He was meeting the normal responses made by any bureaucracy to a reformer who wanted to change things and do it in a hurry. In other words he found that the trouble with fourteenth-century government was that it had become, by medieval standards, a highly efficient administrative machine, a bureaucratic organism, encouraging the spread of an implicit assumption that it was the running and smooth functioning of the existing machinery which mattered more than a reassessment of the purpose for which the machine existed. Moreover the highly factional nature of English politics in the 1370s and 1380s[3] meant that the lay lords, the aristocracy, whom Wyclif saw as a key factor in the *reformatio*, were far more interested in which faction controlled the machine than in asking what it was supposed to be doing. But above all the Aristotelian

[1] According to Wyclif, Gaunt thought that an action imperilling the realm was worse than deflowering the king's daughter: *De Ecclesia*, 12 p 266.

[2] *Responsiones ad Strode*, pp 193–200.

[3] R. H. Jones, *The Royal Policy of Richard II: Absolutism in the Later Middle Ages* (Oxford 1968).

revolution, the growth of an increasingly secularised outlook, had created a great deal of confusion in the minds of contemporaries about the proper relationship between the civil and spiritual ends of society. And when ends are uncertain, there is a tendency to concentrate on maintaining existing arrangements and present equipment, without too much questioning of why the equipment is there and why it exists in that form. Much of the trouble which the controlling forces in the English government found with Richard II was that he proved to be a terrible nuisance, a man who wanted to clarify the purpose of government, to restate, to redefine its nature and function as the king's government, instead of allowing the machine to carry on running as it was, and by itself.

Wyclif's reformation then was a scheme for a revolution, but a revolution which was to be imposed from the top downwards. It was to be literally a *coup d'état*, an act of State, undertaken by the government itself under the guidance of a small élite of right-minded theologians who knew what should be done better than anybody else. The preaching campaigns which Wyclif insisted upon to support the revolution were designed to do precisely that, to provide popular support, not to make the reformation an act carried out by the people themselves. There is nothing in the instructions which Wyclif gave his preachers to suggest other than that the preaching to the laity was to be instruction of the most elementary kind. The reformation was to be a revolution by the head itself.

But what if the head refused to act? We have very little idea of what Wyclif was *doing* between 1379 and 1381: he virtually disappears from view. All we know is that he wrote rather less than usual: it is the one relatively unproductive period in an otherwise incredibly productive literary career. But there is a very significant change between one end of this period and the other. In 1379 Wyclif remarks that he has told the people that the Gospel work of reform would have to go forward slowly. He was still convinced that the king could, he said, bring the reformation about immediately by direct legislative action: but he seems to have accepted that the government had no intention of doing so.[1] In his analysis of kingship, however, Wyclif had accepted that a king who became a tyrant ceased to wield valid governmental power and could be replaced by community action. He had further accepted

---

[1] *Responsiones ad Strode*, pp 197–8, beginning 'Unde in vulgari consuluit quod istud generaliter non fiat subito sed prudenter sicut coeperat paulative' (where he is employing a favourite device of referring to himself in the third person).

the traditional notion that *inutilitas*, uselessness, was to be classified as a species of tyranny, and that the people could move when the ruler failed to carry out his duty of good government. He himself had witnessed the power of the London mob at the hearings of 1377 and 1378. Early in 1381 Wyclif wrote that the faithful few could do little by themselves against the might of clerical power, and would be better advised to retire from public life.[1] But, he added, it would be another thing if the people would rise up under their leadership. If the king will not act, he threatened, there will be a rising of the people under prophetic leadership; refusing to pay taxes, especially tithes; and making new appointments to public offices by popular election.[2] I am prepared to disturb the public peace, he declared on more than one occasion at this time,[3] but this may be justified on the grounds that the clergy have already upset the good order of the realm. If the realm is soon in turmoil, it will have been the fault of the clergy for creating the conditions of disturbance: disorder breeds disorder.[4]

Like other shrewd observers (but unlike the government) Wyclif may simply have been aware of popular discontent – there had been a number of minor outbreaks before 1381 – and was using this as means of threatening Gaunt and trying to force him into action. If there was to be a popular rising, he was not averse to claiming the credit for it in advance. But when the so-called Peasants' Revolt did break out at the end of May,[5] it seems to have been sparked off by nothing more than opposition to a second collection of poll taxes – or perhaps resentment at the virginity tests carried out by the royal officials allegedly in order to assess how many members of a family were eligible for tax. Since it is not my purpose to attempt to investigate the economic causes of the Revolt of 1381 (except to note that professor Postan recently declared that he could not explain the Revolt in terms of oppression and economic distress, because condi-

---

[1] *De blasphemia*, 1 pp 8–9, 18, 'Et tantum inveterata malitia invaluit quod unius simplicis momentanea rebellio parum proderit, cum satraparum suorum persecutione sit statissime extinguendus'.

[2] *De simonia*, 7 p 93; 8 pp 101–3.

[3] *XXXIII Conclusiones*, 25 (*Opera Minora*) p 55, citing Matt. 10: 34, 'Unde doctor christianus non omitteret propter perturbationem pacem talem prudenter dissolvere'; and the similar passages in *De vaticinatione*, 2 pp 170 and 174, where he again uses Christ's remark about bringing a sword, not peace, in order to answer accusations of disrupting the peace, adding 'Sufficeret enim pars regni quae est iam toxice in manu mortua per se debellare vel in iusta causa resistere'.

[4] *De simonia*, 4 pp 44.

[5] [C.] Oman, [*The Great Revolt of 1381*] (2nd ed with introduction by E. B. Fryde: Oxford 1969); [R. B.] Dobson, [*The Peasants' Revolt of 1381*] (London 1970).

tions had been steadily improving, and that the primary cause might well be seditious preaching),[1] let me instead simply call your attention to certain aspects of the Revolt.

In the first place the Revolt was remarkably well organised on a local community basis; it had no difficulty in finding leaders of considerable ability, some of them priests like Ball, others lay priest-kings like Wraw and Litster, and the rebels seemed to know in advance whom they wanted as leaders; and the attack on London was a brilliantly co-ordinated movement, particularly bearing in mind that the initial target of the revolt was not London but Canterbury. We get that remarkable long march of the Revolt from London to Canterbury and back again, not only to pick up recruits on the way, but also to act as a sort of political Canterbury pilgrimage, a travelling classroom for the purpose of teaching the masses on the way the purpose, aims and methods of the Revolt.

The Revolt was more of an urban movement than a rural one – unlike most English popular risings, which used the green lanes and hollow ways of the countryside, it spread along the roads from town to town – and the towns and roads were the pulpits of the poor preachers;[2] and because it was urban, it was often the ecclesiastical centres – like St Albans and Bury St Edmunds – which suffered most. Courtenay himself certainly had no doubt that the movement was primarily aimed against the clergy.[3] And of course the most important victim of the rising was the archbishop of Canterbury, Sudbury – who apparently made the ludicrous mistake of threatening the mob with the pope, and promptly lost his head. After the Revolt had collapsed, Wyclif politely expressed his regrets that the archbishop should have been killed: if there were bad bishops, it was better to preach against

---

[1] M. M. Postan, *Cambridge Economic History of Europe*, I (2 ed, Cambridge 1966) pp 609–10.

[2] See the statute of 1382 against unlicensed preachers 'in certain habits under the guise of great holiness' who move from county to county and from town to town, preaching not only in churches but also in churchyards, fairs, markets and other public places: *Rotuli Parliamentorum*, III pp 124–5; and the mandate against lollard preaching issued by the bishop of Worcester on 10 August 1387, which refers to them preaching publicly in churches, graveyards and on the streets, and privately in halls, rooms, gardens and enclosures: Wilkins, *Concilia*, III pp 202–3. For Swinderby's wayside pulpit of mill-stones, Knighton, II p 192.

[3] [M. E.] Aston, ['Lollardy and Sedition, 1381–1431 '], *PP*, XVII (1960) pp 1–44 at pp 5, 37; Dobson, p 71; compare Walsingham, *Chronicon Angliae*, pp 310–11. For the way in which the Revolt was seen as a vindication of Courtenay's warnings against Wyclif, see J. H. Dahmus, *William Courtenay, Archbishop of Canterbury, 1381–1396* (Pennsylvania and London 1966) pp 70–3.

them and ostracise them rather than indulge in bloodshed.[1] But since Wyclif had remarked that amongst the ranks of the possessed, Sudbury was the archdemon,[2] one need not perhaps take this too seriously.

None of this demonstrates that Wyclif or the Wycliffite preachers were in any degree responsible for the Revolt. On the other hand it does demonstrate that their opponents were perfectly entitled to suggest that they were, and the accusation was duly levelled.[3] But more to the point is Wyclif's reaction afterwards. Not only did he express sympathy for the rebels,[4] and for the conditions which led to the rising – again emphasising that the clergy were mainly to blame for heavy taxation[5] – but, whilst he condemned the Revolt, the only real reason that he gives is that the rebels went about it the wrong way. They had the right idea, but they just carried it out improperly: 'licet maiores bonos instinctus habuerint, non plene fecerunt ad regulam'.[6] The fatal flaw in the movement was that it acted against the clergy without the authority of parliament, of the lay lords who made up the *communitas regni* together with the king. It should have been an act, he writes, of the *totum regnum* undertaken with full public authority.[7] If one recalls that the rebels had made considerable efforts to suggest that they were acting on royal authority; that every care was taken not to harm the members of the royal family; and that the London rebels dispersed as soon as Richard II took over the nominal leadership of the Revolt, then it may be suggested that it is a matter of considerable significance that Wyclif condemned the Peasants' Revolt because, although it tried, it *failed* to be a revolution from above.

I hope I have now said enough to suggest the real answer to my original question: why did a Wycliffite movement under Hus's command succeed where Wyclif failed? Hus had nothing more to say

---

[1] *De blasphemia*, 5 p 76; *XXXIII Conclusiones*, 22 p 49.

[2] *De blasphemia*, 13 p 194.

[3] Aston, pp 2–5, 36; Oman, pp 19–21, 101; Fryde, p xxxvii; Dobson, pp 367, 373–8; compare N. Cohn, *The Pursuit of the Millennium* (London 1957) p 413: all agree that Wyclif was innocent of the charge of complicity, however damaging the revolt undoubtedly was for the future of the lollard movement. Similarly Workman, II pp 236–41; McFarlane, pp 99–100.

[4] *De blasphemia*, 13 pp 197–8. Compare J. Stacey, 'The Character of John Wyclif', *London Quarterly and Holborn Review*, CLXXXIV (London 1959) pp 133–6 at p 134.

[5] *De blasphemia*, 6 p 83; 13 pp 190, 198; 14 p 214; 17 p 267; *Responsiones ad Strode*, pp 198–200.

[6] *De blasphemia*, 13 p 190.

[7] *De blasphemia*, 13 p 197, 'Tertio deficit populus in modo agendi multiplici...et tertio quia exspectari debet totius regni exhortatio sive consilium': the *totum regnum* should have acted 'in parliamento publico', 17 p 269.

than Wyclif about the need for a *reformatio regni*: if anything, he said considerably less; but there was no essential difference between his and Wyclif's scheme for reform. It is true that he succeeded to a well-established and flourishing native reform movement, and enjoyed a very great measure of popular support. But it is arguable at least, in the light of the rising of 1381, that Courtenay and the chroniclers were right to maintain that a reformation of the clergy would have gained massive popular support in England. The essential difference in Bohemia, however, is that the Czech reformation at a crucial period did take on the character of a revolution from above.

The Czech reform movement had grown up to a large degree under royal protection, first from Charles IV and subsequently from Wenceslas, although it can hardly be said to have been state-orientated until after 1400 when the influx of Wyclif's writings provided the Czechs with a groundplan for a national church-state under royal control – a feature which does much to explain why the writings of an obscure Oxford don of twenty years before proved so acceptable in Bohemia. But Wenceslas (who, ironically enough, was soon to be deprived of his claim to Roman emperorship on the grounds that he was *inutilis*, useless) had learned from his contest with John of Jenstein during the 1380s and early 1390s that a king could gain control of his clergy and create a proprietary church if he was prepared to act sufficiently vigorously against his primate. At various times Wenceslas imprisoned the archbishop of Prague, confiscated his estates, killed one of his officials, and eventually forced the archbishop into resignation.[1] It is perhaps significant that one of Hus's earliest writings as a royal pamphleteer deliberately reminds the Czech clergy of Wenceslas's treatment of Jenstein.[2]

Wenceslas saw in Hus and the growing Wycliffite movement in Bohemia the means of recovering his position after the civil war of 1399–1403 and of making himself supreme in his own kingdom. Whilst it suited him, Wenceslas played the part of Wyclif's ideal

[1] See now R. E. Weltsch, *Archbishop John of Jenstein, 1348–1400: Papalism, Humanism and Reform in Pre-Hussite Prague* (The Hague and Paris 1968). A convenient survey of Wenceslas's struggle with the higher nobility during the 1390s, which involved a further contest between the king and bishop John of Litomysl, is provided by F. Dvornik *The Slavs in European History and Civilization* (New Brunswick, N.J, 1962) pp 183–8.

[2] [*Mistra Jana Husi,*] *Korespondence* [*a Dokumenty*], ed [V.] Novotný (Prague 1920) pp 3–4. The tract is written in the form of a letter from Wenceslas to Boniface IX, dated August 1402, in which the king supposedly threatens to throw his opponents into the Vltava, as had happened to Jenstein's vicar-general, John of Pomuk, in 1393.

king, and converted the Czech reform movement into a *reformatio regni* for the benefit of the Bohemian monarchy. In the five years after 1408 Wenceslas deliberately and no doubt cynically used the Hussites to make himself master of *studium*, *sacerdotium* and *regnum*. The decree of Kutna Hora in January 1409 not only gave the Czechs control of the university of Prague, and encouraged the removal of the anti-Hussite German masters, but the effect was to make Wenceslas the real rector and regulator of the university. Wencelas's seizure of archbishop Zbinek's estates and revenues in 1409 and 1410, and his expulsion or imprisonment of all clergy who observed the archbishop's interdict in 1411 – all actions undertaken ostensibly in support of Hus himself – forced Zbinek into death in exile, and enabled the king to appoint his own physician (Albik) as archbishop of Prague. And in 1413, on the plea of ensuring adequate Hussite representation on the city council of Prague, Wenceslas transferred all appointment of councillors to the crown, and gained control over the government of his capital.[1]

Yet that Wenceslas was acting solely for his own royal advantage is made abundantly clear by his treatment of Hus himself over the affair of the indulgences for the Neapolitan crusade of 1412. When Hus preached against the indulgences – and thus imperilled Wenceslas's policy of maintaining good relations with pope John XXIII – Wenceslas decided that Hus had outlived his usefulness and had to be silenced. Hus was driven out of the capital into exile in southern Bohemia (Kozí Hrádek) for eighteen months: he was not recalled even though the question of the indulgences became a dead letter within a month of his departure. Hus had served the royal purpose, and could be dispensed with as soon as the royal supremacy was established. It was almost certainly Wenceslas who engineered Hus's departure for Constance, partly through Henry Lefl of Lazany, the lord of Krakovec, a leading member of the royal council, at whose castle Hus was invited to reside in the summer of 1414, and from which he left for Constance;[2] and partly through the king's brother Sigismund, who encouraged Hus

---

[1] For these events see now [M.] Spinka, *John Hus: [A Biography]* (Princeton 1968); also P. de Vooght, *L'Hérésie de Jean Huss* and *Hussiana* (Louvain 1960).

[2] This supports the testimony given at Constance by the Prague inquisitor, Nicholas of Nezero, according to which Wenceslas obliged Hus to go to the council: Spinka, *John Hus' Concept of the Church*, p 353; *John Hus*, p 220. This statement has been generally decried as being part of evidence obtained under duress and contradicting earlier testimony, and on the grounds that Wenceslas would never have done this for the reason stated by Nicholas, to clear his realm of suspicion of heresy. This does not necessarily clear Wenceslas of blame, although his reasons may have been very different from that given by the bishop.

to take his case to Constance, and whose safe-conduct ensured that Hus never returned.[1] One would very much like to know how far the Czech clergy at Constance who acted as Hus's accusers were acting under royal instructions.

But it is not my intention to open the case of Hus here. My purpose is simply to emphasise that, as Wyclif himself had always stressed, a *reformatio* could only succeed – and subsequently in Bohemia *did* succeed – when it was seen as a revolution from the top downwards. In a sense the real heir of Wyclif in Bohemia was not Hus, but Wences-las. It was Wenceslas rather than Hus who in the end proved that Wyclif was right: that a reformation has to be an act by the head. But England had to wait for a century and a half after Wyclif's death for a king who was capable of understanding the point and of putting it into effect.

[1] For Sigismund's invitation, Novotný, *Korespondence*, p 197. The safe conduct had been offered to Hus before he left Krakovec, since he refers to it on 1 September, although it was not actually issued until 18 October, when Hus had already set out (on 11 October). The document was ambiguously phrased so that it was not clear whether it covered Hus at Constance itself or on a return journey see F. Palacký, *Documenta Magistri Joannis Hus* (Prague 1869) p 238; [M.] Spinka, [*John Hus at the Council of Constance*] (New York and London 1965) pp 89–90. Hus later accused Sigismund of acting like Pilate in betraying him to his Czech enemies: Spinka, pp 259–60, 286; compare *John Hus' Concept of the Church*, pp 331–7; *John Hus*, pp 222–37. Sigismund's sincerity in the matter of the safe conduct is defended by de Vooght, *L'Hérésie*, pp 325–8, 334–5.

5

MISLEADING MANUSCRIPTS: WYCLIF AND THE NON-WYCLIFFITE BIBLE

by MICHAEL WILKS

THE precise nature of Wyclif's connection with the production of the first English bible[1] is shrouded in mystery, a subject for the fierce controversy and debate that is possible only where ignorance and uncertainty prevail. To begin with, there is an almost total absence of reliable contemporary evidence. The first statements explicitly attributing authorship to Wyclif do not occur until the generation after his death. Of these, the earliest is that of the chronicler Henry Knighton, whose contacts with early lollardy might make him appear to be a more reliable source than most.[2] Writing perhaps in the mid-1390s, Knighton referred back to the year 1382 as the time when Wyclif translated the gospel, which Christ had given to the clergy and doctors of the church, into the tongue, not of the angels, but of the Angles. He accused Wyclif of trying thereby to make the gospel easily available to the literate laity – or, as he viewed the matter, of scattering the pearl of biblical wisdom so that it might be trampled on by the swine.[3] There is however no other reference to Wyclif as translator

---

[1] For details of previous translations of individual books of the Bible in England see [M.] Deanesly, [The] L[ollard] B[ible and Other Medieval Biblical Versions] (Cambridge 1920) especially pp 302–18; or the convenient list in H. Hargreaves, 'From Bede to Wyclif: Medieval English Bible Translation', BJLR, 48 (1965–6) pp 118–40 at 118–20. Compare Sir W. A. Craigie, 'The English Versions (to Wyclif)', The Bible in its Ancient and English Versions, ed H. Wheeler Robinson (2 ed Oxford 1954) pp 128–45 at 134–7; F. F. Bruce, The English Bible: A History of Translations (2 ed London 1970) pp 10–11; G. Shepherd, 'English Versions of the Scriptures before Wyclif', CHB, II (Cambridge 1969) pp 362–87.

[2] As canon of the augustinian house of St Mary of the Meadows at Leicester, he was not only in the heart of lollard country, but must have been acquainted with Hereford and Repingdon, and probably Swinderby: Deanesly, LB, p 239.

[3] Knighton, [Chronicon, ed J. R. Lumby], 2 vols RS (London 1889) II, pp 151–2, 'Hic magister Iohannes Wyclif evangelium, quod Christus contulit clericis et ecclesiae doctoribus . . . transtulit de latino in anglicam linguam, non angli-cam, unde per ipsum fit vulgare et magis apertum laicis et mulieribus legere scientibus quam solet esse clericis admodum literatis et bene intelligentibus, et sic evangelica margarita spargitur et a porcis conculcatur.' This section of the chronicle (from 1377) terminates at 1395, which presumably indicates the date

during the parliamentary controversies of 1395–7 about the legality of vernacular bibles,[4] nor in the revival of the dispute at Oxford in 1405.[5] The subsequent condemnation of biblical translation by archbishop Arundel in 1407 mentioned only translations 'made in the time of the said John Wyclif or since';[6] and it was not until 1411 that the archbishop told John XXIII (in a covering letter to a list of 267 wycliffite errors being forwarded to the pope) that Wyclif himself had maliciously instigated the practice of translating the scriptures into his mother tongue.[7] Even this does not have the unambiguous attribution contained in Hus's statement of the same year that Wyclif had actually translated the whole latin bible into English, and Hus himself acknowledged that this was only what the English said.[8] But enough had in fact been said to establish a tradition: there had been a Wyclif bible.

It is true enough that manuscripts of the whole bible in English were in existence by 1400. Many of these manuscripts clearly represent the version thought to have been prepared by Wyclif's erstwhile secretary, John Purvey, and published together with an introductory tract on translating the bible into English about 1396. This version need not concern us here, except to notice that Purvey refers in his *General Prologue* to a previous translation of the bible into English, with an implication that it was in need of correction – although not to the extent, he remarks, of many ordinary latin bibles.[9] It has generally

---

of composition: V. H. Galbraith, 'The Chronicle of Henry Knighton', *Fritz Saxl Memorial Essays*, ed D. J. Gordon (London 1957) pp 136–45.

[4] Deanesly, *LB*, pp 282–3; [H. B.] Workman, [*John Wyclif*] (Oxford 1926) II, pp 193–4, 343–5.

[5] Deanesly, *LB*, pp 293–4; Workman, II, p 169.

[6] Wilkins, III, p 317, '*Ne quis texta s. scripturae transferat in linguam anglicanam. Statuimus igitur atque ordinamus ut nemo deinceps aliquem textum sacrae scripturae auctoritate sua in linguam anglicanam vel aliam transferat per viam libri, libelli aut tractatus, nec legatur aliquis huiusmodi liber, libellus aut tractatus iam noviter tempore dicti Iohannis Wycliffe, sive citra compositus sive in posterum componendus, in parte vel in toto, publice vel occulte.*'

[7] Wilkins, III, p 350, '*novae ad suae malitiae complementum scripturarum in linguam maternam translationis practica adinventa*'; compare Deanesly, *LB*, p 238; Workman, II, pp 186–7 (correcting the date from 1412).

[8] Cited Deanesly, *LB*, p 240; Workman, II, p 187.

[9] '. . . for no doubt he shall find full many Bibles in Latin full false . . . and the common Latin Bibles have more need to be corrected, as many as I have seen in my life, than hath the English Bible late translated': see further Deanesly, *LB*, pp 255 *et seq*. The high standard of Purvey's work as a translator has been stressed by Hargreaves, 'The Latin Text of Purvey's Psalter', *Med A* 24 (1955) pp 73–90; 'The Marginal Glosses to the Wycliffite New Testament', *S[tudia] N[eophilologica]*, 33 (Uppsala 1961) pp 285–300; 'The Wycliffite Versions', *CHB*, II, pp 387–415 at 407–13.

been accepted that the material evidence for this earlier version consists primarily of three manuscripts, two now at Oxford and the other at Cambridge, all of them remarkable in that they appear to suggest a change in the identity of the translator at Baruch 3:20. Bodley 959, written in four or five different hands, stops short at Baruch 3:20 itself. Bodley Douce 369 covers the whole Bible, but contains a break at the Baruch passage with a note: *Explicit translacōm Nicholay de herford.* Whilst the other, Cambridge, manuscript (University Library MS Ee.i.10, an 'abridgement' of the latter part of the old testament) also notes at Baruch 3:20: 'Here endiþ þe translacioun of N and now bigynneþ þe translacioun of j and of oþere men.'[10] The 'N' is presumably Nicholas Hereford, one of the most prominent of Wyclif's circle at Oxford; but the 'j' could relate to Wyclif, Purvey or to somebody else altogether. Moreover, the text of the translation up to this Baruch passage is one of an extremely literal nature, but is far less literal afterwards. Accordingly, the nineteenth-century editors of the wycliffite bible, Forshall and Madden, working mainly on the basis of the two Oxford manuscripts and accepting Bodley 959 as the original manuscript of the first translation, argued that Nicholas Hereford must have translated the old testament up to Baruch in this very literal fashion whilst at Oxford, but had broken off when he left England in 1382 to appeal against his condemnation at the papal curia. The work had then, therefore, to be finished by others, in particular by Wyclif himself, and they had done so in a much less literal style of translation.[11]

In assuming that Bodley 959 was the original manuscript, Forshall and Madden completely ignored the point that the existence of a number of different hands posed a serious problem for this interpretation, and this discrepancy has since opened up the way for more recent scholars, notably the swedish linguistic experts, Fristedt and Lindberg,

---

[10] Hargreaves, *CHB*, II, p 400, amending the reading given by him in 'An Intermediate Version of the Wycliffite Old Testament', *SN*, 28 (1956) pp 130–47 at 133. As Hargreaves comments (p 146), it is not clear why such an abridgement should have been made—although John Rylands Library English MS 89 provides another example—and it is even more difficult to understand why the writer should have copied in a note about Hereford stopping at Baruch which could have had no obvious relevance to his own work.

[11] J. Forshall and J. Madden, *The Holy Bible: made from the Latin Vulgate by John Wycliffe and his Followers*, 4 vols (Oxford 1850) I, p xvii; also F. D. Matthew, 'The Authorship of the Wycliffite Bible', *EHR*, 10 (1895) pp 91–9. Deanesly initially accepted that the translation was by 'Wyclif and his circle' (*LB* p 251), but in *The Significance of the Lollard Bible* (London 1951) pp 3–5, suggested that Wyclif merely inspired the work and that the chief translator was Hereford. Bodley 959 was still accepted here as the original manuscript.

to demolish the Forshall-Madden thesis very thoroughly. Bodley 959 can no longer be regarded as the original manuscript of the first translator. On the contrary, it is a copy of a much corrected version:[12] either the last of a whole series of earlier but no longer extant manuscripts,[13] or at least a fair copy of a heavily revised original draft translation.[14] Either way it is unlikely to be earlier than the last decade of the fourteenth century.[15] This in turn casts doubts upon the existence of a break in the work of translation at Baruch 3:20 caused by Hereford's supposed visit to Rome in 1382. It has been suggested by Lindberg that the break might equally well have been due to Hereford's reported recantation between 1387 and 1391[16] – whilst Fristedt would reject the notion of a break altogether: it is certainly a very odd place for a

[12] [S. L.] Fristedt, [*The*] *W*[*ycliffe*] *B*[*ible*, 2 vols (Stockholm 1953–69)], I, pp 76, 113; 'The Authorship [of the Lollard Bible]', *S*[*tudier i*] *M*[*odern*] *S*[*prákvetenskap = Stockholm Studies in Modern Philology*,] 19 (Stockholm 1956) pp 28–41 at 31; [C.] Lindberg, [*MS. Bodley 959: Genesis—Baruch 3.20 in the Earlier Version of the Wycliffite Bible*, 5 vols (Stockholm 1959–69) I, pp 21–3; III, pp 29–32; IV, pp 18–19.

[13] Fristedt, *WB*, also 'The Dating [of the Earliest Manuscript of the Wycliffite Bible']', *SMS*, ns, I (1960) pp 79–85 at 84–5. As he points out (*WB* I, p 43), this would mean that 'we are not in possession of a single document which is indubitably by the pen of Wycliffe, Hereford or Purvey.' That there was a considerable variety amongst the manuscripts of the English bible by 1400 is suggested by the introduction to an early fifteenth-century wycliffite concordance to the new testament in English: discussing synonyms of the word 'church', the author comments, 'Now it may be so þat in sum Newe Lawe is writen in sum text þis worde *kirke* & in þe same text & in a noþer book is written þis word *chirche*': cited A. McIntosh, 'Some Linguistic Reflections of a Wycliffite', *Franciplegius: Medieval and Linguistic Studies in honor of F. P. Magoun*, ed J. B. Bessinger and R. P. Creed (New York and London 1965) pp 290–3 at 291; and now printed in S. M. Kuhn, 'The Preface to a Fifteenth-Century Concordance', *Speculum*, 43 (1968) pp 258–73.

[14] Lindberg, II, pp 7, 29–31; III, 32–3: all the scribes were working off the same original manuscript and making a fair copy of revisions to it. Thus Bodley 959 is 'the translator's authorised copy, based on his own first version, and written out by several scribes who were also guided by him in revising the text.' In V, pp 95–6, he suggests that it may be Hereford's copy of his own original together with an intermediate Oxford version, in effect making this a third version.

[15] Fristedt, *WB*, I, pp 11–15, 146, was initially prepared to accept the Forshall-Madden dating to before 1390, but has subsequently re-dated to *c* 1400: 'The Dating', pp 84–5. Lindberg also oscillated between *c* 1390 and *c* 1400 (III, p 33; IV, pp 30–1), but has now settled for the latter: V, pp 55, 61, 95.

[16] Lindberg, II pp 30–2; III, p 33; V, pp 95–6: this means that the completion of the translation of the whole old testament cannot be placed before 1390 af the earliest. The original idea of a break in 1382 is still to be found with E. Delaruelle, *L'Église au temps du Grand Schisme et de la crise conciliaire* (Paris 1962) p 969.

translator to stop work, virtually in mid-sentence. He would argue that Bodley 959 is an incomplete manuscript, which simply stops short in the form that we have it at the end of a folio, and that a similar break in other manuscripts must have other explanations.[17] This can hardly be said to provide a convincing reason for the existence of rubrics stipulating that Hereford was the translator up to this point. But it would indicate that there might originally have been a complete literal translation of the old testament, which is now no longer available.[18]

This point aside, however, both writers seem to agree with each other in accepting that these old testament manuscripts provide the key to the genesis of the Wyclif bible, and offer a basis for discussing Wyclif's own part in its production. According to Fristedt, they show that the work of translating the whole bible into English was undertaken at Oxford[19] early in the 1370s by a group of wycliffites centred on Queen's College, with John of Trevisa playing a prominent part,[20] and

[17] Fristedt, *WB*, I, p 145; II, p xlvii: this led to the scribes of later manuscripts changing to a different one at this point, I, pp 86–8. A comparison can, he suggests, be made with Bodley Douce 369, which is not a single work but a fifteenth-century binding together of two separate parts. Craigie, 'The English Versions', p 139, appears to accept that the break in Bodley 959 is due both to] it being the end of the folio and to Hereford stopping the work of translation here.

[18] Fristedt, *WB*, I, pp 107, 135, 145; 'The Authorship', p 31: support for this belief in a complete version of the whole bible translated on strictly literal principles is provided by Christ Church MS E.4.

[19] Fristedt, *WB*, II, pp lxiii–lxiv, although he had earlier rejected the theory of an 'Oxford idiom' (I, pp 39–50, 91) and identified the dialect of the original literal version (I, pp 95–8, 118, 145–6) as being that of Leicestershire, which might indicate Lutterworth, but with some northern idioms, which he first attributed to derivations from Wyclif, but subsequently explained by the argument that Hereford was himself a Yorkshireman too: 'The Dating', p 80. Lindberg identifies the dialect of the original translation and of the various scribes of Bodley 959 as being that of the north-west Midlands: see the detailed discussion in I, pp 13–15, 23–5; II, p 18; III, pp 16–18, 33; IV, pp 30–1; V, p 98; whereas M. L. Samuels, 'The Dialect of MS Bodley 959' = Lindberg, V, pp 329–39 (App. I) prefers the central Midlands; but both would accept a Leicester location.

[20] Fristedt, *WB*, II, pp xlviii–xlix, lxiii–lxiv, revising I, pp 1, 6–7, 118. The case for Trevisa's participation, originally suggested by Caxton, rests primarily on his remarks in *Dialogue between a Lord and a Clerk upon Translation* of the mid-1380s in favour of putting the bible into English, and on the fact that he was at Queen's college for a number of years which coincide with the residence there of Hereford and, to a lesser extent, Wyclif himself. Trevisa and Hereford were members of the southern group of masters who were expelled during the north versus south conflict in the college during 1376–80, and in 1378–9 they carried away a number of books from the college library which might well have been useful to someone translating the bible. See further H. J. Wilkins, *Was John*

was completed at Lutterworth by Hereford and his assistants, possibly Repingdon and Brut,[21] by 1383. It was then revised by Wyclif and Purvey, who objected to the numerous errors and excessively literal character of this first draft, and who therefore produced a 'first revision' or 'intermediate version'[22] (perhaps with further assistance from Hereford) during the course of 1384.[23] In all this Wyclif himself was well to the fore. He can be assumed to have initiated and inspired the project, laying down rules of procedure for the translators to follow, supervising and correcting their work,[24] even if he personally wrote little of the actual original text.[25] Eventually Purvey, seeking to achieve a clearer and more readable translation, must be accredited with a second revision of the whole bible in the middle years of the 1390s.[26]

Lindberg on the other hand regards the first part of the old testament as the work of Hereford in the years between 1384 and 1387,

---

Wycliffe a Negligent Pluralist?: John de Trevisa, his Life and Work (London 1915) pp 100–12; D. C. Fowler, 'John Trevisa and the English Bible', *Modern Philology*, 58 (Chicago 1960–1) pp 81–98.

[21] Fristedt, *WB*, I, pp 115–17; compare Lindberg, IV, pp 30–1. Walter Brut seems to have been a literate layman: at his trial in 1393 he, or an associate, reproached Hereford for his ignorance of latin grammar: see Workman, II, p 337.

[22] The idea of an intermediate version, for which see Hargreaves, 'An Intermediate Version', especially p 145, was previously put forward by E. W. Talbert, 'A Note [on the Wyclyfite Bible Translation]', *University of Texas Studies in English*, 20 (1940) pp 29–38, mainly on the basis of Huntington Library MS HM 134. Fristedt, originally working independently of Talbert, first accepted Talbert's evidence ('The Authorship', pp 28, 33–40), but subsequently rejected it on the grounds that the Huntington MS contained passages from Purvey's version of *c* 1396, and so must be dated after 1400: 'The Dating', pp 81–2.

[23] Fristedt, *WB*, I, p 145. Talbert suggested a continuous process of revision between 1384 and 1395: 'A Note', p 38.

[24] Fristedt, *WB*, I, pp 136, 141–8; II, pp xi, lxiv, lxvi; compare 'The Authorship', p 35. He argues that the same rules were applied to the lollard translation of the pseudo-Augustinian tract *De salutaribus documentis*: I, pp 43–8; II, *passim*; also 'New Light on John Wycliffe and the First Full English Bible', *SMS*, ns, III (1968) pp 61–86. That Wyclif himself conceived the idea of translating the Bible into English is also maintained by P. A. Knapp, 'John Wyclif as Bible Translator', *Speculum*, 46 (1971) pp 713–20.

[25] Fristedt, *WB*, I, pp 95–105, 115–17; II, pp xlviii–xlix, lx–lxi, lxiv–lxvii; compare 'The Authorship', p 37.

[26] Fristedt, *WB*, I, pp 8–9, 140–1. According to this it was Purvey's departure from the literal method in his second revision which explains the need for the *General Prologue*—he was conscious of the need to justify the new method (I, p 137)—and also accounts for Arundel's condemnation, aimed against the revision rather than the original translation: a straight word for word translation might have been tolerated, but not one which set out to make the bible intelligible to all (I, pp 142–3).

that is to say, in the period immediately after Wyclif's death.[27] On the assumption that the translators began at the beginning, this would effectively exclude Wyclif from any direct connection with the wycliffite Bible – as had already been argued by a number of English historians.[28] But Lindberg thinks this so improbable that he has steadily come to the conclusion that Wyclif had already translated the new testament first around 1380[29] (and without help from Trevisa[30]), leaving Hereford to carry on and do the old testament after 1384 – a task which Hereford performed so badly without Wyclif present to guide him that Purvey was later obliged to revise Hereford's old testament up to the point where it stopped at Baruch, and then complete the remainder of the old testament himself[31] about 1390.[32] Whichever version of these diametrically opposed Stockholm stories is preferred, the modern scandinavian account of the Wyclif bible accepts that it remains Wyclif's to a very considerable extent.

No one can reasonably mourn the demise of the superficially plausible and deceptively simple Forshall-Madden interpretation: but we may express regret that a quarter of a century of intensive technical scholarship has only managed to replace it with a situation of excruciating complexity, so that general bewilderment now prevails. We may notice straight away, however, one glaring inconsistency in the swedish approach to the problem. All the elaborate superstructure about the place of Wyclif in the preparation of the English bible is deduced from

[27] Lindberg, II, pp 30–2; III, p 33.
[28] Workman, II, pp 157, 160–2, allowed that Wyclif instigated the translation of the old testament, and the literal quality of the original version was due to his intention that there should be a sentence by sentence translation, but the work was carried out by Hereford first, and then Purvey, and Wyclif himself had no hand in it. But Wyclif was dissatisfied with the result, as shown by his refusal to use it, and set Purvey to the task of revising it. Much the same position was adopted by H. E. Winn, *Wyclif: Select English Writings* (London 1929) pp 7–9; also G. Leff, *Heresy in the Later Middle Ages*, 2 vols (Manchester/New York 1967) II, pp 512 n 3, 578, 591.
[29] Lindberg, II, pp 30–2; III, p 33; V, pp 92, 95. The possibility that translation of the new testament preceded that of the old testament was considered by Forshall and Madden, I, pp xv–xvii; compare Craigie, 'The English Versions', pp 139–40.
[30] Lindberg, II, p 32, who rules Trevisa out on the grounds of dialect. However relevant this may be in an old testament context, it does not necessarily preclude his involvement in translation of the new testament.
[31] Lindberg, III, p 32; and see also S. H. Thomson, *Europe in Renaissance and Reformation* (London 1963) p 175: Wyclif began translating the bible between 1380 and 1384, leaving Hereford and Purvey to complete and revise the work, which was finished by 1388.
[32] Lindberg, II, pp 30–2; III, p 33; IV, pp 30–1.

manuscripts which make no reference to Wyclif whatsoever and which contain within themselves not a shred of real evidence that he was in any way connected with them. These manuscripts have been studied on the presupposition that they represent a Wyclif bible: whereas, if taken without this prior assumption, there would be no intrinsic reason for mentioning Wyclif in this context. Because, in other words, a tradition has existed since the 1390s, namely, that there *was* a Wyclif bible, it is taken for granted that English bible manuscripts must in some way or other illustrate this tradition. If the tradition is ignored, the manuscripts as such can offer no grounds for thinking that Wyclif participated in their production. The only firm conclusion that can be reached amidst this morass of supposition about the manuscripts is that there was an English bible – a matter which was never in doubt. The secondary question of whether Wyclif and/or his followers should be related to it cannot be approached on a manuscript basis: it can only be considered from what we know independently about Wyclif and early lollardy.

Since Wyclif regarded the old testament as a mere prelude, and sometimes a misleading one, to the evangelic law of the new testament,[33] he might naturally have preferred to have the new testament available in English first. It is a pity therefore that so much erudition should have been devoted to this less important section of the bible, especially when genuine evidence exists for thinking that the new testament was in fact available before the old testament, and that Wyclif might have approved of this order of procedure. His own statements clearly indicate that some biblical texts in English were in existence by 1383, but we notice that he always refers here specifically

---

[33] In the *De veritate sacrae scripturae*, 10 (I, pp 218–21) he attacked the 'sophists' who argued that the old testament was not part of scripture: it had to be accepted as canonical, and Christ himself had said that he came to fulfil the old law, not destroy it. But Wyclif's own use of it was decidedly selective, and he was quite prepared to use the pauline principle that the foundation of the church constituted a new age operating on different principles, so that the new apostolic law swept away mosaic ordinances, when it was convenient for him to do so: see for example his refusal to use the old testament to justify warfare in *De civili dominio*, II, 17, pp 247–8, and his denunciation of arguments for papal absolutism based on old testament passages like Jer. 1:10, as in *De potestate papae*, 11, p 273. This did not however deter him from finding 'right' examples in the old testament, for example, 11, p 275; compare *De Ecclesia*, 7, pp 143–4. His overall position does not seem to have changed much from his initial discussion in chapters 7 and 8 of the *De mandatis divinis*, in which he concluded that the old testament contained certain basic truths in conformity with the new testament, but was far from being of equal standing with the *lex evangelica*. All references are to the Wyclif Society editions.

to the gospels, or at least the *lex Domini*, and nowhere mentions an old testament or a complete bible in English. It may also be of significance that the earliest attribution of biblical translation to Wyclif, that of Knighton, only accuses him of having translated Christ's gospel and other parts of the new testament in 1382. There is no positive reason for thinking that a new testament was produced any earlier than this. It is only during 1382 that passages begin to appear in Wyclif's works to justify knowledge of the gospels in English, and here it could very well be argued that they refer only to preaching the biblical texts in English rather than to an actual translation itself.[34] As has been noted, the celebrated case of William Smith, the 'parchemyner' of Leicester, who later confessed to having written books in English since 1381 or 1382 *de evangelio et de epistolis et aliis epistolis et doctoribus* only refers to new testament material, and could be books *about* the gospel and epistles rather than *of* the biblical texts.[35] It was not until the end of this year, 1382, that Wyclif began to urge that the laity should be able to study the gospel in English for themselves;[36] and not until the middle of 1383 do we at last have a direct statement by him that the lay lords can do so,[37] with all its implications that some sort of translation must have been ready. Finally, in 1384, we hear from Wyclif that codices of an English new testament are being burned.[38]

---

[34] The first indication seems to be *Sermones*, III, 45, p 384 (June 1382) where he argues that pronunciation of the gospel is no more important than the language it is written in provided the right meaning is retained. *De nova praevaricantia mandatorum*, I, pp 116–17 (late 1382 or early 1383) refers only to pamphlets preaching biblical truths in English; whilst *De triplici vinculo amoris* 2, p 168 (late 1383) mentions only writings in English and queen Anne of Bohemia's possession of Czech and German translations of the bible: Buddensieg's editorial note is surely correct against Deanesly, *LB*, p 248, in that there is no specific reference here to an English bible. *Of Mynistris in þe Chirche*, ed Arnold, p 293 (about September 1383) merely suggests that the gospels should be known and expounded in English; and similarly *Opus evangelicum*, III, 31 and 36 (II, pp 15 and 132) of 1384, but incorporating earlier material, refers to English preaching.

[35] K. B. McFarlane, *Wycliffe and English Nonconformity* (repr Harmondsworth 1972) p 125, with reference to Knighton, II, p 313. For the re-dating of this see A. Hudson, 'A Lollard Sermon-Cycle [and its Implications]', *Med A*, 40 (1971) pp 142–56 at 152 n 1.

[36] *De amore* = *Ep* V, p 9 (late 1382); *Speculum saecularium dominorum*, I, pp 74–5 (1382–3).

[37] *Expositio Matt. XXIV*, 8, p 378, 'quia temporales domini ... possunt tamen ex Dei gratia studere Christi evangelia in lingua eis cognita'.

[38] *De contrarietate duorum dominorum*, 2, p 700, 'dyabolus ... faciat comburi codices de lege Domini. Lingua enim sive hebraea sive graeca sive latina sive anglica est quasi habitus legis Domini'; and see also 8, p 711, accusing the friars of arranging 'quod libri ewangelici et sensu catholici declarati populo comburantur.'

None of this does more than indicate that Wyclif was aware in his last two or three years that an English new testament existed, and that he gave a rather limp measure of approval to it. There is nothing to suggest that he had a hand in it himself. Otherwise we should have to account for a most uncharacteristic reticence on his part. Considering the extent of his writings at this period, he seldom refers, and then only in passing, to something which one might have supposed would be very close to his heart – a means by which all should be able to understand the bible. How can one explain this unaccustomed modesty? There is no such diffidence when he was talking about the importance of the sermons which he devised for his 'poor priests' to preach.

Since we do not know what this early English new testament was like, it is difficult to say. But much of the difficulty would indeed disappear if our swedish experts are correct to the extent of suggesting that it was a very literal type of translation made on the traditional model, which the lollards would subsequently have to revise extensively. Its very literalness would be the best possible argument for it *not* being a Wyclif bible. The dominant tradition of medieval biblical translation, based on Jerome's discussion of this highly specialised task, was one which assumed that every word of the sacred text was itself sacred, and that even the very order of the words was a divine mystery which made it imperative to preserve this in the translation. The faithful exponent had to make word correspond to word, and there was little scope for an idiomatic expression of what the translator thought the divine author had meant.[39] This might render the meaning almost unintelligible in places, but this was particularly appropriate for use by university masters and the educated clergy generally. The word for word system provided for greater academic accuracy, was of more value for the purposes of debate, and had the immense advantage that it was still possible to make use of the standard latin glosses on the vulgate text in which each individual word was annotated. The 'construe' method produced a work to suit experts, and it is not surprising that the wycliffites should prefer to revise a translation of this type rather than attempt a new one altogether. Insofar as the Wyclif group was a university élite there was hardly likely to be dissatisfaction with the English bible on this score. Wyclif had himself remarked often enough that

[39] W. Scharz, 'The Meaning of *Fidus Interpres* in Medieval Translation', *JTS*, 45 (1944) p 75.

not one syllable of scripture was lacking in significance.[40] But Wyclif's opponents were academics too, and a bible which would have been of equal value to them (given that they could have ignored the canonical prohibition on bible translations[91]) would not have been Wyclif's conception of a good translation. What he wanted was an English bible which would bring out the real essence of the gospel teaching – and so prove his enemies to be falsifiers of scriptural truth.[42] If he had a bible, he would need one which would explain what it meant as it went along.

It only confuses the issue to maintain that Wyclif wanted the bible to be a new legal code to set against the canon law of the papacy and its supporters, and therefore would have welcomed a word for word translation as producing the verbal accuracy needed in a code of law.[43] This not only overlooks the point that the bible had always been regarded as the lawbook *par excellence* of the hierocratic system itself,[44] but also assumes quite unjustifiably that Wyclif was an exponent of *sola scriptura* in the sense of wishing to make the higher law of the bible into an instrument of everyday usage, replacing both human traditions and the positive law itself. On the contrary, however, Wyclif continued to treat the bible, divine law, as very much a higher and therefore – in a fundamental sense – unwritten law, quite unsuitable for general lay use. This can be seen in his incessant demands for reliance on the literal sense of scripture. For what Wyclif meant by the literal *sense* had little

[40] *De Ecclesia*, 1, p 10: the statement 'in tota scriptura non ponitur vel una sillaba sine sensu' is in fact a tautology in that scripture is itself to be defined as those parts of the bible which have a right 'sense'.

[41] *Decretales*, V, vii, 12, which derived from Innocent III's condemnation of waldensians in Metz who were translating the bible into French for use in unauthorised preaching: see *Reg.*, I, 141–2 (*PL* 214 (1855) cols 695–9).

[42] See for example the long attack on the papalists in *De Ecclesia*, 3 pp 48–56, demanding that their actions should be judged against the bible truly understood, and concluding, 'Quae enim posset esse maior adulteratio verbi Domini quam intelligere ipsum ad sensum diaboli iuxta quem defendatur esse haereticum et blasfemum . . . ?' Similarly *De veritate sacrae scripturae*, 7, especially pp 141–2, 148, 158–9, for the argument that those who misinterpret scripture are falsifying it, and so can be accused of saying that scripture is largely untrue: 'Ex istis videtur quod magna pars scripturae foret falsissima . . .'

[43] Deanesly, *The Significance of the Lollard Bible*, pp 8–9; Knapp, 'John Wyclif as Bible Translator', p 714; W. Mallard, 'John Wyclif and the Tradition of Biblical Authority', *Church History* 30 (Chicago 1961) pp 50–60 at 57.

[44] Compare the very pertinent remarks of W. Ullmann, 'The Bible and Principles of Government in the Middle Ages', *La Bibbia nell'alto medioevo: Settimane di studio del Centro italiano di studi sull'alto medioevo* 10 (Spoleto 1963) pp 181–227, 331–6.

enough to do with literal *translation*. One must never confuse the two things. By literal, Wyclif meant true, conforming to the inner divine content of a biblical statement: he was always concerned with what he thought to be the meaning behind the words, not with the words themselves – let alone the ink and parchment which gave them visible form and made them legible.[45] Words were signs, essentially vehicles for righteousness, and their supreme function was to convey the true sense, to carry a correct understanding of Christ's teaching with them.[46] The bible was a *via regia*, a highway to truth, and as with all road systems it was necessary to have guidance along the right way. The underlying assumption here was that translation meant understanding, and understanding entailed exposition by those qualified to interpret the words rather than actual reading by the faithful of the texts themselves – even if they could read and could even afford the cost of having their own bible. Certainly all were to know the scriptures,[47] but by this Wyclif primarily had in mind that all were to know them by being taught what they ought to mean, not by using their own eyes. The reading of texts was a job for the priest rather than the layman (unless perhaps he was a lord), and the priest would then retail to his audience what he thought they should know, taking care to explain and gloss what was being said as he went along. For Wyclif the good priest still stood between the Word and man. His technique for getting the bible 'read' was the sermon or the tract, the explanation of a text by one qualified to reason rightly about it. The sermon was itself the best 'translation' of the bible,[48] the handing on or transfer (*translatio*) of the

[45] *De veritate sacrae scripturae*, 6 (I, pp 107–8), 'Nam, sicut ostendi alibi de lege Dei, est praeter codices vel signa sensibilia dare veritatem signatam, quae potius est scriptura sacra quam codices. Unde solebam describere scripturam quod sit sacra veritas inscripta . . .', and more extensively pp 114–16: the same distinction applies in reverse to heresy: 7 (I, p 140). See also *Trialogus*, III, 21, pp 238–9; *De civili dominio*, III, 1, p 4, 'codices aut habitus corporales vel ritus sensibiles non sunt christiana religio, licet sint quandoque per accidens eius signa.'

[46] For example *De veritate sacrae scripturae*, 3 (I, p 44); 16 (II, pp 5, 15, 19–20, 32).

[47] Note the use of phrases like *De Ecclesia*, 7, p 146, 'scrutetur homo totam scripturam . . .'; p 156, 'Sed scrutetur fidelis evangelium . . .'; and therefore 'nam mille sunt fideles qui habent immediate a Deo fidem scripturae independenter ab illo [papa], etiam plus quam ipse', *De potestate papae*, 10, p 261; also *De officio regis*, 4, p 72.

[48] There is an excellent illustration of this principle in Trevisa's *Dialogue*: 'Also the gospel and prophecye & the right feyth of holy chirche must be taught and preched to Englysshe men that conne no latyn. Thenne the gospel and prophecye and the right feyth of holy Chirche must be told hem in englysshe, and that is not don but by Englysshe translacon, for such *englysshe prechyng is very*

divine truths behind the written words. We might reasonably infer that the wycliffite vernacular sermons were much more closely akin to what he wanted than any translation in the modern sense of the word. The question of the actual authorship of the English sermons raises its own problems, but the most significant thing about them in this context is that the lengthy passages of the bible which do get translated in the course of them bear no resemblance to any other known version. The translator of the English sermons did not have, or did not wish to have, a bible translation to work from. He preferred to make his own – and his own mistakes and corrections.[49] By the time he had finished his work on the sermons, he had produced his own 'selected passages of the New Testament in translation', selections which were so extensive that they may be regarded as forming their own abridged version of the bible.[50] Why should he be anxious for more, for the whole Bible in translation? He had already produced what he thought most important for the benefit of the laity, and had, by putting it in sermon form, ensured its right presentation. This discrepancy between the English sermon version and the so-called Wyclif bible is again a clear indication that Wyclif had nothing to do with the preparation of the latter. The English sermons were not only contemporary, but the translator was working off the manuscripts of Wyclif's latin sermons before these were revised and augmented.[51] This argues for someone, or a group, close to Wyclif, even if it was not Wyclif himself; and the very fact that the alleged early Wyclif bible did not employ the same language means that this first English bible was not a creation of Wyclif's immediate circle in its initial recension. On the contrary, the bible translators may themselves have made use of the English sermons.[52]

Future research into the sources should therefore be concerned with the question of a non-Wyclif bible, not of a Wyclif or even a wycliffite one. It is possible that Wyclif's emphasis on the sense of scripture as

---

translacon, and such englyssh prechyng is good and nedefull, thene englyssh translacon is good and nedefull.' See Wilkins, p 95; Fowler, pp 97–8.

[49] As originally pointed out by [T.] Arnold, [*Select English Works of John Wyclif*], 3 vols (Oxford 1869–71) in notes to I, p 71 and II, p 13.

[50] Workman, II, pp 176–7. Fristedt, *WB*, I, pp 7, 106, glosses rather unconvincingly over this point. A similar situation arises with Chaucer's translations: see now W. M. Thompson, 'Chaucer's Translation of the Bible', *English and Medieval Studies presented to J. R. R. Tolkien*, ed N. David and C. L. Wrenn (London 1962) pp 183–99.

[51] The translator used the 3-part version of the *Sermones* written (as a single work) by Wyclif in 1381–2, not the 4-part compilation of 1384.

[52] The suggestion is made by Arnold, II, p 345 note.

opposed to undue interest in the words apparent in the *De veritate
sacrae scripturae* of 1378 is a pointer to the period when the work of
translating the bible into English began. But we can only assert with
any confidence that some sort of English version of the new testament
had been made available by 1382. We do not know who was responsible for it, nor where it was produced. John of Trevisa, working at
Oxford, may still have as good a claim as any to be considered, but we
can only be convinced that it was not Wyclif, and that this early version was not an authentic wycliffite production. To this was apparently
added an old testament at a later date, on which Nicholas Hereford
and a certain John seem to have been engaged at some stage. But by
this time the work of providing an English bible for general consump-
tion had become very much a group activity, and the text underwent
a process of continuous revision which in due course led to the Purvey
version in the 1390s, but is unlikely to have stopped there. There was
in other words a takeover of an originally independent English bible
project by the wycliffite movement in the decade or so after Wyclif's
death, one more example of the way in which early lollardy moved
fairly rapidly away from the original standpoint of its founder in the
direction of a more radical, populist, lay-centred church. English bible
revision and multiplication was just the sort of work which would be
appropriate to and, I suggest, was appropriated by the wycliffite missionary school or rival *universitas* which Wyclif appears to have established after his virtual expulsion from Oxford, the intensely active and
well-staffed headquarters, a veritable 'Centre for Lollard Studies', combining a wycliffite library and publishing house, whose existence has
been revealed recently by Dr Anne Hudson's profoundly important
and very exciting investigation of early lollard literature.[53] This may
have been located in the Leicestershire area, although not necessarily at
Lutterworth itself,[54] and this is precisely the area to which we may look

[53] 'A Lollard Compilation and the Dissemination of Wycliffite Thought', *JTS*,
ns, 23 (1972) pp 65–81, especially 75–80; 'Some Aspects of Lollard Book
Production', *SCH*, 9 (1972) pp 147–57, especially 155–7; also 'A Lollard
Sermon-Cycle', pp 145–6, 150.

[54] It is possible that this was at Oxford itself ('A Lollard Compilation', pp 73, 75)
but the alternative suggestion of the Braybrooke area ('Some Aspects', pp 155–
6; compare the remarks on dialects, 'A Lollard Sermon-Cycle,' pp 149–50) may
prove to be a more fruitful one, since this was the land of Thomas Latimer,
known to be one of the lollard knights, and a notorious lollard centre in the
early fifteenth century: see K. B. McFarlane, *Lancastrian Kings and Lollard
Knights* (Oxford 1972) pp 195–6.

for the provenance of the Oxford and Cambridge bible manuscripts. But these manuscripts themselves, however significant for the study of late fourteenth-century lollardy, derive from a late stage in the history of biblical translation, and can only be peripheral to the prime question of the relationship between Wyclif and the first English bible.

6
ROYAL PRIESTHOOD:
THE ORIGINS OF LOLLARDY

LOLLARDS, the chroniclers Knighton and Walsingham informed their readers, are called Wycliffites or Wycliffians because they are the disciples of Wyclif (*Wycliff discipuli et Wyclyviani sive Lollardi*) and so belong to his sect.[1] It is however one of the major problems of early Lollard history to know precisely how this came about. What were the mechanics of the process by which an Oxford academic, whose popular reputation outside the university was not likely to have been considerable until he was involved in two spectacular but abortive trials and was the subject of a papal condemnation during 1377–1378, became the acknowledged leader of a movement which was said five years later to have the support of half or more of the kingdom?[2] It is more than a little odd that, despite generations of the most intensive research, the most recent and in many ways the best and most complete analysis and summary of Lollardy is obliged to comment that Wyclif's connection with the actual process of evangelization and dissemination has always been an uncertain one,[3] and to conclude that he inspired 'a movement which outlasted persecution for over a hundred years, produced a literature of its own and a list of martyrs and devoted missionaries right up to the time of the Reformation, without their originator ever apparently having displayed any outstanding powers of personal leadership or even any very direct interest in the practicalities of building up a new religious group.'[4]

Although the history of the Peasants' Revolt of 1381 makes it abundantly clear that fourteenth-century mass movements were capable of a high degree of organisation and discipline seemingly generated spontaneously and from within the movement itself, one would think that some traces must surely remain of the links between Wyclif himself as the isolated figurehead of the

Reset and repaginated from *The Church in a Changing Society: CIHEC Conference in Uppsala, 1977* (Uppsala, 1978), 135–63

movement and the main body of the sect to explain why it was
so successful. What was the nature of his contact with a movement whose members included 'great lords' and 'simple folk'
alike, and whose numbers increased so dramatically that they
were alleged in the course of half a dozen years to have filled the
realm?[5]

During the past hundred years there have been basically two
answers proposed to this conundrum. One, which received its
fullest expression at the beginning of the century from a still
relatively unknown American scholar, H. L. Cannon,[6] restated the
traditional view that during the second half of the 1370s Wyclif
gathered together a large number of disciples and, working out
of Oxford as the headquarters of the movement, instructed them
in his own version of the principles of the faith before
despatching them on preaching tours which soon came to cover
much of the country. Whilst Cannon himself dismissed the notion
that Wyclif saw these poor priests (*poor prestis* or *sacerdotes
simplices*) as a distinct and separate organisation – although, he
acknowledged that they were later charged with conspiring to
form an illicit *confoederatio Lollardorum*[7] – he accepted that they
were highly organised and carefully prepared by Wyclif himself,
aided by his academic lieutenants, and he cited in particular the
Latin and English sermons as evidence that they were thoroughly
trained in preaching techniques and knew how to select suitable
material for their discourses.[8] But little would remain to indicate
their activities in Oxford itself, since few of them were university
men, but rather ill-educated curates from rural parishes and
unbenificed clerks who had to be brought in from outside (which
would in fact make it even more difficult to explain how they
were contacted and selected). Moreover, these simple priests were
to be itinerant preachers, frequently on the move regardless of
their bare feet, preaching both publicly and privately whenever
possible, in streets, fields, churchyards and gardens as much as
in halls, houses and inner rooms.[9] Clad in their long russet
gowns, worn in imitation of the Franciscans and other 'holy
hermits' – a form of attire never openly approved of by Wyclif
himself[10] – the Wycliffite preachers ranged the land, but looking
back always to Wyclif and Oxford as the co-ordinating and
command centre of the movement. It was very much Wyclif's
affair, and it was essentially ecclesiastical: the poor preachers

were to be priests, not laymen; and they were not, at least by implication, to be in the royal service.[11]

More recent research has produced little of substance which can conclusively disprove this account: on the other hand it has not educed very much to support it either. But the redating of most of the Latin texts of Wyclif, which Cannon used, to the early 1380s, and the growing suspicion that he had little enough to do with the English sermons anyway, would seem to offer encouragement to the radical revision of the traditional thesis which has gained general approval during the last quarter of a century and has now become the new orthodoxy. Most modern scholars, largely influenced by the late and much lamented Bruce McFarlane[12] and undaunted by Wyclif's own very rude remarks about the opinions of Oxford *moderni*, have now, somewhat ironically, reached the point where it is virtually possible to dismiss the idea that Wyclif had any real contact with the Lollard movement at all. This distinctly iconoclastic attitude does not deny that there was a somewhat small-scale Lollard movement by 1382, especially in the area around Leicester, but argues that its existence was a coincidence, rather like the Peasants' Revolt, for which Wyclif was given credit and made responsible without any real justification. It certainly looked to him for inspiration: but he took no part in organising it.[13] Thus Wyclif in retirement at Lutterworth during the last three or four years of his life remained immune from persecution because it was recognised that, notwithstanding his voluminous and vitriolic pamphleteering, he was not organising sedition.[14] The real organisers, and the explanation of the connection with Oxford, are to be found in the small group of 'proto-Lollards'[15] like Hereford, Aston, Repton and (doubtfully) Purvey, who had been friends and supporters of Wyclif when he was at the university, and who subsequently undertook a programme of publicising Wyclif's ideas to a popular audience in a simpler and more radical form than they had when they first appeared. By their preaching they did what Wyclif himself failed to do, either because he refused to do it or was unable to do so.[16]

In contrast to the traditional picture of Lollardy, perhaps the most valuable aspect of these more recent studies has been to indicate the extremely important part played in the Lollard movement by the laity, especially men from the middle ranks of society, like craftsmen in industrial areas, notably the cloth industry, and esquires.[17] Whilst the effect of this has been to emphasise the divorce between Lollardy and Wyclif himself, and to underline the character of post-1382 Lollardy as a non-academic popular movement comprising a great many people with no particular pretensions to learning – 'a sect of semi-literates and pious laymen'[18] – it has also somewhat inconsistently given prominence to the importance of the group of lords specified by the chroniclers as having been 'Lollard Knights' – 'huius sectae promotores strenuissimi et propugnatores fortissimi' – whose zeal for God was matched by their lack of intelligence in allowing themselves to be misled by false doctors.[19] Although Knighton's phraseology here might have been taken to imply that these lords took a leading part in the movement after being in contact with people like Wyclif himself, the problems attached to explaining how the Lollard Knights became Lollard have been largely avoided by classifying them as an eccentric if not aberrant fringe group, who did not represent the outlook of the aristocracy generally, and who do not feature in the history of the movement until well into the 1380s and 1390s. In this way the notion of a watershed about 1380 dividing Wyclif himself from Lollardy is reaffirmed instead of being questioned; and this in itself corresponds to the view that Wyclif needs to be seen during the 1370s as having been primarily a dissenting anti-clerical protester and reformer, but not so very remarkable or unique for that. It was only in and after 1380 that he developed far more radical doctrines, notably those concerning the eucharist, and so became heretical properly speaking – as if these later theories were optional extras which in other circumstances he might have left well alone. Either way the notion of a change in the years around 1380 helps to preserve Lollardy as a novelty, the first English heretical movement to assume extensive proportions, to be highly organised, and to become really dangerous politically – something which the ecclesiastical hierarchy found it very difficult to cope with simply because they were so completely unused to anything of the sort and lacked any experience of the way to deal with it.[20]

The yawning gulf between these two quite divergent accounts of the place of Wyclif in the origins of Lollardy can, I wish to suggest here, be at least partially bridged if we are prepared to recognise that the term Lollardy is itself a misnomer, and that our habit of thinking of it in terms of a popular heretical movement generates a number of questions which cannot be properly answered because they should never have been asked. These so-called Lollard Knights provide the key to the problem. The most striking feature about them is that they were all long-established, trusted and experienced royal servants, who were influential members of the royal household administration, for the most part knights of the King's Chamber, men at the very centre of government. They were also closely associated with either Edward, the Black Prince, or his widow Princess Joan of Kent, and subsequently their son Richard II, although some of them had earlier seen service in the retinues of Edward's brother, John of Gaunt, duke of Lancaster. As a group they were frequently in touch with one another, both in public and private life, having their common links and interests as courtiers and royal retainers who had first made their way as career soldiers in Edward III's campaigns. Some of them were the sons of royal officials, members of families with long traditions of service to the crown.[21] Far from being the poverty-stricken landless gentry which they were initially assumed to be, so far down the social scale that they could be thought to have connections and natural sympathies with a Lollard peasant proletariat,[22] the Lollard Knights were an aristocratic body forming part of the cultivated literary circle at court which patronised poets like Chaucer and the author of *Piers Plowman*; and one of them at least, Sir John Clanvowe, was himself capable of writing both a love poem and a distinctly puritanical devotional treatise – illustrating the ability of the glittering, elaborately structured and highly sophisticated culture of the courts of Edward III and Richard II[25] (and the households of great princes like the Black Prince and Gaunt) to combine religious literature and secular poetry in a manner[26] that gave Wyclif and Chaucer an identity of outlook which transcends their common allegiance as retainers of Gaunt himself. As McFarlane very reasonably argued,[27] their pre-eminence and influence at court does much to explain the quite remarkable degree of protection afforded to the Lollards during the last two decades of the fourteenth century: no Lollard was burnt for heresy before 1400, and the bishops generally showed themselves well satisfied with token recantations and assurances of future good behaviour. But it tends to obscure their real significance if we can only see them as a development of the 1380s, indicative of a new trend, instead of considering them as the survivors and

heirs of a previous generation. They were essentially con-
servatives, looking back to the ideals of a court supposedly
dedicated to the pursuit of Christian chivalry, which had
flourished during the reign of Edward III and his sons, and it
makes a great deal more sense to think of them protecting
Wycliffites because they were royal servants, and had always
been brought up to understand that this was the appropriate
thing for royal servants to do.

From this standpoint two further considerations present
themselves. In the first place the presence of Wycliffite support
at the heart of the royal administration suggests that the problem
of the spread and dissemination of Lollard teaching hardly arises.
Lollardy was broadcast because it was official policy. If Wyclif's
teachings were regarded during the 1370s as the expression of an
officially approved reform programme, which carried the seal of
royal authentification, then it would have been entirely normal
and unremarkable for them to have been accepted by a great
many people as an expression of duty and loyalty to their
superior. One of Wyclif's main motives in trying to ensure that
there was a lay-dominated proprietary church system in England,
with the lords responsible under the king as patron in chief and
originator of all ecclesiastical rights for the appointment of
suitable clergy in every church from the cathedral to the chapel,[28]
was to enable the true faith to spread downwards to every level
in society under the guidance and protection of the relevant local
lay magnates. One notices the appearance of a number of
chaplains amongst the names of those who would be cited for
heresy,[29] and it would be better to regard these as cases of clerks
who were Lollard because they knew what was expected of them
by their lords rather than trying to see them as examples of the
lower clergy reaching up to convert their lay superiors. Our view
of the process needs to be reversed, and they are evidence for the
aristocratic nature of Lollardy more than its popular character.
This was entirely in line with Wyclif's own insistence that he was
preaching in the first instance to the lords of England as being the
only people who could really make sure in practice that the
clergy was being reformed. He gave the aristocracy a
responsibility for the teaching of the approved religion in a way
which is an interesting anticipation of Hobbes' view that the
conduct and understanding of the common people depended on
the public teaching and example of their 'immediate leaders,

which are either the preachers or the most potent gentlemen that dwell amongst them,' and that the universities should be filled with the sons of the aristocracy 'so that they might afterwards instruct the vulgar.'[30] Indeed it would be difficult to think of a political writer since the author of the *Song of Lewes* a century earlier who had so elevated an opinion of the capabilities of the English aristocracy (and who saw nothing to fear from making them the beneficiaries of the disendowment of ecclesiastical property). It was rare for Wyclif to discuss the duties of monarchy, especially when it concerned control and correction of the clergy, without specifically mentioning that the same obligations applied to the lords and knights – or else he made use of a generalised terminology so that what was said would apply equally well to other secular lords besides the king. The same principle would follow from his conception of the monarchy itself as pre-eminently the executive organ of an aristocratic council of the realm or *communitas regni*,[32] in which both lay and sacerdotal magnates – *capitales domini* – combined to represent the whole kingdom, Parliament and Convocation taken together.[33] By the same token it was the aristocracy whom he blamed most bitterly after 1381 for their failure to secure the reformation of the realm and to extend effective protection to the true Wycliffite clergy against the persecution of the papalists.[34]

If it remains true that Wyclif's prime concern continued to be that of converting the priesthood to his way of thinking, and that he valued his position at Oxford precisely because it gave him the opportunity to make the greatest impact in this respect, his own preaching in the period between the autumn of 1376 and the spring of 1378 shows[35] that he was far from exclusively concerned with his fellow clergy, but was equally anxious to influence the lay magnates at the same time. His public addresses during the six months in London before the first abortive hearing at St. Paul's in February 1377, when according to Walsingham he ran from church to church corrupting the citizens with many false insanities,[36] were often aimed at mixed audiences of clergy and laity, whom he regarded as equally part of the fraternity or religious order which he was seeking to establish. Wyclif's *Ordo Christi*, which he publicised at just this period,[37] was to be a unique combination of a religious order with a military fraternity reminiscent of Edward III's orders of chivalry such as the Round Table of 1344 and the more famous Order of the Garter of 1348.[38]

Whilst he described it in quasi-monastic terms, seeing Christ as the abbot or prior of the order, he seems to have conceived the organisation on the model of the orders of warrior-monks like the Templars and Hospitallers, whose aim was to combat the opposing forces of evil (in this context the powers of a diabolical papacy) and to bring the world to a new conversion. Thus Lollardy as an organised movement was seen from an early stage as a sort of order of chivalry, part of the whole *militia Christi*, which was designed – as had been the case with Gregory VII – to enrol the lay lords into the service of truth, so permitting the principles of righteousness to percolate downwards to all members of society. If the eventual aim was to turn the entire world into something approaching a gigantic monastery or religious foundation, and so complete the work which the Benedictines and Cluniacs had attempted but failed to achieve, Wyclif insisted that this was no cloistered ideal, but an essentially apostolic and outward-looking conception, which would involve the Wycliffites in a great campaign of going out into the world to do good and live well. Nevertheless he does not at this early stage seem to have been thinking primarily of having special teams or groups of wandering preachers tramping the high roads and declaring the reformation from mill-stone pulpits in town market-places. On the contrary the message was to be conveyed mainly by normal preaching in the ordinary course of events from town and village churches and household chapels rather than by mass public participation in large preaching campaign meetings. He was still at this period quite capable of describing the laity in general as 'contemptible inferiors',[39] who could only be brought to drink from the life-giving waters of scripture if shepherded there by the preaching of their clerical captains,[40] and his whole attitude towards the masses of the population was that they needed to be led from above rather than be sparked into life by spontaneous impulses from below. It is understandable that Wyclif had marked out the mendicant orders as playing a leading part in this process, and initially intended to use the friars as the spearhead of the whole *acies* or battleline of the *Ordo Christi*. He looked with special favour upon the Franciscans, although in February 1377 Gaunt was able to produce friars from each of the four mendicant orders to defend him at St. Paul's,[41] and it was understandably a bitter blow when he effectively lost the support of the friars during the following year or so.[42] But the really significant feature of this relationship with the mendicants is that Wyclif simply intended to use them in the normal way of things. The English people were to be evangelised in the ordinary course of events by traditional and customary means: it was enough therefore to gain control of their superiors – lords, clergy, religious – and this is what we should expect from somebody who saw himself as the exponent of not just the true, but also the officially, i.e. royally, approved version of the faith. The fact that there is no independent evidence of deliberately organised preaching tours until those undertaken by Wyclif's Oxford group of disciples in late 1381 and early 1382 – that is, some five years later – is an indication, not that there was no Lollardy, but that this was not discerned in the first instance to be the most useful method of disseminating reform principles and of gaining support. Wyclifism was primarily designed to operate internally through the medium of the existing structure of the ecclesiastical system, and the justification for this was that Wyclif had from the beginning considered himself to be the spokesman *par excellence* for the king and the court. The gospel of reform was something to be carried out from the central government by lay magnates and university-trained ecclesiastics after the fashion of Carolingian *missi dominici* as part of the day to day duties of administering the realm, whilst Wyclif himself acted like a latter-day Alcuin at the centre advising them on how to do it.

This basic nature of Lollardy as a court-centred movement is further emphasised if we consider, secondly, the general character of English politics during the second half of the fourteenth century. In broad terms, what Wyclif himself was trying to do was to provide a theology appropriate to a political party – and we can only appreciate why a political party should need a theology if we understand what is meant by 'party' in this context. We are only gradually becoming aware of the constantly shifting factional nature of fourteenth-century politics, in which groups of magnates, both lay and clerical, formed round great aristocratic households, each with its strings of client-lords and retainers, ebbing and flowing as they coalesced and quarrelled with each other in their search for political power.[43] But whilst there was no permanent stability in the system, and it needs to be seen as an extraordinarily mobile pattern of alliances, it is at any given moment possible to draw a distinction between those groups which were forming a royalist or court party and those which upheld a hierocratic party, either out of genuine conviction or because it happened to suit their anti-government stance at that particular time. There was adherence, which might be prolonged or very temporary, to either a royalist or a hierocratic party in much the same way that aristocratic groups called them-selves Court and Country in the later seventeenth century or Whigs and Tories in the eighteenth. The hierocrats tended to stand for the principle more than the practice of papal supremacy, and might more accurately perhaps be regarded as episcopalist rather than papalist: but a profession of acceptance of papal supremacy against the powers of the monarchy was the touchstone which distinguished the hierocrat from the royalist clergy. Thus bishops like Brantingham of Exeter, Reader of Chichester, Erghum of Salisbury and probably Buckingham of Lincoln could normally be described as royalists, whilst someone like Sudbury tried unhappily to remain loosely attached to both sides at once, and the effective leadership of the papalists (like Brinton of Rochester and Despenser of Norwich) can be traced through from Wykeham of Winchester to Courtenay and subsequently to Arundel.[44] But the immediate policies of these 'parties' could alter as easily as their components: the crown was able to come to terms with and claim the support of the hierocratic clergy in times of weakness like the minority of Richard II or immediately after the revolt of 1381, just as easily as the hierocrats could find themselves making common cause with 'opposition' magnates like March, Arundel and Stafford during the Good Parliament of 1376 or Thomas of Woodstock and the rebellious Lords Appellant in 1387.[45] For his own part Wyclif acted as spokesman and propagandist for, and was duly protected by, the royalist party, which depended on an alliance between the two main princely factions formed by the royal households of the Black Prince and John of Gaunt during the 1370s – and supported by the massive system of patronage operated by the administration of the royal household itself.[46] By the 1380s the balance had moved in favour of the Black Prince's adherents, now controlled by his widow, Princess Joan, to form a court party from which Gaunt was gradually eased out.[47] But the Lollard Knights were king's men, in the same way that Wyclif called himself a 'king's clerk'. When he claimed in 1379/80 that he and his supporters were in a majority,[48] or the chroniclers lamented that the heretics were the larger part in the realm,[49] they were simply saying that the anti-hierocratic or royalist group had control of the government, witness Bishop Brinton's sour remarks about the same time that the temporal lords, knights and retainers, misled by 'extraordinary doctors' (like Wyclif), respected those who troubled God and the church most and were beyond ecclesiastical control.[50] To read 'royalist' where a contemporary ecclesiastical source would write 'Lollard' does a good deal to suggest why it is no longer very necessary to ask how Wyclif organised the Lollards: as a complex of aristocratic political groupings they were already there in the form of the families who administered the king's government as a court party well before Wyclif joined them himself and set about grafting an appropriate theology (as it seemed to him) onto their anti-papalism.

It would probably be a great deal easier to come to an accurate appreciation of the original nature of the Wycliffite movement if we could avoid the use of this term 'Lollard' altogether and recognise it for what it was: a term of abuse intended to be deliberately misleading. The first application of the expression to Wyclif and his followers that is recorded appears to have been the use of it by Henry Crump at Oxford in June 1382; and he was promptly suspended by the chancellor for doing so: 'suspenditur Henricus Crumps, magister in theologia ... et imponunt sibi perturbationem pacis quia vocavit haereticos Lollardos.'[51] Since Chancellor Rigg had just been soundly rebuked by the Blackfriars Council for not condemning the Oxford Wycliffites and was now supposed to be thoroughly cowed, this belated spurt of defiance suggests that the term was strongly resented. From now on the hierocratic party mounted a very effective propaganda operation designed to equate the royalists with *lollers*, low class idle rascals,[52] and were considerably aided by the failure of the 1381 Revolt, which left the Wycliffites branded not only with heresy and sedition, but worse, with being peasants or 'peasant-lovers'. And, in short, what the Wycliffites were accused of being they eventually became: in course of time they ceased to be a party and became a sect, although it was not until after the collapse of the Oldcastle Rising thirty years later that they finally lost their aristocratic and political character. During the remainder of the fourteenth century political power, albeit on the decline overall, kept Lollardy respectable precisely because it was still seen as royalism

– and monarchies do not normally burn people who seek to enhance the royal power. It was only when Lollardy lost its political nature and became a religion of the politically unimportant that it was deemed desirable to let its members be tortured and executed. Fifteenth-century Lollards welcomed Wyclif's admonitions that true Christians were humble and poor because this was what they literally were for the most part. But their fourteenth-century progenitors had needed to be urged to be humble for the very reason that they *had* great political power and influence – and to be poor, not in the sense of getting rid of their wealth, but in the more specialised meaning of recognising that they had nothing of their own, but held this wealth from God and the realm, not as a matter of inherent private property right. Even the expression 'poor priest' is unhelpful, since it could be stretched to cover any royalist cleric, bishops more than anybody else. Poverty, for Wyclif, was far from being an actual physical lack of goods, but a willingness to accept that one was not the owner of lands and wealth, only a tenant, and that all material possessions were held from the king as vicar of God.[53] A royalist priest was supposed to be a poor priest by definition, just as Lollardy was a theory for royalists.

Finally, it should be emphasised that Lollardy was the outcome of the effective seizure of ecclesiastical sovereignty by the monarchy of Edward III between the 1340s and the 1370s – when the king required that the papal appointment of clergy to the English church by means of the provision system should either be abandoned or operate only under royal licence; when papal taxation virtually ceased in the end to operate at all; and when the crown insisted that it had the right of excluding papal legates from the realm and of forbidding appeals to Rome. There was hardly any need for the English king to claim to be *caput Ecclesiae*. As Wyclif himself commented, it is only necessary for the pope to recognise that he no longer has legal rights in England without the royal consent, and that papal authority in England is subject to the royal supremacy and English law, for the reformation to be complete. To see Wyclif and his movement in perspective one needs to see them against the background of a kingdom which had already largely negated papal power in practice, and had to all intents and purposes come to see itself as an autonomous national church. That this, from a strictly hierocratic standpoint, made it a kingdom of heretics can hardly be in doubt. As Gordon Leff has put it,[54] what distinguished heresy from mere dissent or heterodoxy is not simple disagreement about the content of the faith, but the practical political error of refusing to submit to ecclesiastical authority. Heresy was not deviation from the faith so much as deviation from the faith as defined and authorised by the Roman church. On this basis it is simply not true that there was no widescale heresy in England before 1380: it was so heretical that everybody had to pretend that it wasn't. By the same reasoning it would make much more sense to regard Lollardy as a movement which, as its political power drained away and its adherents became detectable more on account of their views on matters like the eucharist, images and pilgrimages, was one which moved from heresy to dissent. But in practice as it became less dangerous so it was the more vigorously persecuted. It is part of what we might call the hypocrisy of heresy that powerful denials of papal authority stood a good chance of being treated with respect, whilst the full weight of ecclesiastical censure was reserved for the heretic who was least capable of defending himself. If we are going to describe the *secta Lollardis* as a protest movement, it must be seen in the first instance as an official protest by a quasi-theocratic monarchy against the continuing claims of papal supremacy, not as a protest movement in the popular sense of the term. But this may serve as a salutary reminder about the dangers of too readily equating medieval heresy with popular movements, or rather, of seeing popular movements as the most significant form and aspect of heresy.

NOTES

1. Henry Knighton, *Chronicon* (ed. J. R. Lumby, R.S., London, 1895), ii. 184; also 182, 183, 187, 191; Thomas Walsingham, *Chronicon Angliae* (ed. E. M. Thompson, R.S., London, 1876), p. 377. Wyclif himself preferred to call it the *secta Christi*: e.g. *De potestate papae*, 6, p. 110 (all references are to the Wyclif Society editions).
2. Knighton, ii. 185, 'In tantum namque in suis laboriosis dogmatibus praevaluerunt quod mediam partem populi aut maiorem partem suas sectae adquisierunt'.
3. M. D. Lambert, *Medieval Heresy: Popular Movements from Bogomil to Hus* (London, 1977), p. 229.
4. Ibid., p. 220.

5. Knighton, ii. 183; *Eulogium Historiarum* (ed. F. S. Haydon, R.S., London, 1863), iii. 351, 355.

6. H. L. Cannon, 'The Poor Priests: A Study in the Rise of English Lollardy', *Annual Report of the American Historical Association for 1899* (Washington, 1900), i. 451–82. This account was followed for the most part by H. B. Workman, *John Wyclif* (Oxford, 1926), ii. 201–5.

7. See the alleged confession of John Ball in 1381: *Fasciculi Zizaniorum* (ed. W. W. Shirley, R.S., London, 1858), pp. 273–4; and the mandate by the bishop of Worcester of 10 August, 1387; which charged Hereford, Aston, Parker, Swinderby and Purvey as 'conspirati in collegio illicito ... ritu Lollardorum confoederati', Wilkins, *Concilia*, iii. 202.

8. *Eulogium Historiarum*, iii. 355, 'Discipuli praefati Iohannis studuerunt in compilationibus sermonum et sermones fratrum congregaverunt, euntes per totam Angliam doctrinam huius sui magistri praedicabant,...'

9. Wilkins, *Concilia*, iii. 202–3.

10. Walsingham, *Historia Anglicana* (ed. H. T. Riley, R.S., London, 1863–4), i. 324; Knighton, ii. 184–5: who make the inevitable comment that like all heretics they were wolves in sheep's clothing. Unauthorised preaching by men 'in certain habits' was banned by Parliament on 26 May, 1382: *Rotuli Parliamentorum*, iii. 124–5. Wyclif discussed the view that russet symbolized assiduous labour in the Church: *De fundatione sectarum*, 4 *(Polemical Works)* i. 26–7; *Supplementum Trialogi*, p. 435, but it is far from clear whether his objections relate to russet itself or merely to the friars' use of it, and their subsequent fictitious claims 'de sanctitate habitu': *De nova praedicantia mandatorum*, 7 *(Polemical Works)*, i. 143; *Expositio Matthaei XXIII*, 3 *(Opera Minora)* p. 322. A number of cases of russet-wearing by Lollards have been confirmed.

11. E.g. *Of Poor Preaching Priests* (ed. F. D. Matthew, E.E.T.S. 74, London, 1880), pp. 276–7.

12. K. B. McFarlane, *Wycliffe and the Beginnings of English Nonconformity* (London, 1952), pp. 96–105; reprinted as *Wycliffe and English Non-Conformity* (Harmondsworth, 1972), pp. 83–91.

13. M. E. Aston, 'John Wycliffe's Reformation Reputation', *Past and Present*, 30 (1965), 23–51; V. H. H. Green, *Religion at Oxford and Cambridge* (London, 1964), pp. 63–5; G. Leff, 'John Wyclif: The Path to Dissent', *Proceedings of the British Academy*, lii (1967), 143–80 at 143; *Heresy in the Later Middle Ages* (Manchester, 1967), p. 494.

14. Lambert, *Medieval Heresy*, p. 232.

15. Ibid., pp. 234–7. J. H. Dahmus, *William Courtenay, Archbishop of Canterbury, 1381–1396* (Pennsylvania and London, 1966), pp. 78, 225, 322, not only thinks that the number of Wycliffites was very small during Wyclif's lifetime but queries whether there was a connection between Lollardy and Oxford.

16. J. R. Lander, *Conflict and Stability in Fifteenth-Century England* (London, 3rd ed., 1977), pp. 113–14.

17. For discussion and literature see Lambert, pp. 239–42, 257–64.

18. McFarlane, *Wycliffe*, p. 101.

19. Knighton, ii. 181; Walsingham, *Historia Anglicana*, ii. 159, cf. 217; *Chronicon Angliae*, p. 377.

20. M. E. Aston, 'Lollardy and Sedition, 1381–1431', *Past and Present*, 17 (1960), pp. 1–44; Lambert, pp. 217–18, 269.

21. K. B. McFarlane, *Lancastrian Kings and Lollard Knights* (Oxford, 1972), especially pp. 139–76.

22. W. T. Waugh, 'The Lollard Knights', *Scottish Historical Review*, xi (1913), pp. 55–92.

23. McFarlane, *Lancastrian Kings*, pp. 182–5; and note his remarks in *The Nobility of Late Medieval England* (Oxford, 1973), pp. 228f. on the aristocracy as having become generally literate in England from the middle of the fourteenth century.

24. *The Boke of Cupide* and *The Two Ways*: on which see now *The Works of Sir John Clanvowe* (ed. V. J. Scattergood: Cambridge and Ipswich, 1975).

25. G. Mathew. *The Court of Richard II* (London, 1968).

26. Cf. Scattergood, p. 25; and for the unsolved problems of Chaucer's Lollard sympathies see my remarks in *Bulletin of the John Rylands Library*, lii (1958–9).

27. *Lancastrian Kings*, pp. 222–5.

28. E.g. *De civili dominio*, ii. 5, pp. 39–41; iii. 22, p. 463: *De Ecclesia*, 15, pp. 340–1; *De officio regis*, 3, pp. 59–62.

29. For some examples, Lambert, pp. 237–9.

30. *Behemoth* (ed. F. Tönnies, London, 1889), pp. 39, 5; *English Works* (London, 1839–45), ii. 172.

31. J. H. Fisher, 'Wyclif, Langland, Gower and the Pearl Poet on the Subject of Aristocracy'. *Studies in Medieval Literature in honor of A. C. Baugh* (ed. MacE. Leach: Philadelphia, 1961), pp. 139–57; also L. J. Daly, 'Walter Burley and John Wyclif on Some Aspects of Kingship', *Mélanges Eugène Tisserant* (Vatican City, 1964), iv. 163–84 at 170–1, although both writers fail to appreciate that this preference for aristocracy applies equally to the clergy – Wyclif's well known view that the rule of judges is better than kings refers to the rule of priests, provided of course that they follow the apostolic way of life. Ironically Adam Easton, *Defensorium*. I. iv. 42, criticised him for not saying this.

32. *De eucharistia*, 9. p. 320; *De apostasia*, 7, p. 88.

33. *De officio regis*, 7, p. 181; cf. *De civili dominio*, ii. 2, p. 12; *De Ecclesia*, 15, p. 331.

34. E.g. *Trialogus*, iv. 18, p. 307; iv. 19, pp. 312–14.

35. Particularly valuable here is W. Mallard, 'Dating the *Sermones Quadraginta* of John Wyclif', *Medievalia et Humanistica*, xvii (1966), 86–105.

36. Walsingham, *Chronicon Anglia*, p. 117, 'sed de ecclesia in ecclesiam percurrendo auribus insereret plurimorum insanias suas falsas'.

37. In *De civili dominio*, ii and iii, which appear to have been compiled during 1377, but were probably not complete until early in 1378: see in particular ii. 13, pp. 165–6; iii. 1, pp. 1–2; 2, p. 35; 20, p. 417.

38. On which now J. H. Harvey, *The Black Prince and his Age* (London, 1976), pp. 724, 87–8, 92.

39. *De civili dominio*, ii, 14, pp. 174-S, 177–8.

40. *De veritate sacrae scripturae*, 21, ii. 156–7, 171–2; 23, ii. 230.

41. Walsingham, *Chronicon Angliae*, p. 118.

42. Cf. E. D. McShane, *A Critical Appraisal of the Antimendicantism of John Wyclif* (Rome, 1950). As J. P. Whitney argued in *Essays in History presented to R. L. Poole* (ed. H. W. C. Davis: Oxford, 1927), pp. 98–114 at p. 109, it was the loss of support from the friars which was crucial, not the eucharistic issue.

43. M. H. Keen, *England in the Later Middle Ages* (London, 1973), pp. 16–21.

44. The most useful recent studies of Sudbury, Courtenay and Arundel are by W. C. Warren, J. H. Dahmus and M. E. Aston respectively.

45. Cf. G. A. Holmes, *The Good Parliament* (Oxford, 1975); A. Goodman, *The Loyal Conspiracy: The Lords Appellant under Richard II* (London, 1971).

46. J. A. Tuck, 'Richard II's System of Patronage', *The Reign of Richard II. Essays in Honour of May McKisack* (ed. F. R. H. du Boulay and C. M. Barron: London, 1971), pp. 1–20.

47. R. H. Jones, *The Royal Policy of Richard II* (Oxford, 1968); J. A. Tuck, *Richard II and the English Nobility* (London, 1973), and his introduction to the paperback edition of G. M. Trevelyan, *England in the Age of Wycliffe* (London, 1972); cf. G. Mathew, *The Court of Richard II*, pp. 18–19.

48. *Responsiones ad XVIII argumenta Radulfi Strode*, 3, p. 198, 'Ideo faciamus ut fideles Christi milites quod in nobis est, quia certe sumus quod plures nobiscum sunt quam cum illis'.

49. Knighton, ii. 185: See above at note 2.

50. For references see W. J. Brandt, 'Church and Society in the Late Fourteenth Century: A Contemporary View', *Medievalia et Humanistica*, xiii (1960), pp. 56–67 at p. 59.

51. *Fasciculi Zizaniorum*, pp. 311–12.

52. The most convenient short discussion of the term is in Workman, i. 327. Both Knighton, ii. 184, and Walsingham, *Chronicon Angliae*, p. 377, say that the name was given to the Wycliffites by the *vulgus*.

53. See my 'Predestination, Property and Power: Wyclif's Theory of Dominion and Grace', *Studies in Church History*, ii (1965), pp. 220–36.

54. *Heresy and Dissent*, i. vii and 1–5

7

ROYAL PATRONAGE AND ANTI-PAPALISM
FROM OCKHAM TO WYCLIF

by MICHAEL WILKS

O XFORD scholarship in the fourteenth century, focusing on
Ockham and Wyclif, is a topic which might have been ideally
chosen to appeal to the late and much lamented Beryl Smalley
and, had she lived to participate in the Oxford Conference proceedings, it
is hard to imagine that this would not have been in a very real sense her
conference. Regretfully however, it had to become the occasion for the
publication of her volume of memorial essays,[1] to which the present
collection must appear in some sense as a sequel. I hope that the following
pages can be seen as my own personal tribute to a great scholar who,
unlikely as it may seem, I was privileged for a quarter of a century to be
able to regard as a friend and correspondent. Her immediate and
instinctive kindness to a very awkward young student is something to be
remembered with very warm personal gratitude. I had been working on
the publicists of the first half of the fourteenth century, and had been
inclined to draw a line after Ockham: she encouraged me to continue into
the later part of the century and attempt to deal with Wyclif. He became a
common bond between us, despite the great differences in our particular
interests, attitudes and approach. She would occasionally remind me that
someone whose working life was spent in Cambridge and London had no
business to be dealing with Oxford scholarship and had little hope of
understanding it properly. This is, of course, very true. Oxford philosophy
tended to be Aristotelian and nominalistic: its theology, we are told,
neoplatonic, Augustinian, realist. Yet when they left Oxford to find
positions at the royal and papal courts, the Aristotelian nominalists might
end up as exponents of papal supremacy, whereas it was the allegedly
Augustinian realists who are to be found maintaining the rights of the
crown. It is all very mysterious, very Oxford, and I shall not attempt to
solve these problems here.[2] Instead, I shall turn to the safer prospect of
comparing and contrasting an aspect of the political theory of the more
mature Ockham and the not so young Wyclif. That they were the two

[1] *The Bible in the Medieval World* ed. K. Walsh and D. P. Wood *SCH, Subsidia* 4, (1985).
[2] But see my suggestion that Wyclif at least can be absolved from the charge of inconsistency on
this account: 'The Early Oxford Wyclif: Papalist or Nominalist?' *SCH* 5 (1969), pp. 69–98.

most outstanding anti-papal English writers of the fourteenth century is not in doubt. I suggest that even the Oxford Conference cannot manage to rehabilitate them as Catholics, although it might decide that they would find a place in the modern Church of England. Surely, if he was alive today, William of Ockham would be an Anglican bishop—of some safely remote see, like Durham perhaps—whereas Wyclif would, I suspect, still be complaining that he was not, and would remain an academic, possibly Dean of Peterhouse, if he was once again forced out of Oxford.

Despite their common fate as refugees from the same university, William of Ockham and John Wyclif shared the experience of writing against the Avignon papacy on behalf of the English monarchy. They both wrote for the same king, Edward III, one at the beginning, the other at the end, of his long reign. But the comparison is bound to be an unbalanced one. Whereas after 1370 virtually all of Wyclif's enormous output was intended either directly or indirectly for the benefit of the monarchy, and in particular John of Gaunt, Ockham is only known to have written for Edward III on one, not very successful, occasion. Nor did he write at his usual length. The *moderni*, says Ockham sententiously (and one is not clear whether he is referring to his colleagues or his opponents), are sickened by prolix works and rejoice in brevity,[3] and the *An princeps* is in Ockhamist terms a relatively short treatise. As Professor Offler has reasonably argued in his introduction to the text, it probably dates to about 1338, the year that Edward III of England landed in Flanders on the first stage of his proposed invasion of France to secure the French crown; and the year that Ockham's protector, the self-styled Roman emperor Louis IV (Louis of Bavaria, but claiming to be the fourth Louis in descent from Charlemagne), designated Edward as an imperial vicar charged with the conquest of 'the greater part of the kingdom of France', thereby giving Edward formal recognition of his insistence that he was engaged on a just war.

We do not know the circumstances under which Ockham came to write the tract, although the effusive address 'to the most serene and most glorious lord King Edward'

> Magnanimum hactenus et invictum ac per gratiam Dei perpetuis temporibus non vincendum Anglorum regem Eduardum, generis claritate florentem, fama celebrem, corporali venustate decorum,

---

[3] *An princeps, prologus*, 'quia gaudent brevitate moderni super prolixis operibus nauseantes,' *Guillelmi de Ockham: Opera Politica* i (Manchester, 2nd. ed. 1974) p. 228.

> potestate sublimem, affluentem moribus, gratiosum et strenuum
> probitate ac ardua aggredientem intrepide . . .[4]

this effusion may perhaps suggest that, since Edward was due to visit the
Rhineland the following year, the intention was to present the work to the
king in person. Perhaps Ockham even hoped to escape from his exile in
Munich and return to England again. If so, it would have been politic to
have recognised Edward as king of France as well as England, but the tract
does not do this. Indeed, we have no evidence that it was ever completed.
The work exists in only two incomplete copies, one of them itself partially
a summary. As we have it, the work does not reach as far as its announced
intention of justifying the treaty made between Edward and Louis in the
summer of 1337: a third or half of it is entirely missing. Nevertheless, it is
Ockham's first directly 'political' polemic, and, as I have said, the only
known occasion on which he wrote for the king of England.

At first sight this little tract does not appear to be very significant nor,
let us admit it, very exciting. Ockham seems to have done little more than
stick an English label on a short statement of the general principles of
Church and government which he would elaborate later in the great
Dialogue or the *Eight Questions on Papal Power* and other writings. The
prime purpose, he says,[5] is to show whether the king can be helped to
pursue his just war by using ecclesiastical wealth, on the grounds that
defence of the realm and the royal rights in wartime creates a case of
urgent necessity in which the crown can override the normal rights of
private ownership, and the king is entitled to make free use of his subjects'
possessions according to need, even if the pope forbids it. This claim is so
much a commonplace of medieval (and modern) political theory that it
does not merit discussion here.

In any case it is the possibility of a papal prohibition which seems to
have been foremost in Ockham's mind, and to forestall this he

---

[4] I, p. 229.

[5] *Prologus*, p. 228, 'abbreviatum faciendo sermonem conabor ostendere quod serenissimus ac
gloriosissimus princeps et dominus, dominus Eduardus Dei gratia rex Anglorum, non solum
per laicos, sed etiam per praelatos saeculares et religiosos ac ceteros clericos sui dominii de
bonis ecclesiae contra inimicos ipsum hostiliter invadentes iuraque eius usurpantes iniuste,
non obstante quocunque humano statuto, sententia vel processu, prohibitione vel praecepto,
etiam si a vero summo pontifice emanaret, licite et de iure, immo meritorie, si pura assit
intentio, est iuvandus; et quod si contra ipsum etiam a vero summo pontifice aliqua de facto
ferretur sententia propter hoc, quod iustitiam suam prosequitur, nulla esset et minime
formidanda vel servanda'. Ockham cannot of course resist the temptation to doubt whether
Benedict XII was a true pope, and one notes his familiar principle that papal law is only
human law.

immediately launches into an attack on the claim that the pope has a plenitude of power in both spiritual and temporal matters, so that everything and everyone in the whole world (*universitas mortalium*) is subject to his power. Innocent III had declared that when Christ said to Peter, 'Whatsoever you shall bind on earth shall be bound in Heaven', 'whatsoever' meant precisely what it said and nothing was excluded: 'nihil excipit'.[6] The reader of the first half dozen chapters can be forgiven for thinking that the tract was just another convenient peg on which to hang another of Ockham's obsessive diatribes against papal sovereignty, and another rather tedious restatement of the traditional lay theory of dualism, of a duality of temporal and spiritual powers.

True enough, Ockham begins with the need to separate secular and spiritual powers and functions, but there is an indication that he is going to offer us something less hackneyed when he indicates that Christianity has to be a reasonable religion, a matter of right reason based on authentic scriptures.[7] God did not give the pope a general authorisation to say and do anything he pleases: infallibility attaches only to *scriptura sacra et ratio recta* (which is why, he comments, the pope needs a general council to make definitions of the faith binding on all Christians, and, he cannot help adding, to determine when the pope himself contravenes the truth). Holy scripture needs to be sanely amd rightly understood and supported by infallible reason—it is right reason to which infallibility attaches rather than papal power.[8] And one recalls that one of the main reasons why Ockham found himself before the papal court at Avignon in the first place was not that he had impugned the orthodox faith of the eucharist—indeed, as Gordon Leff

---

[6] 1, pp. 229–30, citing *Matt.* xvi:19 and *Decretales*, I. xxxiii. 6, and concluding: 'Christus autem, promittendo beato Petro et successoribus eius potestatem super reliquos, nichil excepit nec determinavit nec diffinivit, sed indistincte et generaliter dixit: *Quodcunque ligaveris*, etc.; ergo nec nobis aliquid omnino licet excipere; papa ergo a Christo talem habet plenitudinem potestatis, ut modo praesupposito omnia possit.' Also 6, p. 250, 'Sed forte dicet aliquis quod papa generali legatione Christi fungitur in terris; ergo omnia absque omni exceptione ei intelliguntur concessa.'

[7] 6, p. 251, 'et quando ratio recta fundata in scripturis authenticis'.

[8] 6, p. 251, 'Huic respondetur quod prima regula et infallibilis in huiusmodi est scriptura sacra et ratio recta; et ideo ad illum spectat per assertionem veridicam explicare et determinare huiusmodi casus, qui quoad huiusmodi scripturam sacram sane et recte intelligit et infallibili innititur rationi. Ad concilium tamen generale, et etiam ad papam, si intellexerit veritatem in huiusmodi, pertinet per diffinitionem authenticam habentem vim obligandi cunctos fideles ne contrarium doceant, explicare et determinare in huiusmodi veritatem. Si tamen papa contra veritatem in huiusmodi determinare praesumpserit, sibi nullatenus est credendum; sed illi, qui per scripturas sacras et rationem necessariam sciunt ipsum errare, loco et tempore opportunis, aliis circumstantiis debitis observatis, eum reprobare tenentur, . . .'

has pointed out,[9] he used his razor to deny the remanence of substance in the bread and wine in favour of transubstantiation—but the complaint was that he went to enormous lengths to try to show that it was reasonable. Transubstantiation was to be accepted not because the pope pronounced on it, but because it could be shown to be right and reasonable.

In the present context, said Ockham, the absolute power of the pope could *not* be right and reasonable because Christ had established Christianity as a law of liberty,[10] in fact as a law which enhances the liberty that men already enjoy naturally. Christianity cannot *reduce*, but on the contrary only *improve*, the liberty of man under the law of nature. The Gospel law, the *lex evangelica*, does not merely liberate Christians from the servitude of sin and the Mosaic law, but also requires that man under government retains the liberties inherent in natural law. The liberties of the faithful come from both God and nature.[11] They are to be upheld by both faith and reason.

---

[9] G. Leff, *William of Ockham: The Metamorphosis of Scholastic Discourse* (Manchester and Totowa, N.J., 1975) p. 599.

[10] 2, p. 230, 'Quod igitur papa in temporalibus et spiritualibus talem non habeat plenitudinem potestatis, multis modis probatur. Lex enim Christiana ex institutione Christi est lex libertatis, ita quod per ordinationem Christi non est maioris nec tantae servitutis quantae fuit lex vetus.'

[11] 2, pp. 231-2, '. . . quod Christiani per legem evangelicam et instructionem Christi sunt a servitute multiplici liberati, et quod non sunt per legem evangelicam tanta servitute oppressi quanta Iudaei per legem veterem premebantur. . . . quod misericordia Dei voluit religionem Christianam esse liberiorem quoad onera, etiam non de se illicita, quam fuerint existentes sub veteri lege; et per consequens lex evangelica non solum dicitur lex libertatis quia liberat Christianos a servitute peccati et legis Mosaicae, sed etiam quia Christiani per legem evangelicam nec maiori nec tanta servitute premuntur quanta fuit servitus veteris legis. . . . Non enim potest quicunque dominus temporalis habere maius dominium vel potestatem super servum suum quam ut possit omnia praecipere ei, quaecunque non sunt contra legem divinam nec contra ius naturale. Ad illa enim, quae sunt contraria legi divinae et iuri naturali indispensabili, nulla potestas imperatoris, regis vel cuiuscunque alterius respectu cuiuscunque servi se extendit'; 6, p. 248, 'Quia, cum libertas naturalis, qua homines naturaliter sunt liberi et non servi, non sit ab universis ablata mortalibus per potestatem gladii materialis, . . . potestas gladii materialis ad illa, quae derogarent libertati et utilitati bonorum, nullatenus se extendit. Unde nec talem plenitudinem potestatis in temporalibus unquam habuit aliquis imperator, nec ante papatum nec post'; p. 251, 'ut per legationem generalem papa non habeat potestatem restringendi vel tollendi libertates fidelium concessa a Deo et natura'. As pointed out by A. S. McGrade, 'Rights, Natural Rights and the Philosophy of Law', *Cambridge History of Later Medieval Philosophy* (Cambridge, 1982) pp. 738-56 at 742-3, both the demand for a reasonable explanation in theology and the relationship between *dominium* and property were already key features of Ockham's position on Franciscan poverty. For the former see further B. Tierney, *The Origins of Papal Infallibility, 1150-1350* (London, 1972) espec. pp. 210-29. As regards the latter, an important source was Marsilius's use of *dominium* as opposed to *proprietas*, lordship versus ownership, to illustrate Aristotle's dictum that every word has many meanings: *Defensor pacis*, II. xii. 13-24 and 33.

I hasten to add that Ockham was not intending to suggest that conversion to Christianity returned man to a golden age of primitive natural equality. He accepted that sin required the introduction of government, private property and even slavery into the state of nature—but all these institutions had to be of a limited character since they were all in their way infringements of natural liberty. In the conditions prevailing since the Fall, kings were necessary and useful: they made the human laws under which societies now, so to speak, naturally operated. Kings might be appointed by God, but it was God acting through the agency of popular election or institution, as for example the Roman emperor was pre-eminently the choice of the people. And their powers were limited by what we would call fundamental natural rights: the power of neither emperor nor king nor anybody else, he declares here, extends beyond the limits of divine and natural law, even over slaves. In fact the rights of property, guaranteed by God and by nature, were essentially the sort of things that rulers were required to uphold—except in special cases. John Locke could hardly have put it better.

But none of this, said Ockham, has got anything to do with the pope. Christian emperors, kings and princes have temporal lordship and jurisdiction (*dominium et iurisdictio*), they have rights of ownership, possession of property, powers of command, not because they are Christian but because they are emperors, kings and princes—because, in other words, they are the successors of those emperors, kings and princes, who governed by natural right long before Christ came to earth.[12] The Bible and the Fathers agreed that pagans and infidels have a natural property right and so are true lords, and he promptly listed some thirty examples, mostly drawn from the Old Testament, in which the chosen people recognised the rights to land, property and possessions of their enemies.[13] Just as Joseph and Mary went to be taxed, and Christ himself

---

[12] 2, p. 235, 'Praeterea, imperatores Christiani, reges et principes ac alii laici et clerici multi habent veram *iurisdictionem* temporalem ac verum *dominium* temporalium rerum, et non a papa; ergo papa non habet in temporalibus huiusmodi plenitudinem potestatis. Antecedens probatur: Quia non veriorem *iurisdictionem* temporalem nec verius *dominium* temporalium rerum habuerunt imperatores pagani et alii infideles, nec ante incarnationem Christi nec post, quam habent nunc fideles.'

[13] 2, p. 235, 'Sed sanctarum serie scripturarum et testimoniis sanctorum patrum aperte colligitur quod multi infideles et ante et post incarnationem Christi habuerunt veram *iurisdictionem* temporalem et verum *dominium* temporalium rerum, et non a papa nec ab alio sacerdote fideli ... Ergo fideles habent vel habere possunt veram *iurisdictionem* temporalem et verum *dominium* temporalium rerum, et non a papa. Quod autem in scripturis divinis reperiatur expresse quod plerique infideles habuerunt veram *iurisdictionem* temporalem et verum

gave tribute money to an unconverted Caesar, so Abraham purchased the burial field of Ephron; Jacob recognised the property rights of Laban, Joseph the rights of the Egyptians (before they became tyrannical). Solomon gave the Galilean cities to Hiram of Tyre, whilst God instructed the Israelites to respect the rights of ownership which he had given to the children of Esau, to the Moabites and to the Ammonites. The powers that were, *were* ordained of God: and the prophets accepted the authority of the Syrian Hazael, the Persian Cyrus, the Babylonian Nebuchadnezzar in the same way and on the same terms that Paul appealed to Caesar and Christ recognised that Pontius Pilate had powers from above. By the time one has worked through this catalogue of pagan possession, one has a distinct feeling that Ockham thinks the purpose of the scriptures is to prove the rights of non-Christians.

Having done that, Ockham is left (as of course he always intended he should be) to face the question that if pagans, who covered the whole world, always had natural and divine rights to hold land and property, what was there left for Christ to give to Peter? It could not be land-lordship, property ownership, since that had already been acquired: neither Christ nor pope could be made into fixers of landmarks. What was there left? Only, Ockham answered, a superior jurisdiction which could be added on to what men already reasonably and rightly have, an additional jurisdiction dealing with other matters.[14] Temporal power means lordship, *dominium*, the rights of land ownership and other property, and has already been allocated: the additional spiritual power that Peter received by the Petrine Commission could only be a matter of *iurisdictio*. In this sense the papalists were right to define the pope as a *nomen iurisdictionis*, because jurisdiction was all he got, the right to issue Christian laws. The distinction between ownership, especially of land, and the power of command, *dominium* versus *iurisdictio*, became the key feature of Ockham's whole politial and ecclesiological system.

As Janet Coleman has recently indicated,[15] we cannot claim that the distinction between lordship and jurisdiction was original with Ockham.

---

dominium temporalium rerum, ita ut opinio contraria haereticalis debeat reputari, monstrari et probari possit aperte . . .': the list includes *Gen.* xxiii:17-20, xxxi:32-8, xli:35; *Deut.* ii:4-19; III *Reg.* ix:11, xix:15; II *Paralip.* xxxvi:22-3; *Dan.* ii:37-8, v:18.

[14] 6, p. 248, 'et ideo pontificium nova legis non est regulariter maioris potestatis in carnalibus, sed in spiritualibus quam fuerit pontificium veteris legis'.

[15] J. Coleman, '*Dominium* in Thirteenth- and Fourteenth-Century Political Thought and its Seventeenth-Century Heirs: John of Paris and Locke', *Political Studies* 33 (1985) pp. 73-100.

He borrowed it from John of Paris, and it seems to have been familiar to the more radical Thomists: John of Paris himself simply lifted it, unacknowledged, from Godfrey of Fontaines—and they all took it from Roman law. But William of Ockham was the first to realise its full potential, and to see that this question of land ownership could to a very large degree emasculate the papal claims. Christ, on earth, really could not have given what he no longer had (which was why the Devil could tempt him with an offer of all the kingdoms of the earth).

It remained true, as Ockham himself said, that Christ as God, Christ in Heaven, possessed everything, *dominium* as well as *iurisdictio*,[16] but this divine potential could not be made into actual ordained power below, since the earth, the land, was *in* time; and from this point of view the Incarnation was too late—landlordship was simply no longer there to be granted out. No vicar of Christ, on earth, could have received the potency which Christ might wield in heaven.[17] There was no ecclesiastical property ownership to be given to the apostles, because there was none left to give: those who seek to follow the *vita evangelica*, the apostolic way of life, must by definition be without *dominium*, property rights, ownership. It was almost as if Ockham was dismissing the whole question of Franciscan poverty which had occupied him so much for the previous decade. There really was nothing left to argue about. There was no such thing as ecclesiastical property in the sense of ownership or *dominium*: no friar, no monk, no cleric as a follower of Christ could do anything but *use* what already belonged to the laity by reasonable natural right. Jurisdiction might give a right to use, but it could not deprive an owner of lordship. They were two separate things.

In this way the *An princeps* not only looked back to the disputes over apostolic poverty, but also forward to the debates on imperial power which occupied Ockham so much in his later works. But here too the distinction between land and jurisdiction had, Ockham felt, already solved the problem: the question of a papal right to the Roman empire ought logically never to have arisen. The emperor, he says in a significant

---

[16] 4, pp. 239–40, 'quod non papa sed Christus universale dominium et possessionem habeat omnium temporalium rerum; quod verum est de Christo tam secundum divinitatem quam secundum humanitatem post resurrectionem et glorificationem; quod de papa nullatenus continet veritatem, quia Christus Petro, qui reliquit omnia propter Christum, omnium rerum dominium in generali non dedit'.

[17] 4, p. 241, 'Cum enim papa sit vicarius solummodo Christi, licet sit successor Petri, et vicarius alicuius ratione vicariatus non sit potestatis aequalis, sequitur quod papa non habet potestatem tantam, quantam habuit Christus.'

phrase, is 'miles in terris':[18] like one of his knights he is essentially a feudal lord precisely because he is a land holder—he operates within the sphere of *dominium*—and at a later date, as Professor McGrade has shown,[19] Ockham would go to considerable lengths to demonstrate that the pope had no *feudal* rights over the Empire—because the Empire was by definition a matter of land-ownership. This, of course, totally evaded the entire Augustinian argument employed by the papalists that the Roman empire had become the Universal Church, so that immediately the pope was *caput imperii*. But Ockham can hardly be criticised for not answering that, when his whole point was that the empire, being a land question, could only be discussed in feudal terms, as a principle of property ownership. Indeed it is ironic to find an English writer of the fourteenth century emphasising the importance of feudalism, just at a time when most English historians hasten to assure us that fourteenth-century feudalism was being bastardised out of existence. To Ockham, at least, there could be few things more important.

He did not wish to give the impression that the pope could not be a feudal lord: nor did he seek to abolish the papal states. But the point was that such lands could only come from the feudal superior, the emperor himself: 'cum patrimonium ecclesiae non a Christo immediate sed ex imperatoris habeat largitate'.[20] Whatever one's views on the morality of clerical possession, Ockham did not deny that clergy, like laity, had a natural right to private property (if they wished to avail themselves of it) and therefore could have holdings and tenures, regulated by the same human laws, the feudal laws, applicable to any tenant. All private property rights devolved from the king in England as the lord of the land, the landlord of the realm.[21] Ideally, the English clergy ought to have all their physical needs supplied by the laity, so that they did not need to possess, only to use. But anything given beyond this, their *possessiones superabun-*

---

[18] 6, p. 247.

[19] A. S. McGrade, *The Political Thought of William of Ockham* (Cambridge, 1974) pp. 87-92, cf. 137, 144-5.

[20] 5, p. 246.

[21] 7, p. 253, 'Quorum primum est quod praelati et clerici regi Anglorum subiecti res non possident temporales, praesertim superabundantes, iure divino, sed iure humano ab ipso rege manante. Quod Augustinus testatur expresse . . . et habetur in decretis, di. viii, c. *Quo iure*, ait, loquens de villis et aliis rebus ecclesiae [*Decretum*, d. 8 c. 1] . . . Ex quibus patenter ostenditur quod iure humano, scilicet regis, possessiones a clericis de dominio regis Angliae possidentur. Quod etiam ex scripturis divinis posset aperte probari pro eo quod Deus ministris novae legis nullam specialem possessionem dedit, sed solummodo ordinavit ut laici eis in suis necessitatibus providerent.'

dantes, was governed by the same laws as applied to anybody else: and therefore was only held conditionally, a grant with conditions.[22] All private property, being held from the king, as the embodiment of the realm, was subject to covenant, to a *pactum*, a contract which might be tacit rather than expressly stated, that the king could revert to his original proprietary rights over the property granted out.[23] He had the right of any patron to recall his grants for the common good and to defend the *patria*,[24] and whilst Ockham failed to make it clear whether he was talking in terms of a partial recovery like war taxation or outright dispossession, one can safely presume that the same principle covered both. Of the former there is no doubt: he refers to Edward III taking a 'iustum subsidium a clericis Angliae'.[25]

Provided that it was just, there was nothing that the pope could do about it. It was a matter of *dominium*, not *iurisdictio*, and the pope was

---

[22] 9, p. 257, 'Ad cuius evidentiam est sciendum quod papa non habet regulariter potestatem super temporalibus, praecipue superabundantibus, collatis a regibus et aliis fidelibus ecclesiis a iure divino, sed solummodo a iure humano, si dantes super datis ei potestatem aliquam concesserunt; et per consequens quantam potestatem reges Angliae vel superiores aut superior eis dederunt vel dedit papae super bona ecclesiastica, quae contulerunt ecclesiis, tantam habet et non maiorem. Hoc multipliciter posset ostendi. Nam . . . clerici res non possident temporales, maxime superabundantes, iure divino, sed solummodo iure humano, quod est ius imperatoris et regum; ergo papa non habet regulariter super temporalibus datis ecclesiis Anglicanis potestatem nisi iure regum'.

[23] 8, p. 255, 'Nam circa res, praecipue superabundantes, collatas ecclesiae a regibus Anglorum et aliis eisdem regibus subiectis, voluntas dantium et intentio est servanda, cum quilibet in donatione rei suae possit pactum et legem, quod vel quam vult, imponere; quod vel quam donatarius sive recipiens servare tenetur, . . . Sed rebus collatis ecclesiae, antequam darentur, tale fuit onus annexum, ut de eis subveniretur regi pro defensione patriae et iurium publicorum, a quo onere res collatae ecclesiis per reges Angliae sunt minime liberatae'; 9, p. 258, 'Rursus, sicut per praecedentia patet, quilibet in donatione seu traditione rei suae potest pactum et legem, quam vult, imponere; et per consequens potest ordinare quantam recipiens vel alius in ea habere debeat potestatem. Res autem concessae ecclesiis Anglicanis prius erant regum Angliae, et non papae; . . . Quare si reges Angliae nec tacite vel expresse super ipsis aliquam potestatem papae dederunt, papa super ipsis nullam habet regulariter potestatem. Dico autem tacite vel expresse . . .'

[24] 8, p. 257, 'Item, magis tenentur clerici regi ratione curae, quam habet de patria et omnibus, qui degunt in patria, quam ratione personae suae . . . Ergo multo magis, si rex pro defensione patriae et iurium publicorum auxilio indiget clericorum, sibi debent de bonis ecclesiae auxilium impendere opportunum.'

[25] 12, p. 266; also 9, p. 259, 'Reges autem Angliae non dederunt summo pontifici potestatem, ut quocunque statuto, prohibitione vel praecepto, sententia vel processu inhibere valeret clericis regi subiectis, ne eidem in guerra sua iusta subventionis subsidium exhiberent.' The development of the natural right of kings to initiate their own just wars during the thirteenth and fourteenth centuries is discussed by J. T. Johnson, *Ideology, Reason and the Limitation of War: Religious and Secular Concepts, 1200–1740* (Princeton, 1975). For the older doctrine that only the pope (or emperor) could authorise just wars see, e.g., F. H. Russell, *The Just War in the Middle Ages* (Cambridge, 1975); *SCH* 20 (1983); and here further literature.

confined to the latter: 'sciat sibi non dominium sed ministerium esse datum'.[26] He could be a lawyer, but not a landowner in his own right. The power of the keys extends 'ad crimina et peccata, non ad possessiones'.[27] He could only deal with issues which involved a question of right and wrong, of morality and justice—although more in the breach than the observance it would seem—but he was not to be involved in the administration of essentially feudal government. One may of course question the validity of the distinction: where does morality stop and property begin? Why should the government of land be essentially amoral? But at least the distinction in itself is clear enough as a simple proposition ... except that, of course, with Ockham nothing was ever simple. Having, perhaps uncharacteristically, allowed that the pope did possess jurisdiction in England, Ockham then did his best on one hand to whittle this jurisdiction down until it was paper thin. Oh yes, the pope could make legally binding court decisions—but in the normal way of things it was not for courts to enforce their own judgements: he was not to have the coercive power which would allow him to enforce his jurisdiction.[28] Enforcement could usually be better left to the lay power. Oh yes, the pope could declare what was right—but this was precisely what he should normally do: declare it, not command it. He could preach, inform, exhort: it ought to be a case of instructing rather than giving instructions.[29]

Yet on the other hand, as is well known, Ockham also adopted the Aristotelian principle of reciprocity. If the king had an occasional right on the basis of necessity to act as an absolute ruler and take his subjects' goods, even those of his clerical subjects, so, conversely, the pope had *in casu necessitatis* the right to intervene in temporal matters and, as Ockham put

---

[26] 6, p. 251.

[27] 4, p. 241.

[28] 4, pp. 241-2, 'Octavum notabile est quod potestas clavium regni caelorum data papae a Christo, ad peccata et crimina se extendens, non est regulariter coactiva, ... Sanctus enim Petrus recipiens claves regni caelorum a Christo generalem potestatem super omnia peccata, nullo excepto, recepit. Sed super peccata et crimina mere saecularia, quae iudices saeculares iuste et sufficienter punire parati fuerunt, non recepit beatus Petrus in foro contentioso potestatem coactivam, ne per potestatem datam beato Petro potestas saecularium iudicium totaliter esset absorpta'.

[29] 6, p. 249, 'Non enim fuit Ieremias prophete [i. 10] constitutus fuit super gentes et super regna, ut dominaretur temporalia regnis et gentibus, et suae arbitrio voluntatis tollere posset res et iura temporalia quorumcunque et ea quibus placeret conferre; sed constitutus fuit super gentes et super regna, ut sarculo praedicationis et exhortationis vitia et peccata evelleret, destrueret, disperderet et dissiparet, et ut virtutes plantaret et aedificaret'; also p. 247, 'Gladius enim materialis dupliciter ad papalem pertinet potestatem. Uno modo, ut eius informatione et exhortatione, immo si necesse fuerit iussione ... ad nutum, id est informationem, exhortationem vel praeceptum, ...' The Marsilian influence seems clear.

it, do all things necessary for the rule and government of the faithful. There was a papal prerogative right, a *praerogativa Petri*.[30] Innocent III had been quite right to urge that the pope could deal with all matters *ratione peccati*, by reason of sin, so long as it was understood that this was an occasionally used higher power which was only to be activated in emergencies: in these circumstances, 'whatsoever' actually meant 'whatsoever', if it came within the ambit of sin and crime.[31] And elsewhere Ockham tells us that the pope even has the right to translate the empire (as he had,done in 800)—so that the most massive transfer of land and property ownership there could be was permissible if it was classified not as a normal property transaction, but as a retaliation for crimes committed against the Roman church.[32]

It is doubtful whether Edward III, had he ever seen it, would have been much impressed by the *An princeps*. There were too many loose ends; and ultimately Ockham was proposing a compromise—uneven perhaps—but manifestly a division between the competing claims of papacy and lay government. That might have suited contemporary imperial policy. Despite the declaration of the princes at Rhense and Louis' own decree *Licet iuris* in 1338, Louis of Bavaria had not given up hope of legitimising himself by coming to an accommodation with the pope, and he became progressively more rather than less anxious to do so. But it is hard to imagine that the work would have been welcomed by Edward III. True, it offered a justification for Edward having a natural right to tax and confiscate the property of churches; but it allowed him to do so on the basis of his power as a king, not as a specifically Christian king. A benevolent pagan could be

[30] 4, p. 240; p. 242, 'Qualem etiam potestatem coactivam habuit beatus Petrus et habent successores ipsius casualiter super crimina saecularis; in quibus autem casibus huiusmodi potestatem habeant coativam, non est exprimendum ad praesens.' Also 6, pp. 248–9, '. . . licet casualiter etiam in carnalibus sive temporalibus non sit minoris potestatis'; p. 252, 'Qui etiam casualiter tam in spiritualibus aliis, quae scilicet regulariter supererogationis sunt et in quibus fideles regulariter licite possunt quod volunt facere, quam in temporalibus, quantam habet plenitudinem potestatis: ut scilicet in casu, quo necesse est talia fieri et nemo est, ad quem talia spectent, qui de ipsis diligentiam habeat congruentem, ipse habeat potestatem de talibus disponendi; cuius dispositioni, si iusta et utilis fuerit, alii obedire tenentur . . .'

[31] 5, p. 245–6, 'Ad auctoritatem autem Innocentii III . . . respondetur quod Innocentius intelligit Christum nichil excepisse a regulari et casuali potestate summi pontificis, super quo pro utilitate communi necessario expedit ipsum potestatem habere. Non autem intelligit quod Christus nichil exceperit nec excipi voluerit a regulari potestate Petri et sucessorum eius, . . .' citing *Decretales* IV. xvii. 13. For Innocent III's use of *ratione peccati* see *Decretales*, II. i 13; *praerogativa Petri*, PL 217. 549 and 915; *nihil excipit*, PL 217. 481 and 1056.

[32] See further Wilks, *The Problem of Sovereignty in the Later Middle Ages* (Cambridge, 1963) espec. p. 316.

allowed as much—hardly the sort of argument to impress a ruler who had just announced that he was *rex Christianissimus*, the most Christian king of all. One can surmise that Edward would have been much happier with an analysis of earlier medieval precedents, such as he later had from Wyclif.

Above all, Ockham's theory urged a dualism of temporal and spiritual powers: an unusual type of dualism, perhaps, not between two types of jurisdiction but between jurisdiction and *dominium*, but nevertheless a division which, if it gave landed rights to the king, still left the papacy with a substantial, albeit circumscribed, measure of jurisdictional power in England. It would not have disestablished the system of ecclesiastical courts: it said nothing about the papal right of appointment to episcopal sees and other benefices. Yet it was precisely the *principle* of papal jurisdiction in England which Edward III specifically denied on a whole series of occasions throughout his reign. For forty years the English government not only regularly taxed the English clergy (technically these were voluntary grants, although that formality did nothing to lessen the level of ecclesiastical protest), but denied that papal authority could be exercised in England without the royal consent, ordering that papal letters considered to be derogatory to royal rights should be seized and their carriers arrested (1338, 1343), restricting papal taxation and (as many Oxford scholars discovered) access and appeals to Rome (e.g. in the Statute of *Praemunire* 1353), confiscating estates and benefices held by foreign clergy (1337, 1346), and in the Statue of Provisors of 1351 asserting that the holy church of England (*sainte eglise d'Angleterre*) had been founded by the king and his ancestors, and the counts, barons and nobles of his kingdom and their ancestors, for the purpose of teaching them and their people the law of God and to do good works . . . a document so extreme that by implication it deprived all clerics of all rights altogether. It was in the Parliament of 1363 that Edward threatened to disendow the clergy for damaging the rights of lay patrons, a decade before Wyclif took up the theme.

But perhaps the feature of the *An princeps* that the English government during the fourteenth century would have found least acceptable was Ockham's treatment of the scriptures, especially the Old Testament. For Ockham, as we have seen, the prime value of the Old Testament was to demonstrate pagan rights to lordship of property. The ancient land of England might (in a rather take it or leave it fashion) have become Christianised as a sort of optional extra, and the Bible merely showed that the lord of the land had lost nothing by the conversion. But what Edward III needed was a justification of his right to act as a supreme ecclesiastical overlord on a Biblical basis—not the Bible recognising natural right—but the Bible as specifically the book of the *ecclesia Anglicana* . . . and that was what Wyclif gave him. Wyclif could of course take full benefit of the spectacular upsurge in Biblical and theological studies which began at Oxford in the 1320s[33] in a way that Ockham never had the opportunity to do. But it is doubtful that Ockham would ever have wished to argue that the English had adopted the scriptures in the way that Wyclif took for granted. I am not referring here to the translation of the Bible into the vernacular (although that might well become a logical concomitant), but to an adoption and absorption of the Bible as the whole book of English life, a *liber vitae anglicanae*; and to a conception of England as a *populus Dei* on the model of the chosen people of Israel, to convince the English, not only that God was an Englishman,[34] but also that England was itself the inheritance, the *haereditas Dei*, the promised land and a new Jerusalem of which the scriptures had spoken.[35]

To take one example, there are the extremely interesting speeches (apparently made together) by two newly-appointed royal officials, the chancellor and the chamberlain, to the Parliament of January 1377. It was the jubilee year of Edward III, his last Parliament, and one in which Richard (II) was officially adopted as the heir to the throne. Both speakers, the chancellor, Adam Houghton, who had been given the royal pocket bishopric of St. David's, and Sir Robert Ashton, the chamberlain, were associates of John of Gaunt of long standing, and were about to be sent to the interminable negotiations with the papal legates in Bruges about papal taxation in England. Wyclif, who had himself been employed on the same business, was now in London, running from pulpit to pulpit,[36] preaching against Gregory XI's claims to jurisdiction in England for all he was worth. Since the French war was at that point going extremely badly, the main purpose of the joint speech was to rouse patriotic fervour by

---

[33] B. Smalley, *English Friars and Antiquity in the Early Fourteenth Century* (Oxford 1960) pp. 30–2; K. Walsh, *A Fourteenth-Century Scholar and Primate: Richard FitzRalph in Oxford, Avignon and Armagh* (Oxford, 1981) pp. 31–2.

[34] J. W. McKenna. 'How God became an Englishman', *Tudor Rule and Revolution: Essays for G. R. Elton*, ed. D. J. Guth and J. W. McKenna (Cambridge, 1982) pp. 25–43.

[35] For French precedents from the twelfth century onwards see my 'Alan of Lille and the New Man', *SCH* 14 (1977) pp. 137–57, espec. pp. 148–9; *Problem of Sovereignty*, pp. 428–30; also J. R. Strayer, 'France: The Holy Land, the Chosen People, and the Most Christian King', *Action and Conviction in Early Modern Europe: Essays in Memory of E. H. Harbison*, ed. T. K. Rabb and J. E. Siegel (Princeton, 1969) pp. 3–16; and in general, P. S. Lewis, *Later Medieval France: The Polity* (London, 1968).

[36] Walsingham, *Chronicon Angliae* (RS, 1874) p. 117.

referring to the many spectacular English victories over France in previous years. The reason for this divine favour, said the chancellor, was that England had experienced (one notices the past tense) a kind of reformation, a 'great amendment' or renewal and enrichment, and under the leadership of Edward III and other members of the royal family had been honoured by God as never before.

> Et que nostre dit Seigneur le Roy soit benoit de Dieu est provez par l'Escriture [*Ps.*, cxxvii.3–6] que dit, 'Uxor tua sicut vitis habundans in lateribus domus tue', & auxint, 'Filii tui sicut novelle olivarum in circuitu mense tue'. Et tantost bien apres l'Escripture dit en meisme le lieu, 'Ut videas Filios Filiorum tuorum.' Et sur ceo y ent suit la conclusion, 'Ecce sic benedicetur homo.' Et regardez, Seigneurs, si unques nul Roy Cristien, ou autre Seigneur al monde, eust si noble & graciouse Dame a femme, ou tielles Filz come nostre Seigneur le Roy ad euz, Princes, Ducs, & autres. Qar du Roi & ses ditz Filz toutes Cristiens ont euz doute, & par eux ad le Roialme d'Engleterre tresnoblement amendez, honurez, & enrichiz, & pluis que unques mes ne fuist en temps de nul autre Roy.[37]

They would, in the words of the Psalm which he was paraphrasing, see the good of Jerusalem all the days of their lives because—and this was the crucial point—England had now become the Holy Land itself.

> Et issint vous avez ce que l'Escripture dist [*Ps.*, cxxvii.6], 'Pacem super Israel', paix sur Israel, pur quel Israel est a entendu l'eritage de Dieu, q'est Engleterre. Qar je pense vraiment que Dieux ne voussist unqes avoir honurez ceste Terre par manere come il fist Israel, par grantes Victories de lour Enemys, s'il ne fust q'il l'ad choise pur son heritage. Laquele Paix nous doine Dieux.[38]

I do truly believe, he said, that God would never have honoured our land with such great victories if they were not given to use in the same way that

[37] *Rotuli Parliamentorum* (London, 1767) ii. 361–2, para. 6. After a somewhat laboured comparison between the king and the converted St. Paul (paras. 5–6), the former is described as the elect of God and a vessel of grace in both temporal and spiritual matters, whom every subject should obey as *pars corporis principis*: '& si Dieux plest, il est & toutdys mais ferra, le Vessel de grace ou le Vessel de election Dieu (cf. *Act.* ix:15). Du quel vessel touz ses Subgitz y treront, et auront grace & comfort de bien faire si bien espirituelment come temporelment'; para. 8, 'Et par cest chief dont j'ai parle j'entende nostre Seigneur le Roy, q'est nostre chief & nostre soverain, & nous touz sumes ses membres & subgitz'.

[38] ii. 362, para. 11.

God gave victory to the Israelites. England is now as naturally and truly the divine inheritance, the *haereditas Dei*, as Israel was then: and he prayed for peace over Israel against all the depredations of the Avignon pope and the French king. It was a peace, he concluded, which we can surely look forward to under Edward's heir, for Prince Richard has been sent to England by God in the same way that God sent his only son for the redemption of the chosen people.[39] The young prince was then taken off to watch a masque in which a procession of mummers played the part of cardinals dressed like devils.

It was a statement that Wyclif might have produced himself. For Wyclif too the king rules over the elect because he was the lord of the chosen, the members of the English church–state seen as the promised land of the new Israel. One should revert, he argued, to the scheme of things in operation before Christ when there was of course no vicar of St. Peter to claim jurisdiction over independent churches.

> Item, tempore ante incarnationem fuerunt multae particulares ecclesiae ... et illarum nullus Romanus pontifex fuit caput praeter Christum; nec dubium quin illae ecclesiae distinguuntur ab universali Ecclesia et ab aliis particularibus ecclesiis: ergo multae sunt particulares ecclesiae, et per consequens *una universalis ex eis collecta*, quae sub iurisdictione nullius Petri vicarii tamquam capitis sunt subiectae ... Si enim Deus servasset totam Ecclesiam militantem tempore viationis Christi usque hodie conversantem in Anglia, et creasset novas ecclesias, sicut de facto fecit in Francia et alibi, tunc distinguerentur. Quare ergo modo non distinguuntur?[40]

The *ecclesia Anglicana*, it seemed, had a degree of antiquity deriving from its direct descent from the time of Christ, which could not be matched by the French church or other new foundations. Therefore, unlike earlier fourteenth-century upholders of lay supremacy, Wyclif did not need to deal in terms of Roman law or natural rights like Marsilius of Padua or William of Ockham: it was enough to equate Edward III with Old

---

[39] ii. 362, paras. 10–11: Edward III is like Simeon 'qi avoit longement attenduz la redemption de Israel, & avoit responce de Dieu q'il ne murroit ja tan q'il eust veu son Salveour Jehu Crist, qy fuist l'expectation du poeple.' But he may now say 'Nunc dimittis ...', leaving his people to embrace the prince in perfect love and 'a lui obeire en touz ses commandementz. Qar Saint Poul dit [I *Pet.* ii:13], 'Subjecti estote &c. tamquam Regi quasi precellenti'; et si vostre Roi vous soit envoiez de Dieu, il est le Vikaire ou le Legat Dieu sur vous en Terre.'

[40] *De Eccles* p. 30.

Testament kingship,[41] to make him lord of the promised land, a land-lord of the realm, the only person from whom the English clergy could derive their rights and possessions, and who correspondingly enjoyed the power of a Solomon or an Ezra to appoint, depose or dispossess them.[42] Priests have no rights of possession of their own in Israel, for as Ezekiel said, they have God for their inheritance. In this sense they need no more than Christ himself hanging naked on the cross.[43]

During the course of the fourteenth century, inspired by an allegedly holy war and the need for propaganda, English political theology under royal patronage forged a most intimate connection between the Church and the land, between Eng-*land*, the national community, and the idea of the regional church as an *ecclesia terrae Angliae*, an *eglise d'Angle-terre*. It was the outcome of a deliberate adoption of the Old Testament (the only part of the Bible, incidentally, which offered a proper theory of divinely approved kingship)[44] for the benefit of the English people as the new chosen race, the heirs to the promised land. Just as the Israelite had seen his physical occupation of the land of the covenant as the guarantee of his entitlement to salvation, so the right-thinking Englishman of the later fourteenth century came to picture himself as a *piers plowman*, the tiller of the soil of a landed church, a co-worker with Christ in the green fields of England. It made no difference that his actual function was far removed from the soil itself: every king or knight, bishop or priest, was a landlord in the sense of an administrator of estates and property—and could accordingly view himself as a 'natural man', a worker on the land. Moreover, the Bible, especially the Old Testament, talked to him very much in those terms. The Old Testament *is* a mass of agricultural

---

[41] Old Testament kings had both temporal and spiritual power and were *rex et sacerdos* after the example of Melchisedech, the Levites and Moses: *De Pot. Pap* p. 10; also *De Civ. Dom.* ii. 60; *De Ver. Sac. Scr.* i. 69—although Wyclif makes it clear here that this does not represent his own ideal form of government, rule by 'apostolic men'. Kings with priestly power are however much better than priests with royal power. The use of the Old Testament judges as a model for his *apostolici viri* is discussed by L. J. Daly, *The Political Theory of John Wyclif* (Chicago, 1962) pp. 97f.

[42] Henry III's deposition of popes at Sutri follows the example of Solomon (III *Reg.* ii: 24–35): 'Tunc enim practizata fuit lex saepe tacta ... quod instar Salomonis rex debet in casu deponere summum pontificem', *De Pot. Pap.* p. 183; similarly with replacements: 'Unde Sadoch praefecit Salomon in summum pontificem loco Abiathar sacerdoti: patet historia, 3 *Reg.* ii.', *De Civ. Dom.* i. 291. For Ezra see *De Civ. Dom.* iii. 28, citing 1 *Esdra* vii:25–8.

[43] *De Eccles* pp. 214–15, citing *Ezech.* xliv:28.

[44] For this problem the best discussion is still P. Beskow, *Rex Gloriae: The Kingship of Christ in the Early Church* (Stockholm, Gothenburg, Uppsala, 1962).

symbolism[45] precisely because the Jews had a very highly developed sense of the land, their promised land, as an essential feature of their divinely chosen character.[46] Their outlook had a far closer attachment to the actual earth of a particular area than it was initially possible for the Christian Church (which was a church of the dispersion) to accept in any full and complete sense. The territorial doctrine, which was so essentially part and parcel of the Jewish idea of a particular people elected by God as the inheritors of heaven, could only be diluted by Christianity by applying it without distinction to the entire *terra*, the Earth itself, the whole world of the Roman empire; and by spiritualising the whole idea so the emphasis fell upon heaven as the true fatherland, the common *patria* of all Christians everywhere. Christ's rejection of all the kingdoms of the earth seemed to sweep away the Old Testament teaching of the church as a territorial landed entity, and the Jewish doctrine of Israel was converted into little more than a series of analogies for heaven, with Christ himself as the great farmer of the Lord's vineyard.

Something approaching the full Jewish principle of the landed church could only be restored when the Christian church began to come to terms with the principle of nationalism and national sovereignty in the later Middle Ages, and equated a church with a regional area, with a specific geographical, territorial unit. In the course of the fourteenth and fifteenth centuries this equation of *ecclesia* and *terra*, church and land, spread to most parts of Europe—although the elements of it were already present in the theories of Capetian France as a most holy nation (most notably in the Gallican doctrines developed under Philip the Fair and, later, Charles V). Luxemburg and Hussite Bohemia provides another excellent example; and one can find the same sort of ideas appearing in the Spanish kingdoms, in Burgundy, in the Swiss Union and elsewhere. The result was that the Reformation became a virtual inevitability as Europe came to accept this territorial doctrine of the Church so being essentially a collection of 'lands', of independent Israels. And this new—or rather, very old—conception of a church as a territory, as a defined geographical area, was bound to be inherently anti-papal.

Because the papacy had always adopted wholeheartedly the traditional Roman view of the best society as a single universal empire, that is to say,

---

[45] E.g. S. A. Barney, 'The Plowshare of the Tongue: The Progress of a Symbol from the Bible to *Piers Plowman*', *Mediaeval Studies* 35 (1973) pp. 261–93. The use of such symbolism by St. Bernard in the second book of *De Consideratione* was particularly influential.

[46] W. D. Davies, *The Gospel and the Land: Early Christianity and Jewish Territorial Doctrine* (Berkeley, Los Angeles, London, 1974).

of the Christian society as a universal whole, an *orbis terrarum*, which—like Gilroy's plum pudding—could be sliced up into portions and each chunk labelled 'province', but with each segment remaining very much part of the sphere, a slice of the one globe, a section of the mass. The territorial doctrine, on the other hand, would produce a view of the Universal Church not as a *cosmopolis* but more like a league or federation of separate polities, or an Anglo-Saxon empire as a chain of distinct and separate kingdoms, a *collection* of parts.[47] Every Christian prayed, Thy will be done on earth *as it is in Heaven*—and there could be no escape from the conclusion that the Lord's Prayer laid an obligation on each Christian to make the earthly order reflect the disposition and layout of Heaven. But what exactly did that mean? By the mid-fourteenth century it was coming to be suggested that Heaven ought to be visualised as a series of habitations, a collection of palaces, rather than one great throne or court from which glory radiated out in all directions. If the Bible was most true when it was being understood most literally, then Heaven was in fact a place of many mansions, and the Bible should be taken to mean exactly what it said. There was not just one universal house of God (a universal house does sound rather peculiar), but rather a *city*, a collection of many houses: just as on earth the *civitas Dei* meant a whole collection of ecclesiastical polities within a universal framework, each house of God being distinct in itself, and whose very multiplicity—many mansions—was a much closer correspondence to the divine order than one physical, universal, body politic.

This federal structure of the Universal Church as an assemblage of separate pieces, a grouping of distinct *terrae*, less one empire than a pattern of islands, found its best expression during the 1370s with Wyclif, although he was by no means alone in this. The whole Church, he maintained, has the unity of a common idea and purpose, and of course a single spiritual head: it is an intellectual unity. But essentially it is also a multitude of parts: it has to be understood *quantitative*, mathematically, in accordance with an atomistic number theory, just as a field is really many blades of grass, and many trees make a forest.[48] It is a nominalistic theory

---

[47] For examples of Wyclif's equation of the *Ecclesia universalis* with *multa regna* see *De Eccles*. pp. 55–6; and p. 30 (cited above p.150 at n. 40); cf. *De Civ. Dom*. ii. 34, 'Et sic de multis regnorum [et] dominiorum christianitatis translationibus . . .'

[48] Against the argument that the *Ecclesia* must be 'continua quoad locum et tempus', *De Eccles*. p. 99, he replies that what looks like 'totum populum et totum genus sibi succedentium' superficially, may in reality be a thinly spaced out succession of the elect, 'sicut enim iuxta naturales et *perspectivos* videns silvam vel campum segetum a longinquo, iudicat totum esse

which has close connections with Mertonian science, and there were many aspects of contemporary Oxford physics which could be adduced here as analogies illustrating a universal law: particle theories of light and velocity, intensity and force—although Wyclif's favourite figure is the well-known principle that many dots placed side by side will make a line.[49] The whole church is a number of national, territorial entities, nestling together like peas in a pod, but each one capable of being taken independently and apart from the others. Or as the court-poet John Gower phrased it about the same time (or perhaps a year or two later), the Christian Church, he said, is a 'whole world composed of lands, each kingdom being a standardbearer of Christ'—each kingdom, in other words, being its own local, national, landed church.[50]

The pope, said Wyclif, is *caput particularis ecclesiae*: the Roman church, whatever else it may be, is still essentially an individual church, one amongst many. Whilst therefore the pope ought to be obeyed by Christians everywhere if (and it was a considerable 'if') he was declaring

---

continuum consitum arboribus vel frumento, sic nos imperfecta fide videntes Ecclesiam a longinquo non obstante quod habeat in se arbusta sterilia atque zizania, iudicamus eam plenam fructuosis arboribus et frumento.'

[49] The long mathematical digression which introduces this discussion of Church membership begins pp. 97–8 with this analogy: 'Et quantum ad lineas, dicitur quod licet resolvantur in *attomos*, manent eedem . . . sicut sensus errat circa magnitudinem et rectitudinem lineae, quia ignorat numerum punctorum ex quibus componitur, sic viantes errant circa magnitudinem dignitatis vel meriti viantis, quia ignorant numerum et mensuram in quibus Verbum aeternaliter disposuit ponere sponsam suam.' The immediate source for this is chapter 6 of Aristotle's *Categories*, which is cited in the continu_.ion of the discussion on p. 104–5. The *Ecclesia* has a formal unity, in having a common end and a spiritual unity of charity—'Si ergo dictae Ecclesiae sit quantitas continua secundum quam est formaliter magna, tunc ipsa est vere continua, ymo non solum quaelibet pars huius Ecclesiae continuatur cum aliqua alia eius parte, sed omnes simul copulantur ad eundem terminum communem . . . Nec distantia localis nec discontinuatio mathematicae quantitatis obest, quia similitas secundum interiorem hominem et adnascentia membrorum Ecclesiae secundum caritatem excedit unitatem sensibilem.'—but the parts may be geographically separated in a mathematically quantitative sense and therefore only form a universal body as an aggregate: 'Pro quo declarando suppono quod, sicut Ecclesia est unum *aggregative*, sic membrum eius et accidentia sua sunt unum aggregative . . . Ex quo patet quod omnes partes Ecclesiae *collective* intellecte copulantur ad eundem terminum communem ex omnibus communibus terminis Ecclesiae aggregatum. Nam iste communis terminus copulat quamlibet partem quantitativam Ecclesiae cum alia, hic secundum unam eius partem et hic secundum aliam. Ymo, ut logice loquar, sicut punctus replicatus est tota substantia lineae superficiei, et corporis quantitative, sic substantia materialis aggregata est universum corporeum, et eius partes sunt proportionaliter partes mundi.'

[50] *Vox Clamantis* vii. 24, 'Singula, que Dominus statuit sibi regna per orbem, que magis in Christi nomine signa gerunt, diligo.'

the law of God[51]—since the scriptures should always be followed—much more significance attaches to this view of regional churches being each a particular church, located in a particular place, in the same way that the Roman church is called Roman precisely because it is an Italian church.[52] There is no reason why one geographically situated church should have jurisdiction over other particular churches. The pope has no right or power of his own in England, except the duty of *advising* the king about divine matters.[53] But he is just as much subject to the laws of England as any other foreign bishop.[54] How can there be a universal jurisdiction in a Church comprising particular churches?[55] And so not only did this belief in the inescapable territoriality of churches alter the make-up of the Universal Church, it also required a thorough-going change in the distribution of power within that Church. It meant not only a denial of papal supremacy in its traditional governmental form— but it also (although this point does not seem to have been appreciated) meant a rejection of the almost equally traditional theory of dualism ... the theory, which had formally been adopted by virtually all lay governments in the thirteenth and fourteenth centuries, that the king's right to be supreme in temporal matters was matched by the papal right to be supreme in spirituals— a divided jurisdiction, or, more accutately

---

[51] *De Eccles* p. 31, 'Ideo dicunt doctores peritiores quod dominus papa non est caput universalis sed particularis ecclesiae: dum tamen perseveranter vixerit tamquam papa ... concedendum quod de possibili sit papa ipso superior hic in terris ... sed supponere excellentiam Romani pontificis super aliis, etiam quoad Deum, quia certum est quod non est superior nisi fuerit superior quoad Deum.'

[52] See for instance the discussion in *De Pot. Pap*. pp. 165–78; and further my 'The Apostolicus and the Bishop of Rome', *JTS*, *n.s.* 13–14 (1962–3) pp. 290–317 and 311–54 respectively, espec. pp. 346f.

[53] *De Eccles*, p. 282, 'Requiretur ergo ut papa in hoc humilis elemosinarius regis petat ratificationem talis elemosinae, cum omnia quae habet in Anglia tenet de rege'; *De Off. Reg.* p. 146, 'Et patet quod regnum Angliae specialiter non tenetur parere papam nisi secundum obedientiam elicibilem ex scriptura. Sed non est elicibile ex scriptura quod ipse dominetur saeculariter super temporalibus regni nostri. Ideo consulere potest super talibus in quae sunt ad Deum, ed non auctoritative praecipere vel dare dominium ... Rex autem auctoritate propria, sed data a Deo, potest conferre clero elemosinam.'

[54] *De Off. Reg.* pp. 70–1.

[55] *De Civ. Dom.* i. 382, 'Verumtamen pie credere possumus et debemus quod Romanus pontifex sit caput particularis ecclesiae, cui obediendum est in terris prae ceteris, de quanto in ipso Christus loquitur legem suam. Si autem homo in honore tali positus non intellexerit istam sententiam, sed credit maniace quod ab ipso dependet essentialiter regimen universalis Ecclesiae, opus caritatis foret ipsos instruere'; cf. p. 384, '... et ad tantum attendere civilitati quod credant Ecclesiam destrui si dominio civili caruerint; credant maniace quod nichil in ecclesiae particulari sit licitum nisi de quanto originatur et autenticatur a sua curia'; also *De Eccles.* p. 37.

in this case, two jurisdictions, one spiritual and one temporal, a double jurisdiction.

This conception of an ecclesiastical headship divided between two heads, pope and lay ruler, had always suffered from severe theoretical difficulties and had never been capable of operating with complete success (primarily because there was always bound to be a clash of jurisdictions along the border between temporals and spirituals—wherever they might be thought to be). Nevertheless, it was sufficiently vague to be extremely useful; and so elastic that it could be adapted and used in their own ways by a wide range of writers from Aquinas to Marsilius and Ockham. Indeed, the Aristotelian-inspired argument that a Christian subject was a member of two societies, a universal church with jurisdiction over spiritual matters, and the political society of the kingdom dealing with temporal matters, had given dualism a philosophical justification and endowed it with a new lease of life. It seemed that dualism could be applied and could continue to be used whether the kingdom was seen as a sovereign national state or not.

English nationalism demonstrated that this was simply not true. To be truly sovereign a kingdom—a state—had to be its own church, an ecclesiastical polity: and there was no more room for a double or divided jurisdiction, properly speaking, in an Anglican polity than there had been in the papal theory of a universal church-empire. If each church was its own particular entity, there could be no justification for allowing any church to have jurisdiction over another, even in spirituals only. But this raised a considerable problem. The theory of a *dualitas* of jurisdictions—a division between temporal and spiritual swords—had been officially accepted and formally adhered to in England for at least two centuries. Now it suddenly realised that it did not want it . . . or, perhaps we should say, that it could no longer afford to pay lip-service to it. One of the great advantages of the Wycliffite theory of the Church was that it solved this problem. Readers of Wyclif's works (including myself) have long been puzzled by his seeming ability to argue both for and against dualism at the same time—to allow that the pope had headship in spiritual matters over the universal Church, whilst denying it to him in England. Even in the same work, in the same chapter, one finds the two positions side by side.

Wyclif's solution was that these two opposed positions might be stated together because they did not apply at the same time. Contrary to all the conclusions of modern scholarship, Wyclif argued that dualism had developed—not as a defensive position against the growth of papal claims in the eleventh and twelfth centuries taken up by kings and emperors (like

Henry IV, or Barbarossa, or in England Henry II)—but that the notion of a *dualitas* of heads was essentially a *papal* theory produced in a period when the papacy was only moderately corrupt. It was a half-way stage towards the later—totally corrupt—papal claims to headship in both temporals and spirituals, which developed after 1200 with Innocent III.[56] It marked a decline, and indicated that the Church was beginning to slide down the slippery slope towards the gaping hell-mouth of Boniface VIII waiting for it at the bottom. All the same, it had been acceptable in the turbulent conditions of the period. The division of jurisdictions, despite its lack of apostolic or Biblical justification, had been permitted with indescribable generosity by the European monarchs as an act of grace for the purpose of maintaining peace in the Church.

It was an adroit argument (if one ignores its lack of historical veracity), because all the weaknesses and deficiencies of dualism as a political system could be blamed on the papacy, for having suggested it in the first place—and it enabled the lay monarchies of the fourteenth century to, so to speak, 'sit loose' to dualism: to be able to dispense with it as an unworkable papal novelty, whose uselessness even the papacy itself had implicitly acknowledged when it abandoned dualism in favour of claims to total and absolute headship in all respects. Once, Wyclif argued, the pope claimed to be the only vicar of God on earth, (and placed the Church in the position of being ruled by a tyrant and a heretic),[57] there was no longer any reason for the English king to continue to stand by a system which he had reluctantly adopted as a concession and mark of good will towards the papacy itself in a previous century, but which he had always recognised was not the true Biblical, evangelical conception of government in a well-organized church.

Now, however, the argument continued, there was absolutely no reason why the lay ruler should not revert to the position approved by the primitive Church. On the contrary there was a positive obligation on him to do so: and the teaching of the *Ecclesia primitiva*, the early Church, on the matter of jurisdiction, as laid down in the New Testament, was naturally

---

[56] See *De Civ. Dom.* ii. 60, for a succinct statement of the three periods:'. . . sic potest contingere quod Ecclesia Christi sit per apostolos, saeculi iudices, optime regulata; secundo per reges, sed male, qui post dotationem ecclesiae constituunt sibi praepositos in suis ecclesiis; sed tertio pessime per sacerdotes qui aspirantes ad principale mundi civile dominium, postposita lege Christi, sollicitentur praecipue per quae media symoniaca possent perplexius mundum sibi subicere'; also *De Ver. Sac. Scr.* i. 69. For further illustration see Wilks, '*Reformatio regni*', *SCH* 9 (1972) pp. 109–30 at pp. 116–18.

[57] *De Civ. Dom.* ii. 112.

essentially the same as that to be found in the Old Testament, since any conflict between the two testaments was unthinkable. In other words, it was now the duty of the lay prince to convert, or reconvert, the kingdom of England into the condition of a Jewish landed church, an *ecclesia terrae*. It was to become a king's church, an *ecclesia regis*,[58] since there should be no aspect of the realm which was exempt from the king's peace, the *pax regis* being the *pax Christi*. There should be a *reformatio*, a great re-forming of the ecclesiastical structure, so that the English church might return to its pristine condition of purity, a 'restitutio Ecclesiae ad statum quem Christus docuit',[59] and suffer a great recovery of its original, true identity.

   The basic principle of this Reform was that there should be a clear recognition of the difference between faith and coercion, between Christian belief and the compulsion to believe it, and it was not difficult to appeal to the authority of St. Augustine for a statement of the point—although the conclusions which English theorists drew from this were the opposite to what Augustine intended, and the theme was more Aristotelian than Augustinian. Law was to be equated with enforcement: jurisdiction was a matter of *vis coerciva* and it was therefore appropriate that political actions—police actions—should be entirely a matter for the laity in the first instance, and for practical purposes this meant the king. Government and jurisdiction, the making and enforcement of law, was an aspect of kingship, an affair of the *regnum*, the ruling, the realm. In jurisdictional terms the church means a national church, a church of the kingdom governed by its laity, an *ecclesia laicalis* or *saecularis*.[60] The king and Parliament act in regulating the Church of the kingdom on behalf of all citizens.[61]

---

[58] *De Off. Reg.* p. 37, 'Et ista subiectio est eo specialius a rege Angliae cum suis militibus observanda, quo ipse copiosius sine subiectione caesarea dotavit gratantius *suam ecclesiam*. Et hinc nimirum clerus Angliae est regi suo singulariter in multis subiectior. Rex enim reservavit sibi in vacationibus, in electionibus, et in castigationibus cleri sui, super collatis elemosinis dominium singulare.'

[59] *De Civ. Dom.* ii. 153.

[60] *De Off. Reg.* p. 110, 'Et sic capiunt [reges] saeculare dominium non a clericis nostris auctoritative, sed a Christo et ecclesia laicali.'; *De Eccl.* p. 156, 'Tertio miratur saecularis ecclesia quod clerus instat erga brachium saeculare . . .' A clergy without temporal possessions would exist simply for the good of the laity, making the Church into essentially its *pars laicalis*, a *populus laicalis*: *De Civ. Dom.* i. 266; i. 392; i. 333, '. . . ecclesiae, id est, cuicunque congregationi fidelium . . . ad demonstrandum quod cuicunque ecclesiae clericorum, laicorum vel mixtim . . .'

[61] *De Euch.* pp. 319–21: the *clerus Anglicanae* is only 'modica pars respectu ecclesiae totius regni nostri', and therefore the disposal of clerical wealth is a matter for the *communitas regni in parliamentis*.

The clergy, by contrast, have no rights as citizens. This is not to suggest that they are not members of society, but to make the point that citizens are political beings, and a cleric—precisely because he is a cleric—has no political capacity of his own.[62] Clergy, Wyclif explained, make themselves non-citizens when they are ordained, not (or one hopes not) because, like slaves, they are too depraved to be citizens, but for exactly the opposite reason that they are too good, too perfect and ideal, too superior to be put on the same level as everybody else. If slaves cannot be citizens because they are beasts, then the clergy cannot have a political role of their own because they are gods, too divine for the mundane cares of administration and government.

Let me finish by trying to emphasize the main point I have been making here: that the national theory of the English Church was forced to operate with a different type of dualism altogether, and therefore predicated a completely new relationship between laity and clergy. It was now to be a dualism, not of temporal and spiritual jurisdiction, but earthly jurisdiction on one side, and spiritualities—the teaching of the faith and the administration of the sacraments—on the other;[63] to be technical, between *potestas iurisdictionis* and *potestas ordinis*, as lay power and priestly power respectively. Or to quote Wyclif again, between the lordship of coercion and the lordship of love:[64] the rod of power in the sense of force must not be mistaken for the pilgrim's staff of the preacher. In another

---

[62] In the *optima politica legis Christi*, *De Civ. Dom.* ii. 152, 'exclusa proprietate temporalium a clericis ut in primitiva Ecclesia, et tota civilitate devoluta ad laicos'; similarly *De Pot. Pap.* p. 83, 'quod laici occuparent totam civilitatem saecularis dominio . . . quod tota civilitas foret contenta in manibus laycorum'; p. 85, 'Unde cum in statu innocentiae et statu patriae deficiet talis civilitas, videtur quod ipsa sapit imperfectionem et est officio cleri dissonum.' In *De Civ. Dom.* iii. 436–8, he advocates adoption of the Aristotelian scheme (*Politics*, iii. 1, 1275a; vii. 9, 1329a) whereby the priesthood is formed out of those who are too old to participate in active civic functions: 'sed honorabilissimi viri in ultima aetate quando non possunt vacare nisi contemplationi . . . sed procedendo ab imperfecto ad perfectum, illis qui bene se gesserint in militari et in iudicativo officio attribuendum est ultimo sacerdotium tamquam proximum felicitati: multo magis debet hoc observari de sacerdotibus Christi . . .'

[63] *De Pot. Pap.* p. 3, 'Secundum hoc itaque inest homini duplex maneries potestatis, scilicet supernaturalis et civilis. Supernaturalis est potestas quam Deus dat homini ad spiritualiter proficiendum Ecclesiae, cuiusmodi est potestas sacerdotalis in conficiendo vel ministrando sacramenta aut alia spiritualia bona Ecclesiae. Potestas autem civilis est potestas dominativa ad cohercendum rebelles Ecclesiae secundum poenam sensibilem.' Both the magisterial and the coercive powers were present in Christ as *sacerdos et rex*: 'Ille enim qui est sacerdos in aeternum, propheta magnus atque magister, exortatus est saluberrime crebrius praedicando. Sed cum sit rex regum, exercuit tam *auctoritative* quam *instrumentaliter* correptionem humanitus coactivam,' *De Civ. Dom.* ii. 73. One notices here how both the Gelasian functions are subsumed into the power of kingship.

[64] *De Pot. Pap.* pp. 12–15.

context, we find him adapting the distinction which the Anglo-Norman Anonymous is always now associated with: the pope is still the vicar of Christ, but of Christ as a priest and in humility; whereas it is the king who is the vicar of God, of Christ in power and majesty.[65] It is the king who continued the character of the Old Testament deity.[66]

This was not of course the first time in the history of the Medieval Church that the lawmaking power had been distinguished from the magisterial capacity and identified with the power of the lay prince. Despite all his fulminations against Roman law as an alien species which had never rightfully operated in England, we can smile wryly when we find Wyclif quoting Justinian's *Novella* 6 as evidence that in the early days of the Church the Roman emperor knew how to behave like a Christian gentleman.[67] But it certainly became the standard theory of lay-sacerdotal relations in the latter half of the fourteenth century amongst the English royalists. Thus Thomas Ashburn, an Augustinian friar, distinguished himself in the early 1370s by arguing at a royal council meeting (or possibly a session of Parliament) that the English clergy as a body was a bird for the plucking, and should be taxed and dispossessed of its wealth.

[65] *De Off. Reg.* p. 137, 'Ideo videtur mihi probabile quod regalis auctoritas praecellit auctoritatem sacerdotalem secundum rationem multiplicem. Primo quia illa habet similitudinem vicariam deitatis et sic vindicandi potestatem; auctoritas autem sacerdotalis habet similitudinem vicariam humanitatis Christi, et sic rationem paciendi iniuriam'; pp. 121-2, '. . . necesse est matrem Ecclesiam habere saeculares dominos ut reges, Dei vicarios, qui potestative ipsam defendant ubi vicarii Christi deficiunt, et illam potestatem immediate habent a Deo. Christus enim simul fuit rex et sacerdos: ideo ipsum caput habuit unde impertiretur utrique brachio potestatem. Sed papa, cum non habet sic potestatem portandi gladium vindicte, non dat ipsum domino saeculari, sicut nec gratiam, sed ministrat ungendo vel alias solempnitates adinventas praeter necessarias conferendo.' For the teaching of the Anglo-Norman Anonymous on this distinction see G. H. Williams, *The Norman Anonymous of 1100 A.D.* (Cambridge, Mass., 1951) pp. 127f.; E. H. Kantorowicz, *The King's Two Bodies* (Princeton, 1957) pp. 42-60.

[66] *De Off. Reg.* p. 13, 'Oportet ergo Deum habere in Ecclesia duos vicarios, scilicet regem in temporalibus et sacerdotem in spiritualibus. Rex autem debet severe cohercere rebellem *sicut fecit deitas in veteri testamento.* Sacerdos vero debet ministrare praeceptum miti modo humilibus tempore legis gratiae sicut fecit humanitas Christi, qui simul fuit rex et sacerdos. Et hinc dicit Augustinus quod rex habet ymaginem Dei sed episcopus ymaginem Christi propter ministerium indubie. Nec est fingendum ministerium huius differentiae verborum nisi quod rex gerit ymaginem deitatis Christi, sicut episcopus ymaginem suae humanitatis.' The reference is to *Quaestiones ex veteri testamento*, 35 (PL 35. 2234), in which Augustine answers the question of why Saul remained the *christus Domini* for David even after God had deserted him (I *Reg.* xxvi: 16f.): cited Wyclif p. 10 as 'David non nescius divinam traditionem in officio ordinis regalis . . . Dei enim ymaginem habet rex, sicut et episcopus Christi. Quamdiu igitur in eadem traditione est, honorandus est, si non propter se, tamen propter ordinem.'

[67] *De Civ. Dom.* ii. 77, although he managed to ascribe this to Constantine—'dicit imperator Constantinus'—generally regarded as the ideal of Christian emperorship.

He rejected the view that England was a papal fief on the ground that the pope could not be a feudal lord, a capacity reserved to laymen. The pope, he declared, is only a vicar of St. Peter, whose duties were to teach doctrine and hear confessions, whereas the king is the vicar of St. Paul, and it was St. Paul who held the sword and determined that kings should not carry it in vain.[68]

Ashburn was presumably one of the friars who supported Wyclif in the 1370s (although he apostasised and repudiated him in the 1380s), and this relatively rare use of St. Paul was probably derived from Wyclif, who often asserted the superiority of Paul over Peter. But this distinction between the king with powers of government as opposed to the priest instructing in the faith becomes commonplace, and appears in a variety of guises. In 1388 the Augustinian canon of Merton, Thomas of Wimbledon, preached in London on the difference between the two orders, although both, he said, have swords. The king has the physical sword with which to enforce the law of God by cutting down malefactors and defending the realm: the priest on the other hand has only the sword of the tongue, with which to cut out false doctrine.[69] And there are others: but they all testify to the way in which from an English standpoint the Church taken by itself as a universal community of Christians had come to be seen as a purely spiritual body, a society of faith, hope and charity, a sacramental union adhering to a common body of belief, the law of God, but without the capacity in its own right to convert divine law into human law and so make the faith into law enforceable within the State.

The point is stressed in Wyclif's eulogising of the Early Church. The *Ecclesia universalis* he declared, *was* in its best condition when it was set in the midst of a pagan world, and literally could *not* enforce its teachings—when it conducted its affairs by the Bible law alone, and had no civil

---

[68] *Continuatio Eulogii* (RS, 1863) iii. 338, 'Augustinensis dicebat quod Petrus in Ecclesia cognoscitur per claves, Paulus per gladium. Papa est Petrus portans claves Ecclesiae in foro confessionis. "Vos, domine princeps, solebatis esse Paulus portantes gladium. Sed quia iam dimisistis gladium Domini, Petrus non cognoscet Paulum. Erigatis igitur gladium, et Petrus cognoscet Paulum."' For the council which should probably be dated to June 1373, see J. I. Catto, 'The Alleged Great Council of 1374,' *EHR* 82 (1967) pp. 764–71. For Wyclif's arguments that St. Paul was equal to, if necessary superior to, St. Peter see e.g. *De Pot. Pap.* pp. 75–9.

[69] *Wimbledon's Sermon: Redde rationem villicationis tue* ed. I. K. Knight (Pittsburgh, 1967), pp. 63–4, 'To prestis it falliþ to kutte awey þe voide braunchis of synnis wiþ þe swerd of here tonge. To knyȝtis it falliþ to lette wrongis and þeftis to be do, and to mayntene goddis lawe and hem þat ben techeris þer of, and also to kepe þe lond fro enemyes of oþer londes . . . for ȝif presthod lackede þe puple for defaute of knowyng of Goddis lawe shulde wexe wilde on vices and deie gostly. And ȝif þe knythod lackid and men to reule þe puple by lawe and hardnesse, þeves and enemies shoden so encresse þat no man sholde lyuen in pes.'

character—when it was a self-sufficient society, an *Ecclesia* 'per se sufficiens',[70] and owed nothing to the Roman empire. Even when the Church did acquire a political character—so that its beliefs could be enforced by earthly law and royal power—this political character, he argued, remained an attribute of the Church in the sense of its constituent political societies, its national church-states, its kingdoms, rather than of the Church itself as a society of faith. The Church was not—and this seems to be a very interesting fourteenth-century anticipation of Hooker's argument—the Church was not a political society in its own right, but simply by being a collection of political societies, the kingdoms as ecclesiastical polities, each national state as its own local geographical church, its own Israel. And this is what justified the rule of the godly magistrate.

In a way Ockham and Wyclif represent the poles of reason and faith in Oxford scholarship. Their objectives might coincide, but the contrast between their approaches is instructive. When Ockham in the *An princeps* considered the objection that the king should not be allowed to tax or confiscate the property of his clergy because such wealth was used for charitable purposes and so belonged to the poor, he retorted curtly, quoting both Aristotle and Cicero, that defence of the common good of the whole community, comprising both rich and poor alike, must take precedence. The good of the *patria*, the fatherland, concerned everybody, not just the minority of indigent individuals in receipt of charity.[71] When Wyclif was faced with the same objection, he insisted that the poor were to be understood in the Biblical sense of the meek who would inherit the earth: they were the saints, the elect, who formed the church in heaven and in whom true *dominium*, lordship, resided, and on whose behalf the king acted below over the actual earth as the vicar of God. Thus dominion and grace meant exactly what it said: nobody could have rights to land and power except by the king's grace.[72]

---

[70] *De Civ. Dom.* ii. 60.

[71] 11, pp. 264–5, in reply to the objection raised in 10, p. 261, but already effectively stated 8, pp. 256–7, 'Praeterea, cum bona ecclesiastica sint collata ecclesiis ad pias causas, quia magis pium est defendere patriam quam pascere pauperes: tum quia, secundum Tullium in sua *Rhetorica* [*De invent.*, ii. 53] per pietatem patriae benvolum officium et diligens tribuitur cultus, et per consequens pietas directe ad patriam se extendit; tum quia bonum commune est melius et divinius quam bonum unius, primo *Ethicorum* [Aristotle, *Nich. Eth.*, i. 1, 1094b]; ex quo infertur quod bonum totius patriae est melius et divinius quam bonum pauperum illius patriae; ex quo concluditur quod magis pium est subvenire toti patriae quam pauperibus patriae.'

[72] For a fuller statement see my 'Predestination, Property and Power', *SCH* 2 (1965) pp. 220–36.

And from this point Wyclif had no difficulty in providing an historical basis for the regalian rights which the king had over ecclesiastical property: his rights of patronage, to reserve benefices, to appoint bishops, to tax the clergy and extract oaths of allegiance from them; his duty to make laws to regulate the priesthood, and his capacity to punish delinquent clerics; his power to revoke his original grants by withholding ecclesiastical revenues or by outright confiscation of church property in time of need—all the familiar features of a traditional proprietary church system under which the king as owner became in effect pope in his own lands. It is fortunately unnecessary to set out all the arguments in detail (although they lend weight to the suggestion that Wyclif must have had some sort of legal training). In recent years, first the late Edith Tatnall, and subsequently Dr. Farr, have given us a thorough account of Wyclif's use of feudal law and historical precedents in his claim that the king as patron-in-chief was entitled like any landlord to dispossess his clerical tenants of their holdings.[73] The Bible and feudalism went hand in hand. Apostolic poverty was to be achieved not merely by depriving the possessioners, the *possessionati* (by which he largely meant the great monastic houses), of their superfluous wealth, but by establishing that all clerics were seen, and saw themselves, as royal tenants. To Wyclif the reformation was largely a land question, and could only be brought about, he declared, by a new Norman Conquest,[74] which would not only secure a radical redistribution of land, but would also reaffirm the ancient principle that all land belonged to the king on behalf of God, because it was *his* land, the chosen land, which was in question. And events were to prove that he was indeed one of the greatest of the prophets.

[73] E. C. Tatnall, 'John Wyclif and *Ecclesia Anglicana*', *JEH* 20 (1969) pp. 19-43; W. Farr, *John Wycif as Legal Reformer* (Leiden, 1970).
[74] *De Euch.* p. 320.

8

THESAURUS ECCLESIAE
(PRESIDENTIAL ADDRESS)

by MICHAEL WILKS

THE theme 'The Church and Wealth' may sound suitable for the Silver Jubilee year of the Ecclesiastical History Society, and perhaps even more relevant to a president who finds himself transformed overnight from a Judas to a *princeps*, a supreme example of what has become known as 'the Peter principle'. Yet in many ways it could hardly seem less appropriate to that institution whose founder commanded his followers to take neither silver nor gold.[1] Christ's admonition to the disciples to 'sell all that thou hast ... and follow me'[2] was to create a problem for the Church which, as the following papers will illustrate, is as live an issue today as it has been for nearly two thousand years. It is undeniable that the post-Constantinian Church has been in many and various ways an immensely wealthy society, and that the acquisition of wealth has remained for most Christians an inescapable natural human desire. From an early stage in its development the Church became the largest landowner in Europe, creating its own princes, and from the proprietary churches of the medieval system to the lavish endowment of churches with treasures and monuments which has lasted into the modern period the Church has often seemed to be the outward and visible sign of an aristocracy at prayer. Even within the deliberate plainness of the Dissenting congregations there were those who took the lead in the industrial and commercial revolutions of the eighteenth and nineteenth centuries (the great Quaker banking-houses are a case in point). Although fortified by Thomism, the baroque splendour of post-Tridentine Catholicism was still ill-equipped to deal with the assaults of the Enlightenment, and has since had to face the challenge of a 'liberation theology' which insists that the Church itself by definition can only exist as a community of the poor. Since the apostolic age there has been a permanent tension between the Church and material possessions, and the noise of conflict which this has generated echoes down the centuries.

The biblical basis of the problem is familiar enough. The Old Testament, from which the Christian Church culled so much of its social and political theory, offered a very mixed legacy. 'Naked I came into the

[1] Matthew 10. 9; compare Luke 9. 3: Acts 3. 6: I Peter 1. 18.
[2] Matthew 19. 21; Mark 10. 21; Luke 12. 33; 18. 22.

world, and naked I shall leave it' was perhaps the most overworked of
biblical texts in early and medieval Christianity.[3] But nobody can read the
Old Testament for long and be in doubt that it is strewn with injunctions
not to covet thy neighbour's lands, house, cattle, wives, and other possessions; and that for much of their recorded history the Israelites were
obsessed with the idea of taking possession of the promised land and
enjoying its overflows of milk and honey.[4] The New Testament on the
other hand was far less ambiguous, and posed the problem of possessing
not just wealth but private property altogether. It was not just a case that
wealth was irrelevant to one whose kingdom is not of this world. On the
contrary, Christ appeared to have stipulated three absolute prohibitions
for Christians on the use and pursuit of wealth of all kinds. First, there was
the principle that possession of wealth was a positive barrier to salvation:
blessed are the poor, for they shall inherit the kingdom of heaven. Thus it
was the rich man who looked up from his torment to the poor man in
Abraham's bosom.[5] In particular, secondly, Christ could be placed in the
Pharisaic or Essene tradition by objecting to the actual use of money: it
was forbidden to the Apostles; the money-changers were thrown out of
the Temple, not just because they were defiling a holy place, but because
they were money-changers. The most significant feature of 'Render unto
Caesar . . .' was not the question of what did Caesar have that God did not,
but that Christ had demonstrated his own poverty by having to borrow a
coin in the first place before he could say it.[6] The third principle which the
Bible apparently endorsed was that of community of possession and the
need for the Christian to renounce the holding of private property as a
personal possession. The Apostles had a common purse: Judas had carried
the bag, which was presumably why he was the one to be corrupted by
silver. The members of the first community at Jerusalem sold all that they

---

[3] Job 1. 21; I Timothy 6. 7. For subsequent use, for example, Augustine, *De civitate Dei*, i. 10, *PL*
41, col. 23; Innocent III, *Libellus de eleemosyna*, 2, (*PL* 217, col. 750), 'Nudus, ait alius, egressus
sum de utero matris meae, nudus revertar illuc'; *De contemptu mundi*, i. 8 (705), commenting
'Nudus egreditur, et nudus regreditur. Pauper accedit, et pauper recedit': Augustinus
Triumphus, *Summa* (Rome, 1584), xxxvii. 2 ad 3, p. 221.

[4] For example, Exodus 20. 17; Deuteronomy 3. 7 and 20; 5. 21. See further, W. D. Davies, *The
Gospel and the Land: Early Christianity and Jewish Territorial Doctrine* (Berkeley, Los Angeles,
London, 1974).

[5] Luke 6. 20; 16. 23; compare Matthew 5. 3; James 2. 5. See also Mark 10. 23–6; and Matthew 6. 19;
Luke 12. 21.

[6] Matthew 21. 12; Mark 11. 15; John 2. 14–15. Matthew 22. 21; Mark 12. 17; Luke 20. 25.
Similarly Peter and the tribute money: Matthew 17. 24–7.

had and paid it into a common treasury administered by the Apostles jointly, from which they distributed to each according to their needs.[7]

The various historical responses to this biblical doctrine fall broadly into two main categories. For many the Gospel teaching has to be seen as a series of counsels of perfection, as if to indicate that there is a hierarchy of permissible ownerships, so that the principles appropriate to ascetics or members of religious orders would not be applicable to lay members of the Church, for whom the possession of wealth or the lack of it were divinely instituted as a *remedium peccati*, and for whom faith and good works were the key to redemption. How could the Christian work ethic be upheld if it was to be denied that the labourer is worthy of his hire? How could one fulfil the scriptural injunction to give to the poor if one was poor oneself? From the widow's mite to modern campaigns for Christian stewardship the virtue of giving has made it sufficient to point to the good uses to which ecclesiastical wealth is put in the educational, charitable, and missionary fields. So for others the principles of the Jerusalem community of saints have provided the basis for the Church's teaching on property: the poverty of all Christians is maintained by recognizing that in reality all belongs to God and his Church—to the just in heaven—and therefore man on earth really owns nothing of his own. He is simply a steward, a *stipendiarius*, of the divine wealth; and to claim actual ownership would, in the words of Gregory the Great, be an act of theft.[8] Since this became the traditional line of argument for most medieval writers, I want to turn now to look at an author whose response to the problem of wealth in the Church was intended, and in many ways does, sum up a millenium of argument and debate.

*　　*　　*

Earthly wealth, remarked John Wyclif in the early 1370s, is the dung of the Church: 'cum ergo mundi divitiae sint stercora corporis Christi mystici . . .'. It was no doubt an unsurprising sentiment to be voiced by a man whose mind was at that time very much concerned with the specially constructed stone-built lockable lavatory (a unique privilege) which was being put up for him in Oxford. But, he continued, since all matter is the creation of God, even waste material has its uses, and can be made

[7] John 12. 6; 13. 29. Acts 2. 44–5; 4. 32–5.
[8] Gregory I, *Homiliarum in evangelia*, ii. 40, 3 (*PL* 76, cols 1304–5): see further 'The Problem of Private Ownership in Patristic Thought', *Studia Patristica*, 6 = *TU* 81 (1962), pp. 533–42.

productive if properly spread over the garden of the Church.[9] As the fore-most biblical scholar of his time, Wyclif was only too well aware that all Christians as true believers were by definition the poor of Christ, the *paupertates Christi*;[10] and that the evangelic law to which he attached so much significance as the only true guide to Christian living displayed the considerable bias against wealth and private property already mentioned. But he argued that the entire question of material wealth and goods could not be separated from the divinely created existence of matter, of the whole material world itself which God had brought into being. He refused to discuss the subject of human ownership in his great *Summa theologiae* until he had dealt with the Creation itself. The world began, he tells us, as one would expect of an act of divine workmanship, in a state of perfection: and he proceeded to elaborate a state of nature theory, a view of the world before the formation of civil society, which easily bears comparison with the better-known views of English writers like Hobbes and Locke three centuries later.

This first condition of mankind was, he begins, a state of innocence, a condition of rational nature—'status innocentiae sit status naturae rationalis'—when man was free from sin ('immunis simpliciter a pec-cato').[11] Therefore, he continues, in a state of nature man must have enjoyed not only spiritual perfection but also bodily, physical blessedness. The absence of sin would have left an emptiness, and since nature abhors a vacuum, this metaphysical space would have been filled with divine grace, making early man into a perfectly good and blessed being. Grace and nature go together: spiritual well-being must have been matched by natural health. Just as man was immune from all the penalties of sin, so he was free from pain and bodily ills, and all the afflictions and misfortunes represented in the story of Job. Even death itself was absent: man was immortal. He considered whether this was true of the other animals in Paradise, but decided that the birds and beasts would have died, although he allowed that they died without pain.[12] But man went on living—and it therefore seemed possible that a population problem loomed on the

[9] *De civili dominio*, i. 22, WS (1885), p. 158; compare 1. 16, p. 115. Similarly *De potestate papae*, 3, WS (1907), p. 59, 'Et haec ratio quare Christus noluit fundare suam Ecclesiam in mundi divitiis tamquam stercoribus vel aquis labilibus, nec in mundi gloria vel fastu saeculi tamquam ventis, sed in stabili paupertate, quae securius, brevius et statui innocentiae conformius facit humiles regnum coelorum acquirere.' For Wyclif's personal latrine at the Queen's College see A. Hudson, *Wyclif and His Followers* (Bodleian Library, Oxford, 1984), p. 12.

[10] See my 'Predestination, Property and Power: Wyclif's Theory of Dominion and Grace', *SCH* 2 (1965), pp. 220–36.

[11] *De statu innocentiae*, 1 (written 1374/5), WS (1922), p. 475.

[12] 1–3, pp. 475–90.

horizon (a question already raised by FitzRalph: demography is a good medieval subject, not an invention by social scientists). Wyclif, incidentally, had his own version of the view that the clergy of the Christian Church were responsible for the manpower shortage of the Roman Empire: he urged Edward III to reduce the number of clerics, so that there would be more laity, who would in turn produce more children to serve in armies defending the realm.[13] But as regards the problem of too many people in the state of natural innocence, this, he thought, would be solved by an all-provident God, who would have siphoned off the surplus population into outer space by regular translation of batches of people to join the saints and angels in heaven.[14]

But whilst on earth, if man's immortality was to be maintained, all his natural needs had to be supplied.[15] The fruits of Paradise would suffice to provide a vegetarian diet, and there would be water from the pure streams of Paradise: which Wyclif suggests might have been made even more palatable by mixing with the juice from the fruit (perhaps the first reference in history to orange squash):

> Hoc tamen probabiliter potest convinci ex scriptura quod solum fructus in paradiso nascentes naturaliter comedisset . . . Utrum autem homo potaverat aquam vel humore fructuum vixisset est magis ambiguum, sed certum est quod nullum artificiosum potasset, et sic ipso potante aquam vel non foret simplex vel simplicia nutrivissent.[16]

It was an implied preference for a temperance movement which can hardly have endeared Wyclif to the Chaucer family. Nevertheless, he continued with remorseless logic, the fruit would not grow unless the soil was fertile, and for this the air had to be healthy and the climate mild. This had been arranged by placing the Garden of Eden in the east on a high point above the rest of the world. The world was circular with a sort of

---

[13] *De Ecclesia*, 16, *WS* (1886), pp. 372–3, '. . . et ad defensionem regni ac augmentum exercitus christiani amplius populosa.'

[14] *De statu innocentiae*, 3, p. 491. To the objection 'quod nec paradisus sufficeret ad totum genus hominum, nec homines habuissent usum nascibilium in nostro habitabili, sed fuissent tam bestiae quam terrae nascentia omnino superflua', he replies, 'Et quoad secundum patet quod translatis hominibus in coelum innocentium paulatim secundum suam maturitatem, attenta quia modesta conversatione innocentium et fertilitate loci, satis potuit toti generi innocentium suffecisse.'

[15] 5, p. 501, 'Homo in ordinatione primaria creatus est ut nullo iuvamine inferioris naturae indigeat . . . sed omnia sibi necessaria habuit naturaliter ordinata . . .'. This largely follows Augustine's commentary on Genesis put into the *Sentences*, ii. 19, of Peter Lombard (but attributed by Wyclif to Isidore: 2, p. 482).

[16] 3, pp. 493–4.

pimple on top which brought it nearer heaven—'quoad pyramidem', he says—and one recalls that Dante had thought the world to be pear-shaped for much the same reason. Even Columbus had expected to sail uphill as he got near the earthly paradise. Being on top of the world, Wyclif added, would mean that the nights barely existed or were very short: just dark enough to allow for sleep, but not long enough to be an inconvenience.[17] Not too little, not too much: in fact, the essence of the situation was the golden mean.[18] The keynote of natural perfection was moderation in all things. With this absence of a population problem, the fertility of the soil, and the temperate climate, man could survive very well indeed, provided that his behaviour was as moderate as the climate—and it was this modera-tion which is the dominant factor in rational human behaviour. When at a later stage Wyclif went on to relate this to the need for temperate govern-ment, government moderated by reason, he was making an interesting anticipation of the theories of Bodin and Montesquieu that the type of government is determined by the climate of the state, a point which all three writers really borrowed from Aristotle.

After this Wyclif settled down to elaborate his theme of temperate behaviour, but a few examples must suffice here. With this temperate climate there would be no need for clothes: 'ambo primi parentes per tempus innocentiae sine erubescentia erant nudi, et ita, subducto peccato, fuisset tota posteritas, cum nec tegumentis nec ornamentis nec esculentis eguisset.' But this posed the problem of nudity.[19] Would not, Wyclif queried, the exposure of their private parts encourage promiscuity and

[17] 3, pp. 490–1, 'Sed Deus ordinavit immortalitatem hominis si persevereret in innocentia, ad quam immortalitatem necessaria foret aeris salubritas etc. Item, dicunt philosophice sancti doctores quod paradisus terrestris in quo positus est homo fuit in oriente habitabilis nostrae, elevatior terra reliqua, et sic ex situ, ex figura et insitis fuit temperatae influentiae coeli capacior et vitae humanae comodior. . . . Nec video quin paradisus sic poterit situari in alti-tudine, latitudine et figura quoad pyramidem umbrae terrae quod nihil noctis reciperet aut quantum foret expediens pro quiete.' Compare W. Oakeshott, 'Some Classical and Medieval Ideas in Renaissance Cosmography', *Essays in Commemoration of Fritz Saxl* (London, 1957), pp. 254–60.

[18] According to Wyclif the theory of the mean was taken from Aristotle, *N.E.* ii. 6, 1106a–b (*De civili dominio*, ii. 16, *WS* (1900), p. 214; iii. 9, *WS* (1903), i. 125), but Christ and the Bible were in agreement (iii. 10, i. 148–51; also *De Ecclesia*, 5, pp. 107–8), and accordingly it was central to Augustine's ideal of poverty: 'Sed Augustinus canonicis dedit caracterem mediocritas, qui distinguitur a caeteris religiosis; hanc commendarunt plurimi gentium, dicentes medi-ocritatem esse auream, quia non habet austeritatem nec superfluitatem ... Nam nimia austeritas parit superbiam et intemperantiam, superfluitas luxuriam, sed mediocritas perseverantiam', iii. 2, i. 19; compare iii. 6, i. 81–3.

[19] *De statu innocentiae*, 5, p. 501; compare p. 502, 'cum philosophice ponitur quod beati in patria habebunt integraliter cum honestate summa omnia membra nuda, et sic habuissent fideliter in statu innocentiae.'

create a permissive society? But he decided that rational man would exercise the same natural moderation in sexual activity as any other naked animal.[20] What would be the effect, he asked himself, of this relentless diet of fruit on the human digestive system? Would there not be an insoluble problem of sewage disposal? Again he answered that man's naturally moderate appetite would prevent the matter getting out of control, so that it would give offence to neither God nor man, and would not pollute the environment.

> Habuisset etiam homo repletionem et evacuationem cum tanto moderamine libratas quod nec intulissent Deo offensum nec homini nocumentum. Fuisset quidem evacuatio partium superfluentium ad complexionem neutram quousque corpus hominis fuisset de se loco indifferens sicut astra, et per consequens quousque non restitisset animae quorsumlibet differenti.[21]

On the whole he considered that the vegetarian diet would improve man's physique. Provided that he took regular exercise and avoided both laziness and excessive fatigue, he would be kept in good bodily trim. This moderate activity would be provided by the need, mentioned in Genesis 2. 15-20, for man to look after the other animals in the garden.[22]

All this faintly puritanical speculation would subsequently be given a deliberately political application, and would be pressed into service to reinforce Wyclif's general line of argument that God was the best paymaster. The state which cultivated spiritual virtue would correspondingly benefit by prosperous material conditions and a healthy economy. He would, for example, explain the social and economic miseries of fourteenth-century England—the plague, famine, the destructive violence of storms and tempests—by reference to the disordered condition of English ecclesiastical life.[23] Grace and nature go together. But perhaps the

---

[20] 3, pp. 501–2: to the objection 'quod inhonestum foret membra genitalia esse patentia sicut et actus eorum et specialiter procreandi, tum quia homo naturaliter in ostensione talium erubescit tum etiam quia exinde moveretur ad actus illicitos. Si enim sanguineus lapsus ex bonitate suae complexionis provocatur ad coitum, multo magis sanguineus in statu innocentiae, complexionis notabiliter melioris', he explains that they would be 'non plus erubescentes quam bestiae, cum omnia membra animalis sicut et eorum actus naturales sint pulchra in suo genere', citing Grosseteste's *De semine* in support; and as regards sexual activity (p. 503), 'Conceditur tamen quod innocens delectaretur naturaliter in actibus generandi, sed solum ad regulam moderatius quam nos lapsi . . . Innocens ergo delectaretur in illis actibus pene quando, quante et qualiter oporteret.'

[21] 3, p. 495.

[22] 3, p. 492.

[23] For example, *De civili dominio*, iii. 23, ii. 490; compare i. 6, p. 43, and i. 18, p. 131, for the

most attractive feature of Wyclif's first state of nature for an academic audience is his emphasis on the absence of mental fatigue produced by study. Just as constant bodily health and the absence of disease made it pointless to study medicine,[24] so this limited physical activity made it unnecessary to bother with other human arts. There was no need for agriculture or other mechanical labours: 'cum cultum terrae et artis mechanicae in statu innocentiae non fuissent', and therefore no relevance in studying the theory behind them.[25] Nor was there any need for the liberal arts or the study of language and grammar: Adam and his posterity were instructed by God and spoke the prime natural tongue, the language of Hebrew:

> Nec legitur quod Adam artificialiter didicit plus loqui, sed habuit notitiam et instructionem naturaliter a Deo . . . et ad hoc credo voces Hebreas habere maiorem efficatiam quam alias variatas.[26]

True, God did not wish man to be empty headed, and like a sort of celestial Aldous Huxley arranged for men to receive informative dreams (*somnia informantia*) whilst they slept,[27] so that they could learn the principles of the theoretical sciences without the need to study them or to use them.[28]

---

general principle that sin infects the air and creates plague. In *De statu innocentiae*, 3, p. 491, disease is created and spread by the corpses resulting from man's loss of immortality.

[24] 4, p. 498. 'Et patet quod non fuisset praxis vel theorica medicinae. Quid, rogo, valet medicina corporea ubi non fuisset discrasia corporis, monstruositas vel peccatum?'

[25] 10, p. 523; also 4, p. 495, 'Ex istis elicitur quod innocens nec arti liberali nec mechanicae intendisset . . . Cum ergo nulla fatigatio in statu innocentiae infuisset homini, patet quod nec eruditio'; pp. 497–8, 'Ulterius quoad dictae artes mathematicus quadruviales . . . arismetrica . . . musica . . . geometria . . . et astronomia . . ., patet quod dictae artes innocentibus non in-essent . . . Quantum vero ad artes mechanicas patet, cum omnes sunt finaliter propter teguamenta, esculenta vel ornamenta corporis relevantia, et homo nullo istorum in statu innocentiae eguisset, non se circa illa curiose vel sollicite occupasset. Deus enim non ordinavit homini exercitium superfluum . . .'; compare 6, p. 509.

[26] 4, p. 496; compare 5, p. 509, 'idioma Hebreum fuisset nobis naturale'. As he points out in 4, pp. 495–6, Adam was instructed, according to Genesis 2. 19, to give the animals names, and this presupposed a form of speech. In any case, how could he talk to them without language? 'Non ergo didicisset innocens a quocunque grammaticam, quia voces naturales quas quidam ponunt linguam Hebream hominibus naturaliter convenissent. Quomodo, quaeso, communicarent bestiae suas intentiones per voces sine eruditione elicitas, et non homines innocentes?'

[27] But no nightmares: 3, p. 494, 'Non enim diu dormivissent ex crapula nec haberent ex humorum excessu vel impressione sensibilium extranea sompnia tortuosa, sed quiete et regulariter dormiens haberet sompnia ipsum informantia. Si enim post lapsum Deus promittit se loqui per sompnium prophetis communibus . . . quanto magis in statu innocentiae ubi dormiens revelatione indigens foret fidelior et in corpore dispositior?'

[28] 4, pp. 495, 498.

Any further intellectual activity that was required could take the form of anticipation of the joys of heaven to come.[29] It is a little difficult to imagine what these could be unless, as Aquinas had suggested, they included watching the torments of the damned.

This is a very elaborate description of man's natural capacity for happiness, for a life of ease and leisured material prosperity. It was the classical *saeculum aureum*, and in this Golden Age there was none of the inequality of contemporary human institutions. There was no private property, since all was possessed by all in common, and in that sense there was no poverty:

> Quibus hic suppositis patet quod in statu innocentiae forent cuncta cunctis communia ... et cum omnis innocens naturaliter domin- aretur omnibus sibi inferioribus in natura, patet quod omnes homines communicarent in omnibus quae haberent.[30]

Man was the master of nature, but between men there was no need for lordship or serfdom: all were equal and self-sufficient ('homo creatus est magis sufficiens sibi ipsi tam secundum corpus quam secundum animam'), and therefore there was no call for either secular or ecclesi- astical government.[31] The just man under a system of communism requires no law:

> Et quoad leges humanas, quae propter transgressores sunt positae, patet quod in statu cui impossibilis fuisset transgressio non fuissent, quia secundum Apostolum, I *Tim.* i. 9, 'Iustis non est lex posita'.... Similiter circa temporalia non foret repugnantia, cum omnia illa forent communia.[32]

But of course women put an end to liberty and equality. Eve took the apple; sin reared its ugly head in the Garden of Eden; and humanity was thrust out of the earthly Paradise. Beyond Paradise there was a harsher

---

[29] 3, p. 495, 'patet quod per se innocens habuisset gaudium de certitudine beatitudinis sine com- possibili timore, poenali tristitia vel dolore.'

[30] 6, p. 505; compare p. 508, 'Et patet quod iustus laudans Deum meritorie in istis transitoriis habet de eis ut sic utilem usum fructus; ex quo patet quod *iusti sunt omnia*, et per consequens omnis iustus et solus huiusmodi est realiter vere dives.' For man's lordship of nature, see 5, p. 501, 'sic quod soli Deo serviens, omnibus naturis corporeis naturaliter dominetur'; and this applies to all parts of the world: 3, p. 491, 'patet quod iustus habet usum cuiuslibet partis mundi'; 6, p. 507, 'Ex quibus plane patet quod innocens utitur qualibet parte mundi.'

[31] 5, p. 500; p. 501, 'sufficiens sibi ipsi, cum sic probat Aristoteles ex per se sufficientia naturam divinam sufficientissimam, naturam animae perfectiorem corpore et felicitatem vitae hominis perfectissimam, cum per se sufficientia sit per se perfectionis conditio.'

[32] 4, p. 499.

nature, another nature of changing and painbearing climates.[33] Quite apart from his new feeling of shame at being naked, man was forced by climatic conditions to clothe himself, and to seek food and shelter.[34] He was obliged to develop the mechanical arts and to translate his dream knowledge into practice.[35] But this knowledge now survived only in a fragmentary fashion in the state of fallen nature. Most men could no longer, for example, speak Hebrew: man lost his prime divine and universal language and spoke in tongues unintelligible to others[36]—a situation which persisted until the Apostles restored the unity of language by receiving at Pentecost command of the seventy-two tongues of Babel[37] (which explains why there were seventy-two disciples), reuniting the different languages by having them all spoken within the *collegium apostolorum*. But now men had to study languages, and learn the arts of grammar and logic along with all the other human sciences.[38] Above all, however, Wyclif insisted, sin had caused man to lose his dignity as a human being in this second state of nature. He no longer had the heroic stature and self-sufficiency which he once possessed automatically. Nature became a hostile force, something which had to be fought and conquered, and yet man began his life as a baby more helpless than the young of any other animal. Here too Wyclif was closely following Aquinas, who had declared that man's fall from human dignity because of sin meant that he had receded from reason, and was now reduced to the status of an animal—indeed Aristotle had said that a bad man was worse than and inferior to a brute beast.[39] We now get from Wyclif the very familiar medieval theory that it was this sinful condition which necessitated the development of human institutions based on inequality: government, law, slavery, and private property were introduced to curb man's depraved nature.

---

[33] 3, p. 491; compare 10, p. 523: after the Fall the whole of nature becomes hostile and fights with God against man to punish sin: 'et sic pugnavit cum Deo orbis terrarum contra hominem ad Dei iniuriam vindicandum.'

[34] 5, pp. 501-2.

[35] 6, p. 509.

[36] 4, pp. 496-7.

[37] 4, p. 497, 'Sunt autem secundum doctores septuaginta duae linguae sicut ex *Genesi* x eliciunt, quia septuaginta duae gentes de filiis Noe processerant. Et hinc Christus septuaginta duos discipulos, ut patet *Luce*, x. 1, ordinavit, ut ostenderet se eundem magistrum qui in veteri testamento linguas superbientium separavit et qui in novo testamento linguas humilium adunavit.' The theory derives from Gregory of Nyssa.

[38] 6, p. 509.

[39] 5, pp. 500-1; compare Aristotle, *De partibus animalium*, iv. 10; Plato, *Protagoras*, 321c.

> Consideret ergo Philosophus quod appropriatio civilis solum inducitur ad refrenandum viciosos, qui aliter abuterentur temporalibus ... et patet quod repugnat statui innocentiae civilis proprietas. ...[40]

Wyclif ran into some difficulty at this point, since he was anxious to make this a gradual process of change. Sin had to be developed before it was necessary to create human lordship to control and restrain it. There had been no sudden transition from one state of nature to the next, and this had enabled him to accommodate Aristotle's principle that human societies had developed naturally by a slow evolution from the family household to the village to the *polis*, a progression which Wyclif extended (as did most of his contemporaries) by adding on the usual medieval categories of kingdom and empire to the hierarchy of communities.

It is clear enough what he was doing. Like Aquinas he had to combine the apparently contradictory positions taken up by his sources: Augustine had stipulated that civil institutions existed *ratione peccati*, as a remedy for sin; whereas Aristotle had regarded the development of the *polis* not only as an expression of man's naturally social and political nature, but also as the end product of man's search for human perfection. Moreover, the Aristotelian theory required this to be a lengthy process, a matter of generations at least. Yet Wyclif's medieval sources all assured him that the change had taken place within a lifetime, the lifetime of Cain. It was Cain who had introduced all the paraphernalia of civilization, and the constant search for power that goes with it: *civilitas* and *libido dominandi* were inseparable. Augustine assured him that Cain had built the first city; Hostiensis told him that Cain was the creator of civil law; and FitzRalph insisted that it was Cain who had originated private property.[41] There was no gradual transition here, and it was a problem which Wyclif never really disposed of. This, however, pales into insignificance when set against the much greater problem of explaining how Wyclif thought that he could persuade his readers to accept the accuracy, or even the possibility of

---

[40] 6, p. 506.

[41] *De civili dominio*, iii. 21, ii. 425, citing Augustine about Cain; compare ii. 433, 'Ius vero gentium creditur originatum a Cayn, et in ipso ius civile ut proximo sui principio, quod post perfectum est ab Atheniensibus, Lacedonibus et Romanis.' The reference is to *De civitate Dei*, xv. 5 and 17 (*PL* 41 cols 441, 460). *De civili dominio*, ii. 14, p. 169, 'ex adverso una communitas contendit contra aliam communitatem ratione proprietas, quae est seminarium totius contentionis civilis. Ideo Hostiensis in principio lecturae suae dicit quod iura civilia per Caym introducta sunt, et post continuata sunt per generationes gentilium'; compare *De Ecclesia*, 22, pp. 517 f. *De civili dominio*, iii. 11, i. 177, citing FitzRalph, *De pauperie salvatoris*, vi. 21: for Fitz-Ralph see further K. Walsh, *A Fourteenth-Century Scholar and Primate: Richard FitzRalph in Oxford, Avignon and Armagh* (Oxford, 1981), especially pp. 392 f.

believing in, this great rigmarole about the condition of humanity in its first natural state, a Golden Age which was so extensive that it might have developed population problems, when every member of his audience knew perfectly well that the biblical account described the state of primitive bliss as stopping short during the lifetime of Adam and Eve. He did suggest that there was nothing to prevent Adam and Eve from having had many children before Cain and Abel, and that their existence should not be denied simply because the Bible did not mention them. But it was a weak argument, especially for one who constantly proclaimed that all truth was in Scripture, and he knew it. Yet, on the other hand, it would be a mistake to dismiss the whole account as an exercise in academic speculation undertaken for its own sake, probable reason, as he put it, applied to the testimony of Scripture and the dicta of the saints.[42] In the first place Wyclif was using this fiction as a device to strip away the institutions of civilization and reveal the nature of man himself. From this point of view the De statu innocentiae was a continuation of the uncompleted anthropological study De compositione hominis of c.1370, in which Wyclif had maintained that he could not discuss the subject of lordship until he had established the nature of man himself,[43] and, more importantly, had enunciated the principle of dual nature or double substance[44] which he was to apply to all theological and political problems as a way of harmonizing apparently contradictory positions.

For our present purposes the value of the work is that it shows Wyclif making the traditional medieval response to the problem of wealth. The primitive natural equality of man and community of property stipulated by the Stoics, and endorsed by the Church Fathers as being in conformity with divine law, had had to be replaced by all the inequalities of private property and government, the lordship of man over man, as a remedy for sin in the corrupted condition of mankind after the Fall. Wealth and kingship developed together because, Wyclif explained, a personal, private right of ownership, private property, is an aspect of civil lordship, the dominium civile exercised by kings: 'Ad civilem dominationem consequitur

[42] De statu innocentiae, 1, p. 475, 'Videndum est igitur quid convenisset humano statui si totum genus hominis perpetuo statum innocentiae observasset, pro cuius indagine utendum est testimonio scripturae, dictis sanctorum et probabili ratione.'

[43] De compositione hominis, 1, WS (1884), p. 2, 'Tertio quia antecedit ad tractatum humani dominii, cum relatio non potest cognosci nisi per notitiam sui principii subiecti. Nec sciri potest quomodo homo naturaliter dominetur atque servat sibi ipsi . . . nisi praecognoscatur quomodo homo est duarum naturarum utraque . . .'; De statu innocentiae, 5, p. 501, 'Oportet ergo considerare ubi humana natura est posita'.

[44] De compositione hominis, 2, p. 35, 'homo est duae substantiae vel naturae'.

tamquam possessio saecularis proprietas'.[45] The fact that it is divinely instituted as a *remedium peccati* is no reason why the clergy should claim to have it. Kings existed to organize property long before there were priests,[46] and there was therefore no reason why the Christian priesthood should have anything to do with private property. Just as the divine approval of private property justified it for kings in the period before Christ, so conversely Christ's condemnation of private property must logically apply to the priesthood after him. Otherwise how could one explain that Christ had apparently rejected an instrument against sin that God had approved? It was precisely the difference between kings and priests which accounted for the adoption of evangelical poverty by the Early Church. For the priesthood there was now a change to the divine law principle of common ownership accepted by the Apostles and practised by the first community at Jerusalem:

> . . . ergo omnia debent esse communia. Et ista ratio notatis praedictis daret cuilibet catholico plenam fidem. In cuius confirmatione, Veritas cum suis discipulis aufugit proprietatem, sed habuit temporalia in communi, . . . et post eius ascensionem erunt eius discipulis omnia communia: 'dividebatur enim singulis prout cuicunque opus erat', *Act*. 4. 35.[47]

And so matters rested until the practice developed by which individuals endowed the clergy with private property.

In England, Wyclif tells us, this process of endowment effectively began with the British Church under Augustine of Canterbury and was

---

[45] *De civili dominio*, iii. 6, i. 80.

[46] *De potestate papae*, 12, p. 319, 'Ordinatio autem regis longe ante haec tempora processit, ut patet *De civitate Dei*, ii. 12, sic quod licet Christus tempore legis veteris approbavit dominium saeculare divinitus, et tempore legis novae approbavit multipliciter imperatorem, regem et dominum saecularem humanitus . . .'; *De officio regis*, *WS* (1887), 6, p. 143. This principle that the Old Testament relates to the laity whilst the New Testament governs the clergy underlies much of Wyclif's theory including (as hinted here) his well-known distinction between the pope as vicar of Christ as a man and the lay ruler as vicar of Christ as God.

[47] *De civili dominio*, i. 14, pp. 96–7. An extensive analysis of this follows at iii. 6, i. 77–80, in the course of which Wyclif makes the point that the Apostles acted as a corporate body ('cum istud collegium iustissime possedit hoc precium, et tamen non civiliter, cum erant illis omnia communia') so that ownership rested with the corporation itself—which accordingly acted unanimously ('unanimis . . . in voluntate et ratione')—with the Apostles themselves distributing as representative agents of the community: '. . . pro bonis pauperum quae ministrat sed tamquam humilis minister Christi et dispensator bonorum suae ecclesiae.' Compare *De. Ecclesia*, 13, p. 289, 'Unde *Act*. iii [2. 44–5; 4. 34–5] legitur quomodo possessores agrorum vendebant et ponebant ante pedes apostolorum, non ut haereditarie vel perpetue possiderent, sed ut dividetur singulis prout cuique opus erat.'

continued by the Anglo-Saxons.[48] It is true that this marked a falling away
from apostolic standards and divine law requirements. But these grants
were made with good intentions; they were useful in the circumstances of
the time; and, above all, the initial contracts of donation carried with
them, if not expressly, at least tacitly, a guarantee that they could be
revoked by the donors or their heirs. They were to be welcomed because
they were conditional and they were concessions,[49] grants made by kings
(or with royal consent) *ex libera voluntate* as acts of free will.[50] There was
nothing inherently permanent about them (so the question of mortmain
should never have arisen) and the Crown remained the real owner *vice Dei*
of the property involved. Granting property to the clergy was an act of
grace, which was quite acceptable provided both donor and recipient
recognized the conditional nature of the grant: namely, that the king was
to be acknowledged as the source of this property right; that the wealth so
granted should only be used for the good of the realm; that the clergy
themselves held it as a symbol of obedience and subjection to the civil
power; and that they had to admit that there could always be a return on
their part to full apostolic poverty. Under these terms there could be no
absolute right to private property. The king remained, in this English
proprietary church, like his Old Testament predecessors, as the real chief
bishop,[51] and the Roman bishops had no power in England. The king,
whose function was to act as the *persona communitatis*,[52] the embodiment of

---

[48] *De Ecclesia*, 15, pp. 336–7, 'et scimus pro tempore antequam Britones et Saxones dotarunt
ecclesiam vel enim fuit ecclesia nostra dotata, et interim tempore Saxonum ante adventum
Augustini fuit fides Christi infideliter praetermisssa, tunc isti principes primo dotantes
ecclesiam nostram non erant moti nisi titulo misericordiae donare plus vel minus nostrae
ecclesiae ut nec Caesar . . . sed potuerant cum donatione sua primaeva adiecisse conditionem
honestam quod elemosinarii non contempnant insurgentes in regem ad sui populi detri-
mentum. Omnia ista suppono.'

[49] *De civili dominio*, ii. 3, pp. 22–3, 'Nam sub illa conditione donantur eis temporalia ut patet ex
indispensabili lege Christi': the condition may be tacit or stated ('nisi sub conditione tacita vel
expressa'), 4, p. 26; 10, p. 107, compare *De Ecclesia*, 15, p. 344, 'Hoc enim fuit pactum dota-
tionis primaevae.'

[50] *De Ecclesia*, 10, p. 228, 'rex autem Angliae debet concedere et condere leges tales privatas de
suo regali dominio ad aedificationem ecclesiae: ideo capiendum est tamquam per se notum
quod regis est illas leges privatas et elemosinas interpretari et in rectitudine sua defendere';
p. 229, 'quod notetur forma et finis et gratia cuius haec privilegia sunt concessa'; and 13,
p. 280, for grants made by the king *ex libera voluntate*; compare 11, p. 244, 'dicitur quod magna
libertas est concessa a regibus ecclesiae Anglicanae'.

[51] For example, *De officio regis*, 6, p. 119, 'Consequenter apparet ex hoc quod episcopus in
quantum talis est nomen officii et per consequens episcopus regis, quidquid fecerit in
quantum talis fecit auctoritate regis, in quo concedendum est quod rex faciat in illo'; *De potestate papae*, 12, pp. 375–9; *De civili dominio*, ii. 5, pp. 39–41, for the king of England as *dominus
clericorum*.

[52] *De potestate papae*, 12, p. 347, 'oportet esse unum caput ad beneficia ecclesiastica partiendum,

the realm itself, was responsible for the creation, filling, and endowment of benefices and the founding of monasteries and religious houses; and in addition to these rights of patronage, he had as *patronus* a continuing duty of protection and a corresponding right of taxation of the clergy for the needs of the realm.[53]

It was a situation which could not last. Faith grew weary and the world got worse. By introducing private wealth the silver age of the lay proprietary church contained the seeds of its own decay. Inevitably, over the course of time, the clergy began to feel that it had a prescriptive right to its own private property: and the more it acquired, the greater grew its *cupiditas* and desire for more. Moreover, the error was compounded by the appearance of the papacy as head of the Universal Church, and its still more greedy claims to supremacy over any national clergy and a right to possession of their property. It brought the world to a third age,[54] an age of lead, of papal bulls. There had, Wyclif explained, been nothing wrong with the bishops of Rome whilst they remained essentially bishops, enjoying a divine equality with other bishops of the Church. It was that most Christian emperor Constantine who had so misguidedly injected the poison of private wealth into the *corpus Ecclesiae*, and by this Caesarean endowment had converted the Church into a universal landed society, the very earth, the *mundus* itself.[55] The Church was now 'our Roman empire', enjoying the fullness of material wealth, no longer a spiritual society concerned only with the faith and the sacraments. Possession was now the

---

nam lex Christi est ad illud sufficiens et persona populi, cui praeficeretur talis praepositus, foret optimus iudex ad discernendum talem praepositum episcopo praesentandum. Sic enim fuit in primitiva Ecclesia, nec cessat ratio quare non sic foret hodie.'

[53] *De Ecclesia*, 15, p. 340, 'Unde ex iure patronatus confert beneficia interim vacantia, et licentiato capitulo ad novam electionem, praesentato sibi electo, approbat vel reprobat sicut placet'; compare 12, p. 274; *De officio regis*, 7, pp. 182–3, 'Cum igitur omnium istorum patronatum remanet penes regem capitale dominium eo quod rex non potest a se alienare nisi deserat regnum suum . . . Cum igitur semper penes regem remanet basis dominii, et officio suo pertinet sub poena admissionis contra tales abusus de remediis providere . . . Res igitur sacra, super quibus rex habet capitale dominium, debent usui quam limitarunt leges ecclesiae mancipare'; also *De civili dominio*, iii. 2, i. 26–8.

[54] As with dominion and grace, Wyclif's idea of the three ages of the Church may have been inspired by Aegidius Romanus. In *De ecclesiastica potestate*, II. iii. 5–8, Aegidius distinguished three periods in the history of the Church: the first when temporal possessions were forbidden; the second when they were allowed; and the present age when the clergy had temporal possessions with God's help to maintain the *Ecclesia* as a perfect society.

[55] For example, *De civili dominio*, ii. 10, pp. 107–8; *De veritate sacrae scripturae*, 31 *WS* (1905–7), iii. 238–9; and see the long argument in *De Ecclesia*, 8, pp. 168–80, that the privilege of relative poverty granted to the clergy by Christ far outweighs the *privilegium* by which Constantine granted the Empire.

keynote of ecclesiastical affairs and, what was worse, the Donation of Constantine had led, or rather misled, the popes into thinking that it was *their* world. Indeed, it was Constantine who had given the pope the very name of pope itself, to indicate his superiority over other sees:

> sic rex terrenus facit suum episcopum esse papam, ut patet de Constantino, et generaliter imperatores fecerunt quod Romani episcopi forent tantae praeeminentiae super alios episcopos . . .

and who had induced the Council of Nicaea to confirm this.[56] Constantine had tried to make his own bishop into a world ruler, to make Rome the centre of the universe, which was (he commented) as absurd as supposing that the conversion of the emperor of China will make Peking into the capital city of the Christian Church.[57]

Wyclif's charge against Constantine was therefore a double one. In the first place, he had created a head bishop where one had not existed before—and was not necessary when there were already kings—but who now claimed jurisdiction over all other clergy, an essentially pagan institution[58] (and it is perhaps significant that Wyclif dated the Donation to 301, well before the Milvian Bridge). Secondly, and much more important in the present context, Constantine had made the pope, and through him the clergy generally, the recipients of civil lordship, the capacity to hold

---

[56] *De officio regis*, 6, p. 145; *De veritate sacrae scripturae*, 31, iii. 232–4. This point merely had to be quoted out of Higden's *Polychronicon*, iv. 36, (*RS*, v. 140), who tells 'quomodo excellentia Romani imperii adinvenit papatum sui pontificis super alios: "Nycena" inquit "synodus hoc contulit privilegium Romano pontifici ut sicut Augustus prae caeteris regibus, ita Romanus prae caeteris pontifex haberetur episcopis et papa velut principalis pater vocaretur",' *De potestate papae*, 8, p. 177; also 9, pp. 215–16. But he also cites FitzRalph, *De quaestionibus Armenorum*, viii. 24, here.

[57] *De potestate papae*, 9, pp. 215–16, '. . . quod imperator terrenus tam irreligiose instituit, ymo ut dicit, si imperator Thartario ecclesiam de Cambalek aut de Cathay conversus ad christianismum caput omnium aliarum ecclesiarum constitueret, cederet caeteris paribus capitalitas Romanae ecclesiae. Horribile itaque atque necessario defectibile fundamentum Ecclesiae a saeculari principe ita inductum.' For further discussion of this and similar passages see 'The Apostolicus and the Bishop of Rome', *JTS*, ns 13–14 (1962–3), pp. 290–317 and 311–54 respectively.

[58] *De potestate papae*, 5, p. 95, 'Unde Deum contestor nec ex scriptura nec ex sanctis doctoribus fundari video istius iurisdictionis extensionem tam vanam, sed ex ritu gentilium sicut institutionem papae et cardinalium introductam'; 10, p. 232, 'Patet autem ex praedictis quomodo Romanus pontifex fuit consocius alii pontificibus usque ad dotationem ecclesiae, et exhinc ex auctoritate Caesaris coepit capitaliter dominari', citing Gratian, d. 96, c. 14, *Constantinus*; *De civili dominio*, ii. 10, pp. 107–8, 'Probatur primo eo quod a fundatione Ecclesiae usque ad tempus beati Silvestri, quod est circa annum Domini ccc, alienata sunt haec temporalia quoad civilitatem . . . Non enim est firmior dotatio Constantini quam fuit regula apostolica de habendo omnia in communi, sed ista disrupta per avaritiam sacerdotum . . . tale dominium ex Dei omnipotentia dissolvi poterit.'

wealth as private property in their own right. The clergy could now defy the provisions of divine law, the evangelical prohibitions on wealth, on the basis of a purely human legal system which made them the effective owners of what they possessed: 'ad civilem dominationem consequitur tamquam possessio saecularis proprietas'.[59] Clerical property ceased to be a form of tenancy held on a conditional grant from the Crown (which had at least circumvented the biblical prohibitions of clerical possession by leaving ultimate ownership with the king), and now became a private-right possession immune from lay control altogether. As clerical possession expanded, so—according to Wyclif—the kingdom was correspondingly reduced and weakened. He argued that by his own time clerical possession had deprived the king of more than a third of England: 'appropriarunt plus quam tertiam partem regni',[60] exhausting the wealth of the realm by treating it as if it was their own. Every century for a thousand years, he declared, served only to increase the need to repair the damage done by the Donation.[61] The clergy must renounce their civil lordship as the only secure way to reverse the ever-increasing effects of this calamity.[62] Just as the priests of the Old Testament had renounced their possessions in a jubilee year,[63] just as even Constantine himself had renounced an

[59] *De civili dominio*, iii. 6, i. 80; and see the long discussion of this point at iii. 8, i. 111-13; also iii. 21, ii. 441, 'Ideo ad distinguendum istos modus dominandi, dico quod layci dominantur civiliter, clerici vero evangelice, cum primi habent proprietatem civilem, alii autem occupant bona communia Ecclesiae, . . . Dominatio enim saecularis est proprietaria . . . sed dominatio ecclesiastica consistit in communicatione bonorum Ecclesiae, quae ut sic debent esse communia.' There is also frequent quotation of Augustine's famous definition ('Iura ergo humano dicitur "haec villa mea est, haec domus mea est, hic servus meus est" . . . Per iura regum possidentur possessiones', *In Ioh. ev.*, vi. 1, 25-6 (*PL* 35 col. 1436 = Gratian, d. 8 c. 1): for example, *De Ecclesia*, 14 p. 301; *De officio regis*, 7, p. 184, to demonstrate that clerical property should be held from the Crown or not at all.

[60] *De civili dominio*, ii. 1, p. 7; compare ii. 3, p. 21, 'Iam vero aspirant insatiabiliter non tamquam Christi discipuli sed Caesaris ad pinguiora dominia et mundo libera, ad exemptiones, privilegiationes et dignitates, ex quibus pecunia regni indebite est exhausta'; also *De veritate sacrae scripturae*, 25 and 27, iii. 20 and 80.

[61] *De potestate papae*, 7, pp. 160-4; *De officio regis*, 11, pp. 252-4; *De veritate sacrae scripturae*, 11, i. 266-7.

[62] For example, *De civili dominio*, ii. 17, p. 240, 'Unde videtur michi quod nunquam ab origine mundi foret plus necessarium quod theologi et ecclesiastici sint vigiles, renunctiantes temporalibus in personis propriis, et hortantes saeculares ne propter nimiam affectionem ad temporalia amittant aeterna'; ii. 18, p. 269; 'Nec credo qod *ista irregularitas umquam evacuabitur* ab Ecclesia antequam ab onere temporalium sit exuta'. In ii. 14, pp. 179-82, he suggests a three-stage programme of renunciation to match a return through the three ages of the Church. Compare *De potestate papae*, 5, p. 101, where the duties of the *papa evangelicus* who is to bring this about include 'secundo quod renueret omnem dotationem caesaream'.

[63] *De civili dominio*, ii. 4, p. 35, quoting Ezekiel 46. 7, 'Si ergo non licuit sacerdotibus corporalibus retinere quicquam de haereditate principis ultra annum iubileum . . . quanto magis non liceret spiritualibus Christi sacerdotibus quibus praecipit relinquere omnia quae possident.'

empire,[64] so the clergy must give up its civil right to private property—or else the king would have to override the private rights of ownership by reverting to the absolute power which he held in reserve as vicar of God and confiscate the Caesarean endowment as a matter of reason of state. Either way the clergy must be restored to the apostolic poverty of the primitive church, so that spiritual health and material wealth would flourish together as never before.[65]

Wyclif's endlessly reiterated demand for the dispossession of a landed clergy and religious orders, the *possessionati*, grown fat on the ownership of houses, estates, property, and grants of every kind, as part of his programme for a reformation of the English church-state is too well known to merit elaboration here. I merely want to underline three aspects of this demand for compulsory poverty. In the first place Wyclif's target was, as I have said, the English clergy's claim to possess wealth in its own right:[66] the objection was less to the possession of wealth in itself as the demand to be allowed to do so on the basis of a private property right immune from royal control and therefore far in excess of the property rights of the laity. The clergy became a collection of independent corporations within the kingdom, bodies in the kingdom but not of it. But if that point was conceded and amended, Wyclif had fairly generous views on what was meant by poverty (and we must remember that he was after all a

---

[64] *De civili dominio*, i. 39, p. 289, 'Unde videtur mihi quod clerici, caecati lege Caesarea, considerarent quomodo Romani principes infideles, ut Octavianus Caesar Augustus et caeteri blasphemi maxime, quoad mundum habundarunt dominio temporalium, et quando imperatores facti sunt christiani quoad mundum decrevit imperium.'

[65] For example, *De civili dominio*, ii. 13, pp. 152–3, 'quia exclusa proprietate temporalium a clericis ut in primitiva Ecclesia, et tota civilitate devoluta ad laicos, foret, si non fallor, maior virtutum ubertas et maior in republica temporalia copia quam est modo . . . Et sic utrobique tam clerici quam laici forent in virtutibus copiosiores, et populi in temporalibus habundantiores; tunc enim exclusa foret radix peccati de domo Domini, et laici multiplicantes temporalia qui eis opportunius possent intendere . . . et per consequens in omni genere bonorum foret tota Ecclesia undique fertilior, et sic politica legis Christi ducens ad hunc finem foret optima, quia pro bono utilior . . . consideret secundo quomodo utilius foret Ecclesiae regi secundum institutionem primariam quam Christus docuit quam secundum institutionem caesaream, et videbit quod inconveniens visum sequi ex doctrina Christi non foret nisi restitutio Ecclesiae ad statum quem Christus docuit.'

[66] *De potestate papae*, 5, p. 89, 'Notandum tamen quod temporalia non occasione ab eis data sed male accepta venenant ecclesiam. Si enim totus clerus diceret effectualiter quod omnia temporalia quae habemus ut clerici forent purae elemosynae saecularium et bona communia pauperum, secundo effectualiter et indifferenter ministraremus de illis magis egentibus, et tertio consumeremus precise de illis quantum est necessarium ad nostrum clericale officium, possemus proprietate usus et ministerii occupare licite omnia temporalia quae habemus.' See also the discussion of the different kinds of poverty in *De civili dominio*, iii. 8, i. 111–12, in which humility is as much a factor as ownership or use: the best is of course that 'statui innocentiae conformissimam'. There is no natural right to private property: ii. 8, p. 81.

cleric himself). Apostolic poverty, whilst variable, could still allow for a moderate amount of possession, as it did in the state of innocence:

> Cuius sensus dependet super isto quod in statu innocentiae purae fuisset naturale civile dominium ... nunc autem sequentes artissimam evangelicam paupertatem ex eisdem principiis sunt igitur pauperes quia ex nudo usu moderato et titulo gratioso originalis iustitiae contentati....[67]

Poverty lay in absence of ownership combined with restricted use rather than denial of possession altogether. Aquinas had shown, he indicated,[68] that Aristotle was quite the best guide to what the Bible meant, and Aristotle had said that the best society, whilst eschewing superfluous, excess wealth, must ensure that there are enough necessities for a sufficient life to be lived. The poor priest must be given his basic necessities like food and clothing[69]—especially clothing, because whilst too much might stifle the word of God, it would be just as bad if he had too little and had to preach naked. He might very well catch cold, and one cannot preach properly with a chill: 'ne ex defectu tegumenti deveniant reumata indispositi cavere verbum Dei.'[70] Besides, too much austerity can easily lead to spiritual pride, and he counselled clergy whose flock would not give them adequate sustenance either to engage in manual labour to support themselves or else to leave their benefices and go off to find somewhere better.[71] Not too little, not too much: the ideal was the mean, a moderate use.[72] In addition to their tithes, he would not condemn private charitable grants being given by laymen to the clergy (although this was more dangerous and they had to be used carefully)—but the crucial factor remained the need for ownership to be retained by the lay benefactor so

---

[67] *De civili dominio*, iii. 8, i. 113.

[68] *De civili dominio*, iii. 21, ii. 443.

[69] *De civili dominio*, ii. 3, p. 21, quoting I Timothy 6. 8; 2. 12, p. 143, 'quod nulli ecclesiastico donata sunt temporalia nisi de quanto sunt media sibi necessaria ad officium'; *De potestate papae*, 5, p. 85; *De mandatis divinis*, WS (1922), 25, p. 381; *De statu innocentiae*, 10, p. 523, 'retardat enim clericos ab officio sacerdotis cum gravat eos ultra alimenta et tegumenta sufficientia.'

[70] *De civili dominio*, iii. 13, i. 239.

[71] *De civili dominio*, i. 41, p. 327, 'Quod si a raro contingentibus unus populus desit sacerdoti in vitae necessariis ad ministerium subeundem, opus supererogationis foret pati penuriam, exhortando et ministrando illi populo, et vivendo stipendiis alterius populi vel labore manuum instar apostoli ... Et aliter subtrahendum est sacerdotale ministerium, et executiendo pulverem pedem a sic obstinatis, ad populum alium convertendum.' The justification cited is that of Matthew 10. 14 and Acts 13. 46–51.

[72] *De civili dominio*, iii. 2, i. 19; iii. 7, i. 93–5: excess in either direction is deadly to *parsimonia evangelica*.

that these benefactions did not come into the category of clerical private property.[73]

Ownership of the wealth of a kingdom must remain with the kingdom itself, not with any of its individual members. But this only transferred the problem to a higher level. How could a kingdom have rights of ownership when all belonged to God? The logical answer was to equate the kingdom with God. Like most contemporary writers, Wyclif accepted that the world formed the patrimony of Christ, the *patrimonium crucifixi*, who was the source of all grace. Indeed, it was precisely because the king acted in place of Christ that he had the right to dispossess the *possessionati*:

> Unde vere dicit quod si patrimonium petit vel fundum suum vel corpus, cum sint de possessione humana, licet in casu invadere et specialiter clerico possessionato a principe et eius legibus rebellante.[74]

Christ possessed all kingdoms,[75] and so the entire Church formed a great treasury of material wealth, a bank or storehouse of temporal goods, matching and corresponding to the spiritual treasury of celestial grace. Christ was said to have two treasuries or banks: there were, said John XXII (following Augustine), two *loculi Christi*.[76] There is the sacramental *thesaurus Ecclesiae*, from which sacramental grace is distributed; and alongside it is the earthly treasury, the material *thesaurus Ecclesiae*, which contains all the material possessions and earthly wealth of the Church.[77] In

---

[73] *De officio regis*, 3, pp. 59–60, 'Videtur igitur mihi secundum veritatem scripturae quod omnes clerici debent pure vivere de decimis, oblationibus et privatis elemosinis laicorum, sic quod omnia civilia dominia in regno debent esse in manibus saecularium dominorum.'

[74] *De officio regis*, 7, p. 184; *De Ecclesia*, 3, p. 51, 'Hodie autem superadditur quod bona pro quorum acquisitione, conservatione et repetitione tantum insistimus sunt bona Ecclesiae et patrimonium Christi: ideo licet pro bona universalis Ecclesiae conservationi eorum insistere'; *De mandatis divinis*, 30, pp. 459–60; *De veritate sacrae scripturae*, 20, ii. 132; *De potestate papae*, 2, p. 23, for *thesaurus Domini* (re martyrdom); compare Bernard, *De consideratione*, iv. 4 (*PL* 182, col. 782).

[75] *De civili dominio*, i. 21, p. 154, 'et scit quod Domini est terra et plenitudo eius, orbis terrarum et universi qui habitant in eo' [Psalm 23 (24), 1].

[76] *Extravagantes Iohannis XXII*, xiv. 5: for further examples see my *Problem of Sovereignty* (Cambridge, 1963), pp. 179–82.

[77] See his condemnation of popes for their readiness to 'expendere corporalem thesaurum domini dominorum', *De potestate papae*, 12, p. 292; and the attack on Clement VII in *De officio regis*, 6, p. 121, 'Sed quis auderet asserere quod non licet dominis temporalibus aufferre villas, castra et thesaurum Ecclesiae quem occupat Robertus Gibonensis cum suis sacerdotibus tamquam suum?' See also *De Ecclesia*, 13, p. 291, for an extended analogy of the two types of food, temporal and spiritual, which go into the stomach of the *corpus Ecclesiae* ('sit tribuit commensurale alimentum spirituale per praelatos distribuendum fidelibus, sic dat escam corporalem partiendam per activos'). But the clergy are like worms in the body: 'Si enim viator haberet vermen in stomacho qui consumeret nutrimentum membrorum, quomodo

Wyclif's version it was of course the king who controlled the purse-strings of both bags. The king was to ensure the distribution of both temporal and spiritual suffrages: one directly by himself; the other, the spiritual, through the actions of good priests.[78] It was however a papal theory in origin, and is another example (like the closely related argument of dominion and grace) of Wyclif's ability to take over hierocratic theory and adapt it to his own essentially national requirements. It was not, in Wyclif's eyes, for the pope to claim that all that men had—*omne quod habet*—derived from the pope as the great banker of the heavenly treasuries. John of Salisbury had said that every *respublica* had its fisc, since every corporate body had a stomach of its own,[79] and whilst Wyclif allowed that there was only one universal bank in heaven—the predestined, he writes, are in the stomach of the Church[80]—he insisted that on earth there was a bank with many branches. Every national kingdom in western Europe or Christendom (*Christianismus*) formed its own celestial treasury here below.[81] Each national church-state was, so to speak, a Nat-West version under its king of the great universal bank of heaven managed by Christ.

It would be a mistake to give the impression that Wyclif was being particularly original or idiosyncratic in describing the *ecclesia Anglicana/ regnum Angliae* as a national bank. It may have been Wyclif's influence

---

servaretur sanitas et valitudo eorum? . . . sic autem est in corpore Ecclesiae cuius virtus regitiva est patris sapientia.'

[78] *De Ecclesia*, 15, pp. 340-2; *De officio regis*, 7, p. 181, 'Debet igitur credi quod rex ex omissione negligenti in isto regimine non minus peccaret fraudando subditos a spirituali suffragio quam iniuste temporalia auferendo vel suos legios occidendo'. Note also that demand in *De civili dominio*, ii. 3, pp. 20-1, that the clergy should be content with their grants from the king: 'Ideo praecipit quod contentur, subducta cupiditate iniusta bonorum proximi, de suis stipendiis a communi aerario ministratis . . . Et revera si permanerent in suis limitibus primitivis, contenti de stipendiis a communi aerario saecularie ministratis, nunquam tantum scidissent christianorum imperium temporale, in civile dominium monstruose atque praepostere surrepentes.' The passage is inspired by the advice given by Christ to the Roman soldiers to be content with their wages in Luke, 3. 14: Wyclif describes them as 'Romani milites imperatorum stipendiarii defendentes Iudaeam'.

[79] *Policraticus*, v. 2; and for the idea of the fisc see further E. H. Kantorowicz, *The King's Two Bodies* (Princeton, 1957), pp. 173-92. In a different context Wyclif quotes the idea that the clergy itself is the stomach of the realm: *De potestate papae*, 12, p. 377, 'totum enim regnum est unum corpus . . . Ideo oportet . . . incipere a clero, cum sit pars principalis et stomachus corporis per quem cibi digestis et sanitas sunt ad caetera membra corporis derivanda.'

[80] *De Ecclesia*, 3, pp. 60-1, 'in stomacho sanctae matris Ecclesiae' where the elect are assimilated by the digestive process, but the hypocritical *lapsi* are expelled again like the wind swallowed whilst eating or 'ut aqua tepida quae provocat ad vomitum'.

[81] For example, Wyclif's charge against papal tax collectors for trying to withdraw wealth from the *patrimonium regni*, *De officio regis*, 5, p. 108: the king should refuse this ('vel negare sibi corporale regni sui suffragium'), pp. 104-5; also 6, p. 119; 7, p. 184.

which inspired the use of the idea by the English government in Edward III's last Parliament of January 1377, when the crown was trying to raise money to finance the French wars.[82] But for two centuries the French themselves had been describing France as a treasury of heavenly grace on the grounds that France was the real *civitas Dei*,[83] and Wyclif himself pointed to Saint Augustine as his authority on the whole subject. 'John, son of Augustine', it was said of him;[84] and he certainly regarded himself as the best Augustinian of the fourteenth century. Nor can there be any doubt that Augustine had used the notion of a *thesaurus Ecclesiae* on many occasions. The Church, he had declared, is the fisc of Christ: 'si non habet rem suam publicam, Christus non habet fiscum suum';[85] and commenting on Matthew 6. 20, 'Lay up for yourselves treasures in heaven', he had referred to Christ as the keeper of the great celestial bank to which all earthly riches ought to be committed.[86] The point is beyond dispute. Yet it is very questionable whether what Augustine said was what Wyclif meant, and I would like therefore to finish off, thirdly, by suggesting that if a comparison is made with the teaching of Augustine himself on the subject of private wealth, at least one very significant difference will emerge.

The problem of wealth and private property, which had greatly taxed so many patristic authors, was an inescapable one for Augustine himself. As an imperial bishop Augustine was automatically a prominent member of a society, the Roman Empire, which had long maintained that the prime justification for state power was the defence of private property rights. As Cicero had urged, without the *res privata* there would be no *res publica*,[87] and however much the imperialization of the Roman Empire

---

[82] *Rotuli Parliamentorum* (London, 1767), ii. 361–2: see *SCH*, Subsidia 5 (1987), pp. 148–50.

[83] *SCH* 14 (1977), pp. 148–9, and here further literature.

[84] H. B. Workman, *John Wyclif* (Oxford, 1926), 1, p. 119. For an example of Wyclif's own praise of Augustine—he has never found the errors which Augustine was alleged to have committed, and therefore 'inter doctores scripturae sacrae citra auctores est Augustinus praecipuus'—see *De veritate sacrae scripturae*, 2, i. 35–9.

[85] *Enarratio in Psalmos*, cxlvi. 17 (*PL* 37, col. 1911).

[86] *Enarratio in Psalmos*, xxxviii. 12 (*PL* 36, cols 423–4), 'Sollicitudini tuae consilium do, Thesaurizate vobis thesaurum in coelo. Hic in terra si velles servare divitias quaereres horreum: . . . Quid si dabo melius? Dicam tibi, Noli commendare huic minus idoneo, sed est quidam idoneus, illi commenda: habet magna horrea ubi perire non possint divitiae; magnus super omnes divites dives est. Iam forte dicturus es, Et quando audeo tali commendare? Quid si ipse te hortatur? Agnosce illum, non solum paterfamilias est, sed et dominus tuus est. Nolo, inquit, serve meus, perdas peculium tuum . . . Est alius locus quo te transferam. Praecedat te quod habes; noli timere ne perdas: dator ego eram, custos ego ero . . . Sed ego, inquis, quomodo pono in coelo? Dedi tibi consilium: ubi dico, pone: quomodo perveniat ad coelum, nolo scias. Pone in manibus pauperum.'

[87] For example, *In Catilinam*, iv. 2–3; *De officiis*, II. xxi. 73; compare I. vii. 20; and for the purpose of law to protect property, *Pro Caecina*, 73–5.

had changed the basis on which property was to be held, the Roman law of property was probably the most highly developed and sophisticated aspect of the Roman legal system. For Augustine the entire business of private wealth in a Christianized Roman Empire was something which could not be lightly brushed aside as if it was something of little consequence to the faithful.[88] It is sometimes said that Augustine's attitude towards the possession of private wealth was one of neutrality, but this does less than justice to a much more complex viewpoint. It was neutral much more in the sense of being double-sided: ambiguous or ambivalent in the best sense; and, as one might expect of a Platonist, his whole approach was fundamentally teleological. In essence it was, to Augustine, a question of desire: what did one want wealth *for*? Wealth, however much or little of it, was inert matter, something which did not *matter* in itself,[89] an aspect of the *civitas terrena*. In fact, in the form of houses, strongholds, estates, and so on it literally was the earthly city, and therefore, like civil society, political power, the whole apparatus of the *pax terrena* —the peaceful enjoyment of one's possessions—it had no positive value if desired for its own sake.[90] Wealth, in itself, offered nothing beyond itself. Surely, he asked, it is happiness to have your sons safe, your daughters beautiful, your barns full, your cattle numerous, neither wall nor hedge falling down, no tumult or clamour in the streets: but peace and quiet, order and abundance, plenty of all things in your houses and cities. Should the righteous shun such things? Did not Abraham's house abound with gold and silver, children, servants, cattle? Yes, this may be happiness: but only on the left hand, the left hand of temporal, mortal, bodily things. I am not asking you to shun them, he continued, but you must never make the mistake of thinking them to be on the right hand, the right of God, of eternity, of the years that fail not. Let us *use* the left hand for the time being, but ardently desire and long for the right hand to achieve eternity.[91]

This passage from his commentary on the Psalms neatly encapsulates the main points of Augustine's teaching, even though his language about wealth was often considerably more savage. Goods are false gods:[92] the

[88] D. J. MacQueen, 'St. Augustine's Concept of Property Ownership', *Recherches Augustiniennes*, 8 (1972), pp. 187–229; also H. A. Deane, *The Political and Social Ideas of St. Augustine* (New York and London, 1963), especially pp. 105–12, 127–49.

[89] *Ep.* clvii. 4, 23 (*PL* 33, col. 686), 'Sed ut nobis ostenderetur nec in isto paupertatem per seipsam divinitus honoratam, nec in illo divitias fuisse damnatas, sed in isto pietatem, in illo impietatem suos exitus habuisse . . .'.

[90] *Ep.* clv. 3, 10 (*PL* 33, cols 670–1).

[91] *Enarratio in Psalmos*, cxliii. 18 (*PL* 37, col. 1903).

[92] *Enarratio in Psalmos*, lxxix. 14 (*PL* 36, col. 989).

world is full of evil to urge us not to desire it, and yet, disfigured as it is, we cannot despise it as we should. The world is evil: oh, it is so very evil—and yet we love it and desire it as if it was good.[93] There was for Augustine no profit in wealth, least of all in money. Money, he tells us, is made round to indicate its mobile nature, its capacity to roll away and leave nothing behind.[94] Gold and silver evaporate, and are no more substantial than wind and smoke: those who seek them are swept headlong into the sea like Gadarene swine.[95] Seeking wealth, like the pursuit of political power, for their own sakes is theft: there is no true property *right*, because wealth cannot be rightful. Property in itself is a *latrocinium*, stolen property,[96] because you cannot have more except at somebody else's expense: they must lose for you to gain; for you to inherit, someone must die. You cannot live without harming others, and trying to prevent them from doing to you what you are doing to them.[97] So, very much like Hobbes, Augustine depicted the life of man in nature as a process of endless desire for more[98] to counteract his permanent fear of loss.[99] But if desire was present, he

---

[93] *Sermo* lxxx. 8 (*PL* 38, col. 498), 'Malus est mundus, ecce malus est, et sic amatur quasi bonum esset'; compare lviii. 8 (398), 'Ipsa est infelicitas hominum: propter quod peccant, morsentes hic dimittunt, et ipsa peccatum secum portant. Peccas propter pecuniam, hic dimittenda est: peccas propter vitiam, hic dimittenda est . . .'; also *Enarratio in Psalmos*, cxxxi. 25 (*PL* 37, col. 1727).

[94] *Enarratio in Psalmos*, lxxxiii. 3 (*PL* 37, col. 1057), 'Quid enim tam incertum quam res volubilis? Nec immerito ipsa pecunia rotunda signatur, quia non stat.'

[95] *In Ioh. Ev.*, x. 6 (*PL* 35, col. 1469), 'Nonne omnia fumus et ventus? Nonne omnia transeunt, currunt? Et vae his qui haeserint transeuntibus, quia simul transeunt. Nonne omnia fluvius praeceps currens in mare? Et vae qui ceciderit, quia in mare trahetur'; *Enarratio in Psalmos*, cxxxi. 25 (*PL* 37, col. 1727), 'Pecunia nihil est: non inde auxilium habebitis. Multi propter pecuniam praecipitati sunt, multi propter pecuniam perierunt, multi propter multam quaesiti sunt a raptoribus: tuti essent si non haberent quaererentur.'

[96] *De civitate Dei*, xix. 12 (*PL* 41, col. 638), 'Ideoque si offeretur ei servitus plurimum, vel civitatis vel gentis, ita ut sic ei servirent quemadmodum sibi domi suae serviri volebat, non se iam latronem latebris conderet, sed regem conspicuum sublimaret, cum eadem in illo cupiditas et malitia permaneret'; compare iv. 4 (115).

[97] *Enarratio in Psalmos*, lxiv. 9 (*PL* 36, cols 780–1). The law uses fear to moderate how much men take from each other: *De libero arbitrio*, I. xv. 32 (*PL* 32, col. 1239), 'Dum enim haec amittere timent, tenent in his utendis quemadmodum modum aptum vinculo civitatis, qualis ex huiuscemodi hominibus constitui potest. Non autem ulciscitur peccatum cum amantur ista, sed cum aliis per improbitatem auferuntur.'

[98] *Sermo* cxiii.4 (*PL* 38, col. 650); lxxxv. 6 (523), 'Radix est enim omnium malorum avaritia. Avaritia est velle esse divitem, non iam esse divitem.' See further my 'Augustine and the General Will', *Studia Patristica*, 9 = *TU* 94 (1966), pp. 487–522.

[99] *Enarratio in Psalmos*, xxxviii. 11 (*PL* 36, col. 438), 'Homo cordatus nihil praetermittis omnino, unde nummus super nummum et in occulto diligentius castigetur. Depraedaris hominem, caves depraedatorem: quod facis times ne patiaris, et in eo quod pataris non te corrigis . . .'; cxxiii. 10 (37, col. 1646), 'Quid ergo tenes? Aurum. Tene ergo, si tenes, non tibi auferatur invito. Si autem et per aurum traheris quo non vis, et ideo te quaerit maior raptor, quia invenit

argued, there was basically no difference between rich and poor: a poor man wanting to be rich was really a rich man who happened to be without wealth—and he had no real hope of gaining satisfaction.[100] From wanting corn, wine, and oil, he would want the farms and estates which produced them: and why stop there? Next, he would want the world, then heaven itself.[101] Similarly, possessing more created pride; desiring more was avarice; taking more was theft: wealth was the root of all evil and led to all the other sins.[102] Private property was a symbol of sin, even if not sinful in itself: it was a mark of man's alienation from his true self.

Nevertheless, however evil wealth and property might become, they were divine creations: even Satan had been created by God, and nothing was so bad that it could not, in other circumstances, become a quasi-good. Most bad things were double-sided: even heresy had its value as a test for faith, just as a slave in the municipal mines should remember that his misery was working to beautify the city.[103] Therefore property, like civil power, like the Roman Empire itself, could cease to be stolen property, would no longer in fact be evil, if, on the contrary, it was made useful for a higher purpose. Wealth could be useful, and should therefore be *used* to

---

minorem raptorem; ideo te quaerit maior aquila, quia prior cepisti leporem: praeda tibi fuit minor, praeda eris maiori. Haec non vident homines in rebus humanis, tanta cupiditate caecantur'; *De civitate Dei*, iv. 3 (*PL* 41, col. 114), 'Sed divitem timoribus anxium, moeroribus tabescentem, cupiditate flagrantem, nunquam securum, semper inquietum, perpetuis inimicitiarum contentionibus anhelantem, augentem sane his miseriis patrimonium suum in immensum modum atque illis augmentis curas quoque amarissimas aggerantem . . .'; *Ep.* cxxx. 2, 3 (*PL* 33, col. 495), 'cum sit eis non indigere quam eminere praestantius; quae plus excruciant adepta timore amissionis quam concupita adeptionis ardore?' *Sermo* cxiii. 4 (*PL* 38, col. 650), 'Quales divitiae sunt propter quas latronem times . . .?'

[100] *Enarratio in Psalmos*, lxxxiii. 3 (*PL* 37, col. 1057), 'Qui vero nihil horum habent, et habere desiderant, inter reprobandos divites computantur: non enim attendit Deus facultatem sed voluntatem'; li. 14 (36, cols 609–10), 'Viderunt enim etiam ipsos pauperes etsi non habentes pecuniam, tamen habere avaritiam.'

[101] *Enarratio in Psalmos*, xxxix. 7 (*PL* 36, col. 438), 'Quo ducit et quo perducit terrena avaritia? Fundos quaereras, terram possidere cupiebas, vicinos excludebas; illis exclusis, aliis vicinis inhiabas; et tamdiu tendebas avaritiam donec ad littora pervenires: perveniens ad littora, insulas concupiscis; possessa terra, coelum forte vis prendere. Relinque omnes amores: pulchrior est ille qui fecit coelum in terram.'

[102] *De libero arbitrio*, I. xi. 22 (*PL* 32, col. 1233), '. . . cum interea cupiditatum illud regnum tyrannice saeviat, et variis contrariisque tempestatibus totum hominis animum vitamque perturbit, hinc timore, inde desiderio, hinc anxietate, inde inani falsaque laetitia; hinc cruciatu rei amissae quas diligebatur, inde ardore adipiscendae quae non habebatur . . . et quaecunque alia innumerabilia regnum illius libidinis frequentant et exercent.' For Nero as an example see *De civitate Dei*, v. 19 (*PL* 41, col. 166).

[103] *Sermo*, cxxv. 5 (*PL* 38, col. 693), 'Ille quidem male vixit: sed non male ordinavit lex. Ex effractore erit metallicus: de opere metallici quanta opera construuntur? Illius poena damnati ornamenta sunt civitatis.'

obtain salvation by good works and good deeds.[104] The earthly city needs to be an agreement about what is necessary and useful for the sake of something beyond itself.[105] Wealth can lead to destruction or to heaven: it depends how it is used and why it is desired and how necessary it is—use, desire, need. In a famous analogy Augustine remarked that just as travellers at a wayside inn needed plates and cups, tables and chairs, for the food and drink to sustain them on their passage, so the pilgrim through human life should use the goods of this world to achieve salvation, without either enjoying them or becoming entranced by them.[106] What should a Christian do? he asked; and replied, he should use, not serve, the world. The world is to be used in the service of God. Augustine was above all a utilitarian, even if he saw utility as the pursuit of the greatest happiness of the smallest number, of the elect.

What then should a rich man, according to Augustine, do with his wealth? It was clearly not enough just to say 'forsake all and follow me'. The man of wealth, he indicated, was faced with a choice between two options. The mere possession of wealth was not wrong, provided it was used for good ends and not desired for itself: the eye of the needle blocked desire for wealth, not wealth itself.[107] Therefore the first choice was to keep one's wealth and use it charitably, for good works on behalf of God. Simply being rich was not immoral so long as the wealth was not prized for its own sake—and he admitted that wealth, although not valuable,

---

[104] *Expositio . . . Ep. ad Romanos*, 72 (*PL* 35, cols 2083–4): obedience to those in power and the payment of taxes (Romans 13. 1 and Matthew 22. 21) is to be accepted 'Cum enim constemus ex anima et corpore, et quamdiu in hac vita temporali sumus, etiam rebus temporalibus ad subsidium degendae huius vitae utamur, . . .'; *Ep.* cxxx. 2, 3 (*PL* 33, col. 495), 'Talibus bonis non fiunt homines boni, sed aliunde boni facti, bene utendo faciunt ut ista sint bona.' Compare cliii. 6, 16 for a further comparison with civil power.

[105] *De civitate Dei*, xix. 17 (*PL* 41, col. 645).

[106] *In Ioh. Ev.*, xl. 10 (*PL* 35, col. 1691), 'Non amat multum nummum qui amat Deum . . . O si Deus digne amemus, nummus omnino non amabimus. Erit tibi nummus instrumentum peregrinationis, non irritamentum cupiditatis; quo utaris ad necessitatem, non quo fruaris ad delectationem . . . Utere mundo, non te capiat mundus. Quod intrasti, iter agis, stabulum est haec vita. Utere nummo quomodo viator in stabulo utitur mensa, calice, urceo, lectulo, dimissurus non permansurus'; *Sermo* lxxx. 7 (*PL* 38, col. 497), 'Duo ergo genera beneficiorum sunt, temporalia et aeterna. Temporalia sunt salus, substantia, honor, amici, domus, filii, uxor et caetera vitae huius ubi peregrinamur. Ponamus nos ergo in stabula vitae huius quasi peregrini transituri, non quasi possessores mansuri.'

[107] *Enarratio in Psalmos*, li. 14 (*PL* 36, cols 609–10), 'Et ut noveritis non pecuniam in divite sed avaritiam condemnari . . . ut noveritis quia non divitiae culpantur: habebat Abraham multum auri, argenti, pecorum, familiae: dives erat; et in eius sinum Lazarus pauper sublatus est. In sinum divitis pauper: an potius ambo Deo divites, ambo a cupiditate pauperes?'

could make for a better life.[108] To be a rich man without desire was better than being the king of a great province.[109]

But how could one tell whether one's property was being rightly used? This was far more difficult, and the answer could never be known for certain in this life (any more than you could be certain whether you were a member of the damned or the saved—a point seized on and made much of by Wyclif). This would have to be determined at the Day of Judgement: but it might well be the case that one's possessions, one's right to hold property, had already been lost through misuse.[110] There was right and wrong ownership in the same way, said Augustine, that even bishops were to be separated into true pastors and mercenaries, elect and foreknown, although for present purposes one should obey the mercenary, since he could at least fulfil his function of preaching to the faithful.[111] Even the evil have their good uses. But conversely even good use carries with it the danger of pride in one's achievement;[112] even lack of desire for wealth hardly balances the sense of loss if property is taken away from you, although one ought not to complain about that.[113] Wealth is always potentially dangerous and carries with it a permanent risk of corruption. The second option of doing without it is really better. Augustine therefore

---

[108] *De moribus Ecclesiae*, xxiii. 42 (*PL* 32, col. 1329), 'Multo enim mirabilius est non inhaerere istis quamvis possideas, quam omnino ea non possidere'; *Enarratio in Psalmos*, cxxxi. 6 (*PL* 37, col. 1718), 'Abstineamus ergo nos, fratres, a possessione rei privatae, aut ab amore si non possumus a possessione . . .'.

[109] *Enarratio in Psalmos*, lxxv. 18 (*PL* 36, col. 970).

[110] *Ep.* cliii. 6, 26 (*PL* 33, col. 665), 'Omne igitur quod male possidetur, alienum est; male autem possidet qui male utitur . . . Pecunia vero *et* a malis male habetur *et* a bonis tanto melius habetur quanto minus amatur. Sed inter haec toleratur iniquitas male habentium, et quaedam inter eos iura constituuntur quae appellantur civilia: non quod hinc fiat ut bene utentes sint, sed ut male utentes minus molesti sint.' This principle that all things belong to the just in heaven meant that the Donatists lost their right to possess in two different ways: they had no divine right, and on earth were subject to imperial decrees confiscating their property by human law: *Ep.* xciii. 12, 50 (345), 'Et quamvis res quaeque terrena non recte a quoquam possideri possit nisi vel iure divino, quo *cuncta iustorum sunt*, vel iure humano, quod in potestate regum est terrae: ideoque res vestras falso appelletis quas nec iusti possidetis et secundum leges regum terrenorum amittere iussi estis.'

[111] See the list of passages cited by S. J. Grabowski, *The Church: An Introduction to the Theology of St. Augustine* (St Louis and London, 1957), pp. 220–1.

[112] *Ep.* ccxi. 6 (*PL* 33, col. 960), '. . . superbia vero etiam bonis operibus insidiatur ut pereant: et quid prodest dispergere dando pauperibus et pauperem fieri, si anima misera superbior efficiatur contemnendo quam fuerat possidendo?'

[113] *Enarratio in Psalmos*, cxxxi. 25 (*PL* 37, col. 1727); compare *Ep.* clvii. 4, 32 (*PL* 33, col. 689), 'Fieri enim potest ut dicatur christiano ab aliqua potestate, Aut christianus non eris, aut si in hoc permanere volueris, domum possessionesque non habetis. Tunc vero etiam illi divites qui in suis divitiis sic statuerant permanere, ut ex earum bonis operibus promererentur Deum, haec dimittant potius propter Christum quam propter haec Christum . . .' The true Christian has nothing and possesses all (II Corinthians 6. 10).

advised Christians to discard their property. One should keep enough for one's needs, but superfluities beyond necessity were best disposed of.[114] It was the best form of insurance. If the end of the world suddenly came, and your wealth had been given away in a charitable fashion, then surely you as the poor of Christ were likely to be saved. And if the end of the world did *not* come, then at least you were relieved of all the cares and bother of looking after it. But how could one give away wealth in a charitable fashion? Would not the handing over of this potentially harmful substance lead to the corruption of the recipient? Would that be charitable, a good deed? Sell all that thou hast and follow me is all very well, but does this not damn the purchaser? Again, there was no merit in a poor man becoming rich. The only way out of the dilemma was not to give one's property and wealth to anybody (shades of Rousseau!), but to return it to its already existing owner. Wealth should be restored, given back, to God, the only true possessor: and in this context God means the Church.[115] A rich man desiring to dispose of his wealth should hand it over to the treasury of the Church, the *thesaurus Ecclesiae*, which will hold this wealth in accordance with divine law.[116]

Although Augustine did not elaborate this last point to anything like the extent that one might wish, the outline of his argument becomes clear. The Christian society, although now both Church and Roman Empire, was to retain a dual system of property administration, human and divine. For those who wished to keep their wealth, rightly or wrongly as the case might be, there was a human system of property rights, organization and distribution: that was why emperors and kings, the civil power, was useful and divinely approved. God, as Augustine put it, distributes human rights to mankind through kings and emperors, despite the fact that the earth

---

[114] *Enarratio in Psalmos*, lxviii. ii. 18 (*PL* 36, col. 864), 'tantum quaere quantum depellendae necessitati satis est. Cum autem superflua quaeris, compedes tuas onerare desideras'; *Sermo* lxxxv. 4, 5 (*PL* 38, col. 522), 'Teneant sibi quantum sufficit, teneant plus quam sufficit. Demus inde quamdam partem. Quam partem? Decimam partem'; also lxxxv. 6 (523).

[115] *Sermo* 1. 1, 2 and 1. 2, 4 (*PL* 38, col. 327): compare Deane, *Political . . . Ideas of St. Augustine*, pp. 292–3, n. 122. Also *Ep.* xciii. 12, 50 (*PL* 33, col. 345), 'Quisquam denique ipsas res pauperum vel basilicas congregationum, quas sub nomine Ecclesiae tenebatis, quae omnino non debentur nisi ei Ecclesiae, quae vera Christi Ecclesia est, non per iustitiam sed per avaritiam tenet, displicet nobis.'

[116] *Ep.* cxxii. 2 (*PL* 33, col. 471), 'Sicut enim ad loca munitiora festinantium migrant qui ruinam domus vident contritis parietibus imminere, sic corda christiana quanto magis sentiunt mundi huius ruinam crebrescentibus tribulationibus propinquare, tanto magis debent bona quae in terra recondere disponebant, in thesaurum coelestem impigra celeritate transferre, ut si aliquis humanus casus acciderit, gaudeat qui de loco ruinoso emigravit: si autem nihil tale fuerit subsecutum, non contristetur qui quandoque moriturus, immortali Domino, ad quem venturus est, bona propria commendavit.'

and the fullness thereof is the Lord's. What is the emperor to me? asks the Donatist, and I tell you that it is by right from him that you possess your land. Take away imperial rights, and who can say that this house, this estate, this slave, this property is mine? It is by rights derived from kings that possessions can be possessed and enjoyed both in right and in peace.[117] But for those who wished to dispose of their wealth there was the alternative of the treasury of the Church, that much of the world which had already been restored to its creator. The *thesaurus Ecclesiae*, in practical terms, did not mean the whole world, but only that part which God had so far been able to reclaim by human donation. In the Christian Roman Empire there was a double treasury of material wealth, a secular one administered by lay rulers, and a spiritual one administered by the bishops and the priesthood. It was a distinctly Gelasian position, allowing one to render either to Caesar or to God, or indeed to both at once.[118]

The logic of the situation, however, was that the treasury of the Church, clerically administered temporal wealth stored in the *thesaurus Ecclesiae*, would gradually increase as more and more wealth and property was given to it. The lay-administered treasury, the fisc of the Roman Empire, from which all lay property was held directly, the public purse into which all taxes still had to be paid, would in course of time diminish and be steadily eroded away. But at present there was a double ownership: it was literally true, in the words of a much-quoted maxim, that *quod non cepit Christus, rapit fiscus*.[119] The city of God on earth was divided territorially in terms of landed wealth between the ecclesiastical treasury under sacerdotal control and the treasury of the realm, the *fiscus reipublicae*.

> Nunquam hoc facietis nisi aliquid de rebus vestris sepositum habueritis, quod cuique placet pro necessitate rei familiaris suae tamquam debitum quasi fisco reddendum. Si non habet rempublicam suam Christus, non habet fiscum suum. Fiscus enim scitis quid sit? Fiscus saccus est, unde et fiscellae et fiscinae dicuntur. Nec putetis quia aliquis draco est fiscus, quia cum timore auditur exactor fisci: fiscus

---

[117] *In Ioh. ev.*, vi. 25–6 (*PL* 35, cols 1436–7), 'Iure tamen humano dicit, Haec villa mea est, hoc domus mea, hic servus meus est. Iure ergo humano, iure imperatorum. Quare? Quia ipsa iura humana per imperatorem et reges saeculi Deus distribuit generi humano . . . Per iura regum possidentur possessiones': see above n. 59. Also *Ep.* xciii. 12, 50 (*PL* 33, col. 345), '. . . iure humano, quod in potestate regum est terrae: ideo res vestras . . . possidetis et secundum leges regum terrenorum.'

[118] *Expositio . . . Ep. ad Romanos*, 72 (*PL* 35, col. 2084): see above n. 104.

[119] Kantorowicz, *King's Two Bodies*, pp. 174–7, citing Gratian, C. 16 q. 7 c. 8.

saccus est publicus. Ipsum habebat Dominus hic in terra quando loculos habebat: et ipsi loculi Iudae erant commissi.[120]

In time the latter, like civil power itself, would gradually wither away, as more and more wealth was transferred to the ecclesiastical holding, and the world would eventually be administered by the clergy alone. But that time was not yet.[121] For Augustine the Church was still pre-eminently a mission Church, an *Ecclesia diffusa*, a Church of scattered estates diffused throughout a largely pagan or nominally Christian world.[122] The conversion of the imperial power had given the Church added force, but it still had to be seen as a growing Church,[123] an entity laid out in the midst of its ordained expansion and development: and that was why a dual system was still necessary.

Emperors in Rome, Augustine once remarked, should take off their crowns before the memorial of the fisherman:

> ... sed melius est ut Romam cum venerit imperator, deposito diademate, ploret ad memoriam piscatoris quam ut piscator ploret ad memoriam imperatoris.[124]

---

[120] *Enarratio in Psalmos*, cxlvi. 17 (*PL* 37, col. 1911).

[121] *De Trinitate*, III. iv. 9 (*PL* 42, col. 873), 'Hoc de aliqua domo ubi aliquorum talium societas est, hoc de civitate vel etiam de orbe terrarum licet cogitare, si penes sapientes sancteque ac perfecte Deo subditos sit *principatus et regimen* rerum humanarum. Sed hoc *quia nondum est*, oportet enim nos in hac peregrinatione prius mortaliter exerceri, et per vires mansuetudinis et patientiae in flagellis erudiri . . .' See also Wilks, 'Roman Empire and Christian State in the *De civitate Dei*', *Augustinus*, 12 (Madrid, 1967), pp. 489–510.

[122] *Sermo* cclxx. 6 (*PL* 38, col. 1243), 'Congregatur enim unitas corporis Christi ex omnibus linguis, per omnes scilicet gentes toto terrarum orbe diffusas'; *De vera religione*, 6 (*PL* 34, col. 127), 'catholica Ecclesia per totum orbem longe lateque diffusa'; *Enarratio in Psalmos*, xliii. 1; lvi. 1; cxxii. 2 (*PL* 36, cols 476; 662; 37, col. 1630): the *corpus Christi* 'diffusus est usque ad fines terrae'.

[123] *Sermo* li. 14 (*PL* 38, col. 341), 'Cum ergo transmigraret etiam per Christum et apostolos Israel in Babyloniam, hoc est, evangelium veniret ad gentes, quid dicit Apostolus quasi ex voce tunc Ieremiae? . . . *Nondum erant reges christiani*, et orabat pro eis . . . et videtis impleri quod figuraliter dictum est, In eorum pace erit pax vestra. Acceperunt enim pacem Christi et destiterunt persequi christianos: ut iam in securitate pacis aedificarentur ecclesiae et plantarentur populi in agricultura Dei, et fructificarent omnes gentes fide, spe et charitate quae est in Christo'; cf. *Ep.* clxxiii. 10 (*PL* 33, col. 757), citing Psalm 71. 11: 'quod utique quanto magis impletur, tanto maiore utitur ecclesia potestate ut non solum invitet sed etiam cogat ad bonum . . . Vide nunc quemadmodum de his qui prius venerunt, dictum est 'Introduc huc'; non dictum est 'compelle': ita significata sunt ecclesiae primordia ad hoc crescentis, ut essent vires etiam compellendi.'

[124] *Enarratio in Psalmos*, lxv. 4 (*PL* 36, col. 789); compare lxxxvi. 8 (37, col. 1107), 'Quales isti principes? Venerunt de Babylone principes, credentes de saeculo principes venerunt ad urbem Romam quasi caput Babylonis: non ierunt ad templum imperatoris, sed ad memoriam piscatoris.'

It is an obscure comment, whose meaning is far from obvious, although the superiority of the fisherman over the emperor is clear enough. Possibly Augustine was referring to the occasion in 390 when Theodosius took off his regalia when seeking absolution from Saint Ambrose of Milan. But it was also a prophetic remark. Half a century after Augustine's death the papal chancery produced a spurious life of Saint Sylvester, which purported to show that Constantine had taken off his crown before the pope: and two centuries later this legend would be converted by the chancery into an actual donation of the empire to the pope.[125] In short, according to papal theory, the whole world now became the *thesaurus Ecclesiae* —although in practice the papacy was remarkably slow in drawing out the implications of this, and it was not until the eleventh century that it explicitly claimed to be the source of all private property.[126] This in turn led to changes in the idea of the double treasury. Augustine's two purses, ecclesiastical and public, dividing the world between them, were now gradually replaced during the twelfth and thirteenth centuries with the view that the whole world was the *thesaurus Ecclesiae*, whilst the spiritual treasury came to be seen as the other treasury, the treasury of sacramental grace. It was this latter version, not the Augustinian one, which was to be adopted by Wyclif—and was suitably changed to suit his own purposes by replacing the pope with the king as the chief treasurer. We should perhaps classify it as a third version of the treasury of Christ theory. But without the intermediate stage of the papal theory Wyclif's version would not have been possible. There was a vital step in between. He was at best only the stepson of Augustine.

Birkbeck College, London

---

[125] The best account of the *Legenda sancti Silvestri* and the Donation is still W. Ullmann, *The Growth of Papal Government in the Middle Ages*, 3rd edn (London, 1970), pp. 74–86.

[126] In 1080 Gregory VII declared that the Roman church was the source of the 'terra imperia, regna, principatus, ducatus, marchias, comitatus et omnium hominum possessiones', *Reg.* vii. 14a (ed. Caspar: Berlin, 1955), p. 487. That this should be distinguished from the *terra ecclesiae* is suggested *SCH* 7 (1971), p. 85.

9

WYCLIF AND THE GREAT PERSECUTION

by MICHAEL WILKS

AS has been remarked often enough, Lollardy was the first real
English heresy, and its progenitor, John Wyclif, inspired what
Anne Hudson has so rightly termed a 'premature Reformation',[1]
a reformation which had far more immediate impact in Hussite Bohemia,
but in England left Wyclif for a century and a half as a voice crying in the
wilderness, a prophet without honour in his own country. Since history is
usually studied backwards, his name is most commonly associated with
the alleged eucharistic heresy condemned at the Blackfriars Council of
May 1382. This was more significant for its timing than its substance. The
actual charges were not only a distortion of Wyclif's theory, and Wyclif
himself was never specifically named, but any reasonably intelligent
scholastic could have worked it out from Wyclif's philosophical
principles at least ten years earlier.[2] But the eucharist had the great
advantage of being a theological matter, which no one could contest the
right of bishops and masters to deal with, and this made it a far more
effective stick with which the papalists could belabour their lay
opponents—and by 1382 the times were far more propitious. The
Peasants' Revolt of 1381, an event with which Wyclif's name was quickly
linked,[3] had thrown the regency government of the young Richard II into
turmoil: and Lollardy, newly introduced as a term of abuse, could be represented as a recipe for any number of horrors, not least the assassination

---

[1] A. Hudson, *The Premature Reformation: Wycliffite Texts and Lollard History* (Oxford, 1988); and
see also her 'Lollardy: the English heresy?', *Lollards and their Books* (London and Ronceverte,
1985), pp. 141–63; and now J. I. Catto in *History of the University of Oxford*, 2, *Late Medieval
Oxford*, ed. J. I. Catto and R. Evans (Oxford, 1992), pp. 175–280.

[2] One should not be misled by the tactic adopted by his opponent William Woodford of claiming that Wyclif was for a long time uncertain in his own mind about his theory of the eucharist. He admitted that he had had to change his view, e.g. *De eucharistia* (all references to Wyclif
Society editions unless noted otherwise), 2, p. 52, 'Unde licet quondam laboraverim ad
describendum transsubstantiationem concorditer ad sensum prioris Ecclesiae, tamen modo
videtur michi quod contrariatur, posteriora Ecclesia aberrante'; and for other examples see
SCH, 5 (1969), pp. 69–98, but he was already aware in his debates with Kenningham in 1371
that the same principles governing philosophy, theology, and politics would have an impact
on the eucharist: see *Fasciculi Zizaniorum*, ed. W. W. Shirley (RS, 1858), p. 453. This however
raises the still unresolved problem of whether the *De logica* should be dated to the 1360s: see
W. R. Thomson, *The Latin Writings of John Wyclyf* (Toronto, 1983), pp. 6–7.

[3] M. Aston, 'Lollardy and sedition, 1381–1431', *Lollards and Reformers: Images and Literacy in Late
Medieval Religion* (London, 1984), pp. 1–47.

of bishops. The murder of Archbishop Sudbury in 1381 had opened up the way for his replacement by Wyclif's leading opponent, the very vigorous bishop of London, William Courtenay. All this was however simply the culmination of a long process against Wyclif which had resulted in two abortive heresy trials in 1377 and 1378.[4] In both cases Wyclif was rescued by royal intervention, by John of Gaunt. Wyclif, as he had proudly proclaimed, was a *clericus regis*, a king's clerk, a member of the royal household: and as Christopher Given-Wilson has recently shown, king's clerks might be few in number (and exceptionally cheap to maintain, since they could—as Wyclif was—be paid out of normal pluralism), but they wielded a degree of influence out of all proportion to their numbers.[5]

Although Wyclif and his supporters escaped effective condemnation in 1377–8 and continued to enjoy royal protection, one of the great problems in Wyclif's personal history is that it was precisely at this point that he began to issue a steady flow of horror stories about the tribulations of the faithful and the way that their numbers were being cut down. If we accept his insistence that the number of his followers was but a few, those few must have suffered massively. It was, he said at one point, as if God had gone to sleep: there was a savage wave of repression on a huge scale.[6] Close analysis of his words, however, suggests that the dangers involved may have consisted more of risks being taken rather than actual atrocities suffered. Poor priests, we are told, were *threatened* with excommunication, loss of office, imprisonment, and death;[7] soldiers of Christ should

---

[4] J. H. Dahmus, *The Prosecution of John Wyclyf* (New Haven, 1952; reprinted Hamden, 1970).

[5] C. Given-Wilson, *The Royal Household and the King's Affinity: Service, Politics and Finance in England, 1360–1411* (New Haven and London, 1986), pp. 175–9. Wyclif's statement 'Ego autem, cum sim peculiaris regis clericus, . . . defendendo et suadendo quod rex potest iuste dominari regno Angliae, negando tributum Romano pontifici . . .' in the *Determinatio* against Uthred of Boldon and William Binham, p. 422, may be compared with his arguments of the same period in the *De veritate sacrae scripturae* that to condemn him would be tantamount to an attack on the king, his council, and the law; and that 'clerici regum et homines simplicis literaturae' can preach the faith better than doctors of theology: 3, i. 354; 24, ii. 234.

[6] 'Licet autem Dominus ad tempus dormiat', *Speculum saecularium dominorum*, 3, p. 84. See also *De officio regis*, 11, p. 258, 'et vix paucissimi christiani remanebunt in Ecclesia sub Christo', but note the use of the future tense.

[7] E.g. *De ordine christiano*, 5, p. 139, 'Sed quis est qui audet contra praelatos Antichristi doctrinam istam defendere vel vicariis suis in hoc contradicere, specialiter cum privatio beneficii, excommunicatio cum censuris aliis consequuntur, et breviter quae secuntur ad hanc fidem suppositam pauci vel nulli audeant pro Christo subicere se martirio? Sed rarenter est hodie invenibile quis sit ille'; *De demonio meridiano*, 1, p. 419, 'Ad quod laborarunt pauperes presbyteri clamando usque ad mortis periculum'; 3, p. 424, '. . . et omnino pessimum est quod fideles in Domino prohibeantur per incarcerationes, privationes et censuras alias dicere palam populo legem Christi'; *Dialogus*, 24, pp. 48–9; 27, p. 56.

expect to be killed, and should *prepare* themselves for martyrdom.[8] One cannot avoid detecting what is almost a note of pride in which he relates the perils facing the movement. Although he occasionally descended to a level of petulant protest about the awful unfairness of the great persecution—they persecute us, but we don't persecute them[9]—nevertheless according to his own account a great retribution was taking place: the faithful were being put to death;[10] his supporters amongst the friars were being incarcerated in foul prisons after secret trials, and presently expired from their maltreatment.[11] The Psalms foretold that the death of his saints was precious in the sight of God, and Wyclif himself would provide an example for them to follow.[12] Like Zachariah,[13] he could prophesy that the people of God would find salvation in Christ, but his own expectation was a new martyrdom, and he assured his followers that he was steeling himself for the coming event. He was under heavy attack: there never had been such a time of peril for the Christian faith.[14]

---

[8] *De veritate sacrae scripturae*, 23, ii. 232, 'Quam gloriosa causa foret michi praesentem miseriam finiendo. Haec enim fuit causa martirii Christi . . .'; *De perfectione statuum*, 4, pp. 466–7, 'Sed quia persecutio est horrenda occisio imminet sic dicenti, ideo cum oratione humili disponamus nos ad martirium, memores coelestium praemiorum'; *Dialogus*, 27, pp. 57–8.

[9] *Opus evangelicum*, iii. 47, pp. 172–3, 'ex hoc prosequitur istos simplices quod publicant istam haeresim et patenter reserant fidem suam. Pars autem huius fidei non persequitur haereticos sibi adversarios, sed humiliter scribit et delucidat viva voce evidentias fidei scripturae quae movent ipsam et moverent cunctos catholicos ad istam partem fidei sustindendum.'

[10] *De ordine christiano*, 3, pp. 133–4, 'Ex hoc enim fingit [papa] se praestare Deo obsequium, occidendo quoscunque huic perfidiae tamquam fidei repugnantes.'

[11] *De incarcerandis fidelibus*, p. 95, 'Sed praelati caesarei . . . ad extollendum suum venenosum dominium incarcerant plus tyrannis. Et idem est iudicium de sectis novellis incarcerantibus fratres suos; et sic Antichristi discipuli in subtillitate et severitate excedunt scolares Luciferi . . . ut legitur *Iohannis*, ix.22 . . .'; also p. 97; *De fundatione sectarum*, 7, p. 40, '. . . fratres professionis eiusdem propter hoc quod detegunt scelera sui ordinis incarcarcerat et occidit'; 10, p. 51, 'fratres proprios immisericorditer usque ad mortem cruciant'; *De versutiis Antichristi* (ed. I. H. Stein, *EHR*, 47 (1932), pp. 98–103), 3, p. 102, 'de incarceratione fratrum suorum usque ad mortem'; *De quattuor sectis novellis*, 12, p. 285; cf. *De eucharistia* 6, p. 183.

[12] *De amore* (*Ep.* 5), pp. 9–10, commenting on Ps. 115. 16–17, 'Hic dico tamquam mihi probabile citra fidem quod quilibet martir Dei potest pertinenter Deo dicere istos versus.'

[13] *Expositio Matthaei XXIII*, 14, p. 352, part of his commentary on Matt. 23. 34 where Christ predicts that his prophets will be killed; cf. Luke 1. 67f. According to medieval tradition Zacharias was slain by Herod in the Temple.

[14] *De perfectione statuum*, 3, p. 461, '. . . ad tantum enim [dyabolus] caecavit saeculares dominos per suos discipulos Antichristos quod reputarent fidelem clericum, qui diceret sententiam evangelicam in hac parte, esse summum haereticum a praelatis et toto populo occidendum. Ideo, si non fallor, a mundi principio usque nunc non fuit fidelibus ewangelizantibus maius periculum quam est nunc in isto meridiano demonio sic regnante. Nunc enim tam clerus quam saeculares domini seducti reputabunt talem esse haereticum, et sic in suo iudicio tam corpore quam anima condempnabunt.' Complaints about teachers of truth being subjected to false accusations of heresy begin as early as the *De mandatis divinis*, 28, pp. 410–11.

The problem is that we entirely lack historical verification for all this. Quite apart from the fact that Wyclif himself died safely in his own bed, as far as we know no Lollard was actually put to death until the beginning of the next century.[15] The most striking feature of the records of the ecclesiastical courts during the last quarter of the fourteenth century is the really very small number of anti-Lollard cases. This might indicate the very small numbers of Wyclif's supporters. But it is much more likely to demonstrate the very great caution, indeed the positive reluctance, of so many bishops, most of whom were royal appointments, to proceed against a group whose chief heresy was the exaltation of royal power. On the whole captured Lollards were treated with tolerance, and released after making purely formal assurances of good behaviour, to an extent which borders on the ridiculous. It amounted to one of the most restrained campaigns against heresy in history, and this is a discrepancy that requires an explanation.

There is no dispute that the charges in 1377–8 concerned Wyclif's views on civil lordship: that he was to be condemned in other words for his antipapalism. He had appropriated the papal theory of dominion and grace for the benefit of the king, creating a version of the theory which made the king rather than the pope the vicar of God, and therefore the effective owner of all the wealth in the kingdom, fully entitled when necessary to dispossess the possessioners, to disendow the monasteries and religious houses, and to reclaim the lay patronage given over the centuries to cathedral and parish churches.[16] It is not surprising that the Pope, Gregory XI, suggested that Wyclif had gone mad,[17] which was not only an expression of shocked disbelief that a doctor of theology could say such things, but was presumably also intended to invite a plea of insanity in mitigation of the offence. But for what the Pope termed wilful misinterpretation of the Scriptures and for preaching theses likely to overturn the good order of the whole Church, Wyclif was to be imprisoned and forced to confess or, if he fled from justice, to be summoned to appear at Rome itself to be dealt with directly by the papal court.[18] The death of Gregory XI in March 1378 and the outbreak of the Great Schism,

---

[15] P. McNiven, *Heresy and Politics in the Reign of Henry IV: The Burning of John Badby* (Woodbridge and Wolfeboro, NH, 1987).

[16] See my 'Predestination, property and power: Wyclif's theory of dominion and grace', *SCH*, 2 (1965), pp. 220–36.

[17] There is a convenient translation of the three bulls in Sudbury's register in Dahmus, *Prosecution*, pp. 39–45.

[18] Ibid., p. 42; H. B. Workman, *John Wyclif* (Oxford, 1926), 1, p. 294.

combined with the collapse of the second trial in London, left Wyclif free to continue his campaign for a *reformatio regni et ecclesiae*, a process which he claimed was going to have more impact on England than the Norman Conquest.[19]

The Pope, whose knowledge of what Wyclif had actually been teaching was limited to what he had been told by the English Benedictines, 'Black Dog and his pups' (perhaps a reference to Cardinal Adam Easton),[20] declared that Wyclif had espoused the political theory of Marsilius of Padua and John of Jandun, the worst heresy the papacy had ever heard of.[21] In point of fact Wyclif's political thought owed rather more to William of Ockham than it did to Marsilius and in that Ockham was a leading exponent of the doctrine of apostolic poverty radical Franciscan theory was perhaps the single most important influence in the themes which Wyclif propounded during the 1370s, and for which he might have been condemned far more successfully than he ever was. The influence of the Franciscan Spirituals (for want of a better title) in the courts of England and the Empire, also in Spain and Naples, during the mid-fourteenth century, is still a largely obscure subject,[22] but it needs to be seen as the background to the development of what we might call Wyclif's third heresy, the heresy of the New, or rather the Last, Age.

However unlikely it may seem to us that Wyclif should be credited by his contemporaries as being the prophet of a new age, it would in no way have seemed abnormal in the context of the 1360s and 1370s.[23] It was a period when official government propaganda, no doubt fuelled by the French wars, insisted that England was the new Israel, the land of the book, especially of the Old Testament.[24] It was a wonderfully useful

---

[19] *SCH.S*, 5 (1987), p. 163, referring to *De Ecclesia*, 13, p. 278.

[20] Although according to Bale (*Scriptorum Catalogus*, i. 495) it was Nicholas Radcliffe and Peter Stokes who were denounced by Wyclif as 'the black and white dogs'. But dogs was a favourite term of abuse with Wyclif—e.g. cardinals as the dogs of the Roman church: *De demonio meridiano*, 2, p. 421—and looks back to Hildegard's 'fiery dog of unrighteousness'. See also W. A. Pantin, 'The *Defensorium* of Adam Easton', *EHR*, 51 (1936), pp. 675–80, esp. p. 680.

[21] The description is Clement VI's, on whom see now D. P. Wood, *Clement VI: The Pontificate and Ideas of an Avignon Pope* (Cambridge, 1989).

[22] M. Reeves, *Joachim of Fiore and the Prophetic Future* (London, 1976), pp. 45–53.

[23] See now *The Apocalypse in the Middle Ages*, ed. R. K. Emmerson and B. McGinn (Ithaca and London, 1992), especially the contribution of P. Szittya at pp. 383–4 and 391–6, and here further literature; also R. K. Emmerson and R. B. Herzman, *The Apocalyptic Imagination in Medieval Literature* (Philadelphia, 1992), although one may question the comment that this English apocalpyticism was 'thoroughly orthodox', p. 148.

[24] *SCH.S*, 5 (1987), pp. 148–52. For Walter Brut's argument that the Apocalypse applied particularly to England because it was the new Israel see Szittya, in Emmerson and McGinn, eds, *Apocalypse*, pp. 396–7.

conception: every victory was proof of divine favour; every defeat another example of the tribulations to be endured by the chosen people before they could take full possession of the promised land. And what was Israel without its prophets? Moreover Wyclif had, so to speak, been brought up into the business. What is to my mind one of the major advances in recent Wyclif scholarship is the book by Jonathan Hughes which deals with the circle of reformers pursuing the aim of a great revival of spiritual life in Yorkshire, which gathered round John Thoresby, royal chancellor during the 1350s and archbishop of York from 1362 to 1373.[25] The Wyclif family were part (to use a fashionable term) of Thoresby's affinity. It may have been under Thoresby's patronage that Wyclif went to Oxford—if he was not already there—and it was Thoresby's encouragement which led to him being enrolled into government service. The chief agent for this was Richard Scrope, the very pious lord of Bolton and Masham, who became royal treasurer in 1371 and was a companion in arms of John of Gaunt. He shared with Gaunt a special interest in promoting advocates of the spiritual life, notably hermits and mystics. It is probably no accident that the finest collection of prophecies and mystical writings in England was to be found in York. The library of the Augustinian Hermits[26] had over 600 works, of which about a third consisted of John Erghome's collection of prophecies, and which included material by other Joachimite and Franciscan-inspired authors like Vincent of Beauvais, William of St Amour, and Robert of Uzès. It also contained writings by John of Rupescissa, an author recently described as a virtual 'clearing-house of medieval prophecy',[27] and a crucial figure in the formation of a 'Northern visionary school' which spread Joachimite influence extensively in northern Europe. Although it has been suggested that all this was a relatively 'quiet apocalypticism',[28] Wyclif is I think positive proof that it was not quiet at all. Whilst there is no evidence that he personally used the

---

[25] J. Hughes, *Pastors and Visionaries: Religion and Secular Life in Late Medieval Yorkshire* (Woodbridge and Wolfeboro, NH, 1988), esp. pp. 127–66. But it should be noted that Wyclif was ordained, and may have gone to Oxford, under the previous archbishop, William de la Zouche, who was not a royalist appointment. This probably explains Wyclif's well-known change of views after the period of his 'youthfulness'.

[26] M. R. James, 'The Catalogue of the library of the Augustinian Friars at York', *Fasciculus J. W. Clark dicatus* (Cambridge, 1909), pp. 2–96; Claire Cross, 'Monastic learning and libraries in sixteenth-century Yorkshire', *SCH.S*, 8 (1991), pp. 255–69 at p. 265. For this catalogue see now *The Friars' Libraries*, ed. K. W. Humphreys (London, 1991).

[27] For John see J. Bignami-Odier, *Études sur Jean de Roquetaillade (Johannes de Rupescissa)* (Paris, 1952).

[28] M. W. Bloomfield and M. Reeves, 'The penetration of Joachism into Northern Europe', *Speculum*, 29 (1954), pp. 772–93.

York library, it is known that he made extensive use of the Franciscan library in Oxford. Sir Richard Southern has shown[29] how Wyclif went to the Franciscan library (like Roger Bacon before him) during the 1360s to read the works of Robert Grosseteste, the thirteenth-century bishop of Lincoln. Grosseteste enjoyed an enormous posthumous reputation in England as the bishop who had opposed the tyranny of Innocent IV to such an extent that he had declared the Pope to be Antichrist, because he had misunderstood the whole character of the Petrine commission. The true *traditio* or grant made to the apostles was to make them like Christ as suffering servants, who would demonstrate that true lordship consisted in sacrificing oneself and repudiating the regal nature which had corrupted the Jewish priesthood of the Pharisees. This was of course grist to Wyclif's mill, but Grosseteste had much more to offer him: the Aristotelian scientific method which was so crucial in Wyclif's own philosophy; stress on the importance of pastoral care and the duty of preaching by the clergy; a call for a logic of scripture which would return the study of the Bible to the basic requirements of the apostolic life: poverty, humility, and love; and above all for present purposes Grosseteste had declared that the number of false clergy, the number of Antichrists, was multiplying so rapidly that the Last Age of the world forecast by St John (I John 2. 18) must be imminent.[30] Grosseteste has been termed a Franciscan by adoption, but I think he must also have been indebted to the prophecies attributed to Joachim of Fiore (although Professor Southern disagrees).[31] There is no doubt however that by the mid-fourteenth century there was a virtually standardized prophecy current in England which was largely a blend, not always a very successful one, of the main theories of Hildegard of Bingen (popularized by the compilation of her sayings by Gebeno of Eberbach in 1220) and Joachim of Fiore, with numerous other spurious items added in. As Henry of Hassia declared,[32] Hildegard and Joachim

[29] R. W. Southern, *Robert Grosseteste: The Growth of an English Mind in Medieval Europe* (Oxford, 1986), pp. 296–305.

[30] Ibid., pp. 296, 307, 317–18; R. C. Petry, 'The reforming critiques of Robert Grosseteste, Roger Bacon and Ramon Lull, and their related impact upon medieval society', *The Impact of the Church upon its Culture*, ed. J. C. Brauer (Chicago and London, 1968), pp. 95–120 at p. 111.

[31] Southern, *Grosseteste*, pp. 281–5.

[32] Henry of Hassia, *Epistola* (*Historische Jahrbuch*, 30 (1909), p. 306): 'Est verum quod Hildegardis et Abbas Ioachim sonant quasi finem mundi et adventum Antichristi praecessurae sint una vel plures reformationes ecclesiae seu reductiones in statum primitivae sanctitatis.' There is an excellent summary of this development in H. Lee, M. Reeves, and G. Silano, eds, *Western Mediterranean Prophecy: The School of Joachim of Fiore and the Fourteenth-Century Breviloquium* (Toronto, 1989). From amongst the now massive bibliography on Joachim and Joachism, to which Marjorie Reeves and Bernard McGinn are major contributors, mention should be

between them had pointed the way not only to the end of the world and the coming of Antichrist, but to a whole series of *reformationes Ecclesiae* which would 'reduce the clergy to a state of primitive sanctity'. This framework of prophecies had become established and enjoyed what was to all intents and purposes official sanction. Wyclif was able to function as a self-proclaimed Messiah because this prophetic programme was so familiar to his audiences: they were expecting the advent of the end of time and a new revelation. Wyclif appreciated this and was able to offer them one.

One of the best recent studies of this programme is by Kathryn Kerby-Fulton, although mention should also be made of the book by her Cambridge colleague Wendy Scase on what she calls the 'new anticlericalism' of the fourteenth century: both however are writing not about Wyclif but that great Middle English poem *Piers Plowman*.[33] I often think that life would be much simpler if one could show that Wyclif was a poet and was the unknown athor of *Piers Plowman*: they clearly came out of the same stable, the royal court during a period when it was dominated by John of Gaunt (who would become the brother-in-law of Geoffrey Chaucer). When the anonymous author of *Piers Plowman* urged the need for a new Peter and a new apostolic priesthood—because contemporary clergy, for all their learning, could not use English, the true apostolic language, and so could not communicate properly with their people[34]—he was voicing sentiments that must have awoken a lively response in Wyclif himself. There are of course discrepancies between them. The author of *Piers Plowman* seems to have been opposed to the friars from the beginning, whereas Wyclif relied on mendicant support during the 1370s and only later accused the friars of treachery and turned so violently against them. None the less, both of them were strongly influenced by Franciscan notions. Both authors adopted the idea that they should appear as holy fools, the

---

made of B. McGinn, *The Calabrian Abbot: Joachim of Fiore in the History of Western Thought* (New York, 1985). Note also Fiona Robb, '"Who hath chosen the better part?" (Luke 10, 42): Pope Innocent III and Joachim of Fiore on the diverse forms of religious life', *Monastic Studies*, 2 (1991), pp. 157–70.

[33] K. Kerby-Fulton, *Reformist Apocalypticism and Piers Plowman* (Cambridge, 1990), although she virtually dismisses any relevance to Wyclif and Lollardy, p. 232 n. 6; W. Scase, *Piers Plowman and the New Anticlericalism* (Cambridge, 1989). Reference should also be made to the seminal study by M. W. Bloomfield, *Piers Plowman as a Fourteenth-Century Apocalypse* (New Brunswick, NJ, 1961); cf. R. Adams, 'The nature of Need in *Piers Plowman*', *Traditio*, 34 (1978), pp. 273–301.

[34] Scase, *Piers Plowman*, pp. 123, 164–7.

minstrels of God,[35] a Pauline theme made popular by the Franciscan Spirituals. Even the name Lollard itself, although it rapidly became a term of abuse meaning idle layabouts—and worse—had a respectable Franciscan origin meaning one who hung about singing the truth against all adversity: Christ was the supreme Loller, because he above all hung on the cross.[36]

Robert Lerner has pointed out[37] that by the fourteenth century there were two versions or variants of the apocalyptic idea, although it might be more accurate to say that the fourteenth-century theory was an amalgam of both. On the one hand there was the older traditional theme that once society had assumed an ideal form under the rule of an emperor of the Last Age, assisted by a *papa angelicus*, an ideal pope, then the end of the world was at hand, a situation marked by the appearance of Antichrist. The best society was in other words essentially a prelude to the final struggle between Antichrist and the Christlike ruler, which would precipitate the Second Coming. By the fourteenth century however it had become more usual to assume that things had become so bad that the Last Age and the rule of Antichrist already existed. The pessimism that this induced was tempered by the belief that this state of affairs could not last indefinitely: it must of necessity be eventually replaced by the establishment of the ideal society under the rule of a perfect prince, who would bring peace to his messianic kingdom, redistributing wealth throughout society, paving the way for the Last Judgement. Of particular significance in this second version was the means to bring it about, and it was here that

---

[35] *The Medieval Mystical Tradition in England*, ed. M. Glasscoe (Exeter, 1982), pp. 1–17, and here further references. In England fools and minstrels were classified together in court records: J. Southworth, *The English Medieval Minstrel* (Woodbridge and Wolfeboro, NH, 1989), p. 167 n. 1. For 'lunatic lollers' as holy fools and divine minstrels in *Piers Plowman* see Kerby-Fulton, *Reformist Apocalypticism*, pp. 128–9, 193–4: the author of the poem comes into this category, although it seems unlikely that the C-text is autobiographical. That *Piers Plowman* was complaining about the failure of friars to live up to the ideals of St Francis rather than friars as such is stressed by L. M. Clopper, 'Langland's Franciscanism', *Chaucer Review*, 25 (1990–1), pp. 54–75. See also P. R. Szittya, *The Antifraternal Tradition in Medieval Literature* (Princeton, 1986).

[36] Scase, *Piers Plowman*, pp. 147–51, 220 n. 21. Note Wyclif's elaborate punning in *Dialogus*, 27, p. 57: he was being suspended; Christ was suspended on the cross; but the real suspension was that of the papalists suspending truth. For the term Lollard see R. E. Lerner, *The Heresy of the Free Spirit in the Later Middle Ages* (Berkeley, Los Angeles, and London, 1972), esp. pp. 40–1, 57, and see here for further references and literature.

[37] R. E. Lerner, 'Refreshment of the Saints: the time after Antichrist as a station for earthly progress in medieval thought', *Traditio*, 32 (1976), pp. 97–144; also 'Medieval prophecy and religious dissent', *Past and Present*, 72 (1976), pp. 3–24; 'The Black Death and Western European eschatological mentalities', *American Historical Review*, 86 (1981), pp. 533–52.

Joachimite theories were so influential. The present Church, the *ecclesia activa*, governed jurisdictionally by St Peter and his successors, was to be replaced by an *ecclesia contemplativa* guided by the doctrines of Christian love committed to St John, creating a spiritual, renovated Church. This was to be achieved by the formation of a new order of poor wandering preachers proclaiming the principles of the Eternal Evangel, the true Gospel of the Scriptures rightly understood in a way which had never happened since the days of the apostolic Church. But it was an essential feature of this new order that they should be small in number, a saving remnant of saints, whose efforts to reform society would be met by horrendous persecution, whose faith would be tested by terrible suffering, but out of whose torment society would be reborn. It would, as it was often suggested, be like a second crucifixion, a prelude or testing time out of which the Christian ideal would be resurrected.[38]

It would be tedious to go through each of these items in turn merely to demonstrate that they can all be found in Wyclif's works. Already by the later 1360s he was citing Joachim as a guide to future events: '. . . praenosticat Abbas Ioachim multiplices eventus in mundo futuros, ut patet in tractatu suo *De speciebus scripturarum*',[39] and from then on the other elements in this pattern of speculation duly make their appearance. His endless complaints that the world was upside down[40] and that the Church had become an *ecclesia carnalis* which could never be in a worse

---

[38] Reeves, *Joachim of Fiore*, pp. 43–4, 48.

[39] *De ente praedicamentali*, 2, p. 18 (this is the anonymous *De semine scripturarum*, apparently originating from Bamberg *c.*1204/5, which Peter Olivi had attributed to Joachim and which became very popular in England: Kerby-Fulton, *Reformist Apocalypticism*, pp. 183–6), although at this stage he seems to have approved of Joachim's condemnation for his theory of the Trinity: *Purgans errores circa universalia*, 5, pp. 45, 47. Later he sought to excuse Joachim, 'si Ioachim ita dixit', on the grounds of ignorance about the nature of universals: *De universalibus*, 11, ed. I. J. Mueller (Oxford, 1985), pp. 263–4; and would argue that Joachim was wrongly persecuted by Innocent III when, like Wyclif himself, he was willing to be corrected if proved to be in error: *De veritate sacrae scripturae*, 7, i. 140–1; *De eucharistia*, 9, p. 278. For a list of other references to Joachim see Thomson, *Latin Writings*, p. 14, although one may doubt Thomson's assertion that these were all borrowings from Higden.

[40] See his use of Isaiah 5. 20, 'Woe unto those who call evil good and good evil' in *De potestate papae*, 5, p. 87: 'et sic de illorum contrariis perversum est nostrum iudicium maniace in contrarium iudicium rationis, et tam multi ac magni inciderunt in istam rabiem quod maior pars mundi arguet docentes et servantes istam sententiam ut insanos, sic quod generalior, accusator et perseverantior est persecutio in paucos docentes licet remisse istam sententiam quam olim fuerat in prophetas'. See also *De mandatis divinis*, 28, p. 410, 'Sed notandum est hic quod mundus est tantum positus in maligno quod doctores detegentes sensum scripturae et Christi consilium dicuntur ex hinc inimici veritatis et perversores Ecclesiae'; similarly *De civili domini*, ii. 16 and 17, pp. 232 and 240; *De veritate sacrae scripturae*, 28, iii. 120; *De Ecclesia*, 12, pp. 264–5.

condition[41] are well known. His appeals to the king to perform an *imitatio Christi*, to pursue a peace policy, and to redistribute the wealth of the religious—not because the laity were particularly deserving, but because apostolic poverty and humility were essential to those who would teach the true gospel of Christian love—all fall into place as parts of a pre-ordained programme. Much mirth has been engendered by Wyclif's initial determination to support the English Parliament's decision to accept Urban VI in 1378 by announcing that Urban (of all people) was an ideal pope, a *papa angelicus*[42]—although it is quite true that in later years he preferred to argue that both Roman and Avignon popes were Anti-christs[43]—but what mattered here was not what Urban was really like, but that it had been written that the Last Age was at hand. So too it was irrelevant whether this final period should be numbered in one way rather than another. Wyclif went to elaborate lengths to divide up world history according to the Augustinian principle of seven ages,[44] so that he could claim to be living in the Saturn-day of the world week, the worst of all times before the coming of the new Sunday, the day of the Lord, only to wreck the entire scheme by reverting to the tripartite Joachimite theme of a third age yet to come.[45] Such inconsistencies only helped to prove that he was fulfilling a prophecy to whose mysteries he alone had the key.[46]

[41] For *Ecclesia malignantium* or *Ecclesia haereticorum*, *De officio regis*, 11, pp. 251 and 257; *De potestate papae*, 7, p. 139 for the pope as 'caput Ecclesiae malignantium et synagogae Sathanae'.

[42] According to *De potestate papae*, 10, p. 233, the Great Schism was caused by Urban's attempt to bring the cardinals to adopt the apostolic life: 'Quam sententiam audivi de papa nostro Urbano VI ipsum dixisse cardinalibus Gregorii qui excessit decalogum ac quia increpans eorum limitavit eos ad vitam apostolicam primaevam, conspiraverant contra eum, eligendo sibi Robertum Gilbonensem, virum ut dicitur dissolutum, superbum, bellicosum et legis Christi ignarum.' Nevertheless both popes could be accepted if *miraculose* they accepted these principles.

[43] *Supplementum Trialogi*, 4, p. 426, 'Et tunc ista duo monstra cum membris diaboli sibi ad-haerentibus sese destruerent, Ecclesia fidelium stante salva. Quod autem istorum capitum sit nequius, est nobis impertinens diffinire, sed creditur probabiliter quod Robertus ... Debemus enim credere ... quod nullus talis papa necessarius est per ordinationem Christi, sed per cautelam diaboli introductus': they are *pseudopapae*, false Christs, and the false prophets of Matt. 24. 23–6 (9, p. 448); similarly *De quattuor sectis novellis*, 3 and 5, pp. 249 and 257, notwithstanding continued use of 'our Urban' (7, p. 265); *De perfectione statuum*, 3, p. 458; *Opus evangelicum*, i. 3, i. 141–2.

[44] Joachim's use of both seven-age and three-age patterns is well known: e.g. Reeves, *Joachim of Fiore*, p. 8. For Chaucer note the interesting suggestions made by P. Brown and A. Butcher, *The Age of Saturn: Literature and History in the Canterbury Tales* (Oxford, 1991).

[45] The threefold division made it easier to accommodate the Donation of Constantine as the turning point between the first apostolic age and the second period which came to an end around 1200 with Innocent III and the *Decretales* on one side and the institution of the friars on the other, making the third age both an age of Antichrist and an Age of the Spirit.

[46] Wyclif's constant insistence that he understood Scripture better than anybody else,

All this suggests that the really dangerous Wycliffite works were less the books on lordship of the first half of the 1370s, nor the *De eucharistia* of about 1380, but his studies of the Bible during the middle years of the 1370s, first in the form of his famous commentary on the whole Bible,[47] followed by his book on the truth of Scripture, the *De veritate sacrae scripturae* of about 1378. From now on he saw himself as expressing Joachim's Eternal Evangel, the true gospel of the Bible understood rightly. These biblical studies not only required him to produce a commentary on the Apocalypse of St John, but also drew his attention to the so-called 'synoptic apocalypse' of Matthew, chapters 23 and 24–5, which he quickly convinced himself contained a special message for himself and his followers, but which the bishops had tried to conceal from the faithful.[48] Discussion of these chapters occasioned numerous pamphlets, and two tracts on the subject were to be included with the Lollard sermon cycle to denote their outstanding significance.[49] As he explained, understanding the Bible required a special gift of knowledge from God:

---

e.g. *De civili dominio*, ii. 10, p. 105, 'Unde audacter non pompatice assero de insolubilitate scripturae sacrae, quae est fides mea, securus quod omnes doctores mundi non possunt veritatem istam dissolvere', would lead him to argue that the rightness of papal and conciliar decrees, as in the case of the eucharist, could be ascertained by measuring them up against his own interpretation: *De eucharistia*, 1, pp. 25–6. The bishops should be grateful to him for teaching them the true nature of the Church: *De Ecclesia*, 1, p. 2.

[47] G. A. Benrath, *Wyclifs Bibelkommentar* (Berlin, 1966); also B. Smalley, 'John Wyclif's *Postilla super totam Bibliam*', *Bodleian Library Record*, 4 (1953), pp. 186–205; 'Wyclif's *Postilla* on the Old Testament and his *Principium*', *Oxford Studies presented to Daniel Callus* (Oxford, 1964), pp. 254–96. Wyclif would also have absorbed Joachimite material through his use of Nicholas of Lyra, on whom see above, pp. 36–7. But the basic character which he assigned to himself came from his extensive use of the biblical text. As J. F. A. Sawyer, *Prophecy and the Prophets of the Old Testament* (Oxford, 1987), esp. pp. 1–2, 15–18, 58f., 87f., has pointed out, the Old Testament prophet had a double function, on the one hand interpreting and proclaiming the truth of Scripture and the nature of righteousness, and on the other hand foretelling the pattern of events leading to the 'day of the Lord'. As an opponent of current ritual practices, he would be rejected by contemporaries and condemned by false accusations, but would survive under the protection of the royal court to which he acted as an adviser. It might almost be a description of Wyclif himself.

[48] The *Expositio Matthaei XXIII* (or *De vae octuplici*) and the *Expositio Matthaei XXIV* cannot however be earlier than mid-1382 and I would prefer to date them to 1383: parts of the latter reappear in the *Opus evangelicum*, which can be firmly dated to 1384 but is largely a compilation of earlier material. Note the use of these chapters of Matthew to attack the friars as hypocrites and pseudo-prophets in the *De fundatione sectarum*, p. 16, which dates to about August 1383. But cf. *De officio regis*, 11, p. 252.

[49] Hudson, *Lollards and their Books*, pp. 202–3, referring to the *Vae Octuplex* and *Of Mynystris in þe Chirche: Exposicioun of Matthew XXIV*, ed. T. Arnold, *Select English Works* (Oxford, 1869–71), 2, pp. 379–89 and 393–423. Note *Of Mynystris*, p. 408, 'þer shal be wepynge and gnasting of teeþ: þis laste word, *unexpouned bifore*, is dredeful to prelatis.' See also now *English Wycliffite*

Cum sapientia Dei patris sit nucleus veritatis in foliis verborum scripturae absconditus, et ipsa promittit suis fidelibus, Ecclus. 24. 31, 'Qui elucidant me, vitam aeternam habebunt', fideles Christi, et specialiter quibus dedit Deus donum scientiae, darent operam ad Christi evangelium declarandum. Et cum capitulum evangelii Matt. 23 multis hominibus est obscurum et includit in se multa notanda fidelibus, quidam fideles satagunt secundum notitiam quam Deus eis donaverat illud capitulum declarare.[50]

It was therefore the proper task of an evangelic doctor to prophesy, and he claimed that just as his colleagues used the writings of Merlin, Hildebrand and the like, so too he could foretell that wars, plagues, pestilences and other tribulations would continue until a gentile clergy was punished for its sins:

Cum secundum sanctos spectat ad officium doctoris evangelici prophetare, et socii mei prophetant ex dictis Merlini, Hildegardis et vatum similium extra fidem scripturae de statibus membrorum Ecclesiae militantis, motus sum etiam, sed fideliori evidentia, prophetare. Dico ergo quod quamdiu clerus Ecclesiae manserit sic gentilitati commixtus, et fimo temporalium irregulariter inpinguatus, non deficient ab Ecclesia pugna, pestilentia et alia plagae in evangelio prophetatae.[51]

To protests that he would disturb the peace of the Church, he retorted sharply that Christ has said he did not bring peace but a

---

Sermons, ed. A. Hudson and P. Gradon (Oxford, 1983–93), 1, pp. 49–50, although it seems unlikely that these tracts were ever actual sermons: the English sermons were based on the Latin sermons, which were produced in 1383 as a treatise, ostensibly on preaching, but were never actually preached.

[50] *Expositio Matthaei XXIII*, 1, p. 313; cf. *Expositio Matthaei XXIV*, 1, pp. 344–5.

[51] *De vaticinatione seu prophetia*, 1, p. 165. Hildegard is cited fairly often for her attacks on clerical abuses, e.g. *De fundatione sectarum*, 14, p. 67; *Trialogus*, iv. 26, p. 338; and Merlin is presumably Geoffrey of Monmouth; but it is difficult to date the *De vaticinatione* precisely. Loserth rather hesitantly suggested about 1378, whereas Thomson would prefer late 1382: but since Wyclif still seems to be at Oxford before the Peasants' Revolt and the eucharistic controversy, a date of 1379/80 seems more probable. But he scorned the use of astrology in making prophecies: *De quattuor sectis novellis*, 10, p. 280, 'Nec credatur pseudoloquentibus in ista materia ut victoria regnis et regibus sicut antea ascribebatur, quia iuxta fidem pax et caritas sunt Deo plus placitae quam dominationis acquisitio, famae, victoriae vel honoris; et profitendo quod nec sum astrologus nec propheta, ignoro si istorum planetarum coniunctio, quae proximo est futura, sit benevola regno nostro, cum luna, quae est planeta infimus, dicitur super Anglicos dominari.' On Lollard use of Hildegard see now Anne Hudson, *Two Wycliffite Texts*, EETS 301 (Oxford, 1993), pp. 96–7.

sword,[52] and he appealed to the king, *athleta Christi*, to protect the heralds of truth (*veritatis praecones*) and listen to one who was 'consiliarius ut confessor et praedicator christianae fidei'.[53] In his last years he became even more openly apocalyptic. The last three books of the *Summa theologiae* against simony, blasphemy, and apostasy were in themselves indications or testimonies to the existence of the Last Age,[54] and the choice of titles like *De solutione Sathanae* or *De versutiis Antichristi* for later tracts seems self-explanatory. The Great Schism came to be seen in his eyes as a climactic event which offered a unique opportunity, and could be compared to the act of creation which brought order out of chaos. It meant Armageddon, the war of the last age of the world against all the forces of evil.[55]

Despite the great deal of blood and thunder involved in this 'reformist apocalypticism' it should be stressed that it evolved out of, and drew its strength from, contemporary spirituality and embraced such very popular ideals as the imitation of Christ and the doctrine of love. Wyclif constantly complained that ecclesiastical life in his own time had been corrupted by unnecessary humanly-devised formalities, by rites and ceremonies, a continual round of meaningless but elaborate services designed to inflate the pride of the clergy and to emphasize their separation from the laity. All this had served to destroy the inner purposes of the

---

[52] *De vaticinatione*, 2, p. 170, 'Sed hii tertio garriunt quod ex talibus sententiis frustra perturbatur Ecclesia, sed ipsi nec attendunt ad qualitatem sententiae nec considerant quodomodo Iesu noster dicit Matt. 10. 34 quod non venit pacem carnalem vel mundanam mittere in terram, sed gladium ad ligas huiusmodi dividendum. Et illud officium executi sunt sancti sequentes. . . .' The king should wage a war of resistance against possessioner clergy in the same way that his predecessors resisted the barbarian invasions: 2, p. 174.

[53] *De vaticinatione*, 1, p. 168. The Pauline notion of the Christian as a champion who wins victory in a race or contest, *athleta* or *pugilis Christi*, is usually applied by Wyclif to his followers generally: *De civili dominio*, iii. 3 and 23, pp. 36 and 564; ironically Gregory XI had told the scholars of Oxford in 1377 that they should be champions of the faith: Dahmus, *Prosecution*, p. 48. For the biblical origins see C. F. Evans, *The Theology of Rhetoric: The Epistle to the Hebrews* (Dr Williams' Library, London, 1988), p. 7.

[54] The point that charity grows cold (Matt. 24. 12) in a three-stage process leading to Antichrist and the end of the world is made by Thomas Wimbledon: see I. K. Knight, *Wimbledon's Sermon: Redde Rationem Villicationis Tue* (Pittsburgh, 1967), pp. 109f. For further examples of Wyclif's use of St Paul (Ephes. 5. 16; II Tim. 3. 1f) to declare that the last days had been reached see *De Ecclesia*, 3, p. 51; *De potestate papae*, 8, p. 193.

[55] In *De officio regis*, 11, pp. 251–2, this is linked to Daniel's prophecy (Dan. 2. 40–5) of the break-up of the Roman Empire, the 'iron monarchy': 'In quo regno oportet, instar ferri, quod terram conterit et seipsum consumit, quod surgat gens contra gentem et regnum adversus regnum, sicut prophetat Veritas xxiii [Matt. 24. 7] . . .'; and see also the use of the Matthew passage to argue that wars, plagues, and earthquakes are evidence of the decline of faith and the advent of Antichrist in *Opus evangelicum*, iii. 31, ii. 113–14. Also Benrath, *Bibelkommentar*, pp. 281, 308.

spiritual life. Accordingly he demanded a simplified form of service, whose prime content was the reading and preaching of the Bible, expounding the true message of Scripture. This message was a message of love: the love of God, love of others, and in particular love of oneself—and love of oneself demanded that a man, a naturally corrupt individual, should subordinate himself and measure himself up to his ideal self. He should become a living exponent of his own greater, truer self as a Christian. To do this he had to perform an *imitatio Christi*, to become what Wyclif termed a *Christicola*,[56] a dweller in Christ in whom Christ himself is to be found. In this way the true Church would become, would be converted into, a society of new men. In its proper sense the Church was nothing but a community of the elect, a *universitas praedestinatorum*, a gathering of those who achieved identity with their true spiritual selves and who would therefore be subsumed into the mystical *corpus Christi* to become one with Christ himself. So the true Christian in his search for salvation was obliged to perform a constant imitation of Christ, a permanent striving to measure and match up his earthly conduct with the pattern of right living defined by his heavenly self. His success would prove that he was indeed one of the elect, and society itself would actually become the Augustinian reflection of heaven on earth. It may be remarked in parentheses that precisely the same lesson was being taught in *Piers Plowman*.

It was a process which men should not undertake unaided. They had to have models to adopt and imitate. They needed Scripture rightly understood, but this itself was something which had to be taught: it needed ministers of the word, a clergy whose aim was not to govern people but to direct by word and deed into the ways of love with learning and humility. This was the function of the poor priests.[57] But the poor priest, the true

---

[56] The term is taken from Marsilius, *Defensor pacis*, I. i. 5. His criticisms of 'rites and ceremonies' are too numerous to specify: e.g. *De civili dominio*, ii. 13, p. 165; cf. I Reg. 15. 22, Isa. 1. 10–17, 66. 3, Jer. 7. 22, Amos 5. 25.

[57] The *sacerdotes simplices* of the *Responsiones ad XLIV conclusiones monachales*, proem pp. 201–2, 'Nec est illis quod vocantur a satrapis ydiotae, quia sic vocabantur apostoli evangelium praedicantes, ut patet Act. 4. 13, . . . non confidunt de ingenio proprio vel potestate humana, sed quod Deus utitur tamquam organis ad hoc opus. Habent autem hoc signum caritatis communicandi altrinsecus quod volunt libenter offere doctrinam suam adinvicem et praedicare populo sine pecunia vel proprietate aliqua acquirenda.' The 'pauperes presbyteri clamando usque ad mortis periculum' only want to preach freely the *evangelium Iesu Christi*: *De demonio meridiano*, 3, pp. 419, 424–5; cf. *De diabolo et membris eius*, 4–5, pp. 371–2, where the *simplices sacerdotes* have the *sensum Christi*, 'sensum ewangelicum divinitus eis datum', and 'qui volunt esse secundum formam ewangelii Dei adiutores' according to I Cor. 3. 9. But they were also to do physical labour, and could teach grammar to children: *Dialogus*, 25, p. 51; and should visit

follower, also had a higher duty: he not only had to preach, he had to suffer. Like Christ himself he was to be the suffering servant of Deutero-Isaiah, the man who sacrificed himself for his people. Just as it was fashionable in the fourteenth century to depict Christ less as a God to be obeyed and more as an example of tormented humanity, so the distinctive feature of the *vita evangelica* for the Wycliffite minister was a denial of self-interest and a willingness to endure suffering in accordance with a predetermined pattern. For Wyclif, the sending out of Lollard preachers into the towns and rural areas was a re-enactment of the great dispersion of the apostles set out in the Bible. Christ's lament over Jerusalem as the city which killed its prophets, juxtaposed to the Olivet discourse on the nature of faithful disciples, was a clear indication to him that the true Church was to be sought by means of the example, preaching, and suffering of a few true men. They would be a church of saints as opposed to the *ecclesia* of the malignants, the false prophets and hypocrites who clustered like vultures round the carcase of the body of Christ, and were inspired by the Roman church, the very synagogue of Satan himself.[58] Salvation was to be looked for from wise prophets sent out as angels with trumpets to proclaim the everlasting Gospel and to prepare the elect for the end of time. But they would first need to endure the ultimate tribulation, the great desolation of a dwindling band of saints who would be vilified, tormented, and crucified like Christ. They should expect nothing except to be persecuted and hounded from city to city.

Wyclif's poor priests were university men: they needed to be highly trained in order to teach. But they were to be classed as simple men, the idiots of God skilled in the ways of unknowing, who like children had come to appreciate the fundamental nature of Christianity as a doctrine of love for others. To be like Christ *in vita et in moribus* was to follow the third

---

widows and orphans (Jas. 1. 27) in the description of them in *De civili dominio*, 1, p. 4, where, in opposition to the 'possessioners', they are secular clergy adopting 'paupertatem, castitatem et obedientiam matri Ecclesiae' and friars following poverty: 'mendicantes vero volentes strictius sequi Christum ... abdicant omnem civilem proprietatem'. See further the valuable comments of M. Schmidt, 'John Wyclifs Kirchenbegriff: Der *Christus humilis* Augustins bei Wyclif', *Gedenkschrift für D. W. Elert*, ed. F. Hübner, W. Maurer, E. Kinder (Berlin, 1955), pp. 92–108. Also Benrath, *Bibelkommentar*, pp. 180, 188–9, 245, 274–305.

[58] For the duty of the prophet to condemn corrupt priests see I Reg. 3. 11–14. A further indication of the time of Antichrist was the loss of supporters: 'Nec confunduntur quod quidam qui inchoarunt, nunc deciderunt, quia sic fuit de Christi apostolis', citing John 6. 66, and I John 2. 18–19. Also Benrath, *Bibelkommentar*, pp. 102, 163, 173, 233, 369.

way, the way of love contained in the hidden gospel of St John,[59] and to realize that doing best of all was to be like Christ in loving all, even one's enemies as they persecuted you,[60] a proposition which Wyclif always maintained he was following the more savagely he denounced them. The ideal apostolic man was by definition an eminently saintly being whose life was bound to be a perpetual struggle against adversity: the *paupertates Christi* proved themselves by their willingness to accept harsh conditions and harsher treatment. They were, he declared, the heirs of the prophets, the sons of the apostles,[61] who committed their lives to the service of God and were stoned for doing so. The Wycliffite had to see himself as an *eroicus*,[62] a member of the heroic order of *pugiles Christi*[63] who would wrestle like champions and endure like soldiers until they had overcome. The Bible could only offer men earthly suffering and urge them to be martyrs for the truth.[64] It is very difficult, he once remarked in later life (and no doubt with John of Gaunt in mind), to understand why men can positively enjoy the miseries and sufferings of making war against the Scots for material gain, and cannot even more joyfully endure the sufferings of the greater Scotland of this world for the sake of the rewards of heaven.[65]

---

[59] On the need for *caritas* 'quae est Dei dilectio', see e.g. *De civili dominio*, ii. 7, pp. 61–2; iii. 23, pp. 492–4, 505; *De fundatione sectarum*, 13, p. 63.

[60] *De civili dominio*, i. 6, p. 46, 'Et tertio exemplificat nobis quomodo debemus inimicis nostris proportionaliter misereri, non contentione tumultuosa scandalisando, sed causam nostram, servando caritatem fraternam, in manu Iudicis committendo'; as required by both divine and natural law, *De mandatis divinis*, 8, p. 69.

[61] *De officio regis*, 11, pp. 256–7. In the Old Testament the sons of the prophets were associations of disciples recording and preserving the teachings of a father figure: I Reg. 10. 5–10; 19. 20; IV Reg. 2. 15; 4.38; Amos 7. 14.

[62] *De veritate sacrae scripturae*, 6, i. 124. For the saints as *eroyci*, *De civili dominio*, ii. 13, p. 156.

[63] *De ordinatione fratrum*, 2, p. 95, 'sacerdotes fideles qui ostendunt in vita et opere quod sunt pugiles legis Dei'; and see above n. 53.

[64] *De veritate sacrae scripturae*, 13, i. 326–7, following a long complaint (pp. 318f.) that the world has fallen into falsehood, making men traitors to the truth and to themselves, and urging them to die for the truth after the example of the martyrs: 'Quomodo, quaeso, sequimur martires vel sanctos confessores qui pro quaestu vel otio non audemus dicere fidem scripturae coram domesticis, quam ipsi ad profectum sui et Ecclesiae confessi sunt coram saevissimis persecutoribus et tyrannis, specialiter cum pro defensione scripturae discernimur a pseudo-apostolis et reportamus ex fide scripturae lucrum beatitudinis' (p. 326); *De mandatis divinis*, 2, p. 8, citing Matt. 5. 10; cf. *De civili dominio*, iii. 3, p. 40.

[65] *Trialogus*, iii. 3, p. 139, 'Quis, quaeso, in Scotia propter legis libertatem et privilegia regis Angliae non laetanter pateretur, si cum hoc foret securus quod integer et vivax rediret in Angliam proportionabiliter ad punitionem a rege Angliae praemiandus? Talis, inquam, granter reciperet tribulationes in Scotia pro spe praemii in Anglia consequendi. Et multo magis tribulatus in valle huius miseriae, et transferendus ad locum patriae . . . certaret viriliter pro praemio beatitudinis consequendo, cum certi sumus ex fide quod oportet nos a Scotia ista

The effect of this was to restore martyrdom to a central place in the conception of the Christian way of life, and was a logical concomitant of Wyclif's desire for a rebirth of the *Ecclesia primitiva*, the original Church of apostles and martyrs. As the 1992 conference of the Ecclesiastical History Society demonstrated,[66] the High Middle Ages had become very hesitant about the question of martyrdom. There was no doubt that those who had died for the faith in opposition to a pagan Roman Empire were worthy of the status. But there was a reluctance to accept the blanket description that all those who died fighting the pagans on crusades were to be put into the same category; and by the fourteenth century the notion of martyrdom was being diluted and applied to such things as the joyful agonies of the mystics and other very pious people. Wyclif complained that the traditional belief in Christian perfection as something that included an individual's willingness to be persecuted to death had become lost in the apparent but false security and stability of contemporary society. The faithful were likely to be misled by the highly organized and materially successful form of the Church into thinking that undergoing persecution was an outworn requirement.[67] He accused his opponents of trying to do away with the ideal of martyrdom on the grounds that modern society could offer more comfortable, conventional, and lucrative ways of demonstrating their belief, whilst dying for the faith had been perverted into highly institutionalized forms like crusades and the defence of national kingdoms against each other. *Pro patria mori* had to be understood in a different way appropriate to a church-state on the verge of collapse. The rotting body of the realm could only be revived and revivified as a *corpus Christi* by an immediate act of corporate suffering. The *reformatio regni et ecclesiae* could not be achieved without a community sacrifice. Just as the Old Testament prophecies had foreseen the messiah as one who would

---

recedere, et correspondenter ad gratitudinem pro passione tribulationis coelestis Angliae perpetuo praemiari vel pro ingratitudine perpetuo cruciari'; cf. *Dialogus*, 27, pp. 57–8.

[66] *SCH*, 30 (1993).

[67] *Trialogus*, iii. 15, p. 181, 'Unde luciferina est excusatio qua hypocritae moderni dicunt quod non oportet hodie sicut in primitiva Ecclesia pati martyrium, quia nunc omnes vel maior pars conviventium sunt fideles: ideo non superest tyrannus qui prosequatur contra Christum usque ad mortem membra eius: et haec ratio quare hodie non sunt martires sicut olim.' This, he added, only helped to demonstrate that a perverse clergy was the abomination of desolation prophesied by Daniel according to Matt. 24. 15, and (iii. 17, p. 186) 'probabiliter ponitur quod Romanus pontifex sit praecipuus Antichristus.'

suffer for the sins of men,[68] so the ministers of Christ were to be willing to die to bring about the salvation of the kingdom as a *populus Dei*.[69] They were the voice of God whose prerogative of understanding righteousness made them the true representatives of the community.[70] It would be as if Christ was being recrucified in his vicars:[71] the prophets would be stoned again for the sake of Israel:

> Et si notemus omnia praelatorum ecclesiae et nomine clericorum qui omittendo et commitendo diminuunt, lacerant vel corrumpunt fidem scripturae, inveniretur hodie multi haeretici prophetas et apostolos occidentes. . . . Et propter hoc quod Ecclesia haereticorum quae olim lapidavit prophetas atque apostolos vivit hodie persequens eos in suis filiis.[72]

The 'holy committee' (*comitiva sanctorum*)[73] of himself and the poor priests would be like Christ and the *collegium apostolorum* redeeming the sins of England through their corporate suffering. Because it was the end of time, the persecution and their readiness to endure it would purchase a new kingdom: out of their deaths the *respublica Anglicana* would be born anew.

That there was Franciscan inspiration in so much of this can hardly be disputed, but it may be appropriate to add a comment on the way in which Wyclif's conception of a group of wandering russet-clad[74] ministers owed much to Franciscan precedent. Although in later life he came to regard the mendicants, orders founded by Innocent III, that worst of all devils, as part of a great plot to intrude papal power into every aspect of religious life,[75] his own order was deliberately modelled on the friars.

---

[68] For the 'suffering servant' theme see Isa. 40–66. The duty of the prophet to intervene with God on behalf of the people is laid down in Amos 7. 2–5, cf. Isa. 6. 11.

[69] For Wyclif on the virtues of Christian suffering see Benrath, *Bibelkommentar*, pp. 195–7, although he allowed a limited right of resistance and permitted flight when necessary.

[70] *Cruciata*, 5, p. 606, 'vere dicitur quod vox populi est vox Dei, populi videlicet simpliciter spiritu Dei ducti'.

[71] *De veritate sacrae scripturae*, 29, iii. 164.

[72] *De officio regis*, 11, p. 255.

[73] *Trialogus*, iv. 33, p. 364.

[74] Russet signified virtuous work: 'russetum vero significat laborem suum in illis duabus virtutibus absconditum, ne sint hypocritae', *Supplementum Trialogi*, p. 435; also *De fundatione sectarum*, 4, p. 27, but he condemned friars who claimed that their holy dress was a guarantee of salvation, when they were covered from head to foot in lies: *Expositio Matthaei XXIII*, 3, p. 322; *De oratione et ecclesiae purgatione*, 4, p. 351; *De nova praevaricantia mandatorum*, 7, p. 143.

[75] See the long list of grievances against Innocent III in *De eucharistia*, 9, pp. 274–8, 311–15; where in addition to persecuting Joachim, Innocent claimed unlimited supremacy over the Empire and England, encouraged war with France, prohibited vernacular Bible translation,

He came to see himself (a remarkable concept for a secular master) as the last of a great line of friar reformers[76] and his followers as an order, the *secta Christi*,[77] with Christ as its prior or abbot.[78] He wrote in glowing terms about St Francis himself;[79] he claimed to have numerous Franciscan supporters[80]—or at least before the great persecution began; and he devised schemes for combining all the religious into one order, his own, to do away with the divisive effects of having so many. It was to be an order to end all orders,[81] and in his more hopeful moments he would suggest that this sect of true Christians, the mendicants of God,[82] would spread to universal dimensions: all men were to become friars in the great

---

established the friars (who then helped to produce the *Decretales*), and of course authorized the false doctrine of transubstantiation, despite the credit he obtained by writing *De contemptu mundi*. In the *Purgatorium sectae Christi*, 4, p. 305, his chief objection to the friars is that they were founded by the pope, 'iste religiosarcha in vita et opere suo ostendit quod est mendaciter et capitaliter contrarius Iesu Christi'; cf. *De perfectione statuum*, 4, p. 463, 'duplex pater istarum fratrum, scilicet dyabolus et papa'.

[76] *De ordinatione fratrum*, 2, pp. 91–5, where he lists his predecessors who have tried to reform the mendicants, including Bonaventure, William of Saint Amour, Grosseteste, Ockham, and 'beatus Richardus' Fitzralph.

[77] The *secta Christi* was a term which clearly began as a reference to his followers, e.g. *De veritate sacrae scripturae*, 14, i. 345, 'ego cum secta mea'; i. 357, 'omnes fautores meos', although he would later argue that they were the only true Christians and therefore the expression meant the whole Church: 'Sic secta christianorum debet includere singulos viatores. . . . Patronus autem huius sectae est Dominus Iesus Christus et regula sua est fides catholica, scilicet lex ewangelica', *De fundatione sectarum*, 3, p. 22; 'Sed quomodo possemus esse in ista caritate confoederati ad invicem nisi Christum et suam sectam principaliter diligeremus, cum ipsum aliter odiremus?' 13, p. 63; cf. 6, p. 37, 'Omnes enim christiani sunt fratres in Domino, et istud nomen est ab istis sectis propter ypocrisim usurpatum'; also *De triplici vinculo amoris*, 8, p. 187, 'Augustinus declarat quod omnis viator est mendicus Dei'. The date of the *Purgatorium sectae Christi* is usually estimated as *c.*1382/3, but it could be earlier. Thomson, *Latin Writings*, p. 295, comments, 'His frequent mentions of the *secta Christi* do not take us any closer in this instance to grasping the dimensions and precise identity of that amorphous group than we were at the outset of this section.'

[78] 'Abbas noster Christus', *Trialogus*, iv. 3, p. 364; 'Christus qui est prior nostri ordinis atque principium, in se virtualiter et exemplariter congregavit', *De civili dominio*, ii. 8, p. 73; also ii. 13, p. 166; iii.1, p. 1; iii. 2, p. 75; *De veritate sacrae scripturae*, 10, i. 206; *De officio regis*, 5, p. 99.

[79] *De veritate sacrae scripturae*, 10, i. 206; and *De civili dominio*, i. 18, p. 129; iii.1, pp. 4–6; iii. 2, pp. 17–18, commending Franciscan poverty. But for a very different view, citing Hildegard as prophesying the friars as diabolical seducers, see *Trialogus*, iv. 26–38, pp. 336–85, especially pp. 361–2.

[80] Note his complaint in *De veritate sacrae scripturae*, 14, i. 354–6, about the Oxford doctor who had been attacking the English Franciscans. According to Walsingham, *Chronicon Angliae* (RS, 1874), p. 118, John of Gaunt appointed a friar from each of the four mendicant orders to help Wyclif at his hearing in 1377.

[81] *De civili dominio*, ii. 13, pp. 164–5; iii. 1, p. 1; iii. 3, pp. 31–6; cf. *De Ecclesia*, 14, p. 308; *De fundatione sectarum*, 4, p. 29; 16, p. 80.

[82] *De civili dominio*, iii. 20, pp. 417–19; *De demonio meridiano*, 3, pp. 424–5; and see above, n. 77.

convent of a reformed world.[83] The whole Church as the house of God would become one huge order, neither monastic nor apostatic but apostolic, whose members would not seek to be enclosed but would go out into the world to perform good works.

Despite these occasional suggestions that he had a universal significance, and his determination that papal power should be destroyed in all kingdoms, Wyclif's prophesies were directed almost entirely towards the prospect of an English reformation. Yet it was this prophetic character which makes it so difficult for the historian to estimate the degree of support that his movement enjoyed. His insistence that he was merely taking his appointed place in a set mystical pattern makes it almost impossible to gauge from his own writings any precise information about the numbers of Wycliffites in the 1370s. If Wycliffism meant essentially the assertion of lay supremacy in ecclesiastical matters, then the chroniclers were perfectly entitled to scream that a substantial proportion of all England had become Lollard by 1380.[84] Given the extent of Lollard support, especially the wide geographical spread of reports of it in the latter part of the century, one might guess that the numbers of Lollard ministers was considerably greater than one would expect. On the other hand it was virtually impossible for Wyclif to admit as much. Not only does he seem to have seen the poor priests as a small group of elite advisers to 'the lords', the crown and the greater magnates, a group which would steer the affairs of the kingdom like a college of apostolic cardinals, but it had become a theological necessity to represent them as a saving remnant,[85] a lodge in the wilderness, a very few amongst the multitudes of the stupid.[86] To the argument that his followers must be heretics

---

[83] *De civili dominio*, iii. 20, p. 417.

[84] But the prize goes to the Austrian chronicler: 'iste draco magister Iohannes Wycleff . . . qui plus quam tertiam partem militantis Ecclesiae in suum errorem pervertit', *Fontes rerum Austriacarum*, SS, vi. 124.

[85] E.g. *De civili dominio*, ii. 7, p. 61, 'Et patet quod si omnes tales essent subtracti ab Ecclesia, pauci in retibus remanerent'; cf. *De Ecclesia*, 9, p. 189, 'Christus autem semper reliquit in una parte Ecclesiae suae vel aliqua aliquos fideles qui mundum deserant et in illis forte abiectis primatibus stat fides et continuatio sanctae matris Ecclesiae', although in *De potestate papae*, 11. p. 272, he could not resist adding the Ockhamist point that God could use his absolute potency to frustrate Wyclif's belief ('Ego autem credo quod est necessarium ex suppositione . . .') that there must be a continuous line of true believers from the Ascension to the Day of Judgement.

[86] *De Ecclesia*, 15, p. 357, 'ideo propter multitudinem, propter famam et propter terrorem istorum satellitum exterriti sunt pauci simplices dicere veritatem'; cf. the use of the 'many are called, but few are chosen' theme in relation to the friars, *De solutione Sathanae*, 2, p. 397, 'sic pauci fideles qui stant hodie in veritate legis Domini . . .'.

because there were so few of them compared to the papalists ('. . . sunt manifesti haeretici et pauci contra cleri multitudinem quae constantius stat cum papa'), he retorted

> Hic dicitur quod argutia illa informis pharisaica dependet super stultitia populari. Cum enim stultorum sit infinitus numerus, ut dicitur Eccles. primo [15], et multi sunt vocati, pauci electi, ut dicitur Matt. 22 [14], idem est ac si Antichristus sic argueret: 'pars dyaboli habet multiplicius falsum testimonium contra Christum, ergo parti illi populus debet credere contra Deum.'[87]

The papalists might be as numerous as the sands of the sea, but this only meant that they required a very wide road to convey them all to Hell.[88] Strait is the gate . . . over and over again we are told how few his supporters were, and how their numbers were constantly declining under the weight of papalist repression. But there was no option in the matter: it was the nature of the saints to be a select few constantly being reduced. They were required to be by definition a permanent minority, regardless of the numbers involved. Wyclif insisted that the opponents could not claim to be a majority simply on the grounds that they had greater numbers:[89] you could not have a majority which was *wrong*. Just as Wyclif's majorities were not to be treated numerically, so his concept of a minority is equally suspect and should be taken with caution. The 'wise and prudent few' who understood their Bibles better than anybody else needed to be under-estimated to secure their place in the great eschatological drama.

Massive persecution should have needed massive numbers to be persecuted, but in this context numbers are as mythical as the persecution itself. It was what *ought* to have happened, and so in a sense rightly *did* happen, rather than what actually took place. Prophecy-fulfilling mythology is much more important here than mere history. Wyclif's close connection with contemporary spirituality led him to produce a political theory more akin to the Passion dramas with their elaborate

---

[87] *Cruciata*, 5, p. 605.
[88] *De solutione Sathanae*, 2, p. 396, citing Matt. 7. 13 and Apoc. 20. 8.
[89] *Dialogus*, 11, pp. 21–2, 'Qui autem credit ut fidem communitati vel populo est in ianuis ut stolide seducatur, quia Eccles. primo [15] scribitur "stultorum infinitus est numerus". Et sapiens Daniel cum populus dampnasset Susannam ex falso testimonio sacerdotum si generaliter multitudo testium approbetur. . . . Ideo est stulta evidentia si maior pars militantum sic asserit, ergo verum, cum sit argumentum topicum ad contrarium concluden-dum, quia Deus scit si nunc militant plures filii patris mendacii quam filii veritatis'; cf. *De potestate papae*, 5, pp. 86–8. One is reminded of Marsilius' *valentior pars*.

embroidery of the details of Christ's trial and crucifixion.[90] Despite some of Wyclif's rude remarks about 'miracle plays', Lollardy was not opposed to the drama as such, and his followers are known to have adapted at least one play to their own purposes.[91] But as has recently been asked of *Piers Plowman*, how far did the author believe in his own drama? Was this apocalyptic speculation simply a cynical manipulation of popular piety to promote royalist propaganda, or do we have here another example of the medieval capacity to believe that enactment of a prophecy would actually bring it about? Should the Lollard persecution be added to the lists of great jousts, the ceremonial battles between the forces of good and evil which often preceded crusades, and might even replace the actual crusades themselves? Whatever the answer, Wyclif takes his place in the long tradition of *ludi de Antichristo*, the plays about Antichrist which were strenuously objected to on the grounds that if one portrayed the end of the world, it was likely to cause it to happen.

If one could ask Wyclif why the Lollard movement eventually failed and became politically helpless during the fifteenth century, I suspect he would answer that it was because the great persecution never happened: the sacrifice was refused. But a more valid answer would be that Lollardy was engaged in the long travail in which its adherents walked in the footsteps of St Paul. Wyclif endless praised the wandering apostle not only for seeking to call St Peter to correction, but also for appealing to Caesar.[92] Wyclif knew that without royal intervention the Reformation would never take place, at least not in England, and his appeals became more and more frenzied as it became apparent that the crown was not willing to act. It weighed little with him that there was a basic contradiction between demanding to be persecuted as a theological necessity in one breath and begging to be saved from it the next. He always accepted that lay supremacy required lay involvement. The saints could declare the truth; they

---

[90] Cf. his comment on the Blackfriars Council: 'Unde in ultimo suo concilio terraemotus in quo illudebant episcopi Christum Dominum nostrum vel membris suis triumphantis Ecclesiae tamquam haereticum condemnando regem nostrum et eius proceres, et per consequens communitatem in castigationem pseudoclericorum haereticando, recoluerunt ex timore patris sui de Romano pontifice . . .', *Supplementum Trialogi*, 8, pp. 445–6.

[91] For the use of the drama as a vehicle for anti-Lollard propaganda see V. A. Kolve, *The Play Called Corpus Christi* (London, 1966), esp. pp. 44–9; and in relation to the Croxton *Play of the Sacrament* see now A. E. Nichols, 'Lollard language in the Croxton *Play of the Sacrament*', *Notes and Queries*, n.s., 234 (1989), pp. 23–5.

[92] *De civili dominio*, ii. 14, pp. 170–1; iii. 2, p. 28; *De potestate papae*, 7, p. 157. St Paul, 'doctor praecipuus', was the ideal of a wandering preacher who was not deterred by popular opposition: *De eucharistia*, 9, pp. 294–5; *Dialogus*, 25, p. 52; *Expositio Matthaei XXIII*, 4, pp. 323–4; cf. *Opus evangelicum*, iii. 6, ii. 22; Benrath, *Bibelkommentar*, pp. 243–4.

could set an example; they could pay the price: but it was the king who had to set his own house in order.[93] Wyclif understood that, like Marsilius and Ockham, he needed the same sort of support from the court in London that the Spirituals had had at Munich. But John of Gaunt was not a Louis of Bavaria.[94] He would gladly employ and protect someone who could be useful in bringing bishops and abbots to heel. Dispossession of the religious, crown appointment of clergy, apostolic poverty and so on, were all things which could find a place in the royal arsenal; even prophecies could be utilized for propaganda purposes: but no government could administer the realm on the basis of apocalyptic speculation. If Wyclif made the mistake of believing himself, we can reasonably doubt whether his patrons did too. As one writer, perhaps Hoccleve, subsequently asked, was the life of a Wycliffite conducive to being a governor?

> Hit is unkyndly for a knight
> That shuld a kynges castel kepe
> To babble the Bibel day and night
> In restyng time when he shuld slepe.[95]

He was asking whether a Lollard knight could be effective: was there not an irreconcilable tension between sanctity and successful politics? Wyclif gave his movement the character of suffering saints, but it meant leaving the real political action to others: people with their minds firmly fixed on the blessed agonies of the prelude to reformation were not likely to be good revolutionaries. And the danger was that what the Lollards professed themselves to be, they were liable to become. A persecuted minority must regard actual success as a dubious asset: a life in which patience under tribulation was a necessary qualification was hardly equipped to handle power and influence. Lollardy therefore accepted far too easily the role it

---

[93] *Opus evangelicum*, iii. 46, ii. 170, 'Pauperes autem presbyteri non possunt aliter facere in ista materia nisi loqui fidem Dei et tangere media per quae regnicolae poterunt esse salvi, quia principum potestas et eorum qui portant gladium debet se extendere ad ista media practizanda'; *Dialogus*, 5, p. 11, 'nec sufficiunt pauperes et pauci fideles sacerdotes resistere, nisi Deus per saeculare brachium vel aliunde citius manus apposuerit adiutrices.'

[94] According to Wyclif the seduction of secular lords by Antichrist was further proof of the end of the world: *Opus evangelicum*, i. 8, i. 26. On John of Gaunt see now A. Goodman, *John of Gaunt: The Exercise of Princely Power in Fourteenth-Century Europe* (Harlow, 1992); S. Walker, *The Lancastrian Affinity, 1361–1399* (Oxford, 1990).

[95] T. Wright, *Political Poems and Songs* (RS, 1861), 2, 244. The point was implicitly raised by Wyclif himself when he remarked that the chroniclers provided few examples of popes who had become martyrs after the papacy obtained temporal power: *De potestate papae*, 7, p. 146.

had given itself of being an underground movement, exciting but ineffective. The notion of the suffering saints sustained the faith and enabled Lollardy to survive the long winter of the fifteenth century, but it had little more to offer. It did not provide a formula for successful government: which is why the Reformation, when it came, sought to abolish Lollardy rather than to revive it.

10

WYCLIF AND THE WHEEL OF TIME

by MICHAEL WILKS

During the 1370s Wyclif wrote to defend a monarchy which made extensive use of bishops and other clergy in the royal administration and yet was faced with aristocratic factions encouraged by bishops like Wykeham and Courtenay who espoused papal supremacy, if not out of conviction, at least as a very convenient weapon to support their independence against royal absolutism. At first sight Wyclif's attempts to define the right relationship between royal and episcopal, temporal and spiritual, power seem as confused as the contemporary political situation. His works contain such a wide range of theories from orthodox two swords dualism to a radical rejection of ecclesiastical authority well beyond that of Marsilius and Ockham that it seems as if his only interest was in collecting every anti-hierocratic idea available for use against the papacy. The purpose of this paper is to suggest that a much more coherent view of episcopal power can be detected beneath his tirades if it is appreciated that his continual demand for a great reform, a *reformatio regni et ecclesiae*, is inseparably linked to his understanding of the history of the Christian Church, and that in this way Wyclif anticipates Montesquieu in requiring a time factor as a necessary ingredient in constitutional arrangements.

Wyclif saw himself as a prophet preaching a message of salvation to a people of God for whom the Bible, especially the Old Testament, had a direct significance. He had so much to say about the importance of Scripture, evangelical liberty, apostolic poverty and the natural innocence of the early Church that it is hardly surprising that some of his later opponents came to criticize him and his followers for ignoring anything the Church had achieved after the first millennium.[1] One has only to consider his use of authors like

---

[1] For examples (Barton, Netter), see Anne Hudson, *The Premature Reformation* (Oxford, 1988), p. 250.

Grosseteste and Fitzralph, let alone less well publicized ones like Aquinas and Ockham, to recognize this criticism as obvious nonsense. Wyclif's was intended to be a universal system, and no one was more eclectic: everything was to be grist for the mill. But it is true that this entailed a refusal to believe that history and historic practices were obsolete and out of date: early sources should still be of relevance to his own time. Was the law of Christ, he once asked, to be allowed to survive for only three centuries whilst the rule of Antichrist went on for ever?[2] Human time might be a linear progression from the Creation to the end of the world, and he followed this scheme in his own work: the *Summa theologiae* ran from the genesis of the divine mandates through an investigation of natural law and civil society to the apocalyptic obsession with Antichrist which characterizes the later books. But this progression led to a Second Coming, the great return of Christ to the world and a new Jerusalem. This idea of return implied a turning round again, a repetition, a revolution not just in the modern sense of a change of government and society but in the classical sense of a movement back to what had gone before. Religion meant for Wyclif, as it had done for the Romans, *religare*, to bind back to the origins, and he adopted the notion that time was a circular process which turned like a wheel. As Aristotle, following Hesiod and Pythagoras, had suggested in the *Physics*,[3] the Greeks accepted that human affairs moved round in a circle through a series of periods in the same way that the heavenly bodies revolved and so must eventually return to their original position, a point marked by a cataclysm and a new beginning. Time, in other words, formed a great year. This great year theory had then been accepted by Cicero and other Roman authors, becoming a staple feature of prophetic material: the Sibylline Oracle, for example, spoke of

[2] *Dialogus*, 7, p. 16. Earlier debates on Wyclif's attitude towards tradition are discussed by M. Hurley, '*Scriptura sola*: Wyclif and his critics', *Traditio*, 16 (1960), pp. 275–352.

[3] *Physics*, 223b; cf. *De gen. et cor.*, 336b; *Problemata*, 916a; *Protrepticus*, frag. 19. Wyclif's commentary on the *Physics* remains unpublished: see W. R. Thomson, *The Latin Writings of John Wyclif* (Toronto 1983), pp. 12–14; otherwise all references are to the Wyclif Society editions (London, 1883–1921).

'the circling years of time'.[4] With Wyclif this great year applies to the whole history of the Church from the beginning to the end of time – 'facta est in magno anno mundi'[5] – but during the Middle Ages there were numerous variants with competing suggestions for different successions and alternations of good and bad periods, and the principle achieved immense popularity in the more common form of the wheel of Fortune.[6]

It is important however to make the point that this was speculation about the nature of human time. Divine time was a different matter entirely: as was often said, a thousand years was but a day in the sight of God – or, perhaps more accurately, that God lived in an eternal present. Past, present, and future were all one in the divine mind.[7] This, Wyclif said, was duration (*duratio*) and must be distinguished from *tempus*, human time,[8] measured in this

[4] The standard account is G. W. Trompf, *The Idea of Historical Recurrence in Western Thought from Antiquity to the Reformation* (Berkeley and Los Angeles, 1979), esp. pp. 11–12, 62–75, 177, 202.

[5] *De Ecclesia*, 17, pp. 389–90; also 9, p. 197 for the succession of the seasons of the year. Plato is credited with the view that the world year lasts 36,000 terrestrial years: *De actibus animae*, i.3, p. 51.

[6] This derives from Boethius, *Philosophiae consolatio*, ii. *prol.* 1–6, where Philosophy is emphasizing the difference between divine and human justice: 'Haec nostra vis est, hunc continuum ludum ludimus: totam volubili orbe versamus, infima summis, summa infimis mutare gaudemus. Ascende si placet, sed ea lege, ne uti cum ludicri mei ratio poscet descendere iniuriam putes.' For a good late fourteenth-century example see *Somer Soneday* (Oxford, Bodleian Library, MS Douce 332), 'A wifman wiþ a wonder whel weue with þe wynde ... And Fortune Y fond', ed. T. Turville-Petre, *Alliterative Poetry of the Later Middle Ages* (London, 1989), p. 143 and fig. 5.

[7] *De Ecclesia*, pp. 106–7, citing Eccles. 3.14–15, and Aristotle on motion in the *Physics*, vii.1. Previous efforts to combine Aristotle's view of time (taken largely from *Physics*, iv.10–14, 218–23; also v.3, 226–7 and vi.1–2, 231–2 on the analogy of time as a line) with an Augustinian conception of God as in an eternal present, notably by Wyclif's predecessor at Merton, Thomas Bradwardine, are well set out by E. W. Dolnikowski, *Thomas Bradwardine: A View of Time and a Vision of Eternity in Fourteenth-Century Thought* (Leiden, New York, and Cologne, 1995), who rightly indicates the contribution of Euclidean mathematics here. The relevance of the *Categories* as a source passed on through Boethius and Anselm has been shown by G. R. Evans, 'Time and eternity: Boethian and Augustinian sources of thought in the late eleventh and early twelfth centuries', *Classical folia*, 31 (1977), pp. 105–18, who cites (p. 112) the significant passage in Abelard's *Dialectica* that time is either an indivisible instant or a composite succession of instants forming past, present, and future. See Dolnikowski, *Thomas Bradwardine*, pp. 42–3.

[8] The term *duratio* was probably borrowed from Augustine. Cf. *De logica*, iii.10,

world by a succession of ages. Once again there was an appeal here to Aristotelian physics: a line was to be seen two ways, either as a single thing or as a succession of dots next to each other – just as in philosophy it was necessary at different times to consider both the universal and the individuals. It was the same with time: it was either, as God saw it, a single eternity; or it was a constant movement of instants (what Chaucer would call degrees)[9] following each other round and round as on the face of a clock, which was how humanity saw it. This was why predestination was such a simple matter. If the future is the same as the past, then God has no difficulty in knowing who is elect and who is damned. But mankind trapped in the wheel of time can have no such certainty and must endure – accept *duratio* – until the succession of ages reveals whether the signs of salvation or perdition to be detected in human life are a true indication of what must be. There can be no sure salvation until human time matches up to divine time, until the circle of periods has completed its course, and there is a return to the perpendicular.[10]

Like so many of his contemporaries Wyclif accepted the Augustinian notion of the seven ages of man, and applied the same idea to the ages of the world.[11] There was what might be described as a world week of seven phases, with the

iii.172, 'et illum mundum durare in transitione successiva est tempus'; and see ii.17, i.224; iii.9, iii.34–5, 80–3; iii.10, iii.181, 196, 211, where he acknowledges that it was reading the *Physics* (apparently in a commentary perhaps by Averroes but probably Aquinas) which led him to change his original view of time through the theory of the line as 'continuatio et contiguatio'. The problem of dating the *De logica* remains unsolved.

9   In the *Nun's Priest's Tale*, vii. 2854–8, the cock crows more strongly 'Than is a clokke or an abbey orlogge. / By nature he knew ech ascencioun / Of the equynoxial in thilke toun; / For when degrees fiftene weren ascended, / Thanne crew he that it myghte nat been amended.' For the *Tales* as political and anti-clerical analogies see now L. Scanlon, *Narrative, Authority and Power: The Medieval Exemplum and the Chaucerian Tradition* (Cambridge, 1994).

10   *De Ecclesia*, 9, p. 198, 'et iterum oportet ut fiat nova appropinquatio ad perpendiculare, quodquam fiat directo post diem iudicii solsticium sempiternum, ut patet *Apocalypsis* ultimo; tunc enim invariabiliter coincident radius incidens et reflexus.'

11   Trompf, *Historical Recurrence*, pp. 207f. The connection between these concepts has already been pointed out by B. Smalley, *Historians in the Middle Ages* (London, 1974); and in general see now J. A. Burrow, *The Ages of Man* (Oxford, 1986).

lifetime of Christ featuring as a halfway stage.[12] The three periods of the Old Testament represented the youth of the world; there had been three ages of decline into old age since; and this led to a seventh or last age of the world, an apocalyptic period of Armageddon, and a prelude to the eighth day of eternal bliss, the great return to another Sunday. Wyclif insisted that his own time was the nadir of the process, the point at which the downward movement had virtually reached its lowest level: the world had never been in a worse condition, and the tyrant priests had brought the Church into the condition of the Last Days.[13] Satan had been bound for a thousand years, and so the history of the Church after Christ had begun in a state of apostolic purity, an age of saints, martyrs, and patristics. The first real downward lurch had occurred with the Donation of Constantine – like an injection of poison into the body of Christ[14] – but it was the eleventh century and the emergence of the Gregorian Church which indicated that the decline was serious and would be fatal.[15] So as a rule of thumb the older a doctrine was, like that of the Eucharist, the more correct and useful it was likely to be: conversely the later the pope concerned, the worse he would probably be.[16] Indeed it was only from around 1200, from the time of

[12] The general principle is in *De mandatis divinis*, 16, pp. 211-14, although this has four ages for the Old Testament period, apparently to relate to Daniel's four world monarchies, as indicated by *De civili dominio*, iii, 15, p. 196. For three Old Testament ages see, e.g., iii.7, p. 60; cf. *De veritate sacrae scripturae*, 15, i.383, 'Nam tempore Crisostomi [who referred to heretical priests] . . . coepit calumnia; tempore Machometi amplius dissipata est; et a tempore editionis *Decretalium* decrevit honor et pruderantia legis scripturae continue, quod videtur esse via praeparatoria Antichristo'; *De civili dominio*, iii.17, p. 247, 'distinguere circumstantias temporum . . .. Aliter enim debent vivere patres veteris testamenti et in iuvenile aetate mundi . . . et aliter provectiones filii mundi senescentis . . ..'

[13] *De Ecclesia*, 3, p. 51; also *De mandatis divinis*, 28, p. 410; 30, p. 474; cf. *De civili dominio*, ii.17, p. 240, 'Unde videtur michi quod.nunquam ab origine mundi . . . cum hodie quod et dolendum est . . .'. On this topic see further M. Wilks, 'Wyclif and the great persecution', in M. Wilks, ed., *Prophecy and eschatology*, SCH.S, 10 (Oxford, 1994), pp. 39-63.

[14] E.g. *De officio regis*, 7, p. 171.

[15] *De eucharistia*, 9, p. 286.

[16] Ibid., 2, p. 32, 'Quare ergo non crederetur tantae vel plus suae sententiae sicut debiliori sententiae succedenti? Ecclesia enim deteriorando quoad fidem scripturae procedit. Et iterum prior sententia plus consonat sensui, rationi, sanctis doctoribus et scripturis . . .'; also 9, p. 278; *De civili dominio*, ii.11, pp. 124-5.

the first really awful pope, Innocent III, that the situation went out of control.[17]

But the period before the 1200 watershed still had much to recommend it,[18] and the work of twelfth-century writers and legislators could be salvaged and reused: Wyclif plundered its intellectual treasures lavishly and shamelessly, thereby giving himself, as he saw it, an irrefutable claim to orthodoxy against his contemporaries. He maintained that moderates like John of Salisbury in philosophy and theology, and the reciprocal dualism between the claims of clerical and lay government in canon law put forward by the Decretists, had achieved a workable compromise. It was only the Decretalists, corrupted by their work on the texts of Innocent III and his successors, who had destroyed the carefully balanced relationship which should exist between king and bishop. That relationship – the king as vicar of God the divine ruler juxtaposed to the human vicar of Christ, the bishop – Wyclif borrowed wholesale from the Christology of the Anglo-Norman Anonymous,[19] a more significant source for the character of medieval English kingship than modern historians like to think. But what this meant in practical terms of the corresponding duties of kings and bishops had been clearly spelt out, he argued, by St Anselm.

It may not have been an Anselm that Sir Richard Southern would recognize, but Wyclif had initially been trained as a papalist, an Augustinian hierocrat, and knew how to make use of his sources for his own purposes, even if it turned the originals on their heads. When, for example, he eventually admitted that his double substance eucharistic theory required that the bread and wine should remain after consecration and conversion into the body and blood of Christ, it was, remarkably, from Anselm (amongst others)

[17] See the lengthy condemnation of Innocent III in *De eucharistia*, 9, pp. 274f., although Honorius III was worse for confirming the Orders of friars and Gregory IX for issuing the *Decretals* (p. 278; also 5, p. 142), and the move to Avignon made matters worse still, 4, p. 106.

[18] *De civili dominio*, ii.14, pp. 178–9.

[19] *De officio regis*, 1, pp. 10, 14; 6, pp. 121–2, 131; although he credits Augustine with this idea. See further G. H. Williams, *The Norman Anonymous of 1100 A.D.* (Cambridge, Mass., 1951). Perhaps after all, he was the Anonymous of York!

that he claimed support.[20] When he insisted that the contemporary Church had become an *ecclesia* of malignants,[21] too corrupt to be a vehicle of salvation, and therefore another covenant with God was needed, a new social contract of good lordship to replace the Petrine Commission, it was from Anselm that he borrowed his term to describe it. It was a chirograph, a document which recognized rights on both sides, and accordingly was made by dividing it down the middle. This, incidentally, is why Piers Plowman tore the pardon in half whilst the contemporary priest could not even recognize it as a contract of salvation.[22] But where Anselm was particularly significant for Wyclif was that he had been responsible for engineering the agreement of London in August 1107, a compromise arrangement which would later provide a basis for the Concordat of Worms in 1122 and the alleged settlement of the Investiture Contest. These agreements had defined a tripartite distinction of episcopal power. The old simple division between a bishop's internal and external powers was coming by the twelfth century to be described as on one side his *potestas ordinis*, the sacramental power given to a bishop by consecration; and on the other side his *ecclesiastica* or *potestas iurisdictionis*, granted by investiture with a ring and staff, the powers and properties of the see which he administered by right of office. But in addition there was a third capacity, the bishop's position as a baron or royal officer, his holding of *saecularia* or *regalia* which granted him powers, duties, and rights which might otherwise have been given to a layman: the custody of cities and castles, official functions, the right to levy tolls and dues, and the feudal obligations of fealty, knight service, and so on which went with them. Faced with a papal insistence that kings should not invest bishops, Paschal II's desire to do

[20] *De eucharistia*, 5, p. 131.
[21] *De officio regis*, 11, p. 251, kings are to act like an aggregate emperor 'contra ecclesiam malignantium . . . quamdiu manet civilitas sublunaris et clerus sic aspirat ad terrenum dominium'; also *De potestate papae*, 7, p. 139.
[22] *De civili dominio*, ii.16, pp. 318–19, citing Anselm, *Cur deus homo*, i.7 (*PL*, 158, col. 368): this cancels the charter of damnation in Col. 2.13–14; cf. *De benedicta incarnatione*, 6, p. 90; G. A. Benrath, *Wyclifs Biblekommentar* (Berlin, 1966), pp. 72–3 (on Jer. 17.13). See also St Bernard, *De consideratione*, ii.6 (*PL*, 182, col. 750); *Piers Plowman*, B.vii.116.

away with the third capacity (episcopal *regalia*), and Henry I's equally strong determination that all jurisdiction should flow from the king, Anselm in 1107 had arranged a compromise by which the king gave up the right to confer the bishop's jurisdictional power by investiture, but retained the right to confer the *regalia*, the bishop's other offices, *per sceptrum*.[23]

Although the fourteenth century normally preferred a simple distinction between a bishop's 'spirituals', which included things like tithes and oblations, and his 'temporals', his estates and offices,[24] the old legal subdivision of jurisdiction was still recognized. Thus when Wykeham came to terms with John of Gaunt in 1377, the bishop agreed to fit out three war galleys with fifty archers and fifty men-at-arms in each, and in return had its temporalities restored to him. It was specified that these temporalities included both the *temporalia* themselves and the bishop's feudal rights (*cum feodis militum*), the custody of castles, manors, and knights' fees. It was in this same year that Wyclif argued that the king had a double basis for refusing to allow papal taxation of the English Church: because it infringed both the royal jurisdiction as patron in chief and the king's feudal rights over his clergy.[25] And to cut a long story short, let me simply make the point that with Wyclif careful analysis of his multitude of condemnations of bishops for having jurisdiction at all – the task of bishops was to preach the truth and leave coercion to the laity[26] – shows that beneath these outpourings

[23]   Eadmer, *Historia novorum*, ed. M. Rule, *RS* (London, 1884), p. 186. See further M. J. Wilks, '*Ecclesiastica* and *regalia*: papal investiture policy from the Council of Guastalla to the First Lateran Council, 1106–23', *SCH*, 7 (Oxford, 1971), pp. 69–85.

[24]   This dualistic position is well stated by M. E. Howell, *Regalian Right in Medieval England* (London, 1962).

[25]   For Wykeham see T. Rymer, *Foedera*, vii.148–9; cf. G. Holmes, *The Good Parliament* (Oxford, 1975), p. 192. *De potestate papae*, 10, pp. 222f. on papal taxation; also *De Ecclesia*, 15, p. 340 on royal rights during episcopal vacancies which allow him to take both feudal and patronage possessions: '. . . in mortibus multorum sacerdotum qui de rege tenent in feudo temporalia cedant regi. Unde ex iure patronatus confert beneficia . . . Unde cum rex praeter istas regalias aufert saepe temporalia . . .'.

[26]   *De civili dominio*, ii.8, p. 73; this distinction of functions follows from the dual nature of Christ. As priest he is 'propheta magnus atque magister', but as king exercises 'correptio coactiva' as defined by Justinian in *Novella*, 6, (p. 77). *De officio regis*, 7, p. 186, 'Dixi autem alias quomodo domini temporales habent potentiam datam eis a Deo ut ubi spirituale bracchium Ecclesiae non sufficit convertere antichristos ewangelica praedicatione, ecclesiastica correctione vel virtutum exemplatione, saeculare bracchium adiuvet matrem suam severa cohercione, et specialiter in pseudo-clericis.'

Wyclif still operated with the traditional (and originally papal) tripartite distinction. Under divine lordship the clergy had a God-given authority which was quite separate from any Caesarean gift,[27] but this magisterial function was essentially non-political, a lordship of love belonging to clergy whose first duty was contemplation of the divine mysteries,[28] and whose superiority rested on their humility, perfection, and ability to provide an example of true Christian living.[29] For this Christ provided them with sacramental power, the indelible character of *potestas ordinis*,[30] but that is all. If therefore the bishops have jurisdiction, as indeed they do (which Wyclif sometimes categorizes as a *potestas executionis*)[31] this can only be a matter of human lordship and so must derive from the king.[32] For instance it was the king who decided that there should be separate civil and ecclesiastical courts.[33] In this way there was a *dualitas* of spiritual and temporal matters, and cases which were a mixture of both.[34] But, more significantly, temporal

---

[27] *De potestate papae*, 10, p. 236, 'Sacerdotes itaque Christi habent potestatem ante istam iurisdictionem caesaream edificandi populum ubicumque terrarum quantum sufficiunt, praedicando sancte conversando vel instar sanctorum doctorum scriptis sententiam catholicam commendando; talem autem potestatem regiminis independentem ab invicem habuerunt apostoli plus et minus . . .'; p. 246, 'sicut ante dotationem tempore quo crevit Ecclesia quando pure regulabatur per legem Christi et regebatur per sacerdotes socios sine praeeminentia humanitus instituta'.

[28] *De dominio divino*, i.1, p. 8, 'Et dominium correspondens voluntario ministerio ad aedificationem corporis Christi mystici voco caritativum dominium sive vicarium, quod habent ecclesiastici, sicut et servitium eo magis quo sunt in ministerio plus perfecti. Aliud autem est dominium coactivum quod quantum ad primam fundationem attinet est ecclesiasticis interdictum . . .'; *De civili dominio*, ii.3, p. 25, 'ecclesiastici quidem ex vi religiònis non possident iuste haec temporalia nisi ipsa meruerint cogitatione contempliva'; also ii.9, pp. 86f. where both St Paul and Aristotle's *Physics* are called in support. In iii.21, pp. 436, 438, quoting lavishly from the *Politics*, he suggests a return to the Aristotelian principle that the clergy, being only a *pars civitatis*, should be drawn from old men no longer capable of being active citizens, only of contemplation.

[29] *De officio regis*, 6, p. 142; 8, p. 196; 12, pp. 275f. In *De potestate papae*, 7, pp. 140-1, clergy have the key of divine knowledge, not the key of power.

[30] *De potestate papae*, 2, pp. 32-3.

[31] *De potestate papae*, 11, p. 307, following FitzRalph, 'omnes potestates ordinis sunt aequales, nec minuitur etiam potestatis iurisdictiionis executio nisi de quanto rationabiliter est restricta'; *sent. ad* 1, p. 398, 'potestas ordinis . . . sufficit sine potestate regiminis vel iurisdictionis superaddita'.

[32] E.g. *De civili dominio*, ii.3, pp. 22-3; *De officio regis*, 6, pp. 118-19.

[33] *De civili dominio*, ii.14, pp. 167f., 173f.

[34] *De civili dominio*, ii.8, pp. 70-1, 'domini temporales regant immediate et directe

jurisdiction is to be distinguished between what the clergy hold *ut clerici* and what is a matter of the general wealth of the kingdom.[35] Feudal functions are distinct from endowed possessions. Following FitzRalph, Wyclif allows that the bishops have held *regalia* or *saecularia*[36] in England since the Conquest,[37] which is to be classified separately from the patronage exercised already by Anglo-Saxon rulers,[38] and which priests may hold in a non-priestly capacity as civil servants, feudatories, and recipients of royal grants.[39] They may have custody of some towns or castles, even be marcher lords;[40] but if so, they do it as if they are laity rather than clergy.[41]

suos subditos quoad temporalia et quoad corpus; consequentur autem et accessorie quoad animam . . .. Econtra autem sacerdotes Christi debent principaliter et directe regere quoad spiritualia carismata ut virtutes; consequenter autem et accessorie quoad bona naturalia et fortunae; et sic oportet suas iurisdictiones esse commixtas et mutuo se iuvantes . . .. Necesse est ergo Ecclesiam fulciri bracchio saeculari ut corpore, et clero ut anima, ut iuvent se reciproce in suis officiis a Domino limitatis instar animae et corporis in eodem supposito'; 12, p. 133, 'iurisdictiones saeculares et ecclesiasticae sunt super clericis commixtae'; also 9, pp. 84–5; 14, p. 173.

35 *De potestate papae*, 5, p. 89.

36 *De civili dominio*, iii.13, p. 223, 'ut redditu et praediis, castris vel aliis adiacentibus et sic militaris foedus, baronia, comitatus, ducatus, regnum et imperium vocantur dominia, quae contingit clericum cum suo clericatus habere sine civilitate ex quod civiliter non dominetur', citing FitzRalph, *De pauperie Salvatoris*, vi.31. For Wyclif's use of FitzRalph see K. Walsh, *A Fourteenth-Century Scholar and Primate: Richard FitzRalph in Oxford, Avignon and Armagh* (Oxford, 1981), pp. 378f.

37 In *De eucharistia*, 9, p. 320, he argues that William I had had to seize all the wealth of the *ecclesia Anglicana* because the Anglo-Saxon clergy were so delinquent.

38 *De Ecclesia*, 15, p. 336, 'et scimus pro tempore antequam Britones et Saxones dotarunt ecclesiam vel enim fuit ecclesia nostra dotata, et interim tempore Saxonum ante adventum Augustini fuit fides Christi infideliter praetermissa, tunc isti principes primo dotantes ecclesiam nostram non erant moti nisi titulo misericordiae donare plus vel minus nostrae ecclesiae . . .'.

39 *De Ecclesia*, 15, pp. 350–1, 'Sed servire civiliter potest esse sine peccato. Nec oportet quod sic homo servit civiliter quod sit servus civilis, cum omnis dominus Angliae sub rege servit sibi civiliter . . . et sic serviunt clerici regi libere qui tenent de illo in capite . . . licet regi eos civiliter cohercere non in quantum sacerdotes sed in quantum regis elemosinarii vel homines eius legii contempnentes'; *De civili dominio*, iii.20, p. 416, 'si enim talis religiosus sit civilis dominus super baronias et comitatus . . . tunc est baro vel comes'.

40 See his apparent approval of the priests of the Old Testament who had 'paucis villis cum suis suburbiis et iliis decimis, oblationibus . . .', *De civili dominio*, ii.4, p. 34; 5, p. 40, 'rex capit temporalia in manibus tamquam eorum dominus'; cf. iii.21, pp. 451–2, arguing that *regalia* cannot be lost from royal control and attacking the pope for trying to intrude foreigners into 'castra episcoporum'.

41 He was still capable of confusing the difference by demanding that the clergy should pay homage for all landholdings and have military obligations: *De civili dominio*, ii.5, p. 39; ii.8, p. 75; ii.18, p. 268.

The real significance of this triple distinction for Wyclif, however, was that it was determined by history. Bishops had three different kinds of power because the history of the Church was to be seen as divisible into three distinct phases, and sources as diverse as St Paul and Joachim of Fiore could be summoned to justify this contention.[42] In the same way that the Old Testament recorded a transmission from the Garden of Eden to an age of innocence in which God's people were priests and kings, a lay priesthood by natural law, followed by the rule of the Levitical priesthood, so since the time of Christ there had been three types of clergy. First, an apostolic priesthood without coercive power; then a shared arrangement with coercion divided between kings and priests, and a dual system of courts and law; and now the worst condition of a clergy claiming all jurisdiction and rendering kings unnecessary.[43]

This meant that there had been three types of Church. In the beginning there had been the Church as a Church pure and simple, living in a golden age[44] of apostolic poverty because kings and emperors owned all the land and wealth, and being pagan were not even part of the Church. In such a self-sufficient community (*per se sufficiens*), clergy only needed sacramental power. This idyllic condition lasted until the time of Constantine, when the conversion of the Roman emperor began the age of endowment with kings and lay lords becoming patrons of a proprietary Church, granting the clergy lands and jurisdiction, and making a Gelasian dualism inevitable. The Donation of Constantine, which initiated the process *ex ritu gentilium*, should be seen, Wyclif maintained, as an endowment – a *dotatio*, not a

---

[42] I Cor. 15.20f.; and for Joachim, Trompf, *Historical Recurrence*, pp. 216–19; E. R. Daniel, 'Joachim of Fiore: patterns of history in the Apocalypse', in R. K. Emmerson and B. McGinn, eds, *The Apocalypse in the Middle Ages* (Ithaca, N.Y., and London, 1992), pp. 72–88. This was a popular theme in the later fourteenth century: see for example 'The Parlement of the Thre Ages', in Turville-Petre, *Alliterative Poetry*, pp. 67–100.

[43] *De civili dominio*, i.27, pp. 194–5; iii.21, pp. 437–8; *De veritate sacrae scripturae*, 4, i.67–70; 15, i.393.

[44] *De Ecclesia*, 23, p. 572, 'saeculum aureum ut in statu innocentiae'. It was equivalent to the state of nature because there was no private property, but first the laity, and then the clergy, abandoned common ownership: *De civili dominio*, iii.6, pp. 77–80; iii.8, pp. 111–13.

donatio[45] – because now the Church was married to the State, and the bishops had jurisdiction in the *respublica*. But now there is the third phase, the worst condition, in which the Church thinks it has become the State and owns everything in its own right.[46] The bishops claim *regalia* as an entitlement: they think they can do anything a layman can do and can staff all the offices of government – whilst the pope imagines he has become the emperor. There is an essential correlation between the three categories of episcopal power and the descent through the three historical periods of ecclesiastical degeneration.

It was however a cardinal principle for Wyclif that what goes down must be capable of going up again. His philosophy had taught him that there were two sides to any circle: there were *ordines descendi et ascendi*, falling and rising motions.[47] The *deformatio*[48] of the downward sweep of time can, and indeed must, be matched by a future upward movement of reformation or restitution, a return out of old age into a glorious new rebirth.[49] But just as the descent had been a periodic decline, so the corresponding improvement would have to be one step at a time. It was to be a Reformation by stages, or, to quote Margaret Aston, 'a

---

[45] *De civili dominio*, ii.7, p. 60, 'sic potest contingere quod Ecclesia Christi sit per apostolos saeculi iudices, optime regulata; secundo per reges, sed male, qui post dotationem ecclesiae constituunt sibi praepositos in suis ecclesiis; sed tertio pessime per sacerdotes qui aspirantes ad principale mundi civile dominium . . . possent perplexius mundum sibi subicere'; cf. iii.2, pp. 445–7; *De potestate papae*, 12, p. 395, 'Constantinum magnum qui dotavit ecclesiam'; 6, pp. 120–1; *De Ecclesia*, 14, p. 300, 'ius plenum ad totum imperium'; and therefore is the *dominus mundi* of Roman law, 'ex lege imperiali post dotationem factam a Caesare', 13, p. 282.

[46] This is the blasphemy of the papal lawyers which drives the bishops mad: 'sunt nimis multi maniaci . . . Et in istam blasphemiam ex defectu intellectus scripturae incidunt multi iuristae, facientes suos praepositos insanire', *De Ecclesia*, 14, pp. 320–1. Wyclif prefers to follow the 'deeper-going doctor of scripture' (possibly himself?) who saw this as the rule of the bramble in the parable of the trees of *Jud.*, 9.8–15: *De veritate sacrae scripturae*, 4, i.67–72.

[47] *De ente in communi*, 1, pp. 13–14; cf. Trompf, *Historical Recurrence*, pp. 167, 192.

[48] *De Ecclesia*, 11, p. 242.

[49] *De civili dominio*, ii.12, p. 153, 'restitutio Ecclesiae ad statum quem Christus docuit'; *De Ecclesia*, 9, p. 189, 'Ecclesia apostolica restituta ad vera privilegia primitiva'; *De potestate papae*, 11, p. 305, 'perfectionem status quem Christus instituit renovandi'.

gradual reconquest of Antichrist';[50] and since the clergy were the superior part of the Church it was appropriate that the process should begin by reform of the clergy.[51] The king should encourage clerical poverty by removing the civil wealth of prelates in particular, by abolishing *regalia* for bishops. But this first stage would leave the bulk of temporals intact: the bishop could still enjoy his episcopal estates and rights of office. He was being reduced to a very Aristotelian concept of poverty, not possessing excess wealth, a moderate sustenance fully sufficient for the ordinary needs of human life.[52] Nor was it a total rejection of the use of bishops and clergy in the work of government. It was a practice which Wyclif increasingly disliked, but the crown had too many clerical allies to abandon them out of hand. What Wyclif, with a long career in royal service himself, really meant was that the monarch should not employ worldly-minded bishops like Wykeham,[53] who accepted *regalia* for all the rewards of civil lordship that went with them, and then bit the hand that fed them by supporting subversive movements like the Good Parliament. It should be relying on spiritually-minded people like himself whose only aim was to serve God and the king. The *regalia*, the castles and towns, of which the

50   M. Aston, ' "Caim's castles": poverty, politics, and disendowment', in B. Dobson, ed., *The Church, Politics, and Patronage in the Fifteenth Century* (Gloucester and New York, 1984), pp. 45–81, reprinted in her *Faith and Fire: Popular and Unpopular Religion, 1350–1600* (London and Rio Grande, Ohio, 1993), pp. 95–131, quotation at p. 131.

51   *De potestate papae*, 12, p. 377, 'Et ex istis primo patet quod rex Angliae primo et principaliter daret operam ad regulandum clerum suum et specialiter episcopos et vivant similius legi Christi; totum enum regnum est unum corpus . . .. Ideo oportet . . . incipere a clero, cum sit pars principalis et stomachus corporis per quem cibi digestio et sanitas sunt ad caetera membra corporis derivanda. Oportet enim regem ab illus incipere secundum leges ordinis naturalis.'

52   *De civili dominio*, iii.7, p. 93; iii.8, p. 109.

53   *De civili dominio*, 11.13, pp. 146f., 'et specialiter praelatos qui secundum Apostolum, *Rom.*, 12.8, praesunt in sollicitudine . . . Unde clerus sollicitans se circa mundum, quod foret in laico licitum, degenerat ut sic a nomine clericali.' The principle that the bishop should act for the good of the king and his kingdom is in *De officio regis*, 6, p. 119, 'Confirmatur ex hoc quod rex fecit quid ex eius auctoritate fecerit legius homo suus: sed episcopi . . . sunt enim tales legii homines regis . . . ad finem ut in exequendo suum officium proficiat regno suo . . . ergo sunt ministri regis', which relates here to *spiritualia*, but see 2, pp. 27–9 for the objection to clergy holding lay offices. Similarly in *De civili dominio*, iii.16, p. 313, trade should be reserved to the laity, and clergy should only engage in it for a modest sustenance, not for private profit.

clergy have proper custody, are those of the kingdom of heaven,[54] and they should be denied earthly ones. But it was enough that the Reformation should begin as a reform.

At one time, for example the twelfth century, such reform might have been enough in itself. But now a return to traditional dualism will not do.[55] The catastrophe of the Age of Antichrist could only be met by an equally cataclysmic[56] upwards shift to complete ecclesiastical disendowment. Bishops must be deprived of the lands, wealth, and powers of their sees: the religious orders must cease to be possessioners. The clergy, Wyclif wrote, were to be dispossessed of both temporal staff and material sword;[57] which can be translated to mean that they should lose not only the *regalia* but the *potestas iurisdictionis* as well. The second stage was to be a real revolution, a returning of the wheel, a great restitution of wealth to the king, who would then redistribute it to the heirs of the original patrons, the lay lords. The living hand of kingship, as Wyclif put it, should counteract the dead hand of mortmain.[58] The king would be acting here as the vicar of God, reverting to his casual absolute omnipotence[59] as an act of necessity, that necessity that knows no law and permits any normally illegal action for the defence of the realm.

---

[54]   *De officio regis*, 4, p. 67, 'Cum igitur quilibet clericus curatus habet commissum ad eius custodiam castrum vel villam regni coelorum, quod est Ecclesia . . .'.

[55]   Thus the Donation of Constantine was made with good intentions and would have remained permissible if, on account of 'human fragility', a Gelasian distinction of powers had operated, *De Ecclesia*, 9, pp. 186–8; and see the use of Hugh of St Victor to argue for dualism in *De potestate papae*, 1, p. 7. The time factor is clear in *De civili dominio*, ii.11, p. 124, 'Olim quidam Romana curia irroravit vineam Domini aqua sapientiae Salvatoris, id est lege evangelica quae est doctrina Christi; sed modo dicitur quod fodiunt sibi cisternas, quae continere aquas non valent, statuendo traditiones humanas . . .'

[56]   *De Ecclesia*, 16, p. 374, 'catheclismum appropriationis'. The idea of a three-stage loss of temporals is in *De civili dominio*, ii.14, pp. 180–1, 'Pro quo notandum quod triplex est renuntiatio bonorum vitae.'

[57]   *De civili dominio*, ii.3, pp. 21–2, 'subtrahendo ab eis baculum temporalium ne furentur sic in simplices christianos. Magna quidem foret elemosina gladium materialiem de manu furiosi eripere . . .'; cf. *De logica*, i.11, i.35, 'Sicut vixerunt apostoli in Ecclesia primitiva, sic etiam tenetur vivere episcopi circa finem mundi.'

[58]   E.g. *De Ecclesia*, 15, pp. 331–2. For mortmain see S. Raban, *Mortmain Legislation and the English Church, 1279–1500* (Cambridge, 1982).

[59]   The references are legion: see for instance *De civili dominio*, ii.2, p. 16; ii.4, p. 28. This would be equivalent to a miracle, as had been the dispossession of the Templars, ii.1, p. 4.

Wyclif, never one to leave a stone unturned, reinforced his argument by pointing out that both English common law and Roman law already recognized the principle that lay patrons had a right to reclaim their patronage.[60] All endowed possessions were held conditionally on good service.[61]

Yet even this drastic remedy must prove in course of time to be insufficient, and would come to be simply a prelude to the third stage of the Reformation. According to the biblical model this must be a return to a Church in which all Christians by right of baptism were priests and kings,[62] and where the laity could function as its own clergy. There would be a lay Church, an *ecclesia saecularis*.[63] Now the laity could activate its basic original ability to hear confessions, to give indulgences, to administer baptism, to dispense with marriage regulations, to consecrate the Eucharist, and to determine controversial points of Scripture.[64] Every saintly man would be his own pope.[65] Understandably Wyclif was

---

[60] The important provisions are in the Statutes of Westminster II (1285) and Carlisle (1307) for monastic property, but should be distinguished from the right of reclamation for failure of feudal service in the Statutes of Marlborough (1267), Gloucester (1278) and Mortmain (1279). For a fuller discussion of Wyclif's use of this legislation see W. Farr, *John Wyclif as a Legal Reformer* (Leiden, 1974), pp. 96–138.

[61] *De civili dominio*, ii.4, p. 26; iii.22, p. 484 (citing FitzRalph).

[62] For the residual spiritual power of the laity, *De civili dominio*, ii.17, p. 240, 'Unde videtur michi quod nunquam ab origine mundi foret plus necessarium quod theologi et ecclesiastici sint vigiles, renunciantes temporalibus in personis propriis, et hortantes saeculares ne propter nimiam affectionem ad temporalia amittant aeterna, quam est tempus instans, cum hodie, quod dolendum est, dicitur quod ecclesia Romana pro civili dominio conturbat contumeliis pauculos oves Christi quos Spiritus sanctus ex fide residente in laycis providebat'; and see the long and involved argument in *De Ecclesia*, 20, pp. 500–10, that *potestas ordinis* pertains in a special sense to all Christians and is not just reserved to the clergy for sacramental duties. Cf. *De potestate papae*, 1, pp. 10–11, 'Potestas ordinis vocatur potestas spiritualis quam habet clericus ad ministrandum Ecclesiae sacramenta ut spiritualiter prosit sibi et laicis, ut est potestas conficiendi, absolvendi et sacramenta ministrandi .... Potestas autem spiritualis communis, quam habet quilibet christianus, in exercendo opera spiritualia misericordiae in se et in aliis . . .'

[63] *De Ecclesia*, 7, p. 156; cf. *De civili dominio*, iii.21, pp. 451, 'ecclesiae laycali'.

[64] *De civili dominio*, ii.8, p. 82; *De Ecclesia*, 23, pp. 576–7; *De potestate papae*, 11, pp. 307–8; 12, pp. 381; *De eucharistia*, 4, pp. 89–99; *De veritate sacrae scripturae*, 6, i.137.

[65] *De potestate papae*, 12, p. 368, 'cum papa dicit principaliter praeeminentiam sanctitatis . . . iuxta hanc viam quilibet debet esse papam, ut debet esse sanctissimus viatorum. Debet enim esse papa et quocunque iam viante sanctior'; also 11, p. 315, 'Sicut enim omnis christianus, et specialiter bonus presbiter, est sacerdos, sic est spiritualiter hostiarius, ceroferarius, lector, exorcista, subdyaconus, dyaconus et sacerdos.'

never too precise about this future ideal state any more than St Paul could give a detailed description of the kingdom of heaven, or Marx spell out the full nature of a truly Communist society; and many of his supporters must have wondered exactly what implications this would have for lay lordship, for the hierarchical arrangement of secular society. But as regards the clergy Wyclif was clear enough: the logic of the wheel of history predicted a return to total apostolic poverty. Tithes might be withheld or granted by the laity according to performance;[66] but all the cleric really needed was his clerical status and the ability to seek alms for bare necessities – all clergy would become mendicants dependent on charity.[67] Even clothing was questionable. He had, he remarked, no real objection to nude clergy, but clerics in a state of nature might catch a cold, and how then could they preach?[68] The distinction of clergy from laity would apparently remain in a functional sense that there had to be a part of the Church which specialized in giving instruction and performing sacramental duties, but that was all. All clergy were equal in terms of *potestas ordinis* as they had been in the apostolic Church: to be a bishop was a matter of office, not order.[69] The third strand of episcopal

[66]   *De civili dominio*, i.40, pp. 310–14; i.42, pp. 335–40, 345, 354–5; *De potestate papae*, 12, p. 351, 'Ex istis videtur sequi quod a quocumque praeposito spirituali notorie deficiente in suo officio licet stipendia mundana subtrahere ut decimas, oblationes et alias elemozinas speciales'; p. 358, 'populus debet decimas et oblationes suas ab ei concorditer et constanter subtrahere et in alios pios usus expendere'.

[67]   *De civili dominio*, ii.3, p. 18, 'relinquitur igitur ex quolibet evidenciis quod tota dotacio ecclesiae sit ex elemosinis dominorum. Quod, ne tradatur in oblicionem cavetur in cartis regni nostri Angliae quomodo rex et alii fundatores in puram et perpetuam elemosinam donarunt talia dominia ecclesiae. Ex quod videtur sequi correllarie quod omnes clerici nedum ad Deum ut omnes homines, sed quoad homines sunt mendici.' The dissolution of monasteries might be inferred from this, but it is more akin to the Cluniac ideal of the whole Church as a great monastery.

[68]   Clothing had not been necessary in the state of nature, but clergy now needed it in the harsher climate occasioned by sin: *De statu innocentiae*, 5, pp. 501–2; 10, p. 523.

[69]   *De potestate papae*, 10, p. 246, 'sic in Europa stat esse perfectos christianos secundum fidem Christi, etsi non recognoscant praeeminentiam pontificis Constantini ... ymo patet ex dictis quomodo corpus Christi militaret securius atque perfectius subducto tali ordine caesareo; nam vivendo omnino exproprietarie sicut ante tempore dotationem quo crevit Ecclesia quando pure regulabatur per legem Christi et regebatur per sacerdotes socios sine praeeminentia humanitus instituta, melius et perfectius vixit quam modo. Nec est ratio quin per idem hodie viaret sic perfctius quem nunc viat, igitur cum hoc sit possibile, patet conclusio'; also 9, p. 199, 'ante dotationem Ecclesiae non fuerunt nomina cleri taliter baptizata et per

power was to be disposed of by effectively abolishing bishops.

There was nothing more important to Wyclif than the need for a proper perspective of the past history of the Church. Like so many reformers, he saw the past as much more than a mere matter of record: indeed, it was a lifeline of hope for the future, because it contained the promise of what was to come and defined the shape of that future as a three-stage process. He believed that the changes of successive moments and periods of earthly time as delineated by history could only be matched up to the eternal present of divine time by completing the circle of human duration until there was an eventual return to the beginning. There was, however, no precise temporal symmetry to this idea of applying the wheel of fortune to the Reformation; no suggestion that the Church would need another 1400 years to climb back once more to pristine condition. Earthly time could always be telescoped for divine purposes. Nevertheless the principle of a Reformation in stages indicated that the Second Coming was not imminent. Hastening on the process was no justification for living in immediate expectation of a new Jerusalem. Eventually there would be another Golden Age, but the initial prospects were for more suffering as the price of greater efficiency in the contest with Antichrist. Indeed, as time went by in England, the prospect of a successful Reformation seemed to become steadily more remote: the torrents of both popular and official piety appeared to have been safely diverted into more Catholic channels during the fifteenth century.[70] For Lollardy the wheel of time must have given the impression of being permanently stuck at the half hour, or even to be running backwards. But the clock was ticking.

Birkbeck College,
University of London

consequens nec dignitatum officia. Idem enim fuit ante dotationem Ecclesiae presbiter, episcopus et sacerdos' (again claiming support from FitzRalph); p. 201, 'sed concludit presbiteros, sacerdotes et episcopos sub nomine apostoli'.

[70] As convincingly shown now by E. Duffy, *The Stripping of the Altars: Traditional Religion in England c.1400–c.1580* (New Haven and London, 1992). It might almost be said that the Counter-Reformation preceded the Reformation.

11

THOMAS ARUNDEL OF YORK: THE APPELLANT ARCHBISHOP

by †MICHAEL WILKS

ISTORY in a very religious or ideologically inspired society is always liable to become a victim of propaganda. A concern for what is right takes precedence over what actually happens, and the justification of events replaces the accurate recording of them: there is what may be termed virtuous reality. In such a climate evidence has not only to be rigorously tested and questioned, but close attention has also to be given to what is not recorded or omitted. At no time in English history is this more true than the years around 1400, when justification of a new government required the condemnation of the reign that had gone before. It is well known that the domestic chronicles of the period are a striking example of Hobbes's dictum that in an intolerant society 'imagination and memory are but one thing'. Despite the long centuries of struggle within virtually all medieval kingdoms for supremacy between laity and clergy, the contest of *regnum* and *sacerdotium*, which reached a climax in England during the fourteenth century,[1] the sources – and therefore modern historians – have concentrated upon an alternative, purely secular interpretation of events. The drama of the later 1390s, which saw the deposition of both Archbishop and King, is treated as if it were all a straightforward contest between absolute and limited kingship, in which a feudal aristocracy sought justice against a tyrannical ruler, and this has served to obscure the overriding significance of the crisis as a matter of ecclesiastical history. It will be suggested here, however, that the archbishop in question, Thomas Arundel, successively Archbishop of

---

[1] For a convenient summary of the earlier half of the century see R. M. Haines, 'Conflict in government: archbishops versus kings, 1279-1348', in J. G. Rowe, ed., *Aspects of Later Medieval Government and Society* (Toronto, 1986), pp. 213-45; and his more detailed studies of Adam Orleton (Cambridge, 1978) and John Stratford (Toronto, 1986). The importance attached by Edward III to his control of the chancellorship is well illustrated by his conflict with Stratford in 1340-1: J. Ferster, *Fictions of Advice: the Literature and Politics of Counsel in Late Medieval England* (Philadelphia, 1996), pp. 72-7. For the contest between clergy and laity for control of the chancellorship see now Anne Hudson, '*Hermofodrita* or *Ambidexter*: Wycliffite views on clerks in secular office', in M. Aston and C. Richmond, eds, *Lollardy and the Gentry in the Later Middle Ages* (Stroud and New York, 1997), pp. 41-51.

York (1388–96) and then of Canterbury (1396–7; 1399–1414), regarded the limitation and eventual disposal of Richard II as an essential step in the removal of obstacles to his campaign to eradicate Lollardy in England. So, too, Lollardy itself was not to be treated as a native reform movement backed by a powerful royalist ideology, but should be represented as a wayward sect, composed mainly of peasants urged on and misled by a small number of extreme academics and secular lords.

This paper will therefore suggest that the reticence of official records and the silences of chronicles have a good deal to tell us about the central phase in the career of a man who must be acknowledged as one of the most eminent of medieval archbishops of York. It not only offers a new perspective on the character and intentions of Thomas Arundel himself, but underlines the importance of the see of York in the national politics of the 1380s and 1390s. We need not doubt that the Archbishop regarded York as a stepping-stone to Canterbury, but the transfer of the archbishopric during the Appellant crisis can now be seen to have led directly to the eventual destruction of Richard II's government. An assessment of Arundel's use of the Appellant movement shows that the reign of Richard II should not be seen as just a phase in the development of the civil wars of the fifteenth century, but as a crucial factor in the history of what Anne Hudson has rightly described as a 'premature Reformation'.[2]

Thomas Arundel was Chancellor no less than four times under Richard II and Henry IV, and this does much to account for the fact that the main English sources reflected the point of view of the victorious Lancastrian party.[3] The continuator of the *Eulogium historiarum*, Adam of Usk, and Favent all had direct Canterbury patronage. Knighton used material supplied by the Appellants. Thomas Walsingham wrote for a house, St Albans, closely connected through the de la Mares with Gloucester, Thomas Arundel's main ally, and himself declared that the Archbishop was a most generous friend to St Albans.[4] Only the Westminster chronicler was ambiguous about opposition to

---

[2] Anne Hudson, *The Premature Reformation* (Oxford, 1988).

[3] For a full discussion see A. Gransden, *Historical Writing in England* (London, 1974–82), 2, pp. 118–93; also L. D. Duls, *Richard II in the Early Chronicles* (The Hague, 1975).

[4] Gransden, *Historical Writing*, 2, pp. 131–8, 155–60; C. Given-Wilson, *Chronicles of the Revolution, 1397–1400* (Manchester, 1993), pp. 4–6, 64; *Eulogium historiarum*, ed. F. S. Haydon, RS (1858–63); *The Chronicle of Adam Usk, 1377–1421*, ed. C. Given-Wilson (Oxford, 1997); T. Favent, '*Historia Mirabilis Parliamenti*', in M. McKisack, ed., *Camden Society* ser. 3, 37 (1926); *Knighton's Chronicle, 1337–1396*, ed. G. H. Martin (Oxford, 1995), pp. xxxii, l–li; T. Walsingham, *Historia Anglicana*, ed. H. T. Riley, RS (1863–4); *Chronicon Anglie*, ed.

the King, and his panegyric about Richard II's piety and love for ecclesiastical liberty is so fulsome as to make one suspect that the author was being sarcastic.[5] As regards the deposition of Richard, the official account as contained in the Rolls of Parliament, of which the Archbishop was in charge and for which he is said to have made 'fastidious selection' of material, was distributed afterwards to the chroniclers as a guideline for their own versions of the event. It may be significant that both sides in the contest accused the other of falsely altering the records,[6] and it gradually becomes apparent that on a number of occasions what the King said according to the Chancellor was the opposite of what the King himself wanted. At the best of times no ruler could be personally responsible for the thousands of official commands, and it has recently been shown how during a time of royal weakness, like a prolonged minority, the royal administration was obliged to issue documents declaring the will of a prince who had never been involved at all.[7] In addition to being the king's official spokesman in charge of issuing royal documents and decrees, the function of the medieval chancellor was also to be what we would term a minister for propaganda. Perhaps the outstanding medieval example is the Staufen literary renaissance inspired for Barbarossa by Rainald of Dassel during the twelfth century, but a more contemporary case would be that of John of Litomysl for Wenceslas in Bohemia. Archbishop Arundel, of course, had the strongest of personal reasons to justify himself and to determine what would best be left obscure as well as his duties of censorship. The evidence for what was virtually a preliminary deposition of Richard II during the Appellant crisis of 1386–8 and the belated completion of the process in 1399 often

E. M. Thompson, *RS* (1874). My thanks to Diana Wood and Anthony Tuck for a reference to V. H. Galbraith, 'Thomas Walsingham and the St Albans Chronicle, 1272–1422', *EHR*, 47 (1932), pp. 12–29.

[5] *The Westminster Chronicle, 1381–1394*, ed. L. C. Hector and B. F. Harvey (Oxford, 1962), p. xlvi; cf. Gransden, *Historical Writing*, pp. 182–7. The main source for the *Westminster Chronicle* was Gloucester's household, and it is not surprising that it is pro-Appellant, anti-Lollard, and unreliable: pp. xxivf., lx–lxiii, 107.

[6] Falsification of records by a corrupt clergy became a regular charge in Reformation polemic: R. Pineas, 'William Tyndale's use of history as a weapon of religious controversy', *HThR*, 40 (1962), pp. 121–41.

[7] See further J. Watts, *Henry VI and the Politics of Kingship* (Cambridge, 1996), pp. 1, 27–8, 36, 106–9, 121, 155; also J. W. McKenna, *Political Propaganda in Later Medieval England* (Brighton, 1988). For the selection of material by the Chancery see *Westminster Chronicle*, p. xlvi.

consists of facts where the only certain thing about them is that they are wrong.

When Richard II abdicated and was deposed for tyranny and incompetent government in September 1399 the official account read out to Parliament, the *Record and Process of the Revolution*, contained a list of thirty-three charges against him.[8] The great majority of these charges concerned Richard's style of kingship, which can be seen to have been of the traditional 'descending' type. For Richard, government was based on the simple proposition that all power came from God, and so initially resided in him as vicar of God.[9]

Royal government was by definition absolute. Both King and opposition were in agreement that Richard acted or should act as the embodiment of the *corpus regni*, but whereas Richard saw himself as the sole personification of the kingdom by a divine birthright – as the Wilton Diptych indicated, he was the descendant of kings with succession back to St Edward the Confessor, and so was the living representative of the patron saint[10] – Parliament complained that he had become an individual distinct from society, seeking only his own profit, treating the *corona regni* as his private property because he alone wore the crown.[11] Richard's frequent demands for freedom of action reflect this. One of the most familiar complaints against him was that his rule became tyrannical because he acted by will,[12] whereas Richard himself believed that he was constitutionally obliged to act by will because the public will of the corporate community could find

---

[8] Conveniently ed. and tr. by C. Given-Wilson, *Chronicles*, pp. 168–84.

[9] R. H. Jones, *The Royal Policy of Richard II: Absolutism in the Later Middle Ages* (Oxford, 1968), pp. 167, 175; E. H. Kantorowicz, *The King's Two Bodies* (Princeton, 1957), pp. 24–41. For the traditional nature of this see in general W. Ullman, *Principles of Government and Politics in the Middle Ages*, 2nd edn (London, 1966), pp. 117–37; R. V. Turner, 'King John's concept of royal authority', *History of Political Thought*, 17 (1996), pp. 157–78. This disposes of the suggestion that Richard derived his idea of royal power via Burley from the *De regimine principum* of Aegidius Romanus: N. Saul, *Richard II* (New Haven, CT, and London, 1997), pp. 249–50, 385–6; 'Richard II and the vocabulary of kingship', *EHR*, 110 (1995), pp. 863–701.

[10] J.-P. Genet, 'La Monarchie anglaise: une image brouillée', in J. Blanchard, ed., *Représentation, pouvoir et royauté à la fin du moyen âge* (Paris, 1995), pp. 93–107. Just as the subject prayed to the saint to intervene with God, so the saint and therefore the king became the channel of either divine grace or displeasure to the subject: to oppose a royal grant to de Vere incurred 'the curse of God, St Edward and the king': *CPR, 1381–5*, p. 542. In the 1390s Richard impaled his arms with those of St Edward.

[11] Charge 1.

[12] Charges 16, 19.

expression only through him. Richard was following the Roman law principle that what pleases the prince has the force of law because the sovereignty of the State, the will of the *populus*, has been transferred to him. Richard's incessant demands for freedom of action were not merely frustration at his prolonged minority, but a permanent feature of his view of kingship as absolute monarchy.[13]

But to his opponents Richard was seeking his own benefit by oppressing his subjects, extorting their wealth, and illegally confiscating their land and possessions. To this end, he had created his own private army in the form of a large bodyguard of Cheshire archers, an army of malefactors who would intimidate his opponents.[14] To avoid established legal procedures, the complaint continued, Richard had resorted more and more to the use of the signet as a personal method of authorizing his commands.[15] To justify this he claimed that he was *legibus solutus*, free of restriction by the ancient customs and laws of the land, in other words, the feudal common law. It was generally agreed that the ancient customs, the good old laws of St Edward, had been put into charter form by Magna Carta, which enshrined the rights of the feudal nobility, particularly against dissipation of the wealth of the kingdom to foreigners and the subordination of English policy to foreign interests (a matter which loomed large with Richard's marriages to foreign princesses).[16] This aspect exemplified Richard's persistent failure to take advice from the right people,[17] justifying this by the claim that he alone made law.[18] He disregarded the traditional right of the nobility and Parliament to be consulted in the making of law, and in every way proved himself false to his coronation oath, by which he had promised to govern with justice and subject to the law of the land. It was a clear breach of the feudal contract which should exist between king and community: and by this act of perjury, it was maintained, the King had in a technical sense denied his own right to be king.[19] Although, as Professor Tuck has indicated, later medieval

---

[13] The point is well made by A. Tuck, *Richard II and the English Nobility* (London, 1973), pp. 91, 105, 116.

[14] Charges 4, 6, 7, 14–15, 21, 26–8.

[15] A. Steel, *Richard II* (Cambridge, 1941), pp. 116–17.

[16] T. Turville-Petre, *England the Nation: Language, Literature and National Identity, 1290–1340* (Oxford, 1996), pp. 5–6, 98–9. For the appeal to Magna Carta see charge 29; cf. charge 12 against Nicholas Brembre in Knighton, *Chronicle*, p. 468.

[17] Charges 1, 10, 15, 29: the 'unworthy persons' include 'interfering foreigners'.

[18] Charges 10–12, 16–17, 30, 33.

[19] Charges 3, 9, 11, 22–3, 27, 30; Knighton, *Chronicle*, p. 410. See also A. Boureau, 'The

kings (with the notable exception of Henry VI) tended to be deposed
not because they were weak and incompetent but because they were
too strong, the tradition persisted that they also had to be effeminate
and unstable – and the childless Richard was an obvious target for
rumours of this kind.[20] Richard had an unusually long minority, until
he declared himself of age in 1389, and was long susceptible to the
charge of being a tyrant by definition, according to the slogan, 'Woe to
the land whose king is a child', a person incapable of governing
himself, let alone everybody else.[21] Richard understandably took the
view that as God, not the nobility, had appointed him, therefore only
God could depose him – by death. He became increasingly anxious to
have the deposition of Edward II recognized as an illegal act, to aid
which he pursued a vigorous campaign to have his great-grandfather
canonized: an ever-living saint would be truly an ever-ruling king.[22]
The nobility's response would be that they represented the *communitas
regni*, and were therefore empowered to deal with a ruler who was
persona communitatis. But this did not really quite address Richard's
point that the making and breaking of monarchs needed to be
governed by consistent principles.

Superficially the crisis of 1399 was another classic confrontation
between two antipathetic conceptions of kingship of a type to be found
at any time in the previous three centuries. The case put forward, first
by the Appellants and then by the Lancastrians, is a clear expression of
what is called feudal kingship, comparable to something like the *Song
of Lewes* in the previous century.[23] It could be explained solely in terms

---

development of ideas of royal contract in the late thirteenth and early fourteenth centuries',
in Blanchard, *Représentation*, pp. 165–75. A concern for *iustitia* as the essence of the feudal
contract is emphasized by M. Lessnoff, *Social Contract* (London, 1986).

[20] A. Tuck, *Crown and Nobility, 1272–1461* (Totowa, NJ, 1985); R. W. Bushnell, *Tragedies
of Tyrants: Political Thought and Theater in the English Renaissance* (New York, 1991).

[21] Eccles. 10.16; cf. Is. 1.2–4, 3.4–5; Ps. 92.1–3; Gal. 4.1–2; also Dio Cassius, *Roman History*,
LII, xiv, 2. It was applied to Richard II by Adam Usk, *Chronicle*, p. 6 and Walsingham,
Historia Anglicana, 2, p. 97, but the theme has a vast literary background, and was used not
only by popes (Gregory VII, Innocent III) and papalists (Augustine, Hincmar, John of
Salisbury, Aegidius Romanus), but was in general later medieval usage: Dante, Wyclif,
Chaucer, Gower. It relates to the still larger practice of condemning one's opponents as *pueri*.

[22] C. Given-Wilson, 'Richard II, Edward II and the Lancastrian inheritance', *EHR*, 109
(1994), pp. 553–71.

[23] *Song of Lewes*, in T. Wright, ed., *Political Songs of England, Camden Society* (1839), 2nd
edn by P. R. Coss (Cambridge, 1996), pp. xxii–xxiii, 72–121. The use of the term 'feudal' in
this context needs careful definition. The feudal system was used by every king as a means
of making his supremacy effective, using his subjects, especially the aristocracy in the first
instance, in the administration of the kingdom and the prosecution of war. Its basic

of the conflict between the King and that group of magnates who had already been responsible for the crisis of the Appellants in 1386–8. As most historians have concluded, the fall of Richard II was pre-eminently a secular affair, a dynastic contest between two cousins, rather than a landmark in ecclesiastical history. Yet it is interesting, and perhaps significant, that the charge about Richard's use of the signet to avoid the normal legal channels regulated by the chancellor appears in the context of a rather vague accusation that he had diminished ecclesiastical liberty. That there was another, ecclesiastical, dimension to the affair is indicated by half a dozen claims that Richard had not only infringed ecclesiastical liberties, but had also misled and confused the pope. But the only example of these distinctly enigmatic charges was Richard's illegal banishing of the Archbishop of Canterbury, Thomas Arundel, without trial, because the King 'planned by all possible means to ruin and bring down the archbishop'. Thomas Arundel was deprived of justice whilst his sentence of exile left his see without a valid replacement.[24] Since Arundel is recognized to have been a leading member of the Appellants, this hardly seems to affect the established picture of a king brought down by a group of magnates acting initially through Parliament and subsequently by the successful Lancastrian invasion of 1399.

The deposition of Richard II was as much a matter of ecclesiastical politics as a dynastic struggle for the crown between two cousins: hence the prominent part played by Thomas Arundel. To understand this, however, it is necessary to look back to the political situation obtaining some fifteen years earlier. By 1384 four fairly clear centres of power had evolved in England. Amongst these groups or factions the single most important figure was Richard's uncle, John of Gaunt, Duke of Lancaster, who had become virtually the uncrowned king of England by the later 1370s. The change from the senility of Edward III to the minority of Richard II made little apparent change in Gaunt's dominant position in the royal government. His influence at court seemed to have been strengthened by the defeat of the 1381 revolt and the failure of the ill-fated Flanders crusade. After his struggle with the Good Parliament, Gaunt was perhaps more careful to

principles, aristocratic rather than monarchic, did not pose an insuperable difficulty for a strong ruler. But during a period of personal weakness, such as a minority, the true anti-monarchic tendencies of feudalism could limit and restrict the powers of the king, changing the nature of the kingship itself.
[24] Charges 22, 25, 29–30, 33.

placate his parliamentary opponents. But as his nephew's guardian, Gaunt could rely on his enormous wealth and grasp of royal administration to maintain a Lancastrian kingship.[25]

This predominance contrasts all the more sharply with the position of his two younger brothers. Edmund of Langley, Duke of York, has been described as a political lightweight who went along with whoever happened to be in control at court,[26] and can be largely ignored for present purposes. But Thomas of Woodstock, Earl of Gloucester, was a very different character. Unjustly deprived, as he saw it, of both lands and income, Gloucester harboured various grudges against the King and his ministers. His remedy was to look for support and political power amongst the opponents of royal supremacy in Parliament. This made him a natural ally for his relative Richard, Earl of Arundel, another very wealthy magnate, who shared with Gloucester an enthusiasm for military prowess as well as parliamentary leadership, combined with a general sense of grievance against the royal administration. There was a substantial body of opinion amongst Members of Parliament, an institution which had been becoming increasingly restive since the later years of Edward III's reign, and which had come to regard itself as the natural counsellor of the kingdom, to which the king and his ministers should automatically turn for consultation and advice, especially where finance was involved.[27] The Gloucester–Arundel coalition was quickly adopted as its spokesman against the royal ministers, who were denounced in traditional fashion as favourites, that is, officers with no more authority than the King's personal preference, but described by Richard by the still more traditional soubriquet of the King's Friends.[28]

Under a barrage of hostile propaganda from the chroniclers,

---

[25] For Gaunt see now A. Goodman, *John of Gaunt* (London, 1992); S. Walker, *The Lancastrian Affinity, 1361–1399* (Oxford, 1990). As Margaret Aston has shown, the Flanders crusade was itself an oblique undermining of Gaunt's influence.

[26] Saul, *Richard II*, p. 163.

[27] Note the perceptive remarks of D. Aers and L. Staley, *The Powers of the Holy: Religion, Politics and Gender in Late Medieval English Culture* (University Park, PA, 1996), pp. 183–92.

[28] E.g. *Westminster Chronicle*, p. 440: 'Ad hec rex aliquantulum substit, dicens ... scio quid faciam amicis meis existentibus iam in partibus transmarinis.' The principle of *amicitia principis*, applied to the political grouping or faction amongst the aristocracy which supported and advised the ruler, had a very extensive pre-Christian history, and was commonplace during the Middle Ages, but then appeared more frequently in the guise of the true Christian as *amicus Christi*, a term popular with the Wycliffites. The expression retained its currency throughout the eighteenth century for members of the Whig aristocracy and the American Loyalists.

Richard's Friends have never enjoyed the kind of reputation that they deserved. As always, the royal court, with its massive powers of patronage, was the centre of political life, and this created a semi-permanent monarchist party to be distinguished from the particular faction which had taken charge of the administration at any one time. The royalists were very much a composite grouping, a mixture of officials and *curiales* for whom royal service was the pathway to advancement. Many of them, like Chaucer, were of commercial or gentry family origins, which earned them the disdain of the nobility. At the centre was the household, the *famille du roi*, the Chamber knights and servants. Then there were the members and staff of royal councils: to these were added anyone who was required to be at court, as opposed to those who attended by right of residence. There is no need to produce a catalogue here. A convenient short list is available from the victims of the Appellants' executions and expulsions.[29] Suffice to point, amongst the favoured families like the Hollands and Mowbrays, to three men, who between them largely controlled the government of the young Richard and were to be destroyed by the purges of 1386/7. Simon Burley, one of the many officials whom Richard inherited from the household of the Black Prince and Joan of Kent as a going concern, was a very experienced warrior, and one who inspired a degree of affection in the young King greater than that which he felt for most of his family. Aided by his relative Baldwin Raddington, Controller of the Wardrobe, Burley was the guiding spirit of the household, of which he was officially Sub-Chamberlain, and took a major share in arranging the King's Bohemian marriage.[30] Robert de Vere, son of another Black Prince service family (his father Aubrey, Earl of Oxford, was hereditary Chamberlain), was created Marquis of Dublin and Duke of Ireland in 1386.[31] He was foremost in raising a royal army against the forces of the Appellants, only to have it soundly defeated by Gloucester and Derby at Radcot Bridge. Michael de la Pole, Earl of Suffolk, was Chancellor from March 1383 to

---

[29] *Westminster Chronicle*, pp. 228–30, 30–2; cf. Jones, *Royal Policy*, pp. 12f., 130–7; J. S. Roskell, *The Impeachment of Michael de la Pole, Earl of Suffolk in 1386* (Manchester, 1984), pp. 32–4.

[30] Steel, *Richard II*, pp. 103ff., 141.

[31] R. Halliday, 'Robert de Vere, Ninth Earl of Oxford', *Medieval History*, 3 (1993), pp. 71–85; Roskell, *Impeachment*, pp. 21–2, 26. According to Froissart 'by him everything was done and without him nothing': cited by R. Mott, 'Richard II and the crisis of July, 1397', in I. Wood and G. A. Loud, eds, *Church and Chronicle in the Middle Ages: Essays presented to John Taylor* (London and Rio Grande, TX, 1991), pp. 165–77, at p. 166.

October 1386. Impeached and sentenced to imprisonment, he eventually died in 1389. Pole's attitude towards rivals amongst the nobility and hostility from the bishops were combined in his impeachment of the Bishop of Norwich, Henry Despenser, after the Flanders crusade.[32]

The royalists were strongly anticlerical, part of the wave of anticlerical sentiment which swept through the European courts in the later Middle Ages.[33] As one anonymous writer put it, the forthcoming time of trouble would be a straight fight between the knights and the evil clergy.[34] This was not necessarily Wycliffite. Wyclif's 'heresies' of antipapalism and calls for a return to a national proprietary church system had an obvious appeal, and it was no accident that of the dozen Lollard knights identified by Waugh and McFarlane, eight or nine were or had been household officials.[35] But whereas Wyclif himself eventually came to consider bishops unnecessary and superfluous, the general royalist view was that bishops and clergy were a desirable, indeed essential, part of the royal administration to superintend the 'goostly health' of the nation, provided that they did not therefore indulge in hierocratic assumptions of innate superiority. Bishops were expected to be obedient, loyal, and useful. As Richard II remarked to Aymard Broutin in 1398, 'I am certain that my clergy and my country will do what I want.'[36] In return, they were entitled to a full share in the magnificence and spectacular hospitality of the court.[37] Thus it is not surprising that one of the leading royalists, to be numbered with the triumvirate above, was Alexander Neville, a prime target for the

[32] See further Roskell, *Impeachment*; Jones, *Royal P 'icy*, pp. 130–6, 143–6, 155ff.; A. Tuck, *Richard II and the English Nobility* (London, 1973), pp. 35ff., 58ff., 127–31; M. Aston, 'The Impeachment of Bishop Despenser', *BIHR*, 38 (1965), pp. 127–48.

[33] P. A. Dykema and H. A. Oberman, eds, *Anticlericalism in Late Medieval and Early Modern Europe* (Leiden, 1992); W. Scase, *'Piers Plowman' and the New Anticlericalism* (Cambridge, 1989).

[34] 'O men þat ben on Cristus half, helpe ȝe now aȝenus anticrist; for þe perelows tyme is comen þa Crist and Powle teldon byfore. But o counfort is of knyȝtus, þat þei saueron myche þe gospel, and han wylle to redon in Englisch þe gospel of Cristus lyȝf. For afturward, ȝif God wole, þis lordschipe schal be take fro preestis, and so þe staf þat makeþ hem hardye aȝenyz Crist and his lawe', *English Wycliffite Sermons*, ed. A. Hudson and P. Gradon (Oxford, 1983–96), pp. 2, 64.

[35] W. T. Waugh, 'The Lollard Knights', *ScHR*, 11 (1913–14), pp. 55–92; K. B. McFarlane, *Lancastrian Kings and Lollard Knights* (Oxford, 1972), pp. 137–226.

[36] N. Valois, *La France et le grand schisme d'Occident* (Paris, 1901), p. 620. For the use of clergy as a civil service see in general C. Given-Wilson, *The Royal Household and the King's Affinity* (New Haven, CT, and London, 1986).

[37] G. Mathew, *The Court of Richard II* (London, 1968); J. Blair and N. Ramsey, eds, *English Medieval Industries* (London, 1991), p. 160.

Appellants. Neville had been appointed Archbishop of York in 1375 as a committed papalist, but after a decade of obsessive litigation was pre-eminent amongst the King's Friends. Partly this was due to the monarchy's tactic (quite apart from the utility of the extensive patronage available in the province of York), going back to the twelfth century, of looking for support from York against a hostile or potentially hostile Canterbury. Neville, for his part, needed royal support against his growing numbers of enemies in the see of Durham and the York chapter and collegiate churches. The troubles of 1381 made him well aware of the enmity of his tenants,[38] at the same time that his ambitions for political power brought him into alliance with the Chancellor, Michael de la Pole. His brother Sir William was for ten years a Chamber knight. He was firmly supported by the Dominican Thomas Rushook, whose service as royal confessor was rewarded with the see first of Llandaff, in 1382, and then of Chichester, in 1386.[39] Other royalist bishops included Robert Bray-brooke, Richard's secretary, a close friend of the Black Prince and Joan of Kent, who became Treasurer and Bishop of London in 1381.[40] Walter Skirlaw, an expert canonist, Bishop of Lichfield and subse-quently Durham, who was Keeper of the Privy Seal from 1382 to 1386, and John Fordham, the Black Prince's secretary, who was given Durham. All three faltered at the height of the contest between Richard and the aristocracy: Braybrooke was too useful an adminis-trator to be lost; Skirlaw apparently fell out over a dispute about the see of Wells and joined the Appellants in 1397; Fordham was demoted to Ely, but his predecessor, Thomas Arundel, later charged him with treason in 1390.

At the other end of the political spectrum were the papalists, deeply conscious of their position as successors of the Apostles, who adhered

[38] R. G. Davies, 'Alexander Neville, Archbishop of York, 1374–1388', *YAJ*, 47 (1975), pp. 87–101; R. B. Dobson, 'The authority of the bishop in late medieval England: the case of Archbishop Alexander Neville of York, 1373–88', *Church and Society in the Medieval North of England* (London and Rio Grande, TX, 1996), pp. 185–94.

[39] C. F. R. Palmer, 'The King's confessors', *The Antiquary*, 22 (1890), pp. 265–6; and for his earlier history as Friar-Provincial, idem, *Archaeological Journal*, 35 (1878), pp. 153–4; *EHR*, 33 (1918), p. 497. After impeachment in 1388 he was banished to Kilmore and died in Ireland in 1393.

[40] Braybrooke, who took a leading part in the arrangements for the Bohemian marriage, seems to have been a covert Wycliffite sympathizer (his brother was one of the Lollard knights). He was reinstated under Henry IV and often participated in Lollard trials, yet it was to Braybrooke that the Bohemians copying Wyclif's works went in 1407.

to hierocratic principles. Their acceptance of papal supremacy might be as much a stick with which to beat their lay opponents as belief in the pope (especially one upheld by Parliament during the Schism), but they stood for the ancient doctrine of the superiority of the bishops over kings and saw the bishops as *eminences grises* behind the throne, controlling the direction of royal policy.[41] The leaders of this group were anxious to fill the chief offices in the royal administration. The effective leader of the papalists during the 1370s, William of Wykeham, had retired to Winchester after his bruising experiences with John of Gaunt and the supporters of the monarchy, and his place had been taken by William Courtenay, the very conservative Bishop of London, who succeeded the murdered Sudbury as Archbishop of Canterbury after the Peasants' Revolt, and immediately established a reputation for his attempts to deal with Wyclif and to root out Lollardy from its Oxford headquarters.[42] In between were the other bishops, an amorphous majority, who oscillated uneasily between the two extremes, more interested in their sees and their careers than abstract principles of government, but liable to side with Courtenay as their archbishop when it came to the crunch. It was not easy for them to present a united front: what to do about Wyclif and early Lollardy was a case in point. Their clear dislike of a movement which stood for unauthorized preaching and the confiscation of ecclesiastical wealth and property, let alone a dubious position on the Eucharist and other theological issues, had to be balanced by the discretion necessary in condemning a movement whose chief offence and claim for protection rested on the upholding of royal supremacy over the clergy. The history of the individual bishops during the 1380s has already been studied in detail,[43] but Dr Davies's analysis needs to be corrected in certain respects. He is wedded to two erroneous assumptions. The first

[41] As the Westminster chronicler wrote of Courtenay, *Chronicle*, p. 138: 'numquam, pro veritatis prolacione, salve semper tramite recte justicie capud eo modo alicui inclinaret aut genu, cum pocius juxta canonicas sancciones regum colla et principum genibus pontificium inclinari debeant et submitti.'

[42] For Courtenay's 'unswerving loyalty' to the papacy see J. H. Dahmus, *William Courtenay, Archbishop of Canterbury, 1381–96* (University Park, PA and London, 1966), p. 192, cf. pp. 13–14, 44–5 – although Dahmus, pp. 21–2, dislikes the idea of there being hierocratic and anti-hierocratic parties amongst the bishops.

[43] R. G. Davies, 'The episcopate and the political crisis in England of 1385–1388', *Speculum*, 51 (1976), pp. 659–93. For the difficulty of assigning bishops to episcopal groups see J. R. L. Highfield, 'The English hierarchy in the reign of Edward III', *TRHS*, ser. 5, 6 (1956), pp. 115–38.

is an acceptance of the distinction between Church and State, which not only obliterates the prevailing notion of England as an ecclesiastical polity in which both clergy and laity were respectively the ordained and unordained members of the same society, but dilutes the political character of all the bishops. More seriously, it leads to an emphasis on the unwillingness of most bishops to become involved in secular issues, or as upholders of 'responsible government' to be a force for mediation when they did.[44] In practice, however, the remainder of the bishops sided with the papalists, reluctantly or otherwise, when they had to take sides, and their determination to let Parliament and the aristocracy deal with the royalist ministers during the Merciless Parliament and Richard himself in 1399 was occasioned more by the canon law prohibitions on the shedding of blood by clergy than, as Davies, argues, a reluctance to show that they were committed to the Appellant cause.[45]

With hindsight it can be seen that 1384 was a crucial year in determining the direction of politics for the rest of the reign. Two things substantially altered the standing of the various groups. First of all, John of Gaunt and the Lancastrians were effectively edged out of their commanding position in court politics. Gaunt, who already suffered from a quite extraordinary degree of unpopularity, especially in London, and deprived of support from the King's mother by the death of Joan of Kent, was spending more and more time in the north, trying to deal with the Scots. On one side, the young Richard and the King's Friends were chafing at the influence wielded by the King's uncle; on the other, the papalists were never going to forgive him entirely for his protection of Wyclif (who died at the end of the year) and Gaunt's harassment of Archbishop Courtenay. Gaunt began to suffer a succession of plots and conspiracies, apparently fairly trivial in themselves, but magnified by the hothouse conditions of court intrigue. The Norwich crusade of 1383 had been, at least in part, a move to thwart Gaunt's desire to mount a crusade against Spain. A year later there was the mysterious affair of the mad Carmelite friar, who allegedly confessed under torture to seeking to kill the King for Gaunt's benefit. While absent in Scotland during 1385, Gaunt was informed that he was out of royal favour, and it was only when he came south that a reconciliation was patched up with Richard. By this

[44] Davies, 'Episcopate', esp. pp. 659–60, 691–3.
[45] Ibid., p. 691.

time Gaunt, understandably, began to be far more interested in a Castilian crown, and eventually departed in 1386 to enforce his wife's claim. He did not return until after the Appellancy had petered out.

The direct responsibility for the series of intrigues against Gaunt is difficult to determine. It is usually taken as an indication of the burgeoning of power by the young Richard and the courtiers of the household. But other explanations are possible, and it is perhaps significant that the Carmelites were involved. The Carmelites had virtually taken over from the Benedictines in leading the anti-heresy campaign against Wyclif and early Lollardy; Gaunt seems to have succumbed to pressure from them. The key figure here was probably Walter Diss, who had become Gaunt's confessor and was Gaunt's main agent in preaching and organizing the crusade. He had been prominent in the condemnation of Wycliffite errors in 1382, and would certainly have regarded the weakening of the connection between Gaunt and the Wycliffites and the removal of Gaunt himself from the equation as prime objectives in defence of the Faith.[46]

The second major factor was the gradual eclipse of Courtenay as effective leader of the papalists and his replacement by Thomas Arundel. Although still comparatively young, Courtenay seems to have worn himself out with his campaign against the Oxford Wycliffites. There is some indication that he was ill.[47] It is well known that Perroy gives a misleading picture of harmony in Courtenay's dealings with the Crown.[48] There was a continuing contest over control of episcopal appointments, and whilst, as Dahmus has argued,[49] Courtenay was more successful than he appeared to be, by wearing down the royalist position, he fell far short of outright victory. Nevertheless, relations between King and Archbishop became so bad

---

[46] Gaunt's increasing attachment to the Carmelites is discussed by Goodman, *Gaunt*, pp. 241–7. That Gaunt 'repented' his previous attitude and came to terms with the papalists seems clear enough, but the question of dating remains. Walsingham's suggested 1381 (*Chronicon Angliae*, pp. 151, 328) must be too early, whilst 1389 (*Historia Anglicana*, 2, p. 194) is too late. Courtenay is alleged (*Westminster Chronicle*, p. 117) to have saved Gaunt from a royal plot to murder him in 1385. In the following century the reconciliation between Gaunt and the bishops was commemorated in the St Cuthbert window of York Minster.

[47] For Courtenay after 1384 see J. H. Dahmus, 'Richard II and the Church', *CathHR*, 39 (1953–4), pp. 408–33. Courtenay became much more active again in hunting Wycliffites in 1389: Knighton, *Chronicle*, pp. 530–4.

[48] As argued by J. J. N. Palmer, 'England and the Great Western Schism, 1388–1399', *EHR*, 83 (1968), pp. 516–22; R. G. Davies, 'Richard II and the Church in the years of "tyranny"', *JMedH*, 1 (1975), pp. 329–62, at pp. 329–30, 335.

[49] Dahmus, 'Richard II and the Church', p. 432.

that Richard apparently tried to kill his archbishop, and it was the autumn of 1385 before Braybrooke managed to engineer a reconciliation. But Courtenay had to kneel and acknowledge royal supremacy.[50] He needed to withdraw from active politics and lie low, at least for the immediate future. His mantle passed to Thomas Arundel, Bishop of Ely.

Thomas Arundel admirably filled the bill. To begin with, there was his family connection: as brother to the earl – and both younger and cleverer[51] – he had immediate access to one of the leaders of the parliamentary opposition to Richard II and partner in the coalition with Gloucester. But on his own merits he had already proved himself by his administration of Ely, a diocese which had suffered severely both from the depredations of the expelled bishop, Thomas de Lisle,[52] and then by the Peasants' Revolt. It has been said that at Ely he was a true bishop and a great lord, who upheld the good of the see with 'dutifully conscientious efficiency'.[53] This not only gave him valuable experience in administration, but also enabled him to create a highly influential circle of ecclesiastical patronage, a tightly knit, carefully organized group of followers, comparable to the network of spirituality and political pressure which Wyclif had commanded at Oxford.[54] At Cambridge the Bishop of Ely was already a dominant figure in the

[50] *Westminster Chronicle*, pp. 116, 139; other accounts listed by Dahmus, 'Richard II and the Church', p. 416, n. 2.

[51] A. Goodman, *The Loyal Conspiracy: the Lords Appellant under Richard II* (London, 1971), p. 9. For a royalist view, Sir John Bussey, 'a most cunning and cruel nature': *Adam Usk, Chronicle*, pp. 155–6. Although Thomas Arundel had already acquired some prominence by his support for Despenser in the Flanders crusade, Davies would see him as a man of limited political experience who came to the fore through his brother's support: 'Episcopate', pp. 663, 682.

[52] J. Aberth, *Criminal Churchmen in the Age of Edward III: the Case of Bishop Thomas de Lisle* (University Park, PA, 1996). It should be borne in mind, however, that de Lisle was a committed papalist who retired to Avignon in 1361, when he fell foul of the King. A recent description of him as 'the Al Capone of Ely' might with justice also be applied to Thomas Arundel.

[53] M. Aston, *Thomas Arundel: a Study of Church Life in the Reign of Richard II* (Oxford, 1967). There is also a good general account of Arundel in P. McNiven, *Heresy and Politics in the Reign of Henry IV* (Woodbridge and Wolfeboro, NH, 1987), pp. 63–78.

[54] J. Hughes, *Pastors and Visionaries: Religion and Secular Life in Late Medieval Yorkshire* (Woodbridge, 1988), pp. 246–7; as with the papacy, spiritual vision and political involvement may well go together. 'Arundel and his clergy extended this principle of strong church government and applied it to the inner lives of parishioners as they set about influencing and monitoring what people thought and felt.' I cannot share Margaret Aston's impression that he was not much concerned with heresy before the 1390s: *Thomas Arundel*, pp. 328–35.

University, a school which specialized in the study of canon law. He was also well placed here to forge links with the Carmelites in the pursuit of Lollard heresy. Beyond this it has been noted that he was most assiduous in attending Parliament and Convocation.[55] Indeed, it might be said of him, as was said of Calvin, that no man loved meetings more. This may be testimony to his dutiful acceptance of the burdens of responsibility, but it is also an indication of Thomas Arundel's ambition and desire to control the direction of events.

What transformed the situation, it was rather belatedly realized, was the revival of the Anglo-Imperial alliance, confirmed by the marriage of Richard II to Princess Anne of Bohemia. The marriage was first proposed by the Emperor Charles IV in 1378 and taken up on behalf of Urban VI in the year following the Great Schism by Pileo di Prata, Cardinal Archbishop and papal legate in England, and organized on the English side by Burley, supported by Gaunt and Robert Braybrooke, Chancellor and Keeper of the Signet, but soon to be Bishop of London. A treaty was agreed by March 1381, and Anne came to London later that year, and was married and crowned in January 1382.[56]

Some historians have questioned the extent of Anne's political influence and her sympathies for native reform movements, both Czech and English, but it is more likely that these have been underestimated. Both Wenceslas and Anne used and approved the use of vernacular translations of the Bible by the laity, at least by people such as themselves.[57] Not only did Richard become extremely fond of his new young wife, but Anne was a prominent member of the imperial family: she was a daughter of Charles IV and sister to his successor, Wenceslas. Richard could hardly have remained aloof from the crisis developing in Bohemia. Wenceslas's struggle with his

[55] R. G. Davies, 'Thomas Arundel as Archbishop of Canterbury, 1396–1414', *JEH*, 14 (1973), pp. 8–22, at p. 11.

[56] I am most grateful to Professor Katherine Walsh for an advance copy of her excellent study 'Lollardisch-Hussitische Reformbestrebungen im Umkreis und Gefolgschaft der Luxemburgerin Anna, Königin von England (1382–1394)', now published in J. Pánek, M. Polívka, N. Reichrtova, eds, *Häresie und vorzeitige Reformation im Spätmittelalter: Herausgegeben von František Šmahel* (Munich, 1998), pp. 77–108. See pp. 81–3, 107 for a list of Bohemian knights in England. This suggests that Anne had greater political influence in English affairs than is allowed for by Saul, *Richard II*, pp. 83–95, 455–7. It is likely that the Virgin Mary on the Wilton Diptych is a portrait of Anne; the way the child Jesus is held shows Bohemian influence.

[57] M. Deanesly, *The Lollard Bible and other Medieval Biblical Versions* (Cambridge, 1920), pp. 79–95.

hierocratic clergy had become a virtual civil war by 1387, and six years later Wenceslas attempted to control his clergy by deposing the Archbishop of Prague, John of Jenstein.[58] Wenceslas became a role model for Richard II, and just as Wenceslas sought help from the Bohemian reform movement (and Gaunt had used Wyclif and his followers during the 1370s), so Richard sought to liberate himself from the stranglehold of episcopal domination. That it was a cynical desire to gain power rather than a genuine desire for reform, which was to be demonstrated in Bohemia by Wenceslas's treatment of Hus, may well be true, but does not affect the argument.

Moreover, the Bohemian connection brought substantial numbers of Bohemians to the English court, where they were treated by Richard with the excessive generosity he reserved for his supporters. Quite apart from the large subvention given to Wenceslas, and the hospitality available to Bohemians at the royal court, there was also an official policy of finding brides, property, and other offices for members of the Bohemian nobility. In the absence of further research it is impossible to quantify the numbers involved. An advance party to negotiate the marriage was followed by a very much larger contingent to form Queen Anne's household. Nor is it known how many were left after the Appellants' attempts to expel them. But it is clear that they continued to come, and that many of them had a 'reformist' bent, and just as the arrival of Bohemian artists and craftsmen made a significant contribution to the magnificence of Richard's court,[59] so the establishment of a Bohemian base in England opened the way for Wycliffite principles to become the inspiration of the Hussite revolution. But the immediate effect was that the royal court became an explosive mixture of anticlerical royalists, Wycliffites, and Bohemian opponents of hierocratic bishops, all wedded to the enhancement of royal power. It was enough for Walsingham to condemn the Bohemians by the single sweeping assertion that they were all heretics.[60] In a sense the Bohemian marriage created the crisis of the Appellancy.

The Roman papacy was slow to appreciate the dangers of a situation

---

[58] R. E. Weltsch, *Archbishop John of Jenstein, 1348–1400: Papalism, Humanism and Reform in Pre-Hussite Prague* (The Hague and Paris, 1968). The deposition of Richard II in 1399 was matched by the rejection of Wenceslas as *rex Romanorum* in 1400: in both cases Boniface IX was involved.

[59] A. Simpson, *The Connection between English and Bohemian Paintings in the Second Half of the Fourteenth Century* (London, 1978 and New York, 1984).

[60] Walsingham, *Historia Anglicana*, 2, p. 119.

which it had largely itself created. The Anglo-Bohemian alliance was regarded as far too useful as a counterbalance to the alignment of France with the Avignon papacy. But to the English bishops it was a very different matter. The need to reclaim control of the government had become urgent. In March 1385 Courtenay accused Richard of aspiring to tyranny.[61] It would be difficult to substantiate a charge of either harsh or incompetent government, the usual grounds of tyranny, against the under-age Richard (although no doubt Courtenay had excellent personal reasons for doing so), but it was much easier if by tyranny was meant heresy, unquestionably a matter for bishops. The principle that rule by heretics was a form of tyranny went back at least as far as Bede,[62] and had been revived and popularized, ironically, by Wyclif, against a corrupt and deluded pope and clergy as well as unjust kings.[63] Whilst Richard personally could hardly be accused of theological error, and was indeed already showing signs of the excessive degree of piety which characterized his later life, the royal administration was a huge target. Walsingham, who indulged in 'almost hysterical abuse' of Lollardy, insisted that the aim of the Lollard knights in the court was to destroy the papacy itself.[64] The danger was not so much the emergence of a Lollard king, but that there was already a king of Lollards, an anticlerical monarchy.

Ad abolendam of 1184 had already made it clear that support for heretics made one guilty of the same offence and ought to deprive a lay official of his office.[65] The solution was the typical papal tactic of employing a dissident nobility to support a true clergy, as had been demonstrated so successfully by Gregory VII against Henry IV in

[61] Goodman, *Loyal Conspiracy*, p. 12, referring to *Westminster Chronicle*, p. 119.

[62] Bede justified the Anglo-Saxon conquest on the grounds that the British were heretics and therefore tyrants, not worthy of anything but to be enslaved: N. J. Higham, *An English Empire: Bede and the Early Anglo-Saxon Kings* (Manchester, 1975), pp. 16–18, 31.

[63] E.g., J. Loserth, ed., *De Ecclesia* (London, 1886), 12, p. 263. Law made by an unjust prince is not to be observed because 'patet quod hoc est contra fidem catholicam . . . et tunc foret indubie lex iniusta et nunquam permittendo'; 15, pp. 340–2, the king can determine what is heretical and therefore can deprive priests who abuse their power 'tamquam ab haereticis Dominus auferatur', because according to Hos. 5. 6, 'God withdraws himself from both priests and kings who spurn the *patrimonium Christi*.

[64] Gransden, *Historical Writing*, 2, p. 131.

[65] *PL* 201, cols 1297–1300; *Decretales*, 5.7.9. The situation, which of course became common enough after the Reformation, had to be faced openly with George I Podebrady of Bohemia in the mid-fifteenth century: F. G. Heymann, *George of Bohemia, King of Heretics* (Princeton, NJ, 1965); O. Odložilík, *The Hussite King (George of Podiebradi) in European Affairs* (New Brunswick, NJ, 1965).

Germany. There were several English precedents: Innocent III's use of Archbishop Langton and the barons against King John; Winchelsea leading a demand for the charters against Edward I; and Reynolds using the lords to get rid of Edward II.[66] Courtenay was in no position to forge such an alliance himself, but Thomas Arundel came forward as the obvious alternative: his access to the Arundel–Gloucester coalition was considerably aided by Gloucester's antipathy to the Bohemians. Embittered by being left relatively poorly off in the share-out of royal estates and offices, Gloucester suffered further by what seemed a deliberate policy to benefit the Bohemians at his expense. Between 1382 and 1384 various properties promised to Gloucester were given to Queen Anne, including Woodstock itself. Gloucester's daughter, married to Robert de Vere, had her marriage cancelled to allow de Vere to marry a Bohemian bride.[67] Whilst Gloucester would now give the appearance of being the leader of the opposition to Richard II, he was doing so as the traditional *brachium* or arm of the Church, acting under ecclesiastical authority. In modern parlance Gloucester and his colleagues supplied the muscle, but the brains of the business was Thomas Arundel.

The diplomatic history of the papacy would suggest that there was nothing very surprising about a pope giving tacit support to one side in a civil dispute well before openly and formally endorsing it, and this was what happened with the crisis of the Appellancy. It is even less surprising that a pope should support a group of hierocratic bishops pursuing a well-tried policy. But it has to be recognized that it represents a distinct change of policy for Urban VI. Urban seems to have assumed at first that he could dominate a new young king in the normal way that popes should control kings. As usual, after an initial period of friendship, the ideological and practical obstacles proved insurmountable. Richard appealed to Urban for support against the growing opposition, but there is no evidence that Urban responded, and the Pope approved all the measures taken by the Appellants without demur.[68] By 1386, assured of papal backing, the alliance was

---

[66] J. H. Denton, *Robert Winchelsey and the Crown, 1294–1313: a Study in Defence of Ecclesiastical Liberty* (Cambridge, 1980); J. R. Wright, *The Church and the Crown 1305–1334* (Toronto, 1980).

[67] Walsh, 'Lollardisch-Hussitische Reformbestrebungen', pp. 91–2. For the Bohemian marriages and grants see the *Westminster Chronicle*, pp. 160–2, 188–90.

[68] Another indication of Urban's change of attitude is Pileo di Prata's transfer of allegiance to Avignon in 1386. Urban was encouraged to support the Appellants in March 1386 by the hope of obtaining a subsidy: Davies, 'Episcopate', p. 678.

ready to strike, and only waited for Gaunt's departure to give itself a clear field. Meanwhile, more support was recruited amongst the nobility. The most senior of the Appellants was Thomas Beauchamp of Warwick, who, despite a long history of royal service,[69] was ill-tempered, quarrelsome, and jealous of his rights. He enjoyed a reputation for supporting Parliament against Gaunt, going back to the Good Parliament of 1376. Thomas Mowbray, Earl of Nottingham, had been a close friend of Richard, but greatly disliked de Vere. Notwithstanding his decision to be an Appellant, Richard regarded him as someone who could be weaned away from the opposition. The one who became the most important adherent, however, was Henry of Bolingbroke, Earl of Derby, heir as the son of John of Gaunt to the Lancastrian inheritance, and Gloucester's nephew. Although the five Appellants claimed to have acted together from the beginning, it is now thought that Nottingham and Derby did not openly join the group until the end of 1387.[70]

The first round of the contest between monarchy and opposition was an attempt to get rid of the two chief royal ministers, Michael de la Pole, Earl of Suffolk, the Chancellor, and the Bishop of Durham, John Fordham, the Treasurer, and it took place at the so-called Wonderful Parliament of October 1386. The choice of target and its outcome suggests that Thomas Arundel was now determining policy, and he had already attacked de la Pole in the Parliament of 1385.[71] It was Thomas Arundel and Gloucester who went to Richard at Eltham 'with a mixture of fear and aggression'[72] and told him that Parliament, as the price of granting war taxation, required the dismissal of the evil counsellors, who, as was said later, were impoverishing the kingdom and seducing the King into thinking that he could ignore the combined displeasure of God, Church, nobility, and people.[73] They

---

[69] For his earlier career see Goodman, *Loyal Conspiracy*, pp. 1–3. For the enormous amounts of territory controlled by the Appellants between themselves, and the family connections between their wives, see the lists in M. McKisack, *The Fourteenth Century, 1307–1399* (Oxford, 1959), p. 460.

[70] Saul, *Richard II*, pp. 166–7, following *Eulogium historiarum* iii, p. 359. Goodman, *Loyal Conspiracy*, p. 153, asks the interesting question of whether Bolingbroke was really representing Gaunt.

[71] Higden, *Polychronicon*, ed. C. Babington and J. R. Lumby, RS (1865–86), 9, pp. 69–70; Walsingham, *Historia Anglicana*, 2, p. 141.

[72] The phrase is Ferster's, *Fictions*, p. 1. An even better example is provided by Knighton's description of the visit by the Appellants to Richard in November 1387, *Chronicle*, pp. 402–4.

[73] '. . . en displesaunce du Dieu et de seynt eglise, en deshonour de uous et de vostre

went with an armed force 'to carry the wishes of the estates of the realm'. Richard had at first refused, arguing that the selection of members of his household was entirely his own affair, and that he was not prepared to move even a scullion from his kitchen at the behest of Parliament.[74] But when reminded of the fate of his grandfather, Edward II, and warned that he could always be replaced by another member of the royal family, one of a series of threats of deposition, Richard gave way, and Pole and Fordham were dismissed from office on 23 October. A day later Thomas Arundel was appointed Chancellor, and John Gilbert, Bishop of Hereford, became Treasurer.[75] Thomas Arundel and the papalists had begun to take over the government, and the 'great and continual Council' set up in November with comprehensive powers to investigate and reform the King's government since the beginning of the reign included, apart from the episcopal officers of state, the new chancellor's backers, Wykeham, Courtenay, and Thomas Brantingham, Bishop of Exeter, and was supported by Arundel and Gloucester.

Although the Chancellor's new council, with its episcopal predominance, claimed to speak in the name of the King, Richard still looked for counsel and advice from his own circle of King's Friends. There were, in effect, two councils, both representing the monarch, but from opposite points of view.[76] The discrepancy was all the more marked when Richard left London in February 1387 and went on a recruiting tour of the midlands and the north. But it is a very significant development in providing a precedent for the 1390s, when official declarations of the royal will seemed to say something very different from what the King wanted. For the royalists, the King's Council continued to be wherever the King was; as one chronicler said, the King's Friends continued like flies to buzz around the King.[77] Their numbers, who had been promised immunity from prosecution, still included de la Pole, although in 1386 he had been put on trial in a

coroune et de tous uoz noblez et gentiles et a touz estatez du dit roialme': Knighton, *Chronicle*, p. 442; also pp. 392, 414, 454–6, and cf. pp. 400–2 for the King's Friends as *seductores regis* and traitors, etc. See also Richard's complaint to Albert of Bavaria cited by Mott, 'Richard II', p. 175.

[74] Knighton, *Chronicle*, p. 354.

[75] Ibid., pp. 360–2. Walter Skirlaw, Bishop of Bath and Wells, was dismissed as Keeper of the Privy Seal and replaced by the Keeper of the Rolls of Chancery, John Waltham.

[76] Roskell, *Impeachment*, pp. 51–2; Ferster, *Fictions*, pp. 68–70. For the argument over the appointment of sheriffs, *Westminster Chronicle*, p. 404.

[77] Favent, 'Historia Mirabilis Parliamenti', p. 2, 'circa regem glomorantes'.

manner which deliberately recalled the process of impeachment used by the Good Parliament, heavily fined, and sentenced to imprisonment. But he was free by Christmas, and back at court.[78] When Richard returned to London in November a showdown was inevitable: Gloucester and Arundel refused to attend court, and Richard ordered the seizure of Arundel's goods. He was being advised to kill Warwick, Arundel, Nottingham, and Bolingbroke for plotting to depose him.[79] Formal appeal against the leading royalists was issued by the Lords Appellant, and a great state trial was arranged for the Westminster Parliament of February 1388. Meanwhile, de Vere had taken the field against the forces of the Appellants and had been soundly defeated by Bolingbroke and Gloucester at Radcot Bridge in December. This sealed the fate of the leading royalists, who were all condemned for treason. De Vere himself fled to the safety of Queensborough and from there went into exile abroad. So did de la Pole, after being returned from Calais in an unsuccessful first attempt. Only two Friends were actually executed at this stage, the Chief Justice of King's Bench, Sir Robert Tresilian, and Nicholas Brembre, Richard's spokesman in the City. The victorious alliance then turned its attention to the core of royal power, the household. Despite anguished pleas for mercy from the Queen, four Chamber knights, beginning with Burley, were impeached for treason and executed in May. The Queen was ordered to dismiss the Bohemians from her household.[80] What Knighton dubbed the Merciless Parliament ('parliamentum sine misericordia')[81] then enacted various measures designed to give Parliament control of the King's Council, to reorganize the royal courts and offices, and to prevent unsuitable people from entering the royal presence without permission. Finally, a new contract of government (which implied that Richard had ceased to be a true king) was made in Westminster Abbey on 3 June 1388: Richard promised to be a good king and lord, and the lords renewed their oaths of allegiance.[82]

The purge also extended to the royalist bishops. There were two principal victims, Thomas Rushook, O.P., Bishop of Chichester, who had been Richard's confessor, was imprisoned in March and threatened

[78] Walsingham, *Historia Anglicana*, 2, p. 149.
[79] *Westminster Chronicle*, p. 208.
[80] McKisack, *Fourteenth Century*, p. 459.
[81] Knighton, *Chronicle*, p. 414.
[82] *Westminster Chronicle*, p. 32; Favent, 'Historia Mirabilis Parliamenti', p. 24; Walsingham, *Historia Anglicana*, 2, p. 172.

with the death penalty, but was banished to exile in Ireland.[83] But the outstanding decision, and one of particular importance here, was the condemnation of Archbishop Neville for treason. He was saved from execution by his clerical status, but deemed it expedient to slip away from York disguised as a priest. It was Thomas Arundel's opportunity for advancement. Since Canterbury was not yet available, York would give him the commanding position as effective head of the episcopalist party. As with the chancellorship, it was not just a dutiful acceptance of an additional burden.

Urban VI was understandably all in favour of this chance to dispose of a leading royalist, and Neville was translated to St Andrews, although Urban was eventually unable to obtain the taxation which he had hoped to gain in exchange.[84] Thomas Arundel filled the vacancy on 3 April 1388, the Bishop of Durham, John Fordham, whose loyalty was suspect, being in effect demoted to replace him at Ely, where he could more easily be disciplined. Ralph Erghum, Bishop of Salisbury, was reduced to Bath and Wells. Thomas was now arguably the most powerful ruler in the kingdom, certainly in 1388–9, able to control both *regnum* and *sacerdotium*. He was too busy with affairs of the kingdom generally to appear frequently in York itself,[85] but he established a circle of academic and spiritual patronage there as he had done at Ely, and many Ely officials were in fact transferred to York.[86]

Archbishop Arundel had achieved what he wanted, and it is generally recognized that the Appellant movement was beginning to lose momentum by 1389, allowing Richard to start the process of a slow recovery of a degree of royal power. Manipulated by Thomas, the savage attacks on Richard's kingship faded away. Although this is often explained by the return of Gaunt to England in late 1389, the fact of the matter is that the alliance between bishops and nobility was no longer needed: Thomas Arundel allowed it to disintegrate. Gloucester and Arundel were expelled from the Council in May 1389 and left to

---

[83] Favent, 'Historia Mirabilis Parliamenti', p. 21; Higden, *Polychronicon*, 9, pp. 156–7; cf. Davies, 'Episcopate', pp. 672–3.

[84] *Westminster Chronicle*, pp. 332–4, 354, 472; Higden, *Polychronicon*, 9, p. 264. Richard was thwarted in his attempt to bring Neville back to England in 1391.

[85] J. Raine, *Historians of the Church of York and its Archbishops*, RS (1879–94), 2, pp. 425–6. Arundel had attempted but failed to obtain a prebend at York in 1370: A. D. M. Barrell, *The Papacy, Scotland and Northern England, 1342–78* (Cambridge, 1995), p. 112.

[86] For details see Hughes, *Pastors and Visionaries*, pp. 173–216, 227, 298.

mutter quietly in isolation; Warwick was deemed too old and spent as a political force; and Derby/Bolingbroke and Nottingham drifted back to court.[87] The phasing out of the Appellancy owed far more to the episcopal supremacy than it did to Richard, and was intimately connected to the government's attitude towards heresy. The eradication of heresy, especially Lollardy, was the other side of the coin to the limitation of the monarchy. One of the chief results of the Appellancy was the strengthening of the legislation against heresy and a new and much more determined effort to root it out. However much Wyclif denounced the forty-day rule, relatively little was done to implement it.[88] Now, however, the Cambridge Parliament of September 1388 revised the supplementary procedures against heretics, and made it clear that this was seen as a restriction on Richard himself, by declaring that the liberties of Holy Church, Magna Carta, and other such ordinances were to be firmly observed.[89]

It has been argued that the young Richard, brought up in the anticlerical atmosphere of the court, showed sympathy for Wycliffite aspirations by taking no action against the Lollard Knights and others, and virtually ignoring the question of heresy in his documents. But suddenly, in the later 1380s, there was a mysterious change of heart on Richard's part, and he increasingly sought to demonstrate a conventional piety and orthodoxy. Denunciations of heresy now became commonplace.[90] That this was the fulfilment of a basic Appellant objective could probably have been demonstrated earlier, had it not been the case that a form of censorship seems to have operated. The day after Sir Simon Burley and three other Chamber knights were formally charged on 12 March 1388, the full Parliament engaged in discussions about the government of the kingdom for the next four days.[91] The contents of these were not specified, but the *Westminster Chronicle* hints that this lengthy debate was largely concerned with the question of what to do about Lollards, whose preaching and production of books in English was corrupting all levels of society. Four unnamed Lollards were cited to appear before a tribunal headed by the

[87] Saul, *Richard II*, pp. 235, 268–9. Adam Usk, *Chronicle*, p. 35, called Warwick 'a wretched old woman'.

[88] H. G. Richardson, 'Heresy and the lay power under Richard II', *EHR*, 51 (1936), pp. 1–28.

[89] Knighton, *Chronicle*, pp. 506–8, 526; *Westminster Chronicle*, pp. lxiii, 356–68.

[90] Saul, *Richard II*, pp. 298–304.

[91] *Westminster Chronicle*, pp. 318, 330.

papal sub-collector, Thomas Southam, and a bench of bishops, theologians, and lawyers two days after Parliament began the Easter recess. A month later, and a week before the fate of Burley was sealed, the Lollards were pronounced guilty: two recanted and two were imprisoned.

That there was a reluctance to report the discussions in full is readily understandable. The bishops, as we have said, were determined to give the impression by their absence from the actual trials of the King's ministers that this was a matter for the laity. It was still felt that admission of heresy was to confess to failure in the regulation of the Christian community, and none of the bishops wanted to acknowledge that they were having to deal with a kingdom which was, in their terms, substantially heretical. Condemnations of heresy began to appear more and more frequently in royal documents, many of which emanated from the Council, and there is no evidence that Richard personally was ever involved with them.

Just as Gregory VII three centuries earlier had forced Henry IV to forsake his claims to be *caput Ecclesiae* as *rex et sacerdos*, so now Thomas Arundel achieved acceptance of the principle of dualism. There was a tacit compromise. Richard was allowed a relatively free hand in temporal matters, whilst the hierocratic party could apply its predominance in spiritual. This predominance was clearly indicated in 1396, when Courtenay died on 31 July: Thomas Arundel moved smoothly from York to Canterbury, although the King would have preferred the appointment of the Treasurer, Roger Walden.[92] It is puzzling, all the same, that in 1388 the parliamentary process should be halted for so long by a seemingly irrelevant topic. Knighton, however, is more helpful here. He tells us that the Lollards, whose numbers were increasing, were Members of Parliament, although much reviled by their colleagues.[93] This alters the whole character of the affair. The

[92] Davies, 'Thomas Arundel as Archbishop of Canterbury', pp. 9–22. See further Aston, *Thomas Arundel*, p. 299.

[93] Knighton, *Chronicle*, pp. 432–4. The editor comments (p. 433, n. 6) that it is interesting that Knighton should be so concerned with Lollardy that he deals at this point with an episode which was secondary to the melodrama of the Parliament's principal business. He follows McFarlane's view, *Lancastrian Kings*, p. 199, that this was connected with the arrest of Nicholas Hereford the previous year because Knighton includes a copy of the commission of enquiry and seizure (pp. 436–42). But it may be argued that this has no more significance in this context than the stereotyped list of Lollard errors usually cited in the record of a heresy trial (pp. 434–88). McFarlane, pp. 193–4, suggests that the *Westminster Chronicle* account refers to the charges against Sir Thomas Latimer in May 1388.

'Lollards' were opponents of the Appellants: in other words, they were the royalists, the King's Friends, and it was perfectly explicable that Parliament should spend four days in the middle of its destruction of the King's supporters in discussing them. Richard's claim to absolute power, his 'tyranny', and 'Lollardy', the subjection of the clergy to royal power, were seen as aspects of the same problem.

With the approval of the episcopal king's Council, Arundel resigned the chancellorship on 3 May 1389, the Council taking over the office directly by transferring it to the safe hands of William of Wykeham.[94] It was to be nothing more than a temporary holding operation. Arundel not only had to reform the York province after Neville, but there was the still more important task of mounting the new campaign against Wycliffite heresy on the basis of the revised legislation of the previous year. The increase in Lollard heresy trials was directly due to fear of the Archbishop, according to Knighton.[95] The revival of the Oxford campaign of 1392, which was still in full vigour five years later, showed that the struggle for supremacy between King and Archbishop continued unabated.[96]

Arundel now had to cope with Richard's direct rejections of papal authority. His reissue through Parliament of Edward III's Statutes of Premunire and Provisors (17 January 1390 and July 1393),[97] which Boniface IX annulled (4 February 1391), was a direct challenge to the Pope. In the 1390s he toyed with the idea of joining the French in a move to end the Schism by withdrawing recognition from both popes, the so-called *via cessionis*.[98]

But the crucial period was early in 1395. A move to condemn the Bible translated into English, in the January Parliament, is said to have been stalled by the intervention of John of Gaunt and a petition from the Lollard knights calling for ecclesiastical reformation. A document containing twelve heretical conclusions inspired by Wyclif was

[94] This should not be seen as a royal dismissal of the chancellor, e.g. Goodman, *Loyal Conspiracy*, pp. 53–4. Arundel regained the chancellorship on 27 September 1391. His subsequent resignation on becoming Archbishop of Canterbury was in accordance with custom: Hughes, *Pastors and Visionaries*, pp. 131–2. In 1396 Arundel arranged for his replacement by Edmund Stafford.

[95] Knighton, *Chronicle*, pp. 532–4.

[96] The best account is still H. B. Workman, *John Wyclif* (Oxford, 1926), 2, pp. 342–401.

[97] E. Perroy, *L'Angleterre et le Grand Schisme d'Occident* (Paris, 1933), pp. 332–5. A compromise was eventually reached by the concordat of November 1398.

[98] Perroy, *L'Angleterre*, pp. 352–76.

allegedly nailed to the door of Parliament.[99] On 18 February Convocation asked the government to take action against a movement whose numbers had increased 'into a multitude', and on 17 September, Boniface IX urged the two Archbishops to suppress 'the crafty and daring sect who call themselves the poor men of Christ's treasury.' According to Walsingham, this Lollard activity alarmed the Archbishop so much that, accompanied by Braybrooke, Bishop of London, he went to Richard, who was with his army in Dublin, and insisted that he must return to England to deal with the threat. Richard, we are told, was so incensed that he returned from Ireland in mid-May, vowing that he would hang all Lollards. The story is highly suspect. Not only do the *XII Conclusiones* look like another of those stereotyped lists of Lollard heresies, in which case it was the papalists who pinned them up, but Arundel went to Ireland to put pressure on Richard, and Richard returned to offer what protection he could to his Friends.

The episode bristles with unanswered questions. Why did Arundel want the King to cut short his Irish expedition? What did he say to persuade Richard to do so? The most likely explanation is that Arundel, on behalf of Boniface IX, threatened Richard with a revival of the Appellant alliance. At all events, Richard decided that it was time to reverse the humiliation of the Appellancy. After the bishops, in early 1397, had urged the imposition of the death penalty for Lollardy,[100] Richard struck suddenly. He had returned to England far from having been converted, as some historians have argued, to a policy of exterminating Lollardy, but now determined to protect himself and his supporters by taking a long-delayed revenge on the Appellants.

The deterioration of Anglo-papal relations under Boniface IX had been matched by the resurgence of opposition in Parliament under the Arundel–Gloucester coalition. The Earl insulted Richard in 1394 at Queen Anne's funeral,[101] and it was reported that Richard was so furious that he struck Arundel with a rod and then imprisoned him in the Tower on a charge of disloyalty. Against a background of increasing parliamentary opposition to royal expenditure and the

---

[99] Walsingham, *Annales*, p. 173; A. Hudson, *Selections from English Wycliffite Writings* (Cambridge, 1978), pp. 24–9; M. Aston, *Faith and Fire: Popular and Unpopular Religion, 1350–1600* (London and Rio Grande, TX, 1993), pp. 109–10.

[100] McKisack, *Fourteenth Century*, p. 522.

[101] Ibid., pp. 469–70; for Anne's death see Knighton, *Chronicle*, pp. 548–50.

policy of peace with France, Arundel and Gloucester refused to attend meetings of the royal Council.[102] They were alleged to be planning to seize Richard in the summer of 1397 and imprison him, and Richard used rumours of plots and conspiracies as a justification for his action.[103]

The intention was to arrest the Appellants so that they could be dealt with by the Parliament scheduled for September 1397: they had already the previous year been exempted from the pardons granted after the Appellancy itself. But subterfuge was required. An invitation to a banquet which Walsingham compared to that of King Herod, at which Salome sought the head of John the Baptist, succeeded only in netting Warwick. He confessed and 'like a wretched old woman' was banished to the Isle of Man. Gloucester was taken by force and was eventually murdered whilst being held at Calais. The Archbishop, apparently ready to sacrifice his brother to save himself, persuaded Arundel to surrender under a spurious safe conduct: he was condemned by Parliament and beheaded. Thomas himself was not allowed a trial on the claim that like an heretical pope his crimes were notorious. The Pope was summarily informed that Richard had deposed him and the royal Treasurer, Roger Walden, would replace him. He was to be translated, like Neville, to St Andrew's as a see under Avignonese jurisdiction. Thomas did not go willingly. He gave a very vigorous sermon denouncing the avarice and arrogance of the royal court. When he eventually left, at the end of October, he went straight to the Pope at Rome to urge him to continue the fight.[104] But Richard's victory was to be short lived, and events now moved inexorably towards the final tragedy.

Only Bolingbroke had so far escaped, presumably because Richard was reluctant to fall out with John of Gaunt, Bolingbroke's father. But Gaunt's protection was a wasting asset. Bolingbroke was banished in September 1398, even before his father died, on 3 February 1399. Richard denied Bolingbroke's right to inherit and shared out the Lancastrian estates. It was to be a fatal mistake. Bolingbroke established himself in Paris, where he was joined by Thomas Arundel: together they plotted the invasion of England. Richard's departure to complete

---

[102] *Westminster Chronicle*, p. 209.
[103] Saul, *Richard II*, pp. 366–7. It is odd that Walsingham dates the beginning of Richard's tyranny to 1397, unless he saw this exclusively in ecclesiastical terms.
[104] *Eulogium historiarum*, 3, pp. 376–7; Aston, *Thomas Arundel*, p. 372.

his unfinished business in Ireland presented a golden opportunity. Bolingbroke and the Archbishop landed at Ravenscar early in July, and were soon joined by 'all the people of the north'.

Thomas had now become a kingmaker. It is possible that Bolingbroke initially intended only to regain his inheritance. But Thomas was 'an unforgiving opponent of Richard': he encouraged Henry to become 'a master of lies and dissimulation'. At a council held at Doncaster in mid-July, Henry appears to have claimed that he only wanted to reform the King and bring him under control, not to depose him – thereby laying both himself and the Archbishop open to a charge of perjury.[105] Richard was persuaded to surrender at Conway by an assurance that his kingship was not threatened, although it is not clear whether Thomas went to him in person.[106] When it came to advancing a justification for Henry's usurpation – he took the crown by right of conquest confirmed by popular consent – a mythology was constructed alleging divine approval by right of direct descent[107] from Henry III. Thomas Arundel, who had resumed the chancellorship for a couple of weeks whilst Henry's title was determined, preached a sermon on the text *Vir dominabitur populo*.[108] By this he declared that not only was there a new king, but also that he himself had put him there.

The deposition of Richard II sealed the political fate of Lollardy. Had he been a more successful ruler, the subsequent history of Wycliffism as a 'failed reformation' might have been very different. It is true that his reign had created the Bohemian connection which ensured that the torch of Wycliffite reform would be carried on. But as regards the *ecclesia Anglicana* Richard suffered from several crippling disadvantages. Given the background of papal support for the Appellants and the long series of disputes between the King and the papacy, it was hardly surprising that his downfall was engineered by Boniface IX: in a sense Richard was deposed by the Pope. The fact that the popes of the Schism were to a large extent clients of the national

---

[105] This follows J. Sherborne, *War, Politics and Culture in Fourteenth-Century England* (London and Rio Grande, TX, 1994), pp. 131–53; also Saul, *Richard II*, pp. 414–15. One may take with a pinch of salt Arundel's assurance to the Lords after Richard's deposition that his life was not threatened: Saul, *Richard II*, p. 424.

[106] Sherborne, *War, Politics and Culture*, pp. 140–3; Saul, *Richard II*, p. 413.

[107] McKisack, *Fourteenth Century*, p. 495.

[108] Given-Wilson, *Chronicles*, p. 186: the theme was that a true king had replaced a tyrannical child. For a full account see Aston, *Thomas Arundel*, pp. 268–73.

monarchies does not mean that the traditional assumptions of papal supremacy had ceased to operate. In Thomas Arundel, Richard was faced with an archbishop eager to repeat the papal lesson of 1207–13 that a king who loses control of his bishops cannot continue to govern. He was a participant in a triangular ideological struggle for sovereignty between king, pope, and aristocracy, who never realized that ideological conflicts cannot be determined by one person in a single generation. In 1399 Arundel had a ready-made alliance with the aristocracy, stretching back over ten years. It is important to remember that Henry IV had himself been a prominent Appellant who always regarded himself as a better alternative king. The success of Henry's usurpation enabled Arundel to drive Lollardy underground. Henry was not going to dispense with the support of the great network of career royalists who were willing to exchange Richard for him, and the Archbishop had to proceed with caution. But the tempo of heresy trials increased steadily, and the first execution of a Wycliffite followed in 1401, shortly before the passing of *De haeretico comburendo*.[109] The English Bible attributed to Wyclif was prohibited in 1407,[110] and the universal condemnation of Wycliffite doctrine was secured at the Councils of Pisa and Constance. England in the fifteenth century became far more orthodoxly Roman Catholic than it had been in the previous century, and it was Arundel who more than any other made it so. It is small wonder that to the chroniclers he was the 'most eminent bulwark of the English Church', 'light and delight of Church and clergy and an unshakeable pillar of the Christian faith'.[111]

Birkbeck College, University of London

---

[109] P. McNiven, *Heresy and Politics in the Reign of Henry IV: the Burning of John Badby* (Woodbridge, 1987).

[110] Wilks, 'Misleading Manuscripts', *SCH*, 11 (1975), pp. 147–51.

[111] Adam Usk, *Chronicle*, pp. lxxxi, 246; Walsingham, *Historia Anglicana*, 2, p. 300.

12
ROMAN CANDLE OR DAMNED SQUIB:
THE ENGLISH CRUSADE OF 1383

*Inaugural lecture delivered 5 November 1980
at Birkbeck College, University of London*

I believe we are, or were, charged in these lectures to tell our colleagues in the College something of the sort of thing that we do. As my colleagues in the department will know, I tend to roam creakingly about and straddle the centuries in most ungainly fashion. But I am by preference a medievalist – although I sometimes wonder when the Middle Ages are going to stop – and if I am left to my own devices, I find myself indulging in what *The Times* this morning called the 'poisoned delights' of politics and religion. I like nothing better than a good juicy debate on the powers of the medieval pope, or the divine right of kings, or any other aspect of the theology of the medieval state as a mystical body.

All this, however, is an acquired taste, and I have been uneasily aware, ever since I have been in the College, that this is not what medievalists are supposed to be for. Medievalists are supposed to know about horses, and when Peter Murray gave his own characteristically brilliant hail and farewell inaugural valediction, he excused himself from dealing with knights on horseback – I leave that, he said, to the medievalists. So obviously I had to talk about horses and knights in armour. In view of the date [5 November] I thought we ought to commemorate the Gunpowder Plot, so I chose the Flanders crusade of 1383, which certainly employed gunpowder (gunpowder had been used in the Hundred Years War since the mid-1340s), and where there was a great deal of plotting, and where, according to Wyclif – one of the leading and most vocal opponents of the crusade – the real aim of the crusade was to make the pope king of England. By any standards, it was an interesting event. Unlike so many crusades, it did not go to the East; it went instead to Ostend.

As historians will know, it's a subject which features in all textbook histories of the fourteenth century. It has had two books written about it, both published in the 1890s. One was by a gentleman from Toronto, who suffered under the disability of being called Professor Wrong; the other an even more obscure German work (*Skalweit*) published in 1898 at Königsberg. Both of these relied mainly on the chronicle accounts and established that, provided one makes allowance for his known prejudices, by far the most reliable account is that given by Froissart, largely because he had access to a good deal of political gossip. Since then we have had the most thorough study of the official background documents and the Rolls of Parliament in a London thesis of 1931 by A. P. Coulborn, which ought to have been published; and some fifteen years ago Margaret Aston produced a most illuminating article on the trial of Bishop Despenser, which tried to analyse what had gone wrong with the crusade. So it is not an original subject, but it is a good story, and it will bear repetition.

The crusade grew out of three major but intrinsically unrelated events. The first was the revival half a century earlier, in the 1330s, of the long-standing English claim that there was a single Anglo-French monarchy, a Britannic *imperium* from Iceland to the Pyrenees, and the claim by Edward III that the government of France belonged to him by right of inheritance. It is one of the curiosities of history that this claim was first made effective in Flanders. In 1338, after declaring himself to be king of France, Edward III had seized Flanders, Brabant, and Hainault, which were in revolt against increasing French control exercised through the count of Flanders. The Flemish weavers, under Jacques van Artevelde of Ghent, had driven out the count, and at a Parliament held in Ghent in 1340, Edward III had solemnly assumed the arms and seal of France. And for the next twenty years he very successfully maintained that claim, until by 1360 almost half of the French kingdom was – as a result of the so-called Edwardian War – English territory.

The next twenty years had, however, almost restored the *status quo*. By 1380 the so-called Caroline War (of Charles V) had reduced the English occupation to a narrow coastal strip in Aquitaine (south west); Brittany was about to decide under the de Montforts that it preferred to be French rather than English;

both kingdoms were now ruled by new young kings – both of whom subsequently went mad – Richard II had been ten at his accession in 1377; Charles VI was twelve in 1380 – and the whole character of the Hundred Years War had changed to a long, drawn-out war of attrition.

The English policy, making a virtue of necessity, was to hold a circle of heavily fortified seaports all round the French coast – known as barbicans of the realm – Calais, Cherbourg, Brest, Bordeaux, and Bayonne (and unsuccessful attempts to add Harfleur, St Malo, Nantes, and La Rochelle to the list). The intention was stated to be to deny the French invasion ports – by the 1370s the English government and the southern counties were almost paranoid with hysterical fear of a French invasion – and on the other hand to provide 'fine and noble entry-ports' to grieve the French. And, in fact, the war was fought very largely by *chevauchées*, the long rides or marches, by small, very mobile English forces, averaging about 5,000 troops, which criss-crossed France between these entry-ports at great speed and set out to do as much damage as they could, and leave a trail of destruction behind them in the rural areas. They usually failed and got caught if they tried to deal with towns. In essence, the English crusade of 1383 was just another of these.

The second factor was that throughout this period the papacy was resident in Southern France, at Avignon. It was technically independent, but under the protection of the French king as *rex christianissimus* and to some extent influenced by French wishes, one of which was to prevent the return of the Roman Church to Rome and to establish Avignon as a *Roma secunda* instead. The details need not detain us. But it is important to know that early in 1378, having at last got back to Rome the previous autumn, the papacy found the Romans even more unspeakably awful than they had been painted and had decided to return to Avignon. For this purpose it was intended to elect a cousin of the French king, Cardinal Robert of Geneva, as the new pontiff in the election of April 1378. In fact, the French cardinals were so busy quarrelling amongst themselves that they inadvertently allowed an Italian archbishop to be elected as Pope Urban VI instead. 'There were', writes Professor Walter Ullmann, 'definite signs of mental derangement in Urban' – or, at least, the shock of finding himself pope instead of merely being head of a curial department, drove him insane – and the French cardinals only managed to put up with him for three months. By the end of September 1378 they had declared him deposed, and replaced him with their original choice, Robert of Geneva, as Pope Clement VII. He eventually, in 1379, having failed to get possession of Rome, took the papacy back to Avignon. Urban VI retaliated by torturing all his remaining cardinals in case they too wanted to go to Avignon, and in one day created a complete new College.

So there was by 1380 a major constitutional crisis in the Western Church, a Great Schism which nobody knew how to end because canon law insisted that no one could tell the pope what to do. In any case, nobody knew who was the pope and who was the usurper. Both popes excommunicated and condemned each other, and all their supporters, so that one way or another everybody was excommunicated, and Christendom had technically ceased to exist. At best there were liable to be two clerics trying to occupy every benefice; at worst there were no more Christians.

The English government had, with very little hesitation, decided that anybody who was not a Frenchman must be the true pope and had declared for Urban VI and the Roman papacy as early as October 1378. It was declared both treason and heresy to support Clement VII. The Crown confiscated the property of his supporters, arrested and tried his ambassadors, and employed John Wyclif to depict 'Urbanus noster', 'our Urban' as a *papa angelicus*, and Clement VII as Satan himself in human form. From the end of 1378 preachers and missionaries began to come to England in large numbers to preach the need for a crusade against Avignon, although nobody, as far as I know, ever explained *how* the English were to get there.

The French, on the other hand, were much slower about declaring for Clement VII, and only did so during 1379 under considerable pressure from the court. But by 1380 we have the position that the French and the English were both able to claim that their war against each other was a holy war, something which could now legally be determined by crusading endeavour. The Schism made the Flanders *chevauchées* into a crusade.

And it was a *Flanders* crusade because of the third factor, that between 1378 and 1382 Europe was swept by a wave of social unrest, which brought out both artisans and peasants in open revolt against the governments who were held responsible for the economic troubles and social grievances which had afflicted Europe since the Black Death in the middle of the century. The revolt of the Ciompi, the Florentine cloth-workers, from 1378; of the English and Norman peasants in 1381; the Tuchins of Southern France in 1382; and, above all for our purposes, the revolt of the weavers of Ghent, under Philip van Artevelde in 1379 – which, despite appalling atrocities, was kept in being and maintained against the count of Flanders, Louis de Male, and the rival cloth-working towns of Bruges and Ypres. The Flemish revolt reached a climax in 1382. Ghent seized the great staple port of Bruges, and van Artevelde declared himself regent. In April a certain Gherkin Tolwin, clerk to the bailiff of Nieuport and chief Flemish spy-master for the count of Flanders, reported to the count that representatives from Ghent had paid a secret visit to London, offering to recognize Richard II as king of France and count of Flanders, and – so it was said – offering him the support of 120,000 Flemings if he could send an expeditionary force of 50,000 men and 80 large ships. This was duly reported by the count of Flanders to the French government, and especially to his son-in-law and prospective heir, Philip the Bold, Duke of Burgundy. The result was that the French king, Charles VI, took the *oriflamme*, the banner proclaiming a holy war to defend the sacred land of France – and with Flemish and Burgundian help swept right across Flanders in November of that year, 1382, recaptured Bruges, killed van Artevelde, and garrisoned the whole area except for Ghent itself. A small Flemish fleet escaped to England, where there was consternation at the expectation that the Anglo-Flemish wool and cloth trade would be interrupted by the French occupation. In fact, apart from a few initial expulsions of English merchants, there was very little disruption to trade; English wool-farmers and Flemish weavers needed each other too much. But this did not prevent the English mercantile interest from raising an enormous outcry that they were being deprived of their markets overseas – and everyone knew that the wealth of England depended on wool, the golden fleece.

****

All these strands came together in the person of Henry Despenser, bishop of Norwich, self-styled *pugil ecclesiae*, champion of the Church. Despenser's qualifications for leading a crusade in person (on the grounds that if a pope was allowed to do it, then so was he) were perhaps spirited more than spiritual. We are told that his favourite text was 'The earth is the Lord's'; and this gave him the right to trample all over it.

Descended from a family whose members seemed with remarkable consistency to die violent deaths, and said to have a great liking for jars of green ginger, which kept him in a permanent state of choleric heat, this aristocratic young tearaway (he is described as arrogant, headstrong, insolent, greedy, and none too bright) had seen military service with the papal mercenaries against Milan in the war of 1369, with the result that the pope appointed him bishop of Norwich the following year, 1370, at the age of twenty-six. His lack of discretion is exemplified in 1377, when he insisted, against town custom, on processing with his mace-bearer through the town of Lynn, thereby provoking a riot amongst the townsfolk, who fell upon the procession, killing the mace-bearer and injuring the bishop. It may have been the memory of this which led him to take the lead, charging at considerable personal risk, into the encampment of the Norfolk rebels in 1381, putting down the rising with great severity, and only narrowly escaping a plot to murder him afterwards.

It seems astonishing, but the evidence is that Despenser had apparently decided as early as the beginning of 1380 to lead a crusade to establish Urban VI as the true pope. He got his clerk, Henry Bower, to Rome on government business in February, and in due course the matter was arranged. Canon law had established from the twelfth century that popes should authorize each crusade individually, and in March 1381 Urban VI duly furnished the bishop with two bulls authorizing him to preach the crusade against Clement VII and to grant indulgences to anyone taking part or supporting the expedition financially. By the time the bulls reached England the bishop was too busy executing revolting peasants – 'ribaldos', he called them – in the summer of 1381; but he arranged for the papal bulls to be reissued to him in May and June 1382.

There were as yet many unanswered questions. Who was to lead the crusade? Despenser was appointed organizer, but that was not the same thing as leading it personally – and whilst precedents for bishops as military commanders were by no means lacking, it was still unusual. Where was it to go? As late as the summer of 1382 there was no statement from the bishop about the destination of the crusade: it was still a crusade with nowhere to go, waiting for bids. All that Despenser would say was that it would be against the Antichrist of Avignon and his supporters. Since all Englishmen now knew that the Antichrists began at Calais, it was assumed that the French would be the target.

But, above all, would it get the support of the English government, and thereby qualify for a government grant? It has recently been shown that in view of the economic position in 1381 and 1382, Parliament had taken the almost unprecedented step of refusing three out of four government requests for wool subsidies. In effect, over a three-year period the government got together only enough money to mount one overseas expedition. It is this which perhaps explains the unprecedented fervour with which indulgences for the crusade were sold, largely by friars, and the very large amounts of money which poured into the collectors' coffers. According to Wyclif, the bishop had killed thousands of Englishmen by his false promises before the crusade even started, since all who contributed were damned; but this did nothing to stem the flow, especially of jewellery, and particularly from old ladies, whose riches had so far debarred them from salvation. But perhaps most money came from people who wanted to *avoid* going on the crusade and were prepared to pay for exemption. The crusade was short of troops from the beginning, and Despenser was accused of trying to cajole knights more than eighty years old to take part, which suggests a certain desperation.

But his real problem now was political, and to understand this I ought to digress for a moment to remark that English governments in the fourteenth century were, like most governments, formed by a combination of a constantly shifting ebb and flow of different factions and groups. This was something which stretched right down to the local level. But for practical purposes, at any given moment around the early 1380s, these groups would coalesce into three main interests:

1. The old royalists or king's men, led by Edward III's son, John of Gaunt, Duke of Lancaster, the *rex incoronatus*, who had virtually governed England during the last years of his senile father and the youth of his nephew Richard II. For ten years Gaunt had struggled against a constant succession of crises to uphold the royal authority – and, in effect, his own – against other aristocratic factions and against unruly bishops. He was anti-papal, Wycliffite, and insistent that bishops were just royal servants. Gaunt had spent most of 1382 in Scotland. He was aware that there was considerable danger of Scots incursion, and in fact a Scottish invasion did take place in the summer and autumn of 1383. He wanted men and money concentrated in the north. If it was not to be used here, then he wanted to lead an expedition to Aquitaine against the French, or southwards into Spain, where he had a claim through his wife to the throne of Castile, and where he had authority to crusade against the Castilians and Portuguese, who had declared for Clement VII. The one thing he did not want was an independent papal crusade, organized by a bishop acting virtually as papal legate in England, and demanding support from the English monarchy as a matter of right, debasing, in his eyes, the English government into being a mere servant of the Roman Church.

2. The second group were the new royalists, led by Princess Joan of Kent, the king's mother, by the de Veres and the Burleys, with Richard II himself coming to be more of a political factor since he had won his spurs in the Peasants' Revolt. The spokesman in 1383 was the new chancellor, Michael de la Pole.

3. Those English bishops, led by the new archbishop of Canterbury, William Courtenay, who were bitterly opposed to John of Gaunt and Wyclif, and who used the principle of papal supremacy over the English kingdom and church as a battle-cry against the royalist politicians.

Since 1377 England had virtually been governed by a precarious alliance between the old and the new royalists. But the new king's friends would probably have preferred not to have a crusade at all. On the other hand, they were far more willing to work with the bishops than John of Gaunt was. They recognized that the demand for an expedition to support the men of Ghent was too strong to be ignored, and they were quite prepared to support an expedition to which Gaunt was opposed for the sake of inflicting a political defeat on him, and thus diminishing his political influence. In the autumn of 1382 the government therefore gave its rather lukewarm support to the third group, the bishops.

Archbishop Courtenay saw the crusade as one more round in the interminable guerilla warfare against the royal supremacy and gave Despenser his full support. He preached the crusade; he declared prayers for it throughout the realm; he issued special bulls for it; and he sent two nephews on it. The success of the crusade would not only be a rejection of the royalists by frustrating the plans of John of Gaunt; it would also be an assertion of the supremacy of the pope – and indeed the crusade acted under the name of the army of Urban and denounced all who opposed it as heretics.

Just before Christmas 1382 Despenser and the English government worked out a compromise arrangement, despite the bitter protests of John of Gaunt and Wyclif. Despenser agreed to Flanders as the first priority, although he was not enthusiastic. He appreciated that this was likely to cause problems from the simple fact that Flanders had already declared for Urban VI, and there was a basic contradiction in an Urbanist crusade attacking an Urbanist territory. For its part, the English government between 6 December 1382 and 17 March issued a series of orders for support for the crusade. Parliament made a grant, and all shipping between 16 and 100 tons was confiscated by the Crown and ordered to assemble at Sandwich by 8 April 1383. Meanwhile, for six months, Despenser waged energetic warfare to prevent a royalist takeover of the crusade, by refusing to allow a lay executive lieutenant of any seniority to be appointed. There were even threats to land him with John of Gaunt or Richard II in person. Every effort was made to delay him at the end, during April and early May, to force him to agree to surrender command. The indomitable bishop was eventually faced with a point-blank demand to wait; and he did the only thing possible – he sailed.

The bishop of Norwich's reports to the government on the progress of the crusade have not survived, although there is one letter which he wrote to another bishop detailing the events of the first week. Beyond this the details are often obscure, and the chronology of events provided by the chroniclers is confusing and contradictory. Hostile sources generally tried to make it a bigger and more prolonged affair than it was: Froissart's account tells us what the bishop was doing in Flanders for some six weeks – before he actually left England; the main Flemish chronicle adds on an extra three months at the other end. Like so much medieval history, the only certain thing about it is that it is usually wrong.

But it seems clear from his own version that Despenser sailed from Sandwich on Saturday 16 May for an overnight crossing which brought him to the English fortress of Calais on the following day, Trinity Sunday, 17 May. His troopships took several days to load and straggle over, and whilst they were waiting, his senior captain, and the nearest person there was to a royal lieutenant, Sir Hugh Calverley, went off to visit his cousin in a nearby garrison. When he returned he discovered to his consternation that another of those ubiquitous Flemish embassies had arrived from Ghent, that a council of war had been held in his absence, and that the decision to clear the French out of Flanders had been confirmed. Despite the small size of his force, Despenser wanted immediate action, and the Flemings offered him all the troops he wanted if he would go east towards Ghent to meet them. Calverley's plea that they should wait for the English reinforcements under Sir William Beauchamp and then march south into France was angrily brushed aside: the bishop was determined to go it alone, untrammelled by any, more senior, royalist commander.

It is difficult to estimate the size of his army with any precision: estimates vary between 3,000 and 8,000. He was certainly paid for 5,000, divided equally into archers and lancers: but he was later accused of having taken only about half this number (and of having pocketed the difference), and of making up the number with a motley crowd of priests, monks, and friars. Their enthusiasm for battle and booty made up for their lack of military expertise, although there is a record of one party of monks who returned very quickly: they could not, they complained, cope with the long marches in the summer heat, and they were disgusted and their stomachs upset by the putrid water which they were given to drink – this was no way to conduct a crusade.

The other person who accused the bishop of improper conduct was, of course, the Count of Flanders. Louis de Male complained bitterly to his advisers that the English had attacked and ravaged Flemish towns without, he said stiffly, giving 'due notice of their intentions to the lord of that country (the count himself)'; and he sent an embassy to Despenser to point out that Flanders had accepted Urban VI as the true pope, so there could be no justification for an Urbanist crusade against it. Despenser is reported to have replied that if the count really was a supporter of Pope Urban, he should join the crusade at once – presumably to attack his own towns – but that the bishop had no doubt that the real lords of Flanders were the French king and the duke of Burgundy. He therefore rejected the count's protest and began to move eastwards along the coast. This was not the road to Ghent, but by sticking to the coastal ports he could receive reinforcements easily; and he was probably conscious that this secured him a means of escape if things went badly. But at first all went very well. Under the guidance of the Flemish leader, Francis Ackerman, the English army quickly captured Gravelines, and the hinterland towns of Bourbourg and Berghes, and then, on 25 May, the port of Dunkirk.

They had not had to do a great deal of fighting. At Gravelines the port was defended only by a stockade. Froissart comments with his usual aristocratic sniff that it would have held out longer if the palisades had been manned by gentleman and not just common sailors. Most of the well-to-do townsfolk had taken themselves and their possessions to the nearby monastic church, which was protected by a stone wall and a ditch, and most of the French garrison. Despite barrages of stones, molten lead, and quicklime, the English assault overcame all resistance in less than twenty-four hours. No male prisoners were taken, but were immediately slaughtered, and the women were given over (*feminis reservatis*) to the pleasures of the army. One of the virtues of holy war was that the enemy had no rights. A great deal of wealth was seized, not only the personal possessions of the townspeople, but also the contents of the warehouses on the docks and the ships in the harbour. There was also a large French military stable, whose seizure was particularly welcome, in that it allowed a much larger proportion of the English army to be mounted cavalry.

After this it was hardly surprising that there was little resistance from the other coastal towns. Only at Dunkirk, on 25 May, did the French garrison bring out the Flemish militia in an attempt to stage a pitched battle, and, as on so many previous occasions in the French wars, the massed French formations were decimated by the English archers before the English pikemen – maddened, we are told, by the murder of the English herald sent out to parley, and in a state of mystical exaltation from the discovery that this was St Urban's Day – fell upon the enemy and butchered them (I quote) 'by the thousand'. The chroniclers' estimates range between 5,000 and 17,000 French and Flemings killed. Froissart, as a hostile source, gives the number of English killed at 400–500, but all the English accounts put the English casualties at less than 20 – all of which only goes to suggest that the battle of Dunkirk was more of a skirmish, decided by a single charge.

Nevertheless, the crusade was making far better progress than had been expected, even if in the opposite direction. By early June, Despenser's army had reached Ostend, and had linked up with the main contingents of Flemish troops from Ghent and the neighbouring small towns controlled by Francis Ackerman. In about three weeks he had cleared some fifty miles of coastline; he had boosted the size of his forces considerably (the army was now overestimated at between 30,000 and 60,000); and the attitude of the English government became noticeably more favourable, ready to take any benefits that were accruing from the campaign, and giving Despenser much wider powers to arrange and administer Flemish affairs.

But the bishop was still nagged by awful doubts about whether a crusade ought to be turning itself into an army of occupation in Flanders. What ought he to do next? English commercial interests clearly dictated a continuing drive to the east towards the great ports and commercial centres of Bruges and Sluys. Despenser himself felt that he had done as much as could reasonably be expected in Flanders, and that he should now go into reverse and strike southwards into France itself by invading Artois and attacking the industrial towns of the northeast. In the event he did neither: on 9 June he decided to compromise by moving inland to attack Ypres. His enemies subsequently said that he did so because he was lured on by a story that there were three barrels full of gold in the cellars of the castle. But the truth of the matter was that this was largely in response to Flemish wishes. Ghent wanted revenge for its loss of control over Ypres as a result of the French occupation the previous year; and Ackerman argued that Ypres could be the keystone of a defensive block against any further French attack. Despenser estimated that the capture of Ypres would be another easy victory and would still serve as an indication that he was turning south towards Artois and into anti-papal France. Once Ypres was taken, he could leave the Flemings to mop up the rest of the French garrisons in the east of Flanders, conscious that he had done his duty by them.

The siege of Ypres lasted for exactly two months and marks the turning-point of the crusade. Although Despenser solemnly excommunicated the defenders, burnt the suburbs, bombarded the city with the great gun of Canterbury, specially brought over with the blessing of the archbishop, and rained arrows into the streets, so that the defenders did not dare to appear on the walls, the attackers could not get through the walls – indeed, could not even reach them until they cut down enough wood to fill up the defensive ditches. And the longer the siege went on, the more the Gantois slipped away home to Ghent to see to their affairs, and the more English deserters went missing and legged it for the coast.

But the bishop stubbornly refused to raise the siege when he found Ypres so unexpectedly well defended – even when offered a change of allegiance by the count of Flanders if he would do so. He argued that he was still doing what he had been doing ever since the crusade began, waiting for the government to send out reinforcements. In fact, had Despenser realized it, a considerable political struggle was going on in England over this point.

By the end of July, when he realized that the bishop was bogged down outside Ypres, John of Gaunt, always an astute political manipulator, appreciated that he had his opponent at his mercy – and the future of the crusade. In essence, he had a simple choice between two courses of action. The bulk of a relief army had already assembled on the Isle of Thanet, waiting for shipping to be collected for it. Gaunt had originally intended to use this army for an expedition to Gascony, from where it could either be diverted into Spain or, if Despenser's crusade was successful, it could strike up across France to meet the bishop coming down from Flanders (or so it was said). But now it could be used to save the crusade, and indeed to take over the crusade. Such a powerful force would have to be commanded either by the king in person or one of the royal family – Gaunt or his brother Thomas of Woodstock. The royal family might even campaign in strength to save the bishop from his own incompetence.

The alternative was to *pretend* to be doing this, whilst in practice doing nothing at all – a procedure much more attractive to the duke's cautious, bureaucratic nature. He would ensure that help was available but was never sent until it was too late. This policy of masterly inactivity was greatly assisted by the bishop's continued refusal to accept troops under a royal commander of any seniority who might replace him. He continued to demand the supply of a large army without generals. Contingents under the command of the Earl of Arundel, Sir William Beauchamp, and Sir William Windsor were all rejected for no apparent reason, other than that Despenser would have had to yield precedence to such distinguished and experienced soldiers. As a result, the only reinforcements who actually reached Ypres were gangs of untrained volunteers, who, as the bishop complained, brought no arms with them, only great appetites and a fine selection of plagues and diseases from the London underworld. They were either peasants and workers, who knew nothing about fighting, or criminals, undisciplined and unruly, who joined the crusade in search of loot, and terrorized the countryside round about. He insisted that the shipping agent, Sir John Philipot, should stop sending him this rabble.

John of Gaunt was naturally delighted. How could he reinforce the bishop if he kept refusing people? Throughout August he continually announced that he was poised to send an army to Flanders: he just needed the royal consent and a decision whether the king would command in person. But it was not until mid-September (between 12 and 15 September) that the government formally appointed Gaunt as 'Special Lieutenant and Captain General' to take over the crusade in France and Flanders – significantly with full diplomatic powers to make peace if this became desirable. A general call to arms was issued to the English lords to send help to the army on Thanet waiting to go to Calais. But by then, as quickly became obvious, it was too late: the relief force never sailed.

With hindsight we can see that the prolonged siege of Ypres dug the bishop's political grave. It also ruined his chances of military success. Throughout July the French king, Charles VI, despite the urgings of the Duke of Burgundy, had been almost as inactive as Richard II. But the prolongation of the siege convinced Charles that this was no mere raid, which, if left long enough, would go away. At the end of the month he issued a general summons for troops to go to Flanders, and on 2 August went to St Denis to raise the *oriflamme*.

It was claimed to be the largest army ever assembled in France, so that old men who remembered previous French armies stood open mouthed with astonishment as it passed. Besides the main French, Flemish, and Burgundian troops, there were Bretons, Lorrainers, Savoyards, and Bavarians, totalling 80 or 90,000 men, although Froissart's report of 26,000 is probably more accurate. It was certainly a highly mobile force: by mid-August it had reached Arras, only to receive the news that the English had made their final assault on Ypres on 8 August, and having completely failed to penetrate the walls, had raised the siege two days later when they heard of the approach of the French forces. They were now in full retreat towards the coast. On the last day of August the French crossed into Flanders and caught the English rearguard at Cassel and wiped it out.

Despenser now fell back on the two small towns, Berghes and Bourbourg, which defended the ports of Dunkirk and Gravelines respectively. But the shock of defeat appears to have made him mad. He argued that it was only a tactical withdrawal in order to regroup, and that the crusade was no worse off than it was before it attacked Ypres. Indeed, the Ypres episode had very cleverly decoyed the French king into Flanders, so leaving the way clear for the crusade to slip past and invade France itself. As every day that passed brought the arrival of reinforcements nearer, they would soon be on their way. He even sent out a reconnaissance force to the west.

This incurable optimism appalled his senior commander, Sir Hugh Calverley, who now becomes more obviously identifiable as a royalist agent, and who appears to have been receiving his own separate orders from John of Gaunt and the government at home. It seems clear that he realized that there was not going to be a relief force from England, and that he was told to get the bishop out of the way, to put on a good show, and then close down the crusade as best he could.

He abandoned Berghes as indefensible. It had only a wooden fence round it, and as the French vanguard marched in on one side, so the English marched out on the opposite side, setting the houses on fire as they went. He concentrated the English forces at Bourbourg, being careful to leave the bishop's men in command, Sir William Elmham, Sir William Farringdon, and Sir Thomas Trivet, whilst he himself hustled the bishop safely out of the way, back to Gravelines and the sea. One need not doubt that he was told to bring him back alive. In due course he was bundled into the greater safety of Calais to await the remnants of his forces.

These were still sizeable. There is no need now, I think, to discuss the sieges of Bourbourg and Gravelines. Both were well defended and then saved by an unexpected diversion created by the men of Ghent – Ackerman suddenly seized Oudenarde (on the Scheldt, and well to the east, the far side, of Ypres). The French armies, which had not been prosecuting the sieges with any vigour, and had spent the time in jousts, tournaments, and what can only be described as a sort of medieval 'horse of the year show', enjoying a hot summer and waiting for the English to get tired of it and go away – were now suddenly needed on the opposite side of Flanders. The duke of Brittany was brought in to mediate and, in effect, buy off the bishop's captains. When they were subsequently accused of having been bribed they defended themselves by arguing that this was money for their horses, which they had sold back to the French, because they could not take them with them. They also pointed to the fact that they had looted and razed these towns before evacuating them and returning to Calais, in late September.

As I hope is clear, the Flanders crusade was never at any time a serious attempt to remove the anti-pope Clement VII, and is of doubtful value in terms of the English prosecution of the war effort against France. It was far more significant as an elaborate playing out of a factional contest within English domestic politics.

The English papalists (for want of a better term) amongst the episcopal hierarchy sought to demonstrate their independence of and control over the royal government, whilst at the same time frustrating and embarrassing and, it was hoped, destroying the coalition of royalist groups, the king's friends, who managed that government, and, above all, to bring down John of Gaunt. The failure of the crusade meant the, at least, temporary triumph and survival of Gaunt, and for the time being, until the next crisis, reestablished his dominance over the royalists.

When the bishop landed at Dover, Gaunt, we are told, was waiting on the beach to arrest him. A political trial was now arranged. Technically the bishop was impeached, using the procedure established by the Good Parliament of 1376 for the prosecution of ministers. But here Parliament, in the sense of the House of Commons, was allowed to play no part: Despenser was simply interrogated by the chancellor, de la Pole, on behalf of the Crown. He was not allowed to call witnesses or produce written evidence. Whilst he was speaking the bishop was repeatedly heckled and jeered by the officials and other people present, so that he lost his temper and became inarticulate. He complained that he was so flustered by the way he was being treated and trapped into appearing a fool that he had (I quote) 'forgotten large part of the defence' that he had wished to make. He was allowed an adjournment for a month (from 26 October to 24 November) to repair his case, but the second hearing only allowed the Crown an opportunity to bring forward new charges and showed that the bishop had forgotten what he had said at the first hearing and was now seen to be contradicting himself.

Essentially there were four charges, and he was found guilty on all four counts. Two were charges of embezzlement – that he had not provided himself with strong enough forces, despite having been given government grants to do so. The third was in effect a complaint that he had diminished the rights of the Crown (that is, of John of Gaunt and the royalists) by insisting on commanding the expedition himself instead of a member of the royal family or a king's man as executive commander. And the fourth was that he had been bribed into surrender by the French without waiting for reinforcements that the government was preparing to send him, which Despenser regarded as particularly unfair, when it was the deliberate withholding of reinforcements which had ruined the crusade.

But all his protests were, naturally, in vain. He was sentenced to lose the profits from his expedition and was deprived of the temporalities – that is, the income – of his see. But the government was careful not to antagonize the bishops too much, and Archbishop Courtenay spoke strongly in Despenser's favour. He got off considerably more lightly than his clerks and captains, who were heavily fined and sent to the Tower – with the notable exception of Sir Hugh Calverley, who now appeared as an accuser for the Crown to denounce what he termed 'the most shameful campaign that ever issued out of England'.

In short, the whole affair was carefully rigged and elaborately stage-managed, and there was little real effort to pretend otherwise. All the participants knew the rules of the political game, and that it was only a matter of waiting and surviving until the cut and thrust of factional in-fighting altered the political alignments. Richard II himself appears to have offered Despenser the prospect of quick re-employment if he would learn his lesson and become an obedient royal servant – such holy bellicosity was not to be wasted. Two years later, in 1385, he took part in the summer campaign against the Scots, and was rewarded afterwards by the return of the temporalities of his see; and for two years after that he even returned to Flanders, or at least the Flemish coast, in the naval campaign of 1386–7. He was one of Richard's main supporters during the second half of that unhappy reign. Not that the bishop was unhappy: for the remaining twenty years of his life he enjoyed himself and his reputation as the martial bishop (*episcopus martialis*), fortifying his manor houses, hunting Lollards, quarrelling vigorously with his cathedral chapter and the East Anglian towns, and making a collection of metrical romances and prophecies. He was, on the whole, a happy bishop, and when he died, in 1406, he was still repeating his favourite text: 'The earth is the Lord's...', and I want it.

Meanwhile John of Gaunt had been able to enjoy a short triumph as the great peacemaker, the man who had to clear up the mess that the bishop had left in Flanders, the professional hero who saved the day and patched up the peace that the amateur soldier had disrupted. He went straight to Calais and negotiated a truce with Charles VI, the Treaty of Lelighen/Lalingham of January 1384, which had the effect of stopping the French campaign against Ghent for the rest of the year. The men of Ghent were so delighted that they presented Richard II with two ostriches for the royal zoo. Ghent was not protected but increasingly isolated, and it was only a matter of time before (by the Tournai treaty of 1385) it had to accept its destiny within the framework of Burgundian Flanders, a Burgundy which was, ironically, for the next century virtually independent of France. The crusade had done nothing to halt the expansion of Burgundy. Its main achievement, as I have said, was to maintain John of Gaunt's weakening political status against his episcopal antagonists and his royalist rivals, and to prolong his hold on the government of his nephew to a greater degree and for a few years longer than might otherwise have been the case. Dr Palmer has recently argued, and he is probably right, that it had a negative effect in furthering the prospects of a peace policy in the Hundred Years War, the policy associated with Michael de la Pole, and leading to the prolonged truce of a quarter of a century that began at the end of the 80s. Not that it cured the English of crusades. A dozen years later even John of Gaunt was to organize another expedition, led by one of his illegitimate sons, when at Nicopolis, 1,500 Englishmen rode out in 1396 to drive the Turks out of Europe, and vanished for ever on the great Hungarian plain.

But as regards the professed purpose of the crusade, the great reunion of Christendom in the light of the Roman obedience, and the crushing of the Antichrist of Avignon, the whole business was supremely irrelevant, and might just as well never have taken place. In this sense it *was* the ultimate lunacy that Wyclif proclaimed it to be before it began. But, as one of Gaunt's retainers, dependent for his safety on government protection, Wyclif had had to pretend to take it seriously and depict the crusade as the beginning of Armageddon, which could only lead to the conquest of the world by Antichrist, and the beginning of the final contest with God. It is an interesting example of the way in which the crusades continued to be seen as the earthly expression of a great cosmic struggle between Good and Evil which went on over and beyond the armies below. But it is also a salutary reminder that in history it is often the mythology which matters, and that the actual facts are usually quite different from what is recorded.

Printed sources: Wyclif's references to the crusade occur in a number of his works: 'Sermones viginti', in *Sermones iv*, ed. J. Loserth, *WS* (1890), nos 4, 13–22; *Polemical Works*, ed. R. Buddensieg, *WS* (1883), i.241–90, ii.449–92, 570–6, 588–632, 653–92; *Opera minora*, ed. J. Loserth, *WS* (1913), pp. 3–6, 98–128, 201–57; *Supplementum Trialogi*, ed. G. V. Lechler (Oxford, 1869); *Opus Evangelicum*, ed. J. Loserth, *WS* (1895–6). The main chronicle accounts are in *The Chronicle of Adam Usk 1377–1421*, ed. and tr. C. Given-Wilson, *OMT* (1995); John Capgrave, *The Chronicle of England to 1417*, ed. Francis C. Hingeston, *RS* (1858); *Chroniques de J. Froissart*, ed. Gaston Raynaud, *Société de l'histoire de France*, 134 (Paris, 1899), bk 2, vol. 11, cap. 19; *Knighton's Chronicle 1337–1396*, ed. and tr. G. H. Martin, *OMT* (1995); Ranulf Higden, *Polychronicon*, 9, ed. C. Babington and J. R. Lumby, *RS* (1886); Thomas Walsingham, *Historia Anglicana*, 2, ed H. T. Riley, *RS* (1864); *The Westminster Chronicle 1381–1394*, ed. and tr. L. C. Hector and Barbara F. Harvey, *OMT* (1982).

Secondary works. The works in English specifically devoted to the Crusade are R. Coulborn, 'The economic and political preliminaries of the Crusade of Henry Despenser, Bishop of Norwich, in 1383', Ph.D. thesis (University of London, 1931) and George M. Wrong, *The Crusade of 1383, known as that of the Bishop of Norwich* (London, 1892). See also Margaret Aston, 'The impeachment of Bishop Despenser', *BIHR*, 38 (1965), pp. 127–48; M. McKisack, *The Fourteenth Century 1307–1399*, Oxford History of England, 5 (Oxford, 1959); J. J. N. Palmer, *England, France, and Christendom 1377–99* (London, 1972); H. B. Workman, *John Wyclif. A Study of the English Medieval Church*, 2 vols (Oxford, 1926), repr. in 1 vol. (Hamden, Connecticut, 1966), 2, pp. 64–70.

WYCLIF: POLITICAL IDEAS AND PRACTICE

Michael Wilks's highly significant contributions to
Wyclif scholarship have for long been considered
essential reading for both colleagues and students.
This collection of twelve of his papers (two previously
unavailable) answers a long-felt need. With his
characteristic learning, clarity, and wit, Wilks analyses
Wyclif's fundamental ideas, demonstrating their
unexpected debt to the political theory of the medieval
popes, reconciling many apparent contradictions, and
setting them within their contemporary political
context. It is hoped that the volume will provide a
small compensation for the keenly anticipated political
biography of Wyclif which Wilks did not live to write.

The illustration on the cover is presumed to be a representation of
Wyclif. It is taken from a Bohemian copy of his *De veritate sacr*
scripture now in Prague National Library

Oxbow Books

ISBN 1-84217-009-
9 781842 170090